BRAIDING LEGAL ORDERS

BRAIDING LEGAL ORDERS

Implementing the United Nations Declaration on the Rights of Indigenous Peoples

John Borrows, Larry Chartrand, Oonagh E. Fitzgerald and Risa Schwartz, Editors

Centre for International Governance Innovation

ISBN 978-1-928096-81-8 (cloth)
ISBN 978-1-928096-80-1 (paper)
ISBN 978-1-928096-82-5 (ePUB)
ISBN 978-1-928096-83-2 (ePDF)

Library and Archives Canada Cataloguing in Publication

Title: Braiding legal orders : implementing the United Nations Declaration on the Rights of Indigenous Peoples / John Borrows, Larry Chartrand, Oonagh E. Fitzgerald, and Risa Schwartz, editors.
Names: Borrows, John, editor. | Chartrand, Larry N., editor. | Fitzgerald, Oonagh E., editor. | Schwartz, Risa, editor.
Description: Includes bibliographical references.
Identifiers: Canadiana (print) 20190092025 | Canadiana (ebook) 20190092122 | ISBN 9781928096818 (cloth) | ISBN 9781928096801 (paper) | ISBN 9781928096825 (ePUB) | ISBN 9781928096832 (ePDF)
Subjects: LCSH: United Nations. General Assembly. Declaration on the Rights of Indigenous Peoples. | LCSH: United Nations—Canada. | LCSH: Indigenous peoples—Legal status, laws, etc. | LCSH: Indigenous peoples—Civil rights. | LCSH: Indigenous peoples (International law) | CSH: Native peoples—Legal status, laws, etc.—Canada. | CSH: Native peoples—Civil rights—Canada.
Classification: LCC K3247 .B73 2019 | DDC 341.4/852—dc23

CIGI gratefully acknowledges the support and collaboration of the Wiyasiwewin Mikiwahp Native Law Centre, University of Saskatchewan, in the development of this publication.

Published by the Centre for International Governance Innovation (CIGI).

Cover and page design by Melodie Wakefield.

Centre for International Governance Innovation

Centre for International Governance Innovation
67 Erb Street West
Waterloo, ON Canada N2L 6C2

www.cigionline.org

Contents

Part II: Indigenous Law Perspectives

Part III: Domestic Law Perspectives

Part IV: Concluding Thoughts

Preface

Larry Chartrand, Oonagh E. Fitzgerald and Risa Schwartz

In Canada, implementation of the United Nations Declaration on the Rights of Indigenous Peoples (UNDRIP)[1] is an opportunity to explore and reconceive the relationship between international law, Indigenous peoples' own laws and Canada's constitutional narratives.

In May 2016, Indigenous and Northern Affairs Minister Carolyn Bennett addressed the Permanent Forum on Indigenous Issues at the United Nations and officially endorsed UNDRIP[2] — without the qualifications attached by the previous government, which considered the declaration to be aspirational and not legally binding. While this announcement did not change the legal relevance of UNDRIP in Canada, it did express the political will to begin implementation and signalled that Canada might be on a path toward reconciliation with Indigenous peoples. Thus, the announcement also raised legal and policy questions about how the federal government intends to adopt and implement this human rights instrument.[3]

1 *United Nations Declaration on the Rights of Indigenous Peoples*, GA Res 295, UNGAOR, 61st Sess, Supp No 49, UN Doc A/RES/61/295, 46 ILM 1013 (2007).

2 Minister of Indigenous and Northern Affairs Carolyn Bennett, "Announcement of Canada's Support for the United Nations Declaration on the Rights of Indigenous Peoples" (Statement delivered at the 15th Session of the United Nations Permanent Forum on Indigenous Issues, 10 May 2016).

3 See e.g. Gib van Ert, "Three Good Reasons Why UNDRIP Can't Be Law — and One Good Reason Why it Can" (2017) 75:1 Advocate 29.

The minister's words — "We intend nothing less than to adopt and implement the declaration in accordance with the Canadian Constitution" — were somewhat ambiguous, raising questions as to whether they simply recognized that no Canadian government could operate outside the Constitution, acknowledged that implementation of UNDRIP would require action by the provinces and territories as well as the federal government, or implied that Canada's Constitution will act as a constraint on UNDRIP implementation. The language of section 35 of Canada's Constitution, which provides that "The existing aboriginal and treaty rights of the aboriginal people in Canada are hereby recognized and affirmed,"[4] arguably is broad enough that interpreting the Constitution in light of implementation of the declaration could lead to an expansive view of inherent rights and treaty rights. Bennett seemed to acknowledge this when she stated, in the same speech, "By adopting and implementing the Declaration, we are excited that we are breathing life into Section 35 and recognizing it now as a full box of rights for Indigenous peoples in Canada."[5] Subsequent developments, however, as discussed below, may suggest that the federal government views UNDRIP implementation as being subject to Canada's Constitution, which is seen as paramount over UNDRIP. This approach would suggest that the Canadian Constitution would prevail if UNDRIP rights are found to conflict or be inconsistent with it.

Since the Government of Canada's "embrace" of UNDRIP at the United Nations Permanent Forum of Indigenous Peoples in May 2016, much has happened to set the stage for an ambitious implementation agenda. Yet progress remains haltingly slow and arguably more illusory than real. It is fair to recognize the numerous positive steps taken by the federal government. In February 2017, Prime Minister Justin Trudeau announced that his government would form a working group of ministers to "examine relevant federal laws, policies, and operational practices to help ensure the Crown is meeting its constitutional obligations with respect to Aboriginal and treaty rights; adhering to international human rights standards, including the United Nations Declaration on the Rights of Indigenous Peoples; and supporting the implementation of the Truth and Reconciliation Commission's Calls to Action."[6] The federal Department of Justice articulated 10 Principles Respecting the Government of Canada's Relationship with Indigenous Peoples, noting that "The implementation of the United Nations Declaration on the Rights of Indigenous Peoples requires transformative change in the Government's relationship with Indigenous peoples."[7] As well, the Department of Justice issued a complementary Directive on Civil Litigation Involving Indigenous Peoples[8] aimed at promoting an approach to conflict resolution between the Crown and Indigenous peoples that is consistent with reconciliation. The old department of Indigenous and Northern Affairs was dissolved and replaced by two new departments: Crown-Indigenous Relations and Northern Affairs Canada; and Indigenous Services Canada.

---

4 *Constitution Act, 1982*, s 35(1), being Schedule B to the *Canada Act 1982* (UK), 1982, c 11.

5 Bennett, *supra* note 2.

6 Prime Minister of Canada, News Release, "Prime Minister announces Working Group of Ministers on the Review of Laws and Policies Related to Indigenous Peoples" (22 February 2017), online: <http://pm.gc.ca/eng/news/2017/02/22/prime-minister-announces-working-group-ministers-review-laws-and-policies-related>.

7 Canada, Department of Justice, "Principles respecting the Government of Canada's relationship with Indigenous peoples", online: <www.justice.gc.ca/eng/csj-sjc/principles-principes.html>.

8 Canada, Department of Justice, "Directive on Civil Litigation Involving Indigenous Peoples", online: <www.justice.gc.ca/eng/csj-sjc/ijr-dja/dclip-dlcpa/litigation-litiges.html>.

In September 2017, on the occasion of Canada's 150th anniversary, Trudeau made an impassioned speech to the UN General Assembly in which he acknowledged that Indigenous peoples on this continent had a history that stretched back many millennia before the arrival of Europeans, and that the nation called Canada was best seen as "a work in progress."[9] He referred to Canada's colonial legacy, the broken promises and the harms that racist policies have inflicted on Inuit, Métis and First Nations peoples, and he renewed promises to use domestic implementation of UNDRIP as "a way forward" to correct past wrongs, support nation-to-nation, government-to-government and Inuit-Crown relationships, and achieve reconciliation.

In February 2018, Trudeau announced "that the government will develop — in full partnership with First Nations, Inuit, and Métis people — a new Recognition and Implementation of Indigenous Rights Framework that will include new ways to recognize and implement Indigenous Rights."[10] This was to include "new recognition and implementation of rights legislation" and going forward he asserted, "recognition of rights will guide all government relations with Indigenous Peoples," with the contents of the framework being built together "through a national engagement, led by the Minister of Crown-Indigenous Relations and Northern Affairs, with support from the Minister of Justice."[11] According to the government website, this "will ensure that the Government of Canada recognizes, respects and implements Indigenous rights, including inherent and treaty rights, and provides mechanisms to support self-determination. The framework will support Indigenous peoples' rights as recognized and affirmed in section 35 of the Constitution Act, 1982, while also aligning with the articles outlined in the United Nations Declaration on the Rights of Indigenous Peoples. It will also be consistent with the Principles Respecting the Government of Canada's Relationship with Indigenous Peoples."[12] However, the initiative seems to be stalled, with little buy-in from Indigenous peoples. In September 2018, a Cabinet Committee on Reconciliation was formed to replace the ministerial working group, build on what it had accomplished and "strengthen the relationship with Indigenous peoples and advance the commitment to a renewed nation-to-nation, Inuit-Crown, and government-to-government relationship with First Nations, Inuit and the Métis Nation based on recognition of rights, respect, co-operation, and partnership."[13] Meanwhile, other federal departments have taken initial, tentative steps to work with Indigenous peoples in the development of policy on such matters as climate change, environmental assessment reform, international trade, intellectual property law reform and protection of traditional knowledge, and preservation and revitalization of Indigenous languages.

9 "Prime Minister Justin Trudeau's Address to the 72nd Session of the United Nations General Assembly" (21 September 2017), online: <https://pm.gc.ca/eng/news/2017/09/21/prime-minister-justin-trudeaus-address-72th-session-united-nations-general-assembly>.

10 "Remarks by the Prime Minister in the House of Commons on the Recognition and Implementation of Rights Framework" (14 February 2018), online: <https://pm.gc.ca/eng/news/2018/02/14/remarks-prime-minister-house-commons-recognition-and-implementation-rights-framework>.

11 *Ibid.*

12 Canada, Crown-Indigenous Relations and Northern Affairs Canada, "Overview of a Recognition and Implementation of Indigenous Rights Framework" (14 February 2018), online: <www.rcaanc-cirnac.gc.ca/eng/1536350959665/1539959903708>.

13 Prime Minister of Canada, News Release, "Prime Minister announces changes to the Cabinet committees" (28 August 2018), online: <https://pm.gc.ca/eng/news/2018/08/28/prime-minister-announces-changes-cabinet-committees>.

In May 2018, Bill C-262, introduced as a private member's bill by Member of Parliament Romeo Saganash, passed in the House of Commons (206 votes in favour, 79 against)[14] and proceeded to the Senate where it has passed first reading.[15] The bill, if passed into law, would affirm UNDRIP "as a universal international human rights instrument with application in Canadian law," require the Government of Canada to "take all measures necessary to ensure that the laws of Canada are consistent with" UNDRIP, "in consultation and cooperation with indigenous peoples, [to] develop and implement a national action plan to achieve the objectives of" UNDRIP and to report annually to Parliament for 20 years on progress with implementation. In February 2019, the government introduced new legislation to protect Indigenous languages, timed with the International Year of Indigenous Languages.[16] Acknowledging "the extraordinary work done by the Assembly of First Nations, the Inuit Tapiriit Kanatami and the Métis National Council" to reclaim, revitalize, strengthen and maintain Indigenous languages in Canada, the Honourable Pablo Rodriguez, Minister of Canadian Heritage and Multiculturalism, introduced Bill C-91, the Indigenous Languages Act, in the House of Commons.[17] The federal government has also introduced Bill C-92, an Act respecting First Nations, Inuit and Métis children, youth and families. The preambles of these bills affirm a government commitment to implementation of UNDRIP.[18]

While these are steps in the right direction, many of the contributors to this collection explain that more is needed to effect actual change on the ground for First Nations, Inuit and Métis peoples in Canada. UNDRIP represents the concerted efforts of Indigenous leaders from around the world to stem the destructive and disempowering effects of colonialism and to create conditions for Indigenous peoples to reclaim their social, cultural, linguistic, spiritual, political, economic, environmental and legal autonomy. As such, its embrace by the Government of Canada should create opportunities to make substantial progress in recognizing Indigenous peoples' rights in Canada. Yet many of the contributors to this book — much like the authors of the Yellowhead Institute's report on Canada's Indigenous Rights Framework[19] — express concern that Canada's vision of Indigenous jurisdiction over lands and resources remains too narrow, and may be little more than a modified version of the status quo.

14 Bill C-262, *An Act to ensure that the laws of Canada are in harmony with the United Nations Declaration on the Rights of Indigenous Peoples*, 1st Sess, 42nd Parl, 2016 (as passed by the House of Commons 30 May 2018), online: <www.parl.ca/DocumentViewer/en/42-1/bill/C-262/third-reading>.

15 As of the time of writing, the bill had passed through first reading in the Senate and was proceeding slowly through second reading. Indigenous organizations were urging the Senate to expedite the bill's passage.

16 Canada, Canadian Heritage, News Release, "Government of Canada introduces historic legislation on Indigenous languages" (5 February 2019), online: <www.canada.ca/en/canadian-heritage/news/2019/02/government-of-canadaintroduces-historiclegislationonindigenous-languages.html>.

17 Bill C-91, An Act respecting Indigenous Languages, 1st Sess, 42nd Parl, 2016 (first reading 5 February 2019), online: <www.parl.ca/DocumentViewer/en/42-1/bill/C-91/first-reading>. In response, Natan Obed, president of Inuit Tapiriit Kanatami, expressed disappointment with the proposed act, and his organization is seeking amendments to make Inuktitut an original language throughout Inuit Nunangat (Inuit homeland), so that Inuit would be entitled to obtain federal services in their own language: Amber Bernard, "Inuit leaders ask for amendments to language act at committee", *APTN News* (25 February 2019), online: <https://aptnnews.ca/2019/02/25/inuit-leaders-ask-for-amendments-to-language-act-at-committee/>.

18 Bill C-92, *An Act respecting First Nations, Inuit and Métis children, youth and families*, 1st Sess, 42nd Parl, 2016 (first reading 28 February 2019), online: <www.parl.ca/DocumentViewer/en/42-1/bill/C-92/first-reading>.

19 Hayden King & Shiri Pasternak, *Canada's Emerging Indigenous Rights Framework: A Critical Analysis*, Yellowhead Institute, Special Report, 5 June 2018, online: <https://yellowheadinstitute.org/wp-content/uploads/2018/06/yi-rights-report-june-2018-final-5.4.pdf>.

International declarations such as UNDRIP are not binding in international law, but are solemn and significant instruments that embody principles of great and lasting importance. While in the legal form of a non-binding declaration, UNDRIP is widely recognized as expressing the minimum standard for the rights of Indigenous peoples around the world. It reaffirms that all the existing human rights treaties apply to Indigenous peoples, extending "the existing corpus of individual human rights to a collective" as well.[20] UNDRIP builds from other human rights treaties and is grounded in a broader context of self-determination than is found in other human rights agreements, recognizing a wealth of political, social, economic, cultural and environmental rights of Indigenous peoples. We need to understand UNDRIP in part through the lens of those human rights treaties, but also take note of its significant difference in explicitly drawing on Indigenous peoples' own legal traditions, customs and institutions. The preamble of UNDRIP tells a great story of the recognition of Indigenous peoples as part of the humanity of the world, with equal but different rights. UNDRIP provides guidance for how dominant political orders should relate to Indigenous peoples based on justice, equality and good faith.

Canada generally takes a dualist approach to international treaties, meaning that such treaties operate as commitments between sovereign nations, and do not automatically impact domestic law or the rights of individuals within Canada. With this dualist approach for treaties, the most obvious way for international law to become part of domestic law is for the legislature with jurisdiction over the subject matter to enact implementing legislation.[21] Customary international law, meaning norms that are recognized and followed in practice by the community of nations as legally binding,[22] can seep into Canadian law through judicial decisions[23] under the common

20 Megan Davis writes, "According to the Special Rapporteur on the rights of Indigenous peoples, S James Anaya: '[t]he Declaration does not attempt to bestow Indigenous peoples with a set of special or new human rights, but rather provides a contextualized elaboration of general human rights principles and rights as they relate to the specific historical, cultural and social circumstances of Indigenous peoples.' These rights are considered to be the extension of the existing corpus of individual human rights to a collective." Megan Davis, "To Bind or Not to Bind: The United Nations Declaration on the Rights of Indigenous Peoples Five Years On" (2012) 19 Austl J Intl L 17 at 27, referring to S James Anaya, Report of the Special Rapporteur on the Situation of Human Rights and Fundamental Freedoms of Indigenous People, UN Doc A/HRC/9/9 (11 August 2008) 24 [86], online: <www.austlii.edu.au/au/journals/AUIntLawJl/2012/3.pdf>.

21 Canadian courts have taken a more liberal approach through the presumption of conformity to develop Canadian law in line with the values and principles underlying Canada's human rights obligations. See *R v Hape*, 2007 SCC 26 at para 53, [2007] 2 SCR 292 [*Hape*], online: <https://scc-csc.lexum.com/scc-csc/scc-csc/en/item/2364/index.do>.

22 International Committee of the Red Cross, "Customary IHL", online: <https://ihl-databases.icrc.org/customary-ihl/eng/docs/v1_rul_in_asofcuin>: "It is generally agreed that the existence of a rule of customary international law requires the presence of two elements, namely State practice (*usus*) and a belief that such practice is required, prohibited or allowed, depending on the nature of the rule, as a matter of law (*opinio juris sive necessitatis*). As the International Court of Justice stated in the *Continental Shelf* case [(*Libyan Arab Jamahiriya v Malta*) [1985] ICJ Rep 13 at para 27]: 'It is of course axiomatic that the material of customary international law is to be looked for primarily in the actual practice and *opinio juris* of States.'"

23 In *Baker v Canada (Minister of Citizenship and Immigration)*, [1999] 2 SCR 817, online: <https://scc-csc.lexum.com/scc-csc/scc-csc/en/item/1717/index.do>, the Supreme Court of Canada (SCC) considered whether Canada's obligations under the International Convention on the Rights of the Child could influence interpretation of the Immigration Act. Justice Claire L'Heureux-Dubé for the majority quoted Ruth Sullivan at para 70: "[T]he legislature is presumed to respect the values and principles enshrined in international law, both customary and conventional. These constitute a part of the legal context in which legislation is enacted and read. In so far as possible, therefore, interpretations that reflect these values and principles are preferred." In *Hape*, *supra* note 20, the SCC stated: "Every principle of customary international law is binding on all states unless superseded by another custom or by a rule set out in an international treaty.... These principles must also be drawn upon in [interpreting] the Charter" (at para 46); "In interpreting the scope of application of the Charter, the courts should seek to ensure compliance with Canada's binding obligations under international law where the express words are capable of supporting such a construction" (at para 56); "Absent an express derogation, the courts may look to prohibitive rules of customary international law to aid in the interpretation of Canadian law and the development of the common law" (at para 39). Importantly, scholars have also concluded that many, if not most, of the principles in UNDRIP reflect international customary law principles already established, notwithstanding the non-legally binding status of a UN declaration itself: see Brendan Tobin, *Indigenous Peoples, Customary Law and Human Rights: Why Living Law Matters* (London: Routledge, 2014).

law. For international human rights obligations, the Canadian practice has been to conduct an internal governmental review of laws and policies to determine whether they already meet the international standard and, if they do, proceed to ratification. This internal legal review is not normally tabled in Parliament or the provincial legislatures, or otherwise made public, and there may be no obvious implementing legislation, especially if officials conclude that an existing law provides rights equivalent to those in the treaty under review.

After years of uncertainty, the SCC now seems to be coalescing around the notion that the Canadian Charter of Rights and Freedoms should encompass all of Canada's binding international human rights obligations.[24] Whether this clarification will have an impact on how section 35 of the Constitution Act, 1982 is interpreted in light of UNDRIP has yet to be seen. In particular, questions remain about how the rights declared in UNDRIP will influence the interpretation of section 35 of the Constitution Act, 1982 as well as the Charter, and what this will mean for the future relationship between international law, Indigenous peoples' laws and Canadian constitutional law. In a 2015 Federal Court case,[25] Justice Cecily Strickland seemed to adopt the notion that UNDRIP could be used contextually to reinterpret domestic law so as to favour an interpretation that respected relevant international law values, but drew the line at reinterpreting constitutional language, making a curious interpretative distinction between different parts of the Constitution. In a 2016 decision, the Canadian Human Rights Tribunal cited Canada's international obligations (referring to UNDRIP earlier in its decision) to find that First Nations children on-reserve must be provided child and family services of comparable quality and accessibility as those provided to Canadians off-reserve.[26] However, most notable in recent Canadian jurisprudence is the absence of a mention of UNDRIP in the SCC's decision in *Mikisew Cree First Nation v Canada (Governor General in Council)*, in which the question of whether the duty to consult Indigenous peoples applies to the law-making process was addressed.[27] One can hope that if Bill C-262 passes into law, both future case law and legislation will be developed and interpreted through an UNDRIP lens.

The origins of this book go back several years. At a round table on UNDRIP Implementation and the Extractive Industry, organized by Terri Mitchell[28] and David Dewitt in Waterloo in December 2014, former Prime Minister Paul Martin and former National Chief for the Assembly of First Nations Ovide Mercredi urged the Centre for International Governance Innovation (CIGI) to help address the overwhelming governance challenges in the relations between the federal, provincial and territorial governments and Indigenous peoples of Canada, challenges that are exacerbated by the pressure to develop natural resources when land claims

24 Early on in jurisprudence under the Charter, SCC Chief Justice Brian Dickson, in a dissenting opinion in *Reference re Public Service Employee Relations Act (Alta)*, [1987] 1 SCR 313 at para 59, stated: "I believe that the Charter should generally be presumed to provide protection at least as great as that afforded by similar provisions in international human rights documents which Canada has ratified." It took another 20 years for the court to embrace this principle with some degree of confidence. In *Divito v Canada (Public Safety and Emergency Preparedness)*, 2013 SCC 47 at para 23 (quoting *Health Services and Support — Facilities Subsector Bargaining Association v British Columbia*, 2007 SCC 27 at para 70), the SCC stated, "the Charter should be presumed to provide at least as great a level of protection as is found in the international human rights documents that Canada has ratified."

25 *Nunatukavut Community Council Inc v Canada (AG)*, 2015 FC 981 at paras 101–06.

26 *First Nations Child and Family Caring Society of Canada v Canada (AG)*, 2016 CHRT 2 at para 455, [2016] 2 CNLR 270.

27 *Mikisew Cree First Nation v Canada (Governor General in Council)*, 2018 SCC 40.

28 See also Terry Mitchell, ed, "The Internationalization of Indigenous Rights: UNDRIP in the Canadian Context" CIGI, Special Report, 4 December 2014, online: <www.cigionline.org/publications/internationalization-indigenous-rights-undrip-canadian-context>.

are unresolved and many Indigenous peoples, Métis and Inuit are living in developing world conditions without access to justice or enjoyment of basic human rights.

CIGI's International Law Research Program (ILRP) saw this invitation as a matter of international and domestic human rights that cut across its research on international economic, environmental and intellectual property law. The ILRP was interested in responding to the Truth and Reconciliation Commission's Calls to Action[29] by providing a forum for exploring important international law and governance questions related to Indigenous peoples' rights. The ILRP research project commenced in earnest with discussions in 2016 in Victoria with John Borrows, Brenda Gunn, Joshua Nichols, Larry McDermott, Risa Schwartz and Oonagh Fitzgerald.

The metaphor of braiding international, domestic and Indigenous laws emerged from a conversation in the garden café at the University of Victoria, where young turtles were basking in the late May sunshine. The braiding metaphor was seen as relevant to many Indigenous traditions in Canada. For example, the various strands of the braided Métis sash represent different Métis values and experiences (and is like a record of Métis constitutionalism in that respect).[30] The braiding of sweetgrass indicates strength and drawing together power and healing. A braid is a single object consisting of many fibres and separate strands; it does not gain its strength from any single fibre, but from the many fibres woven together. Imagining a process of braiding together strands of constitutional, international and Indigenous peoples' own laws allows one to see the possibilities of reconciliation from different angles and perspectives, and thereby to begin to reimagine what a nation-to-nation relationship justly encompassing these different legal traditions might mean.

Under John's leadership, CIGI invited Indigenous legal academics and policy leaders to write short essays exploring UNDRIP implementation and using the metaphor of braiding international, constitutional and Indigenous peoples' own laws to provide insight, analysis and recommendations to policy makers. The contributing authors then met in Tucson, Arizona, in December 2016 to discuss their draft papers at a CIGI symposium, warmly hosted by Robert A. Williams, Jr., and the University of Arizona's Indigenous Peoples Law and Policy Program. Graduate students from the University of Arizona's Indigenous Peoples Law and Policy Program also participated in these discussions.

A first collection of papers marked the tenth anniversary of the adoption of UNDRIP, which also happened to coincide with the 150th anniversary of Canada, providing an opportunity to reflect on the history of treaty making with Indigenous peoples and to envision what the future might hold for this country and its relationship with its Indigenous peoples. A second phase of research on the theme of braiding international, constitutional and Indigenous laws was developed in partnership with the Wiyasiwewin Mikiwahp Native Law Centre at the University of Saskatchewan College of Law, beginning with a workshop in Saskatoon to discuss draft papers and culminating with several contributors presenting their research at the annual conference of the Indigenous Bar Association in the fall of 2018. The present book is the result of these two research projects.

29 Truth and Reconciliation Commission of Canada, "Calls to Action" (2015), online: <http://trc.ca/assets/pdf/Calls_to_Action_English2.pdf>.

30 While there are some variations on the meaning of the colours of the sash, depending on location and community, this is a general guide: red is for "the blood of the Métis that was shed through the years while fighting for our rights"; blue is for "the depth of our spirits"; green is for "the fertility of a great nation"; white is for "our connection to the earth and our creator"; yellow is for "the prospect of prosperity"; black is for "the dark period of the suppression and dispossession of Métis land": Métis BC Nation, "Métis Sash", online: <www.mnbc.ca/pdfs/order_of_the_sash.pdf>.

The focus of this book is less on the legal character of UNDRIP and more on the normative content of its principles which, over time through implementation, are expected to imbue Canadian constitutional and domestic law and Indigenous peoples' own laws with legal force. UNDRIP provides a normative language to inspire hope and replace despair. UNDRIP implementation provides an opportunity for scholars to draw on Indigenous peoples' own laws to shape future law and governance in Canada. UNDRIP provides an opportunity to decolonize Canadian law and rediscover and promulgate Indigenous peoples' own laws.

The doctrine of discovery[31] seems to be a suitable target for UNDRIP-inspired law reform. UNDRIP highlights the fact that Canadian constitutional jurisprudence is built on a fallacy. The SCC has acknowledged that it can revisit issues and come to different conclusions, most recently in reversing the prohibition on assisted suicide. This is indicative that the scope of Aboriginal and treaty rights can also be reconsidered. Many scholars agreed that the decision in *R v Van der Peet*[32] needs reconsideration, and perhaps a place to start is the dissent in that decision. Rather than seeing Aboriginal rights as frozen in time, the dissent in *Van der Peet* recognized that Aboriginal rights must maintain contemporary relevance so that practices, customs and traditions can continue to evolve. Aboriginal rights are inherent rights, grounded in Indigenous legal traditions. Therefore, the SCC might be persuaded to rethink Aboriginal and treaty rights in light of UNDRIP.

UNDRIP is also a linguistic tool, with language that is much more consonant with how Indigenous peoples think of themselves. It could provide new ways of talking and teaching, with everyone having a responsibility to implement UNDRIP domestically, internationally and within Indigenous law. Implementation of UNDRIP should contribute to reconciliation. The Canadian constitutional concept of the duty to consult is a framework for infringement of rights, without safeguards, whereas there are safeguards in UNDRIP's numerous requirements for "free, prior and informed consent." Instead of treating consultation as a burden under constitutional law, UNDRIP describes governance partnership and participation in decision making. UNDRIP shows that the framework for reconciliation needs to be shaped by Indigenous peoples' own beliefs, laws, languages and governance approaches. Thus, UNDRIP and international law form one segment of the braid, with domestic constitutional law and Indigenous laws providing the other two segments to create a strong braid of legal reconciliation.

The contributors to this book explain how Indigenous peoples' own laws offer world views that must be given an opportunity to develop and flourish. Implementation of UNDRIP into both the international and domestic legal landscape will require legal change to recognize and accommodate different legal orders. With the metaphor of braiding, contributors to this book examine the potential opportunities and risks entailed in trying to bring coherence and harmony into the strands of international law, domestic constitutional law and Indigenous peoples' own laws, while taking seriously nation-to-nation relations and reconciliation.

31 The doctrine of discovery has its origins in common law in the United States (*Johnson v M'Intosh*, 21 US [8 Wheat] 543 [1823]) and can also be seen in Canadian law (*St Catherine's Milling and Lumber Co v R*, [1888] UKPC 70, 14 App Cas 46). The effect of the doctrine is that upon "discovery" of North America by Europeans, they gained absolute right to the lands. Europeans thereby acquired sovereignty, legislative power and underlying title, which left Indigenous peoples as occupants on the land, with only some rights of possession and use that could be unilaterally revoked. Underlying the doctrine's foundation were papal bulls from the fifteenth century that gave Christian explorers the right to claim lands they had discovered on behalf of their monarchs. Non-Christian inhabitants of those lands were treated as "savages" who could be converted, or killed.

32 [1996] 2 SCR 507.

Introduction

John Borrows

The Centre for International Governance Innovation (CIGI) has worked with Indigenous and other scholars over the past few years to consider Indigenous issues from various international, domestic and Indigenous legal perspectives. The goal of this effort has been to "explore and reconceive the relationship between international law, Indigenous peoples' own laws and Canada's constitutional narratives" in order "to reflect on the past and envision what the future may hold for this country and its relationship with...Indigenous peoples."[1] As a result of these efforts, on May 31, 2017, a CIGI Special Report was released that addressed the braiding of these three legal approaches as they relate to the United Nations Declaration on the Rights of Indigenous Peoples (UNDRIP).

That report, *UNDRIP Implementation: Braiding International, Domestic and Indigenous Laws*, showcased nine papers that argued UNDRIP could not be implemented without bringing international and domestic law in line with Indigenous legal traditions. This work generated constructive conversations across Canada, while Parliament and the Department of Justice also took action in the field. These developments created a demand for further work, and thus, the following year, CIGI released another report on October 30, 2018, entitled *UNDRIP*

1 Oonagh Fitzgerald & Risa Schwartz, "Introduction", in Oonagh Fitzgerald & Risa Schwartz, eds, *UNDRIP Implementation: Braiding International, Domestic and Indigenous Laws*, CIGI, Special Report, 31 May 2017 at 13.

Implementation: More Reflections on the Braiding of International, Domestic and Indigenous Laws. The 14 papers in that volume continued the theme of braiding that was begun in CIGI's earlier publication.

Bringing international and domestic law in line with Indigenous peoples' own laws is not a linear process. Lines can be parallel, but they can also weave, cross and entwine with one another. Indigenous peoples do not want to see their own legal norms and decision-making processes obscured or extinguished through their interaction with other legal systems. The threads of Indigenous law must be vibrant, strong and recognizably distinct when they interact, affect and are influenced by other legal traditions. Braiding was chosen as a metaphor for the first CIGI report to reinforce this view. Oonagh Fitzgerald and Risa Schwartz introduced the metaphor's importance in the following terms:

> The braiding metaphor is relevant to many Indigenous traditions in Canada. For example, braided Métis sashes represent the weaving together of different traditions. The braiding of sweetgrass indicates strength and drawing together power and healing. A braid is a single object consisting of many fibres and separate strands; it does not gain its strength from any single fibre that runs its entire length, but from the many fibres woven together. Imagining a process of braiding together strands of constitutional, international and Indigenous law allows one to see the possibilities of reconciliation from different angles and perspectives, and thereby to begin to reimagine what a nation-to-nation relationship justly encompassing these different legal traditions might mean.[2]

The chapters in this book examine the relationships between international law, national law and Indigenous law in helpfully perceptive ways. While some scholars braid all three sources together within specific chapters, others pick up one or two strands to examine how they might interact with one another in more general terms.

Regardless of the precise approach, the broader message of this book remains the same: the sources of law must positively react and respond to one another in ways that give effect to Indigenous peoples' laws, values, customs, norms and traditions. The language of Indigenous rights is the language used by international and national law to accomplish this objective, yet, as Sa'ke'j Henderson reminds us in this book, Indigenous peoples have their own ways of describing what is meant by Indigenous rights within their own systems.

The challenge for people working in this field, as the authors of this book acknowledge, is to see Indigenous laws as possessing their own histories, contexts, powers and meanings. Indigenous peoples' own laws may be more broadly construed than either international law or domestic law envisions or allows. As a result, it may not always be easy to place these legal traditions in conversation with one another. Yet these deeply rooted differences should not prevent us from recognizing Indigenous laws on their own terms.

Indigenous laws flow from specific landscapes, ecosystems and peoples, as Aimée Craft and Cheryl Knockwood illustrate in their work. Indigenous laws should be recognized for what they are, without necessarily altering them to fit international or national law sensibilities. Yet

2 *Ibid* at 3.

their profound differences may challenge some practitioners and theorists of international and national law. For example, international law, in particular as it relates to human rights, is often presented as being universal, while Indigenous law might at times be more context specific. Moreover, national law is thought to be paramount in its sphere. These views about international and national law often leave little room for Indigenous law to question and perhaps even overturn the assumptions of practitioners in these other traditions. While Indigenous peoples' laws may contain so-called universal principles (at points), and they may interact with national laws in some ways, they cannot be wholly contained within either approach. Indigenous peoples' law is *sui generis*; it is not a creation of either international or national law, although it might be recognized and affirmed by other systems.

The braiding of Indigenous law with international and national law is thus a unique undertaking that helps us to reconceive the very idea of law. As suggested, Indigenous peoples' law questions the claims of both international and national laws to universality and supremacy. Law can be multidirectional in sources and application. It might be created by clans, flow from experiences with glaciers or rivers, or be sourced in custom and grassroots practices, as well as being created by legislatures, courts and executive authorities. In this light, some sources of Indigenous law might not make sense or even seem like law to people working in other legal traditions. Therein lies the challenge in braiding Indigenous law with international and national law: authority, responsibility, obligation, enforcement and persuasion, *inter alia*, may be differently construed in Indigenous contexts. Law is a social institution that has normative, analytical and specifically cultural components — it differs in time and place, and from group to group, when measured against the broader sweep of history.[3] It does not flow only from Westphalian, religious, secular or other so-called conventional sources.

The chapters in this collection explore how Indigenous law is both similar to and different from international and national law, and where Indigenous law and international and national law might combine to mutually support each other's objectives.

Part I: International Law Perspectives

In "The Art of Braiding Indigenous Peoples' Inherent Human Rights into the Law of Nation-States," Sa'ke'j Henderson starts the collection with a chapter on the inherent human rights of Indigenous peoples. He believes that further recognition of inherent human rights is inevitable for a new order of humanity, based on promoting and protecting inherent human rights and exercising Indigenous peoples' right to determine the development of their lives.

Sheryl Lightfoot, in "Using Legislation to Implement the UN Declaration on the Rights of Indigenous Peoples," writes about UNDRIP's future implementation through national legislation. She explains how national Indigenous organizations, the Truth and Reconciliation Commission (TRC) and the Canadian Parliament's Bill C-262[4] are important for this goal to be realized. The role of national legislation is to help bring clarity, consistency and momentum around UNDRIP's full implementation and to create open space for repealing the Indian Act,

3 Brian Tamahana, *A Realistic Theory of Law* (Cambridge, UK: Cambridge University Press, 2017).
4 Bill C-262, *An Act to ensure that the laws of Canada are in harmony with the United Nations Declaration on the Rights of Indigenous Peoples*, 1st Sess, 42nd Parl, 2016 (as passed by the House of Commons 30 May 2018), online: <www.parl.ca/DocumentViewer/en/42-1/bill/C-262/third-reading>.

accommodating Indigenous law and overturning discriminatory laws through the principles of free, prior and informed consent.

In my chapter, "Revitalizing Canada's Indigenous Constitution: Two Challenges," I focus on two important points. The first is that UNDRIP should cause the Canadian Parliament and courts to reject constitutional distinctions based on pre- and post-contact, since UNDRIP is focused on "peoples" and rights are vested in peoples, rather than asserting the existence of a right from a point before European contact. This "constitutional originalism" is contrary to Canada's "living tree" jurisprudence. My second point is that UNDRIP allows for more explicit recognition and application of Indigenous law within Indigenous nations across Canada. I recommend that Indigenous governments implement UNDRIP in accordance with their own legal and cultural worldviews, in order to strengthen their governance and provide for protection of their members.

Joshua Nichols, in "'We have never been domestic': State Legitimacy and the Indigenous Question," asserts that Canada should use the process of UNDRIP implementation to expose the problems with the current legal framework and remove the doctrine of discovery from Canadian law. He believes that UNDRIP offers Canada the opportunity to be a true world leader in the area of Indigenous rights, but only if the declaration is implemented in a historically informed manner that allows Canada to reconsider the history of the struggle for Indigenous self-determination. Only then will Canada be able to move toward a real nation-to-nation relationship with Indigenous peoples.

Gordon Christie explains, in his chapter entitled "Indigenous Legal Orders, Canadian Law and UNDRIP," that he believes the real challenge of UNDRIP implementation is for Canada to recognize and accept the strong legal pluralism of Indigenous and Canadian law. The intent of UNDRIP implementation is for Canada to work in a collaborative fashion with Indigenous nations. Gordon provides some recommendations for the Canadian government that, if followed, would allow for Indigenous law and Canadian law to be interwoven in light of principles and provisions contained in UNDRIP.

Brenda Gunn discusses how UNDRIP can be used to address the special needs of Indigenous women in a Canadian context in her chapter entitled "Bringing a Gendered Lens to Implementing the UN Declaration on the Rights of Indigenous Peoples." She points out not only that Indigenous women are in a deficit position when it comes to rights implementation (due to violence and discrimination), but also that Indigenous women have much to offer in positive terms to UNDRIP's application. She argues that using a gendered lens to enact UNDRIP can help parties to resist fundamentalism in the interpretation of Indigenous rights and to appreciate how rights are indivisible, interdependent and interrelated, thus avoiding troubling hierarchies that otherwise might be inadvertently embedded in the implementation of this document.

Part II: Indigenous Law Perspectives

Sarah Morales discusses, in "Braiding the Incommensurable: Indigenous Legal Traditions and the Duty to Consult," how free, prior and informed consent could be used to braid together the duty to consult and Indigenous legal traditions in a manner that may allow Canada to come closer to achieving the constitutional goal of reconciliation. Her chapter examines why the duty to consult and accommodate, as recognized under section 35 of the Constitution Act, 1982, has been unable to achieve reconciliation, and questions whether free, prior and informed consent can be a useful interpretive framework for the duty to consult. As well, Sarah emphasizes the importance of Indigenous legal traditions in implementing the duty to consult.

Larry Chartrand's chapter, "Mapping the Meaning of Reconciliation in Canada: Implications for Métis-Canada Memoranda of Understanding on Reconciliation Negotiations," issues a challenge to Métis leaders to account for the agreements they sign with governments in Canada. He argues that the concept of reconciliation found within their work falls far short of international standards and those found in the TRC because the agreements reproduce narrow interpretations of Aboriginal and treaty rights in Canada's constitutional jurisprudence. Larry questions whether Métis leadership is "selling out" by adopting watered-down versions of reconciliation found in the Aboriginal and treaty rights section of Canada's Constitution. While Larry considers the Canadian government's potential hypocrisy in pushing a deficient reconciliation agenda when its public comments are much broader, his chapter is important because it raises the question of Indigenous peoples' own complicity in failing to follow the higher standards of reconciliation in documents such as the TRC and UNDRIP.

In "Our Languages Are Sacred: Indigenous Language Rights in Canada," Lorena Sekwan Fontaine writes about some of the challenges that may be faced by the Canadian government on its recent announcement that it will work on an Indigenous Languages Act to support the revitalization of Indigenous languages. The objective of Lorena's chapter is to provide a survey of Indigenous customary law regarding Indigenous languages, as well as examples of how countries have implemented Indigenous language rights. She also provides recommendations on promoting and advancing Indigenous language rights in a timely chapter that should provide policy depth for Canadian lawmakers as they proceed with Canada's commitment to revitalize Indigenous languages.

Aimée Craft discusses article 25 of UNDRIP, which references, *inter alia*, Indigenous peoples' spiritual relationship with their waters and their responsibilities to future generations in this regard. Her chapter, "Navigating Our Ongoing Sacred Legal Relationship with *Nibi* (Water)," outlines an Anishinaabe approach to implementing this provision by reference to Anishinaabe peoples' own laws. She suggests this is done through advancing Anishinaabe peoples' sacred treaty relationships with "*nibi* [water], water beings and all of Creation," in an argument that is particularly attentive to how Anishinaabe language describes these relationships. The chapter highlights the role of relationality in deepening Anishinaabe responsibilities toward water through spiritual, natural, customary and human ways.

Cheryl Knockwood provides, in "Rebuilding Relationships and Nations: A Mi'kmaw Perspective of the Path to Reconciliation," a road map for Mi'kmaw governance to be recognized and affirmed through UNDRIP's implementation. She breaks this process into the smaller pieces of Mi'kmaw relationships with Mother Earth, experiences of injustice at the hands of government, the implementation of treaties and Aboriginal rights, including developing a Mi'kmaw Aboriginal and Treaty Rights Implementation Act, and hosting a Mi'kmaw Summit to develop a nation-building action plan. Along the way, Cheryl discusses the role of Mi'kmaw legal traditions, including stories, language and teachings about sustainability. By focusing on principles of being responsible, honourable, wise and respectful to rebuild the Mi'kmaw Nation, this chapter highlights the role of Indigenous law in resurgence and reconciliation.

Sarah Morales writes about the importance of UNDRIP for addressing violence experienced by Indigenous women in the extractive industry sector in "Canary in a Coal Mine: Indigenous Women and Extractive Industries in Canada." She explains that some of the specifically gendered impacts of extractive industries are related to personal safety, health, environment, culture and economic participation. Using a human rights framework, Sarah suggests that rights to culture, religion, health and physical well-being, and decision making hold the potential to break the worst abuses faced by Indigenous women when extractive industries operate within Indigenous territories. The chapter is significant because it shows how Indigenous peoples' right to sustainable development must reflect the concerns and solutions of both Indigenous men and Indigenous women to achieve reconciliation and implement Indigenous legal traditions in specific contexts.

Part III: Domestic Law Perspectives

Brenda Gunn provides a juridical path forward for implementation of UNDRIP in "Beyond *Van der Peet*: Bringing Together International, Indigenous and Constitutional Law." In Brenda's view, this will require resetting the relationship between Indigenous peoples and Canada by recognizing and protecting Indigenous peoples' rights, according to their own legal traditions. Canada's pledge to implement UNDRIP provides the ideal moment to reconsider the federal government's relationship with Indigenous peoples, which should include how Indigenous rights are defined and protected. Implementation also affords the opportunity to no longer apply the "central and integral to the distinctive culture" approach adopted by the Supreme Court of Canada in *Van der Peet*, and to find a more appropriate way to articulate the scope of section 35(1) of the Constitution Act, 1982.

Joshua Nichols, in "UNDRIP and the Move to the Nation-to-Nation Relationship," contrasts what he identifies as status quo reconciliation, which contains Indigenous jurisdiction within federal and provincial power, with nation-to-nation federalism, which would reject "racist fictions of discovery and *terra nullius*" and replace them with "processes of mutual agreement and consent that are found in the histories of treaty making." The significance of Joshua's chapter is that he identifies why it is necessary to change the narrative from an assimilatory one to one that recognizes Indigenous self-determination in flexible and mutually beneficial ways.

Jeffery Hewitt provides insight as to why many Indigenous people remain skeptical about Canada's intention to implement UNDRIP in accordance with the Canadian Constitution in his chapter, "Options for Implementing UNDRIP without Creating Another Empty Box." Hewitt explains that section 35 of the Constitution Act, 1982 provides for the potential that Canada could make the rights found in UNDRIP — such as the right to self-determination, the right to free, prior and informed consent, and the right to lands and resources — less meaningful. He is concerned that implementation that is consistent with the common law stemming from section 35 will only serve to maintain the status quo. The chapter provides recommendations for other means of implementing UNDRIP rather than through section 35, which Jeffery believes will meaningfully contribute to Canada's reconciliation discussion and advance the nation-to-nation relationship.

In "Asserted vs. Established Rights and the Promise of UNDRIP," Robert Hamilton writes about how UNDRIP's definitions of self-determination and of free, prior and informed consent do not fit within section 35(1) of the Constitution Act, 1982's doctrines of consultation and accommodation. Robert argues that section 35(1)'s reliance on categories of "asserted" and "established" rights is incompatible with UNDRIP implementation. The reason for this difference is that UNDRIP supports "a model of legal pluralism and negotiated jurisdictional sharing which the domestic Aboriginal rights framework has difficulty accommodating." Robert interrogates these distinctions in his chapter and concludes by providing examples of Indigenous-Crown relations that remove the asserted/established rights distinction from Canadian law.

Ryan Beaton, in "Articles 27 and 46(2): UNDRIP Signposts Pointing beyond the Justifiable-infringement Morass of Section 35," looks at UNDRIP's article 46, which recognizes that Canada can justify infringements of Aboriginal and treaty rights if it does so to "respect...the rights and freedoms of others and for meeting the just and most compelling requirements of a democratic society." Ryan's chapter argues that article 46 cannot be applied in isolation. Specifically, he notes that article 27 of UNDRIP requires governments to co-create dispute resolution processes with Indigenous peoples to address potential infringements before they occur. In making this point, Ryan asserts that this means that section 35(1)'s justification for allowing governments to infringe Aboriginal and treaty rights cannot be sustained in light of UNDRIP's implementation.

Kerry Wilkins begins his chapter, "Strategizing UNDRIP Implementation: Some Fundamentals," by discussing the political cost of implementing UNDRIP for Canadian governments, and details some ways in which UNDRIP challenges the status quo. He also discusses the costs for Indigenous peoples of not pursuing the implementation of UNDRIP. To examine these issues in greater depth, Kerry details four pressing questions that must be answered in the course of implementing UNDRIP: who are the Indigenous peoples that are to benefit from UNDRIP, what are the territorial spaces to which it will apply, how might it be enacted as domestic Canadian law and what is the Crown's role toward Indigenous peoples after implementation? The chapter represents a valuable contribution to the literature because it clearly identifies the most pressing challenges that Indigenous peoples and the Crown must face if they are going to successfully realize UNDRIP's promises.

In "UNDRIP Implementation, Intercultural Learning and Substantive Engagement with Indigenous Legal Orders," Hannah Askew discusses how the implementation of UNDRIP requires a significant investment of time and resources to learn about Indigenous legal orders. Drawing on former British Columbia Court of Appeal Chief Justice Lance Finch's phrase "duty to learn" in relation to Indigenous law, Hannah highlights resources that can be accessed to learn more about Indigenous legal traditions, including: "traditional stories; online audio recordings of storytellers and speakers; language lexicons; nation and band council websites; cross-disciplinary Indigenous scholarship, including graduate theses; anthropological writing, past and present (treated with caution, as it is often authored by non-members); public lectures; visual art such as carvings, poles and weaving, as well as dance, music and film." Moreover, Hannah discusses the place of land-based learning, social media and Indigenous leadership in this work. She expresses caution about some of the dangers involved in reinvigorating Indigenous law, all while acknowledging the gift that Indigenous law might provide for other Canadians as Indigenous law becomes a more significant force in the land.

Part IV: Concluding Thoughts

Gordon Christie's second chapter, "Implementation of UNDRIP within Canadian and Indigenous Law: Assessing Challenges," critiques conservative commentators who express caution about UNDRIP's implementation in the Canadian context. He warns that these critics are attempting to undercut measures designed to address structures of domination forged by colonialism, dispossession, oppression, loss of self-determination and cultural genocide. Gordon deconstructs these critics' arguments or concerns along three lines: first, that a broad interpretation of UNDRIP would require a fundamental restructuring of Canada; second, that UNDRIP would use non-Western notions of property and jurisdiction to address Indigenous territoriality; and, third, that UNDRIP would provide a veto to Indigenous peoples in relation to development of their lands. Gordon addresses each of these issues by pointing out the critics' "aversion to the notion Canada should relinquish absolute power over lands and resources unjustly taken from Indigenous peoples."

Joshua Nichols and Robert Hamilton's concluding contribution, "Conflicts or Complementarity with Domestic Systems? UNDRIP, Aboriginal Law and the Future of International Norms in Canada," discusses how Indigenous peoples might receive a fair and equitable distribution of benefits arising from the use of their genetic resources should they decide they want to allow this to occur. Examining the Nagoya Protocol on Access to Genetic Resources and the Fair and Equitable Sharing of Benefits Arising from their Utilization to the Convention on Biological Diversity, adopted as a supplementary agreement to the 1992 Convention on Biological Diversity, the authors propose a system for access and benefit sharing based on UNDRIP's standards that facilitates nation-to-nation dealing in this field.

Cheryl Knockwood speaks to the hopes of the Mi'kmaw Nation of eastern Canada for the full implementation of self-determination and the full implementation of Aboriginal and treaty rights through UNDRIP. In "UNDRIP as a Catalyst for Aboriginal and Treaty Rights Implementation and Reconciliation," Cheryl provides examples of the hard work that Mi'kmaw communities are currently undertaking to implement the spirit of UNDRIP in their communities.

Sa'ke'j Henderson completes this book with a discussion of how the concept of inherent dignity underlies many international rights norms and instruments. In "The Necessity of Exploring Inherent Dignity in Indigenous Knowledge Systems," Sa'ke'j encourages us to understand inherent dignity by engaging Indigenous knowledge systems and languages when interpreting this term. The benefits of this approach include seeing more clearly how Eurocentric concepts of dignity treat humankind as distinct from other life forces. Sa'ke'j also considers how the concept of inherent dignity might relate to inherent Indigenous rights and to the correction of historical wrongs suffered by Indigenous peoples.

This book reveals that while UNDRIP's implementation will draw from a variety of sources, Indigenous peoples' own legal judgments about this process must never be ignored. It shows how Indigenous law is an important source of authority in advancing the economic, political and other relationships that are key to Indigenous peoples.

In the past year, I have been involved with my colleagues in teaching Indigenous law in a braided way at the University of Victoria Law School in British Columbia. In the fall of 2018 we launched the world's first professional educational program in Indigenous law, which teaches Indigenous law alongside common law legal traditions. This experience has reinforced the value of comparing and contrasting legal traditions to understand where the gaps, inconsistencies and taken-for-granted assumptions are present in conventional law school teaching. As I teach Anishinaabe constitutionalism alongside Canadian constitutional law, it is very apparent that neither approach is universal, neutral, immutable or flawless in how they regulate action or resolve disputes. My colleagues who teach Cree law and criminal law, Gitksan law and property law, Salish law and tort law, WSANEC and other legal traditions find the same thing. Braiding legal traditions encourages greater nuance in applying law to the complex affairs of life where Indigenous peoples are involved. Triangulating legal sources and cross-referencing decision-making patterns allows us to better identify colonialism's biases, with greater clarity and precision. Braiding legal sources creates a richer tapestry of possibilities for pursuing justice when Indigenous peoples are involved, as the chapters in this book demonstrate.

PART I

International Law Perspectives

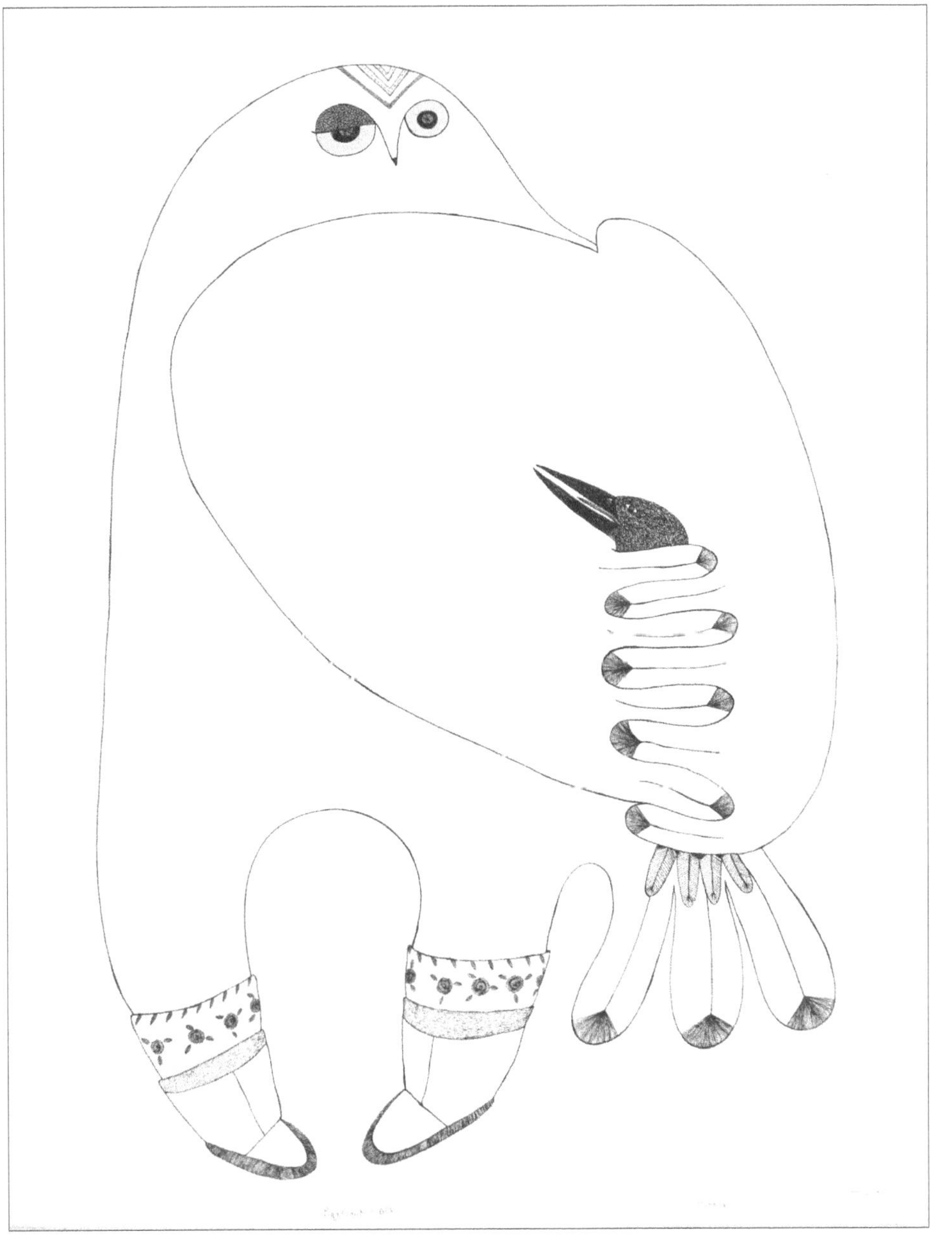

Previous page:

Piqatiglik BFF
Ningiukulu Teevee

2018, 76 x 58.5 cm, ink on paper

1

The Art of Braiding Indigenous Peoples' Inherent Human Rights into the Law of Nation-States

James (Sa'ke'j) Youngblood Henderson

In 1977, Elder and medicine person Phillip Deere (Muscogee Nation) delivered his "Longest Walk" speech in Washington, DC, after hundreds of others had walked across the United States to support tribal sovereignty and conduct talks at the White House. He declared, "We must understand that we are all human beings, it is important to be human beings, it is important to act like one. But if you can't act like one, you might as well not be one."[1] Elder Deere stressed that we must follow the natural laws of love, peace and respect that define Indigenous humanity, proclaiming that "[t]he freedom that the Native people is seeking today is to be free to be who they are. They have a right to be who they are. That's why I encourage the Indian people, you can be nobody else, there is no failure in life until you tried to be somebody else. So, you have to be who you are."[2] He also acknowledged that "we must know both ways of life, and that way no matter how much education you get, you will never forget who you are."[3] He insisted that Indian youth could not continue to stand around any longer. At that time, Elder Deere told me

1 A version of Elder Deere's speech can be found online at <http://descendantofgods.tripod.com/id108.html> [Deere, "Longest Walk"]. The reassertion of the inherent rights of Indians was articulated by the National Congress of American Indians in the 1961 *Declaration of Indian Purpose*, drafted by D'Arcy McNickle from the Flathead Reservation, online: <www.declarationproject.org/?p=32>. Elder Deere and others were also influenced by George Manuel and his book with Michael Posluns, *The Fourth World: An Indian Reality* (Toronto: Collier-Macmillan Canada, 1974).

2 Deere, "Longest Walk", *supra* note 1.

3 *Ibid.*

that our next longest journey was to fly like an eagle to the nest of the nation-states in Geneva to reclaim for all Indigenous peoples the humanity and dignity that was being denied to them in the United States, Canada and beyond.

Elder Deere and his vision of human rights guided me and other young Indigenous attorneys and activists to the multi-faceted UN system in Geneva, Vienna and New York, and to the Russell Tribunal in Rotterdam to assist in negotiating the recognition of our humanity, personhood and human rights in international law for the benefit of Indigenous peoples and the states parties. We were guided by an ancient teaching that humans have to search for their vision. This vision quest is difficult and requires many sacrifices, but the knowledge learned has tremendous potential for the people. To unleash the potential of this blessed vision, people must perform their vision before their relatives. The act of performance of the vision — by discussion, song, dance and story — empowers the vision in the rhythmical cycles of life. To keep the vision private, however, is to ignore the collective source of the vision and its purpose.

Our involvement in declaring our human rights is an example of the validity of this ancient teaching. Three protracted decades later, Elder Deere and others' visions were pronounced as part of UN law in the International Labour Organization's Convention No. 169 on Indigenous and Tribal Peoples (1989);[4] the United Nations Declaration on the Rights of Indigenous Peoples (UNDRIP) (2007) (in which the UN General Assembly affirmed Deere's vision);[5] the outcome document from the World Conference on Indigenous Peoples (2014);[6] and the Organization of American States' American Declaration on the Rights of Indigenous Peoples (2016).[7] We demonstrated that, together, Indigenous peoples can master complexity and build the framework of inherent human rights for an extraordinary era.

In general, the idea of inherent human rights is an entirely new frame of reference in the history of Eurocentric legal thought and traditions. While theories of natural and civil rights existed in Eurocentric legal thought, it was not until after 1966 that the inherent human rights of individuals in the UN human rights covenants[8] began to replace political utopian thought constructions about the state and justice.[9] Samuel Moyn argues that 1977 was the "breakthrough year" for individual human rights. This was the same year that Elder Deere and the Indigenous delegations formed the International Non-Governmental Organization Conference on Discrimination Against Indigenous Populations in the Americas in Geneva,

4 *Convention concerning Indigenous and Tribal Peoples in Independent Countries* (27 June 1989) (ILO No 169), 72 ILO Official Bull 59, 28 ILM 1382 (entered into force 5 September 1991).

5 United Nations Declaration on the Rights of Indigenous Peoples, GA Res 295, UNGAOR, 61st Sess, Supp No 49, UN Doc A/RES/61/295, 46 ILM 1013 (2007).

6 *Outcome document of the high-level plenary meeting of the General Assembly known as the World Conference on Indigenous Peoples,* GA Res 69/2, 69th Sess, UN Doc A/Res/69/2 (2014).

7 AG/Res 2888 (XLVI-0/16).

8 *International Covenant on Economic, Social and Cultural Rights,* 16 December 1966, GA Res 2200A (XXI), 21 UNGAOR, Supp No 16 at 49, UN Doc A/6316 (1966), 993 UNTS 3, Can TS 1976 No 46, 6 ILM 360 (entered into force 3 January 1976) [*ICESCR*] (Canada acceded to this covenant on 19 August 1976); *International Covenant on Civil and Political Rights,* 19 December 1966, GA Res 2200 (XXI), 21 UNGAOR, Supp No 16 at 52, UN Doc A/6316, 999 UNTS 171, Can TS 1876 No 47 (entered into force 23 March 1976) [*ICCPR*] (Canada acceded to this covenant on 19 August 1976); *Optional Protocol to the International Covenant on Civil and Political Rights,* 16 December 1966, GA Res 2200A (XXI), 21 UNGAOR, Supp No 16 at 59, UN Doc A/6316, 999 UNTS 302 (entered into force 23 March 1976) [*Optional Protocol*] (Canada acceded to this protocol on 19 August 1976).

9 Samuel Moyn, *The Last Utopia: Human Rights in History* (Cambridge, MA: Harvard University Press, 2012); RL Barsh & JY Henderson, "International Context of Crown-Aboriginal Treaties in Canada," CD-ROM: *For Seven Generations: An Information Legacy of the Royal Commission on Aboriginal Peoples* (Ottawa: Libraxus, 1997).

which was the first direct voice for Indigenous peoples and delegates at the United Nations. This conference began the process of reclaiming the inherent rights of Indigenous people based on Indigenous knowledge systems and law. The conference gave rise to Indigenous diplomacy and legal warriors.[10]

One starting point in implementing human rights is the need to comprehend the deep tension between inherent human rights and Eurocentric legal traditions of sacred and immanent order and the will of sovereigns.[11] Human rights are related to, but not derivative from, the Eurocentric idea of law as immanent order: an inherent or moral order latent in an intelligible and justifiable scheme derived from either an order pre-existing in nature, a discovered divine revelation or an artificially constructed social or cultural life that produced sacred laws and legal doctrines. For thousands of years, humans have viewed nature and society as expressing an immanent or sacred order, self-subsisting, if not self-generating, and independent of the human will or reason. Discovering that implicate order has been the essence of the work of jurists in constructing legal doctrine throughout Eurocentric thought and jurisprudence. This quest led to some knowledge systems discovering that human life or society could be artificially made, devised and ordered by a sovereign ruler or reason, rather than apprehending the hidden harmony of nature and submitting to it. Thus, the search for implicit order was displaced by an imposed order. This led to the idea of law as the will of the sovereign, and the sovereign's distinct law-making institutions' established law. The sovereign or state imposes law on society and humans to make a legal order. The source of all law is in the decisions of the constitutionally legitimated institutions; the sovereign or state delegates all private rights to its subjects or citizens. The assertion of the existence of inherent and inviolable human rights, arising either by nature or from other sources, becomes the antithesis of the will of the sovereign, even when the sovereign is viewed as residing in the people.

These two views of law — legal doctrines as founded on the latent normative order and law as the will of the sovereign — are incompatible; their relation to each other is that each of them is fundamentally incomplete and depends on religious beliefs or indigenous laws of the peoples that formed communities and societies.[12] The Eurocentric legal tradition of the imposed order of a sovereign has never been able to exclude the immanent or sacred, or customary, law. These residual laws have resulted in several legal revolutions or transformations in the Eurocentric legal tradition.[13]

10 James [Sa'ke'j] Youngblood Henderson, *Indigenous Diplomacy and the Rights of Peoples: Achieving UN Recognition* (Saskatoon: Purich, 2008).

11 Roberto M Unger, *The Universal History of Legal Thought*, online: <www.robertounger.com/english/pdfs/UHLT.pdf>.

12 See *ibid* at 2–3; John Rawls, *The Law of Peoples* (Cambridge, MA: Harvard University Press, 1999); LM Findlay, "Always Indigenize! The Radical Humanities in the Postcolonial Canadian University" (2000) 31 Ariel: Rev Intl English Literature 307: H Patrick Glenn, "Doin' the Transsystemic: Legal Systems and Legal Traditions" (2005) 50 McGill LJ 863.

13 Harold Berman, *Law and Revolution: The Formation of the Western Legal Tradition* (Cambridge, MA: Harvard University Press, 1983); Harold Berman, *Law and Revolution II: The Impact of the Protestant Revolution on the Western Legal Traditions* (Cambridge, MA: Harvard University Press, 2003) [Berman, *Law and Revolution II*]. Berman stated that "the word 'revolution' is often dated from the outbreak of the French Revolution of 1789, when the duke of Liancourt brought the news of the storming of the Bastille to King Louis XVI at Versailles. 'But that is a revolt,' exclaimed the king. 'No, Sire, 'said Liancourt, 'it is a Revolution'"; Berman, *Law and Revolution II* at 3. The national revolutions were the Lutheran (Protestant) Reformation in Germany (1517–1648), the English revolution (1640–1689), the French Revolution (1789), the American Revolution (1776–1783) and the Russian Revolutions (1905 and 1917).

UNDRIP is the latest revolution in legal thought. The inherent rights expressed in UNDRIP exist as a holistic reflection of the elusive implicit order of human life and behaviour developed by Indigenous thought and law. In the history of Eurocentric legal thought and transformations, inherent human rights have existed as a shadow realm that reveals and reflects the concept of law both as an immanent order and as the will of the sovereign. Both concepts have attempted to disguise or deny this implicit order of inherent human rights, which is now unfolding, by asserting that all rights are derived from the positive enactments of God or the sovereign.[14] The Eurocentric attempt to reconcile the conflict between inherent human rights and the idea of law of the sovereign based on social control and violence is a perennial, unresolved challenge. Indeed, Canada's assertion during constitutional talks in 1980 that the right to self-determination in ratified human rights covenants[15] did not apply to Indians because Indians were the wrong kind of people instigated our quest for the declaration of the human rights of Indigenous people.[16]

With the successful creation of a global consensus on inherent human rights of peoples, we have to find a way of braiding or implementing human rights of Indigenous peoples into national law of the states. The braiding will be more like contrapuntal music, rather than architectural blueprints. The quandary of how to implement the human rights of Indigenous peoples within the law of the nation-state is an important, pressing and daunting challenge, as these rights present an enigma to theories of Eurocentric law, as well as to Eurocentric theories of humanity and society. Indigenous peoples' human rights undermine and unsettle the arrangement of most nations, societies and politics, making these arrangements, derived from the institutions of the state, seem contingent, precarious and defective. These human rights reveal the innermost secrets of both Indigenous and Eurocentric approaches to humanity and leave unanswered many questions about the rule of law in forming or designing social order.

The initial goal of Indigenous peoples in articulating their human rights at the United Nations was to decolonize the colonized Indigenous peoples. It was to remind ourselves of our Indigenous teachings about how to be human and of the value of relying on these teachings, rather than following the Eurocentric version of humanity. Our vision of human rights was to have ourselves implement our ancient knowledge and laws in our daily lives and struggles, through

14 Groups have always existed, and they have asserted rights against other groups. Eurocentric international law has vested the nation-states with a monopoly over group rights and the regulation of the conduct of nation-states, although nation-states have the ability to recognize rights in certain collectivities and individuals, such as minorities and Indigenous peoples. Self-determination as a human right in juxtaposition to the "nation" and "state" is a manifestation of the Eurocentric concept that the sovereign can establish rights and entitlements by legislation. In Eurocentric law, the sovereign can establish or recognize the collectivities of individuals, usually identified as ethnic, linguistic, gender and religious groups. Although numerous Eurocentric theorists' works have contained drifting references to group rights or collective rights, few have developed an analysis; Jeremy Waldron, "Taking Group Rights Carefully" in Grant Huscroft & Paul Pishworth, eds, *Litigating Rights: Perspectives from Domestic and International Law* (Oxford, UK: Hart, 2002). Most have avoided or refused to discuss these collective rights, choosing to focus on individual rights; Linda Cardinal, "Collective Rights in Canada: A Critical and Bibliographical Study" (2000) 12 NJCL 165; Dwight G Newman, "Collective Interests and Collective Rights" (2004) 41:1 Am J Juris 127.

15 The UN law establishes that the right of self-determination is a matter of state law affirming a people's right to determine political, economic, social and cultural development; *Charter of the United Nations,* 24 October 1945, 1 UNTS XVI, Can TS 1945 No 7, art 55; *ICCPR, supra* note 8; *ICESCR, supra* note 8. As the *Optional Protocol, supra* note 8, signals, the state must respect self-determination in its national or provincial laws to be entitled to protection of its territorial integrity. In juxtaposition to this, as an aspect of external self-determination, is the recognized right of colonial peoples to break away from imperial powers that continue to subjugate, dominate or exploit them; *Declaration on Principles of International Law concerning Friendly Relations and Cooperation among States in accordance with the Charter of the United Nations,* 24 October 1970, GA Res 2625, UNGAOR, 25th Sess, UN Doc A/RES/2625(XXV).

16 See "Mi'kmaq Society v. Canada: The Right of Self-Determination and to be Involved in Public Affairs", online: Native Law Centre, University of Saskatchewan <www.usask.ca/nativelaw/un-human-rights--first-nations/mikmaq-society-v.-canada.php>.

community or collective solidarity and individual sensibilities. To renew these sensibilities in our legal traditions remains a challenging responsibility, the activation of which is commencing in most Indigenous communities. To live up to the concept of being a self-determining human, as expressed in UNDRIP, is our responsibility as Indigenous peoples; it is a new way to reform and empower our traditions and versions of humanities, to create a teaching to make us greater, individually and collectively.

A supplemental goal was to have the colonizing nations recognize and respect our inherent rights to Indigenous humanity and self-determination. This respect of our rights was designed to operate not only as a process to allow for mutual dignity and influence but also to distribute mutual competencies among the diversity of knowledge. This respect was reflected in the subsections of UNDRIP; the first subsection stated the affirmation of human rights, and the second subsection stated ways in which the states parties could braid these minimum inherent rights into their constitutions and laws. The general orientation of the second subsection was articulated in article 38 of UNDRIP: "States in consultation and cooperation with indigenous peoples, shall take the appropriate measures, including legislative measures, to achieve the ends of this Declaration."

No obvious way exists to reconcile each of the inherent human rights with contemporary law as the will of the sovereign, although they coexist with the drafting of UNDRIP, the American Declaration on the Rights of Indigenous Peoples and a number of other instruments and devices. A positive model was presented in 2008 when the Canadian House of Commons passed a motion in favour of implementing UNDRIP. The motion recommended "that the government endorse the United Nations declaration on the rights of indigenous peoples as adopted by the United Nations General Assembly on 13th September, 2007, and that Parliament and the Government of Canada fully implement the standards contained therein."[17]

Beyond gaining the recognition and compliance of the consenting states, Indigenous peoples had low expectations that the colonizing nations and their institutions would implement our inherent human rights.[18] Our apprehension was that the colonizing states would attempt to appropriate our inherent rights or dilute them in their attempt to implement our human rights. Inherent human rights belong to the people, not to the will of the sovereign, states or

17 See Grand Council of the Crees, "Ottawa Adopts International Declaration on the Rights of Indigenous Peoples", online: <www.gcc.ca/newsarticle.php?id=133>.

18 Canada has a dismal record of implementing human rights covenants that it has ratified; see Senate, Standing Senate Committee on Human Rights, *Promises to Keep: Implementing Canada's Human Rights Obligations: Report of the Standing Senate Committee on Human Rights* (December 2001), online: <www.parl.gc.ca/Content/SEN/Committee/371/huma/rep/rep02dec01-e.htm>. In Canada, no constitutional requirement exists for the involvement of or approval by Parliament or the provincial legislatures in the ratification or acceptance of UN legal obligations, the customary international law or UN treaties or declarations. However, Canadian legal conventions arising from its colonial status before constitutional reform in 1982 suggest that Parliament needs to enact the ratified UN human rights covenants and declarations. The colonial approach viewed the League of Nations and UN covenants and declarations as not being self-executing by executive ratification. Rather, the covenants ratified by the executives of the federal and provincial governments had to be implemented through domestic legislation in order to have full force and effect. Such covenants and declarations can and do influence judicial interpretations of related constitutional or statutory rights; see *Suresh v Canada (Minister of Citizenship and Immigration)*, [2002] 1 SCR 3 at para 60. The validity of this colonial convention is questionable in light of constitutional reforms and the principles of fundamental justice. The Supreme Court of Canada has recognized that the exercise of patriated constitutional authority in Canada includes the global system of rules and principles that recognized the rights of a people to self-determination; *Reference re Secession of Quebec*, [1998] 2 SCR 217 at paras 32, 113–33. The resistance to implementation or the failure to implement these international obligations, which were consensually ratified by Canada or the provinces, makes them into false promises, which is contrary to the spirit of consensual promises and the terms of the international human rights instruments themselves.

governments. All aspects of our inherent human rights belong to and serve our distinct and diverse knowledge systems, languages and laws, rather than the artificial settler states or their Eurocentric legal traditions of civil or common law. The Indigenous peoples' view was that none of our human rights affirmed in the conventions and declarations could be delegated to any states or their institutions through consultation and cooperation. They could only be recognized and promoted by the state with our cooperation for the purposes of preventing violence or discrimination against, or assimilation of, Indigenous peoples in our full enjoyment and effective exercise of our humanity. Indigenous peoples have pointed out that the Eurocentric state, with its reliance on violence, rather than persuasion, to make law binding and its many attempts to enact non-discriminatory laws, has failed to make significant changes in its citizens' thoughts or behaviour or to protect vulnerable peoples.

As Indigenous peoples enter the twenty-first century as self-determining people, the need is great to restore the Indigenous concept of humanity, to regenerate a consciousness that enables all peoples to enrich their situation and restore their dignity. To renew and live in accordance with concepts of Indigenous humanity, law and human rights, both collectively and individually, is the meaning and goal of UNDRIP. This meaning amplifies not only the existing treaties and agreements of Indigenous peoples but also the fundamental rights of Indigenous peoples, according to their Indigenous knowledge, legal systems and new agreements. Canada has affirmed that the inherent rights in UNDRIP will be promoted through the constitutional rights of Aboriginal peoples, as set out in section 35 of the Constitution Act, 1982,[19] and will not be imposed on them. The appropriate measure of braiding or implementing these inherent rights in Canadian law will be through initiatives undertaken by Aboriginal peoples of Canada in their nation-to-nation approach.[20]

The concept of implementing the inherent human rights of Indigenous peoples through treaties, agreements, constructive arrangements and partnerships with the states to achieve the ends of UNDRIP appears to most Indigenous peoples as a preferred option. The actual spirit and intent of the consensual agreements, both old and new, have always been based on these inherent powers and rights, and may not be interpreted as diminishing or eliminating the inherent powers or rights of Indigenous peoples. The consensual arrangements can be sufficiently restructured with the state to empower the exercise of inherent human rights. In the inner unity of overarching and respectful arrangements, no need exists to devise a legal order that accommodates antagonistic or divergent ideas, interests and wills of other groups. This approach does not require braiding inherent human rights with the will of the sovereign. However, this approach requires a deeper insight into the higher order and prophetic nature of legal traditions

19 *Constitution Act, 1982*, s 35, being Schedule B to the *Canada Act 1982* (UK), 1982, c 11.

20 Statement of Prime Minister Justin Trudeau, online: <http://pm.gc.ca/eng/minister-indigenous-and-northern-affairs-mandate-letter#sthash.o5wcHSgS.dpuf>; Minister of Indigenous and Northern Affairs Carolyn Bennett, "Announcement of Canada's Support for the United Nations Declaration on the Rights of Indigenous Peoples" (Statement delivered at the 15th Session of the United Nations Permanent Forum on Indigenous Issues, 10 May 2016). See also Canada's 2010 Statement of Support on the United Nations Declaration on the Rights of Indigenous Peoples, online: <www.aadnc-aandc.gc.ca/eng/1309374239861/1309374546142>: "We are now confident that Canada can interpret the principles expressed in the Declaration in a manner that is consistent with our Constitution and legal framework. Aboriginal and treaty rights are protected in Canada through a unique framework. These rights are enshrined in our Constitution, including our Charter of Rights and Freedoms, and are complemented by practical policies that adapt to our evolving reality. This framework will continue to be the cornerstone of our efforts to promote and protect the rights of Aboriginal Canadians."

and consciousness among Indigenous peoples and their right to self-determination than the present stage of my inquiry permits.

The vision of Elder Deere and the Indigenous advocates has been affirmed in the global consensus of the United Nations and has been endorsed by the states parties. Many challenging negotiations between the states and Indigenous peoples remain to be carried out to implement our inherent human rights, according to our choice and traditions, and to allow us to determine and nourish our own lives, as well as those of future generations. These negotiations are no longer seen as impossible, but rather as inevitable. Indigenous peoples are aware that in their attempts to live cooperatively and to braid their human rights into the national law of states through the development and implementation of national action plans, strategies and appropriate measures, they will be entangled in struggles with the states and other peoples. Nevertheless, these relentless struggles will unfold a new order of humanity based on promoting and protecting the inherent human rights of Indigenous peoples and on Indigenous peoples exercising their right to determine the development of their lives. These struggles will transform and decolonize the existing governance and legal systems, and will generate new visions of systemic justice to replace systemic injustices. To create systemic justice in the states, Indigenous peoples must encourage hope to prevail over past experiences, creativity over impossibility, constitutionalism over domination, prophecy over habit, kindness over the impersonal, place over time, solidarity over individualism, serenity over vulnerability, and empathic love and relationship over everything.

2

Using Legislation to Implement the UN Declaration on the Rights of Indigenous Peoples

Sheryl Lightfoot

"Effective implementation of the Declaration will be the test of commitment of States and the whole international community to protect, respect and fulfill indigenous peoples collective and individual human rights. I call on governments, the UN system, Indigenous Peoples and civil society at large to rise to the historic task before us and make the UN Declaration on the Rights of Indigenous Peoples a living document for the common future of humanity."

Victoria Tauli-Corpuz, chairperson of the United Nations Permanent Forum on Indigenous Issues, on the occasion of the adoption of the UN Declaration on the Rights of Indigenous Peoples, September 13, 2007

In the celebrations immediately following adoption of the United Nations Declaration on the Rights of Indigenous Peoples (UN Declaration)[1] by the UN General Assembly on September 13, 2007, minds were already turning to crucial questions of its implementation, both on the international level and in domestic contexts. The UN Declaration, which calls on all states to fully restructure relationships with Indigenous peoples, was a transformational moment in world politics. As Victoria Tauli-Corpuz, chairperson of the UN Permanent Forum on Indigenous Issues, noted in her celebratory remarks on the passage of the declaration, "This is a Declaration

1 *United Nations Declaration on the Rights of Indigenous Peoples*, GA Res 295, UNGAOR, 61st Sess, Supp No 49, UN Doc A/RES/61/295, 46 ILM 1013 (2007) [*UNDRIP*].

which sets the minimum international standards for the protection and promotion of the rights of Indigenous peoples. Therefore, existing and future laws, policies and programs on Indigenous peoples will have to be redesigned and shaped to be consistent with this standard."[2]

In the decade since its passage, the UN Declaration has gained universal consensus as an international human rights instrument and has been reaffirmed by consensus eight times in the General Assembly.[3] A report to the Human Rights Council by the Expert Mechanism on the Rights of Indigenous Peoples (EMRIP) on the 10-year progress of the UN Declaration noted that it now informs the work of many global actors, has influenced the drafting of multiple new state constitutions and statutes and has contributed to the development of laws and policies pertaining to Indigenous peoples worldwide.[4] A similar 10-year anniversary report by the Permanent Forum on Indigenous Issues recounted progress in the areas of increased constitutional recognition of Indigenous peoples and a growing body of jurisprudence, including important legal victories for Indigenous rights in the African Commission, Bangladesh, Belize, the Caribbean Court of Justice and Indonesia.[5]

Even with these positive steps, however, full implementation of the UN Declaration remains elusive around the world and in Canada. Even in countries with strong legal frameworks for supporting Indigenous peoples' rights and well-being, severe implementation gaps between legal recognition and concrete action steps on the ground remain, and, therefore, actual implementation on the rights of Indigenous peoples has been limited.[6]

Barriers to implementation, common to all states with Indigenous peoples, include difficulties operationalizing Indigenous rights due to a lack of awareness about the rights and standards, difficulties in identifying practical steps for implementation and conflicting interpretations of the content of Indigenous rights.[7] The 2014 UN special rapporteur's report on Canada's implementation progress noted that "the numerous initiatives that have been taken at the federal and provincial/territorial levels to address the problems faced by Indigenous peoples have been insufficient."[8] Yet, as New Democratic Party Member of Parliament Romeo Saganash (Abitibi–Baie-James–Nunavik–Eeyou) has aptly pointed out, "Implementation of the Declaration is a political, moral and...legal imperative, without qualification."[9]

2 UN Permanent Forum on Indigenous Issues, Press Release, "Message of Victoria Tauli-Corpuz, Chairperson of the UN Permanent Forum on Indigenous Issues on the Occasion of the Adoption by the General Assembly of the Declaration on the Rights of Indigenous Peoples" (13 September 2007), online: <www.un.org/esa/socdev/unpfii/documents/2016/Docs-updates/Statement-Press-Release-IDWIP-2007.pdf>.

3 Paul Joffe & Sheryl Lightfoot, "Legislative Framework Essential for UN Declaration", *The Hill Times* (10 January 2018) at 13.

4 EMRIP, *Ten years of the implementation of the United Nations Declaration on the Rights of Indigenous Peoples: good practices and lessons learned — 2007–2017*, UNHRC, 10th Sess, UN Doc A/HRC/EMRIP/2017/CRP.2 (2017).

5 UN Permanent Forum on Indigenous Issues, *Tenth anniversary of the United Nations Declaration on the Rights of Indigenous Peoples: measures taken to implement the Declaration*, UNESC, 16th Sess, UN Doc E/C.19/2017/4 (2017).

6 Sheryl Lightfoot, *Global Indigenous Politics: A Subtle Revolution* (Abingdon, UK: Routledge, 2016).

7 Victoria Tauli-Corpuz, *Report of the Special Rapporteur on the rights of indigenous peoples*, UNHRC, 27th Sess, UN Doc A/HRC/27/52 (2014).

8 James Anaya, *Report of the Special Rapporteur on the rights of indigenous peoples, Addendum, The situation of indigenous peoples in Canada*, UNHRC, 27th Sess, UN Doc A/HRC/27/52/Add.2 (2014) at para 81.

9 *House of Commons Debates*, 41st Parl, 2nd Sess, No 206 (4 May 2015) (Romeo Saganash) (debate on Private Member's Bill C-641, *United Nations Declaration on the Rights of Indigenous Peoples Act*).

The Need for Legislative Frameworks in Implementation Efforts

Former UN special rapporteur on the rights of Indigenous peoples James Anaya stated that the UN Declaration, as a consensus international human rights instrument, "reflects legal commitments that are related to the UN Charter, other treaty commitments and customary international law."[10] Because the UN Declaration is a pivotally important international human rights instrument, states have a political and moral obligation to implement it in domestic law and policy. The UN General Assembly has called for full implementation of the UN Declaration at both the national and international levels.

Implementation of Indigenous rights in domestic settings is expected to be comprehensive and systematic. Implementation has always been thought to include judicial reform, policy reform and legislative avenues, the synergy of which will lead to full implementation. A national legislative framework, one that includes mandates for a review of existing laws and policies, a national action plan, annual reporting mechanisms and a complaints mechanism, is an especially powerful first step toward full implementation.

As article 38 of the UN Declaration sets out, "States, in consultation and cooperation with indigenous peoples, shall take the appropriate measures, including legislative measures, to achieve the ends of this Declaration."[11] Former UN special rapporteur on the rights of Indigenous peoples Rodolfo Stavenhagen wrote, "[T]he rights in the Declaration can be seen as a framework of reference, a point of departure leading perhaps, among other things, to new legislation, to a different kind of judicial practice, to institution building and also, whenever necessary, to a different political culture."[12] As Stavenhagen describes it, a process of "glocalization" will occur where global-level standards, such as the UN Declaration, influence and contribute to changes in national and local-level political processes, and "it is precisely at the regional and country levels that the rights of the Declaration must be made to apply."[13] EMRIP's 10-year report on the UN Declaration implementation reads: "As States have the principal responsibility for adopting legislative measures and public policies to implement the rights recognized in the Declaration (article 42), they should adopt measures to achieve this aim, including through the implementation of recommendations and decisions of all human rights bodies referred to above."[14]

The UN special rapporteur noted in her 2017 report to the General Assembly, "The effective implementation of the rights of indigenous peoples requires States to develop an ambitious programme of reforms at all levels to remedy past and current injustices. This should involve all the branches of the State, including the executive, legislative and judiciary, and implies a combination of political will, legal reform, technical capacity and financial commitment.

10 James Anaya, *Interim report of the Special Rapporteur on the situation of human rights and fundamental freedoms of indigenous people*, UNGA, 65th Sess, UN Doc A/65/264 (2010) at para 62.

11 *UNDRIP*, *supra* note 1, art 38.

12 Rodolfo Stavenhagen, "Making the Declaration Work" in Claire Charters & Rodolfo Stavenhagen, *Making the Declaration Work: The United Nations Declaration on the Rights of Indigenous Peoples* (Copenhagen: International Work Group for Indigenous Affairs, 2009) 352 at 357.

13 *Ibid* at 356.

14 EMRIP, *supra* note 4 at 15.

Implementation should be measured against compliance with these requirements, and not on the basis of rhetorical claims of commitment or isolated measures."[15]

The handbook for parliamentarians on implementing the UN Declaration, published by the Inter-Parliamentary Union and several UN agencies, cites the law-making role of parliaments as of particular importance in the implementation of the UN Declaration.[16] The handbook suggests that legislative review and reform are essential first steps in implementation efforts and that all future national legislation should be evaluated for compliance with the UN Declaration as an ordinary part of the legislative process. The handbook provides existing examples of national implementation legislation already adopted by Bolivia in 2007 and the Republic of the Congo in 2011. A similar manual for national human rights institutions states that national legislation is an important first step toward domestic implementation, but "legislation alone is generally not sufficient"; thus, a national action plan should also be developed that includes legislation, a review of existing laws and policies, a complaints mechanism, stakeholder education, and active involvement of Indigenous peoples in the development and implementation of the action plan.[17]

The World Conference on Indigenous Peoples, at the UN headquarters in New York in September 2014, was held specifically to share best practices on Indigenous rights and their implementation. The more than 1,000 participants of the World Conference included member states, Indigenous organizations, non-Indigenous non-governmental organizations (NGOs), UN agencies and organizations, and independent experts. Plenaries were held on specific issues shared by Indigenous peoples around the world, such as land, territories, development and resources, and also about system-wide implementation of the UN Declaration within the UN system as well as in individual national contexts. The outcome document of the World Conference clearly stated the necessary elements for national implementation of the UN Declaration and the collective commitment of the UN member states participating: "We commit ourselves to taking, in consultation and cooperation with indigenous peoples, appropriate measures at the national level, including legislative, policy and administrative measures, to achieve the ends of the Declaration....We (also) commit ourselves to cooperating with indigenous peoples, through their own representative institutions, to develop and implement national action plans, strategies or other measures, where relevant, to achieve the ends of the Declaration."[18]

While no state has yet achieved full implementation, it stands to reason that implementation of Indigenous rights can ultimately be achieved — methodically — through a comprehensive approach including national legislation, a national action plan, policy reform and litigation. Maori legal scholar Claire Charters argues that Indigenous rights norms in both legal and political contexts are mutually enforcing. She finds that their repeated use in Indigenous political and legal advocacy, over time, will enhance the political and legal value of the UN Declaration

15 Victoria Tauli-Corpuz, *Report of the Special Rapporteur of the Human Rights Council on the rights of indigenous peoples*, UNGA, 72nd Sess, UN Doc A/72/186 (2017) at para 22.

16 Inter-Parliamentary Union, UN Office of the High Commissioner for Human Rights, United Nations Development Programme & International Fund for Agricultural Development, *Implementing the UN Declaration on the Rights of Indigenous Peoples: Handbook for Parliamentarians No. 23* (Geneva: Inter-Parliamentary Union, 2014) at 38.

17 *The United Nations Declaration on the Rights of Indigenous Peoples: A Manual for Human Rights Institutions* (Sydney & Geneva: Asia Pacific Forum of National Human Rights Institutions & Office of the United Nations High Commissioner for Human Rights, 2013) at 78.

18 *Outcome document of the high-level plenary meeting of the General Assembly known as the World Conference on Indigenous Peoples*, GA Res 69/2, UNGAOR, 69th Sess, UN Doc A/RES/69/2 (2014) at paras 7–8.

as states internalize the need to comply with Indigenous rights norms. Charters' study finds that "norm conformity can be achieved not only through legal sanctions or compulsion but also through the gradual normalisation and acceptance of the legitimacy of norms by the state and also the public at large."[19]

Calls for a National Legislative Framework in Canada

Calls for concrete national legal and political reform measures in Canada began as early as 2011 at the UN Permanent Forum on Indigenous Issues when the Canadian Indigenous Rights Coalition of Indigenous organizations and non-Indigenous NGOs issued a joint statement, delivered by National Chief Shawn Atleo of the Assembly of First Nations, on behalf of the coalition. The statement called on all UN member states to formulate national action plans to implement the UN Declaration with clear priorities and timelines and annual reporting, as well as a full review of existing laws and policies to assess their compliance with the UN Declaration.[20]

In June 2015, the Truth and Reconciliation Commission of Canada (TRC) announced the release of its summary report: *Honouring the Truth, Reconciling for the Future*.[21] This announcement concluded six years of intense and highly emotional work on the part of the TRC, which was created by the Indian Residential Schools Settlement Agreement.[22] The TRC was authorized to settle class action legal claims brought forward by residential school survivors. It conducted an extensive study of the century-long, church-run and government-funded Indian Residential Schools program in Canada, in order to reveal the truth about the program and its legacy impacts on Indigenous peoples.

The TRC summary report notes that healing the harm done to the relationship between Canada and Indigenous peoples, lasting more than a century and a half, will be hard. But, reconciliation, the report states, "is about establishing and maintaining a mutually respectful relationship between Aboriginal and non-Aboriginal peoples in this country."[23] While finding out the truth of residential schools was important, it was only the initial step in what is to be a very long process. The process of reconciliation will need to involve actions — actions that will fundamentally change behaviour at all levels of government and in all facets of society.

19 Claire Charters, "Use It or Lose It: The Value of Using the Declaration on the Rights of Indigenous Peoples in Māori Legal and Political Claims" in Andrew Erueti, ed, *International Indigenous Rights in Aotearoa New Zealand* (Wellington, AU: Victoria University Press, 2017) 138.

20 Joint statement of Assembly of First Nations, Chiefs of Ontario, Grand Council of the Crees (Eeyou Istchee), First Nations Summit, Haudenosaunee of Kanehsatà:ke, Innu Council of Nitassinan, Indigenous World Association, International Organization of Indigenous Resource Development, Louis Bull Cree Nation, Montana Cree Nation, Native Women's Association of Canada, National Association of Friendship Centres, Samson Cree Nation, Union of BC Indian Chiefs, Amnesty International, First Peoples Human Rights Coalition, Canadian Friends Service Cornmittee (Quakers), Amnistie Internationale, Hawai'i Institute for Human Rights, KAIROS: Canadian Ecumenical Justice Initiatives, "Implementation of UN Declaration" (19 May 2011) UN Permanent Forum on Indigenous Issues, online: Assembly of First Nations <www.afn.ca/2011/05/19/permanent-forum-on-indigenous-issues-free-prior-and-informed-consent/>.

21 TRC, *Honouring the Truth, Reconciling for the Future: Summary of the Final Report of the Truth and Reconciliation Commission of Canada* (2015) [TRC, *Honouring the Truth*], online: <www.trc.ca/websites/trcinstitution/File/2015/Findings/Exec_Summary_2015_05_31_web_o.pdf>.

22 *Indian Residential Schools Settlement Agreement* (8 May 2006), online: <www.residentialschoolsettlement.ca/IRS%20Settlement%20Agreement-%20ENGLISH.pdf>.

23 TRC, *Honouring the Truth*, *supra* note 21 at 6.

The TRC included 94 sweeping Calls to Action[24] as part of its report. These 94 recommendations, which were intended to form the blueprint for reconciliation into the future, call upon all layers of government — federal, provincial, territorial and municipal — to make fundamental changes in policies and programs in order to repair the harm caused by residential schools.

In its 2012 interim report,[25] the TRC first suggested that the UN Declaration could play an important role in any reconciliation project in Canada and suggested further exploration of this avenue. In the 2015 summary report, the TRC stated that it "remain(s) convinced that the *United Nations Declaration* provides the necessary principles, norms, and standards for reconciliation to flourish in twenty-first-century Canada."[26] The report goes on to note that an appropriate reconciliation framework would be one where the various legal and political systems of Canada, its educational institutions, religious institutions, corporations and civil society all operate in ways consistent with the principles of the UN Declaration, which provides a guiding framework for the sweeping changes necessary for Canada to work toward respectful relationships between Indigenous and non-Indigenous peoples.

TRC Call to Action 43 states: "We call upon federal, provincial, territorial, and municipal governments to fully adopt and implement the *United Nations Declaration on the Rights of Indigenous Peoples* as the framework for reconciliation."[27] Then, Call to Action 44 states: "We call upon the Government of Canada to develop a national action plan, strategies, and other concrete measures to achieve the goals of the *United Nations Declaration on the Rights of Indigenous Peoples*."[28] In all, 16 of the 94 Calls to Action refer to the UN Declaration.

Yet, as the Inuit political organization Inuit Tapiriit Kanatami (ITK) has observed, Canada's position to date on implementing the UN Declaration is one of "inaction"; ITK notes that more than 10 years since the declaration's adoption by the General Assembly, seven years since Canada's first endorsement and nearly two years since Canada's full endorsement, without qualification, of the UN Declaration at the UN Permanent Forum, Canada's commitments are more rhetorical than reflective of any concrete actions toward implementation.[29] The Assembly of First Nations has passed three separate resolutions calling for implementation of the UN Declaration through a legislative framework and national action plan.[30] A legislative framework is also supported by numerous other Indigenous organizations, non-Indigenous NGOs and churches.[31]

24 TRC, "Calls to Action" (Winnipeg: TRC, 2015) [TRC, "Calls to Action"], online: <www.trc.ca/websites/trcinstitution/File/2015/Findings/Calls_to_Action_English2.pdf>.

25 TRC, *Truth and Reconciliation Commission: Interim Report* (Winnipeg: TRC, 2012), online: <www.myrobust.com/websites/trcinstitution/File/Interim%20report%20English%20electronic.pdf>.

26 TRC, *Honouring the Truth*, *supra* note 21 at 20.

27 TRC, "Calls to Action", *supra* note 24 at Recommendation 43.

28 *Ibid* at Recommendation 44.

29 ITK, "Position Paper: Implementing the UN Declaration on the Rights of Indigenous Peoples" (2017), online: <https://itk.ca/wp-content/uploads/2017/01/ITK-Position-Paper-Implementing-the-UN-Declaration-on-the-Rights-of-Indigenous-Peoples-English.pdf>.

30 Assembly of First Nations, Resolutions 38/2015, 28/2016, 60/2016, online: <www.afn.ca/resolutions/>.

31 See e.g. KAIROS Canada, online: <www.kairoscanada.org/what-we-do/indigenous-rights/undrip-campaign>; "Open Letter to All Members of Parliament: Bill C-262 provides principled framework for implementing the UN Declaration on the Rights of Indigenous Peoples" (28 May 2018), online: <https://quakerservice.ca/wp-content/uploads/2018/05/Open-Letter-to-All-Members-of-Parliament-re-Bill-C-262-May-28-.pdf>.

In September 2017, the Committee on the Elimination of Racial Discrimination (CERD), which is the monitoring body for the International Convention on the Elimination of All Forms of Racial Discrimination (which Canada signed in 1966 and ratified in 1970), conducted its periodic review of Canada. The CERD report on Canada applauded the current government's commitment to implement all of the TRC's 94 Calls to Action but mentioned that the CERD is "concerned at the lack of an action plan and of full implementation."[32] The CERD recommended that Canada develop, in consultation with Indigenous peoples, a concrete action plan to implement the TRC's 94 Calls to Action and that it implement the UN Declaration, and adopt a legislative framework to do so, along with a national action plan, annual public reporting and a full legal, policy and regulation review to ensure that all laws and policies are consistent with the UN Declaration.[33]

On May 30, 2018, a private member's bill, C-262, An Act to ensure that the laws of Canada are in harmony with the United Nations Declaration on the Rights of Indigenous Peoples,[34] brought forward by Saganash, passed the House of Commons by a vote of 206 to 79, with only Conservative members of Parliament opposing.[35] It then proceeded to the Senate.

The Benefits of National Legislative Frameworks for Implementation (in Canada and beyond)

A national legislative framework to help implement the UN Declaration has been called for by international human rights institutions, the TRC, Indigenous organizations, non-Indigenous NGOs and churches. The UN special rapporteur on the rights of Indigenous peoples, EMRIP and the CERD have all advised that Canada move forward with a full national implementation plan, including a legislative framework. Doing so would be a major step toward bringing Canada into compliance with international human rights standards and the TRC's expectations.

A legislative framework would also help provide clarity and consistency in implementation efforts and demonstrate the priority status of implementation. It would affirm the centrality of the UN Declaration to reconciliation. Importantly, a legislative framework would compel the government to act promptly to harmonize its laws and policies with the UN Declaration and provide an accountability mechanism for implementation efforts. A national legislative framework would help produce momentum toward completion of a national action plan, legal and policy reform, and annual reporting on progress.

Implementation efforts will have more stamina with a national legislative framework in place. It would thereafter be difficult for future governments to arbitrarily roll back progress toward implementation.

32 *Concluding observations on the combined twenty-first to twenty-third periodic reports of Canada*, UN CERD, 93rd Sess, UN Doc CERD/C/CAN/CO/21-23 (2017) at para 17.

33 *Ibid* at para 18.

34 Bill C-262, *An Act to ensure that the laws of Canada are in harmony with the United Nations Declaration on the Rights of Indigenous Peoples*, 1st Sess, 42nd Parl, 2016 (as passed by the House of Commons 30 May 2018), online: <www.parl.ca/DocumentViewer/en/42-1/bill/C-262/third-reading>.

35 "Vote Details: Vote No. 684", online: House of Commons Canada <www.ourcommons.ca/Parliamentarians/en/votes/42/1/684>.

A national legislative framework would set a precedent for provincial and territorial governments to follow suit and pass their own implementation legislation, as recommended in TRC Call to Action 43. Implementation legislation in Canada would also provide a role model for other countries to follow.

Judicial interpretation could be aided by a national legislative framework, which — if it enshrines the principle of free, prior and informed consent — could help provide an alternative pathway to litigation and adjudication; this should eventually lead to a decreased need for court action. As the UN Declaration is being increasingly cited by courts, in Canada and overseas, legislation could help support legal implementation.

The TRC Calls to Action require explicit repudiation of all colonial doctrines, laws and policies, and a national legislative framework would help bring this into reality. It would also aid efforts to repeal and replace the Indian Act, and other colonial and discriminatory doctrines and laws, with more appropriate mechanisms, based upon the requirement of free, prior and informed consent of Indigenous peoples. Because the repeal of colonial and discriminatory laws is a requirement under the UN Declaration, legislation would help propel this major agenda item forward in Canada, building a coalition of support across several political parties.

A national legislative framework could also potentially support an opening for the accommodation of Indigenous law and legal traditions within Canadian law. Such progress is also required by the TRC Calls to Action.[36]

In sum, a national legislative framework is an important first step toward implementing the UN Declaration, in particular when that framework mandates many of the other crucial steps in the implementation process, including national action plans, a review of existing laws and policies, and an annual reporting mechanism. It would also set an important, positive tone for the wider implementation efforts required by provinces and territories, municipalities, corporations and civil society under the TRC Calls to Action.

36 John Borrows, *Canada's Indigenous Constitution* (Toronto: University of Toronto Press, 2010) at 191–92.

3

Revitalizing Canada's Indigenous Constitution: Two Challenges

John Borrows

Canada's Constitution is Indigenous in at least two respects. First, it is not merely the product of its European origins. Its colonial seeds were cultivated in North American soil and transformed in the process. In this sense, Canada's Constitution is Indigenous, homegrown in a distinctively North American context. Second, the ground from which Canada's Constitution grows first belonged to non-European peoples. Indigenous peoples' governance and lifeways are rooted in this place. Indigenous peoples variously resisted, incorporated, assimilated and rejected colonial actions throughout their lands. These facts have had a significant impact on Canada's wider constitutional trajectory. In the process, Indigenous peoples' own laws became a broader source of Canadian law.[1] The recognition and affirmation of Aboriginal and treaty rights is simultaneously commingled with their persistent denial. Canada's Constitution has been shaped by this tension; its "living tree" is both nourished and constrained by Indigenous peoples' presence throughout the country.[2]

1 *Connolly v Woolrich* (1867), 17 RJRQ 75 (Sup Ct), affirmed as *Johnstone v Connelly* (1869), 17 RJRQ 266 (QB).

2 The leading case on the Constitution as a living tree is *Edwards v Canada (Attorney General)*, [1930] AC 124. A history of the case is found in Robert Sharpe & Patricia McMahon, *The Persons Case: The Origins and Legacy of the Fight for Legal Personhood* (Toronto: University of Toronto Press, 2007). An example of contemporary references to the living tree are found in *Reference re Same-Sex Marriage*, [2004] 3 SCR 698 at para 22.

Unfortunately, more than 20 years ago, the Supreme Court of Canada (SCC) created a fiction that said Aboriginal rights could only be recognized and grow if they arose prior to European contact.[3] This was the *Van der Peet* case, which prevented Indigenous peoples from claiming constitutional rights related to practices, customs and traditions that developed after European arrival. This has stunted Canada's constitutional evolution. Aboriginal peoples have not been able to persuade courts or legislatures that they have constitutionally protected rights to governance, education, health care, justice and so on, and thus they have been cut off from taking appropriate responsibility for their own affairs. Because Aboriginal peoples have had difficulty proving that these activities were integral to their distinctive culture prior to European arrival, they cannot shield the exercise of their rights from Crown restrictions and interference.

The United Nations Declaration on the Rights of Indigenous Peoples (UNDRIP)[4] should cause the Canadian Parliament and courts to reject constitutional distinctions based on pre- and post-contact or assertions of sovereignty.[5] UNDRIP's application to Indigenous peoples does not rest on proof of pre-contact or pre-non-native sovereign assertions.[6] Rights are vested in peoples; peoples as identified in section 35(1) of the Constitution Act, 1982[7] should draw their meaning from international law and be regarded as a political category.[8] Peoples' rights within UNDRIP are also expressed in universal terms. Their exercise is not contingent on a non-Indigenous event (such as European contact with Indigenous peoples or the assertion of foreign sovereignty, as problematically required in Canadian case law). Article 1 of UNDRIP exemplifies this broad-based approach: "Indigenous peoples have the right to the full enjoyment, as a collective or as individuals, of all human rights and fundamental freedoms as recognized in the Charter of the United Nations, the Universal Declaration of Human Rights and international human rights law."[9]

The incorporation of universal human rights standards in the recognition of Indigenous law and governance is an important step in rejecting pre- and post-contact distinctions found in *Van der Peet* and the *Pamajewon*[10] decision (which measures Indigenous governmental rights by whether they were integral to the distinctive culture of Aboriginal peoples prior to the arrival of Europeans).

The *Pamajewon* case from the SCC problematically held that Aboriginal people did not have a "broad right to manage the use of their reserve lands" because "any asserted right to self-government, must be looked at in light of the specific circumstances of each case and, in

3 *R v Van der Peet*, [1996] 2 SCR 507 at para 46 [*Van der Peet*].

4 UNDRIP was enacted by the United Nations in 2007. GA Res 295, UNGAOR, 61st Sess, Supp No 49, UN Doc A/RES/61/295, 46 ILM 1013 (2007) [*UNDRIP*].

5 This idea is further developed in John Borrows, "Indigenous Law & Governance: Challenging Pre-Contact/Post-Contact Distinctions in Canadian Constitutional Law" (Article written for the Marx–Chevrette lecture, University of Montreal, September 2016) [unpublished].

6 For an argument that UNDRIP represents the development of international customary law relative to Indigenous peoples, see James Anaya, *Indigenous Peoples in International Law* (New York: Oxford University Press, 1996).

7 *Constitution Act, 1982*, s 35(1), being Schedule B to the *Canada Act 1982* (UK), 1982, c 11.

8 Catherine Bell, "Métis Constitutional Rights in Section 35(1)" (1997) 36 Alta L Rev 180 ("Rights arising from peoplehood are uncertain because the word 'peoples' is not defined in Canadian constitutional law and minimal domestic judicial opinion has been rendered on this point. However, it is a term which was used frequently in international political discourse at the time s. 35 was negotiated to distinguish colonized indigenous populations from nation states and ethnic minority immigrant populations within those states" at 185).

9 *UNDRIP*, *supra* note 4, art 1.

10 *R v Pamajewon*, [1996] 2 SCR 821 at para 27.

particular, in light of the specific history and culture of the aboriginal group claiming the right."[11] As noted, this narrow conception of self-government built upon the court's earlier decision in *Van der Peet*.[12] Since the regulation of high stakes gambling at issue in the *Pamajewon* case was held to be not integral to the Ojibwe people prior to European arrival, the SCC applied the *Van der Peet* case to find that Ojibwe people could not claim governance rights over the activity on their lands in the present day.[13]

Restricting Aboriginal rights to historical analogues prevents Aboriginal peoples from governing in a contemporary context, since many governance fields will not rest on practices that were central to them when Europeans arrived. This form of constitutional originalism is contrary to Canada's living tree jurisprudence.[14] Freezing the development of Aboriginal rights at the "magic moment of European contact"[15] is also contrary to the broad framing of rights found in UNDRIP, as illustrated in article 1. In my view, UNDRIP's constitutionalization in a Canadian context should be used to challenge and overturn the SCC's jurisprudence, which rests on pre- and post-contact distinctions.

Fortunately, Canada has committed itself to implementing the Constitution in light of UNDRIP's provisions.[16] In 2010, Canada passed a Statement of Support for UNDRIP, which stated that by endorsing UNDRIP, Canada was "reaffirming its commitment to build on a positive and productive relationship with First Nations, Inuit, and Métis peoples to improve the well-being of Aboriginal Canadians, based on our shared history, respect, and a desire to move forward together."[17] In 2016, Minister of Indigenous and Northern Affairs Carolyn Bennett further announced to the United Nations that "[t]hrough Section 35 of its Constitution, Canada has a robust framework for the protection of Indigenous rights."[18] Minister Bennett said, "We intend nothing less than to adopt and implement the declaration in accordance with the Canadian Constitution....By adopting and implementing the declaration, we are excited that we are breathing life into Section 35 and recognizing it as a full box of rights for Indigenous Peoples in Canada."[19] The "full box"

11 *Ibid.*

12 *Van der Peet*, *supra* note 3 at paras 45–47.

13 For a critique of *Van der Peet* and *Pamajewon*, see Bradford W Morse, "Permafrost Rights: Aboriginal Self-Government and the Supreme Court in *R. v. Pamajewon*" (1997) 42 McGill LJ 1011; John Borrows, "Frozen Rights in Canada: Constitutional Interpretation and the Trickster" (1997) 22 Am Indian L Rev 37; Russell Barsh & James Youngblood Henderson, "The Supreme Court's *Van der Peet* Trilogy: Native Imperialism and Ropes of Sand" (1997) 42 McGill LJ 993.

14 John Borrows, "(Ab)originalism and Canada's Constitution" (2012) 58 SCLR 352.

15 *Van der Peet*, *supra* note 3 at para 247.

16 *The Globe and Mail* reported that "[t]hirteen out of the 94 recommendations of the Truth and Reconciliation Commission invoke the United Nations Declaration on the Rights of Indigenous Peoples — including, naturally, the one that calls on Canada to adopt and fully implement the declaration itself." See "Adopting UN Indigenous Rights Declaration Could Worsen Damaged Relationship", Editorial, *The Globe and Mail* (19 June 2015), online: <www.theglobeandmail.com/opinion/editorials/adoptin-un-indigenous-rights-declaration-may-only-make-damaged-relationship-worse/article25048043/>.

17 Canada, Aboriginal Affairs and Northern Development Canada, "Canada's Statement of Support on the United Nations Declaration on the Rights of Indigenous Peoples" (12 November 2010), online: <www.aadnc-aandc.gc.ca/eng/1309374239861/1309374546142>. Furthermore, Canada stated, "We are now confident that Canada can interpret the principles expressed in the Declaration in a manner that is consistent with our Constitution and legal framework" (*ibid*).

18 Minister of Indigenous and Northern Affairs Carolyn Bennett, "Announcement of Canada's Support for the United Nations Declaration on the Rights of Indigenous Peoples" (Statement delivered at the 15th Session of the United Nations Permanent Forum on Indigenous Issues, 10 May 2016).

19 *Ibid.*

approach to section 35 should also cause courts and governments to reject pre- and post-contact distinctions in implementing Aboriginal rights.[20]

The minister's promise to adopt and implement UNDRIP in a constitutional context puts the Crown's honour squarely on the line. As the SCC wrote in R v Badger, "the honour of the Crown is always at stake in its dealing with Indian people."[21] Minister Bennett's pledge to implement UNDRIP in order to "breathe life" into section 35(1) must lead the Crown to work diligently toward the fulfillment of her promises.[22] As the SCC wrote in the *Haida* case, "In all its dealings with Aboriginal peoples, from the assertion of sovereignty to the resolution of claims and the implementation of treaties, the Crown must act honourably."[23] A promise to implement UNDRIP in relation to Canada's constitutional duties toward Aboriginal peoples must be interpreted generously and fulfilled in a diligent and timely manner.[24] Failure to advance UNDRIP's implementation in the ways discussed would be a serious setback for Indigenous-Crown relations, although it must be noted that failure to achieve the minister's promise would not necessarily, in itself, be a breach of the Crown's honour (if the Crown was diligent and other factors had prevented the fulfillment of its promises).[25]

The role of international law in Canada's constitutional system should also play a role in UNDRIP's implementation. Although international norms are not binding without legislative implementation,[26] such norms should be relevant sources for interpreting rights domestically.[27] While UNDRIP is technically not binding on Parliament because of its status as a declaration,[28] it should nevertheless inform the executive's (the Crown's) interpretation and implementation of the Constitution. For instance, the Crown could use its power to make arguments before the courts to directly insert UNDRIP into submissions related to Aboriginal and treaty rights, rejecting pre- and post-contact distinctions. The Crown could also do the same thing when developing, enacting and implementing statutes and policies to ensure that UNDRIP is the standard that animates its actions in the House of Commons, Senate, Cabinet and ministries. When the Crown more fully embraces UNDRIP's provisions, pre- and post-contact qualifications on Aboriginal rights can be rejected. The Crown's influence on Parliament is significant in our Westminster system. The Crown's active engagement in implementing UNDRIP would help to ensure, as the SCC wrote, that "the legislature is presumed to respect the values and principles enshrined in international law, both customary and conventional.

20 For a deeper discussion of the full box analogy of Aboriginal rights, see Ardith Walkem & Halie Bruce, eds, *Box of Treasures or Empty Box? Twenty Years of Section 35* (Penticton, BC: Theytus Books, 2003).

21 *R v Badger*, [1996] 1 SCR 771 at para 41.

22 Gib van Ert, "Three Good Reasons Why UNDRIP Can't Be Law — and One Good Reason Why it Can" (2017) 75:1 Advocate 29 at 30–31.

23 *Haida Nation v British Columbia (Minister of Forests)*, [2004] 3 SCR 511 at para 17.

24 *Manitoba Metis Federation Inc v Canada (Attorney General)*, 2013 SCC 14 at paras 76–79, [2013] 1 SCR 623.

25 *Ibid* ("However, a persistent pattern of errors and indifference that substantially frustrates the purposes of a solemn promise may amount to a betrayal of the Crown's duty to act honourably in fulfilling its promise. Nor does the honour of the Crown constitute a guarantee that the purposes of the promise will be achieved, as circumstances and events may prevent fulfillment, despite the Crown's diligent efforts" at para 82).

26 *R v Sharpe*, [2001] 1 SCR 45 at para 175 [*Sharpe*], referring to *Reference Re Public Service Employee Relations Act (Alta)*, [1987] 1 SCR 313 at 349–50 and *Baker v Canada (Minister of Citizenship and Immigration)*, [1999] 2 SCR 817.

27 *Sharpe*, *supra* note 26.

28 Under this view, Parliament is presumed to act in compliance with its international obligations and to respect the values and principles enshrined in international law through the presumption of conformity, as the courts have recognized; *R v Hape*, 2007 SCC 26 at para 54, [2007] 2 SCR 292. For reasons that UNDRIP is not directly applicable as law in Canada, see van Ert, *supra* note 22.

These constitute a part of the legal context in which legislation is enacted and read. In so far as possible, therefore, interpretations that reflect these values and principles are preferred."[29]

In following the paths outlined above, for example, articles 4 and 5 of UNDRIP challenge the idea that Indigenous peoples can only exercise governmental power if that power was "integral to their distinctive culture" prior to the arrival of Europeans. Article 4 states, "Indigenous peoples, in exercising their right to self-determination, have the right to autonomy or self-government in matters relating to their internal and local affairs, as well as ways and means for financing their autonomous functions."[30] Article 5 states, "Indigenous peoples have the right to maintain and strengthen their distinct political, legal, economic, social and cultural institutions, while retaining their right to participate fully, if they so choose, in the political, economic, social and cultural life of the State."[31]

These articles contest Pamajewon's narrow view of Indigenous governance because they construe governance in a broad light. Self-determination in political, legal, economic, social and cultural matters is the subject of Indigenous self-determination. Indigenous peoples' own laws become a more prominent part of Canada's Constitution under this approach.

Article 27 supports this conclusion through its recognition that Canadian law must give effect to Indigenous peoples' law. It demonstrates that Indigenous law should form a part of how the Constitution recognizes and adjudicates in relation to Indigenous peoples. Article 27 reads: "States shall establish and implement, in conjunction with indigenous peoples concerned, a fair, independent, impartial, open and transparent process, giving due recognition to indigenous peoples' laws, traditions, customs and land tenure systems, to recognize and adjudicate the rights of indigenous peoples pertaining to their lands, territories and resources, including those which were traditionally owned or otherwise occupied or used. Indigenous peoples shall have the right to participate in this process."[32]

Article 27's standard requires states to recognize Indigenous peoples' laws in their adjudicative processes. While there is much more work to do, Canada has already implicitly recognized Indigenous law as a foundation for Aboriginal title under the Constitution, as demonstrated in the *Tsilhqot'in*[33] case. Tsilhqot'in law had a pre-existing and continuing force that was prominent in establishing title.[34] As I have argued elsewhere:

> Tsilhqot'in Elders testified about the continuity of their ways of life in their own language using their legal traditions.[35] Indigenous law was key to establishing a

29 *Sharpe*, *supra* note 26, citing Ruth Sullivan & Elmer A Driedger, *Driedger on the Construction of Statutes*, 3rd ed (Toronto: Butterworths, 1994) at 330.

30 *UNDRIP*, *supra* note 4, art 4.

31 *Ibid*, art 5.

32 *Ibid*, art 27 [emphasis added].

33 *Tsilhqot'in Nation v British Columbia*, [2014] 2 SCR 256.

34 Continuity of occupation through social organization was necessary to prove Aboriginal title; *ibid* at paras 45–46, 57.

35 *Tsilhqot'in Nation v British Columbia*, 2007 BCSC 1700 at paras 149, 167, 176, 360, 362, 381, 397, 399, 403, 431–35.

sufficiency of Indigenous social organization that was necessary to prove title.[36] Tsilhqot'in rules of conduct were central to proving that the Tsilhqot'in historically and presently occupied land in the contested region....[37] [T]he SCC implicitly affirmed that Indigenous legal traditions can give rise to enforceable obligations within Canadian law.[38] Social organization should be treated as a synonym for self-government.[39] When a nation organizes itself socially on a territorial basis, and through its own laws controls land, makes decisions about its use and excludes others, we should conclude that such a nation governs itself.[40] First Nations governance is an important dimension of Aboriginal title.[41]

Implementing UNDRIP within Indigenous Communities

Furthermore, the significance of Indigenous peoples' laws for internal governance matters should also be recognized as part of Canada's Indigenous constitution through UNDRIP's implementation. Article 18 makes this clear: "Indigenous peoples have the right to participate in decision-making in matters which would affect their rights, through representatives chosen by themselves in accordance with their own procedures, as well as to maintain and develop their own indigenous decision-making institutions."[42]

The adoption of UNDRIP clears the path for a more explicit recognition and application of Indigenous law within Indigenous nations across Canada. As part of this development, Indigenous peoples themselves could also implement UNDRIP within their own nations to ensure that their own people are both empowered by and protected from their own

36 *Ibid* ("'the Tsilhqot'in had laws, and that those for which there is evidence appear to have been broadly similar to the laws of other many North American Aboriginal groups'...[T]here was evidence 'that supports the view that chiefs had specific lands within Tsilhqot'in territory and that these lands descended on some sort of hereditary principle.' I too am satisfied that an examination of the historical records leads to a conclusion that Tsilhqot'in people did consider the land to be their land. They also had a concept of territory and boundaries, although this appears to have been enlarged following the movements of the mid-nineteenth century" at para 429).

37 *Ibid* ("Some of the stories and legends told to the Court by Tsilhqot'in elders include: Lhin Desch'osh, the legend of how the land was transformed and the animals made less dangerous; Ts'il'os and Eniyudl; How Raven Stole the Sun; A Story of Raven Stealing Fire; The Story of Salmon Boy; The Story of the Woman and the Bear; The Story of Lady Rock; The Story of Qitl'ax Xen, a boy raised by his grandmother; The Story of Guli, the Skunk; A Story About a Brother and a Sister; A Story About an Owl; Two Sisters and the Stars; and, Frog Steals a Baby. This is not a complete list, but it is representative of the legends I heard. Each carries with it an underlying message or moral that is intended to instruct and inform Tsilhqot'in people in the way they are to lead their lives. *They set out the rules of conduct*, a value system passed from generation to generation" at paras 433–34 [emphasis added]). See also *ibid* ("Various Tsilhqot'in elders testified about dechen ts' edilhtan (the laws of our ancestors)" at para 431).

38 A similar point is made in Val Napoleon, *Tsilhqot'in Law of Consent* (on file with author). See also Jeremy Webber, "The Public-Law Dimension of Indigenous Property Rights" in Nigel Bankes & Timo Koivurova, eds, *The Proposed Nordic Saami Convention: National and International Dimensions of Indigenous Property Rights* (Oxford, UK: Hart, 2013) 79.

39 In *Delgamuukw v British Columbia*, [1997] 3 SCR 1010 at para 159, Chief Justice Lamer observed, "the foundation of 'aboriginal title' was succinctly described by Judson J. in *Calder v. Attorney-General of British Columbia*, [1973] S.C.R. 313, where, at p. 328, he stated: 'the fact is that when the settlers came, the Indians were there, *organized in societies* and occupying the land as their forefathers had done for centuries'" [emphasis added].

40 For a discussion of contemporary Tsilhqot'in legal traditions as they relate to governance, see Hadley Friedland, Jessica Asch, Maegan Hough, Renee McBeth & Al Hanna, from the Indigenous Law Research Unit, *Tsilhqot'in Legal Traditions Report* (2014) [unpublished, archived with Val Napoleon and Tsilhqot'in National Government]. For related materials, see Indigenous Bar Association, online: <http://indigenousbar.ca/indigenouslaw/>.

41 John Borrows, "Aboriginal Title and Private Property" (2015) 71 SCLR 91 at 109 [footnotes in original].

42 *UNDRIP*, *supra* note 4, art 18.

governments. In this respect, UNDRIP would be further entrenched as part of Canada's Indigenous constitution.

UNDRIP is an Indigenous instrument; it was created broadly by Indigenous peoples as it was negotiated for more than 30 years at the United Nations.[43] Internal adoption of UNDRIP's principles would positively and radically challenge the calibration of Indigenous governance by reference to pre- and post-contact categories.

Rights identified by UNDRIP should be available within self-governing Indigenous nations across Canada. Once adopted, they can be interpreted in accordance with the Indigenous peoples' own legal traditions,[44] in Indigenous adjudicative forums.[45] While UNDRIP was drafted with the intent of securing UN recognition of Indigenous peoples' rights as against nation-states, its broad statements can also be construed as recognizing, affirming and protecting the human rights of Indigenous individuals in their relations with their own governments.[46] For instance, article 1 of UNDRIP indicates that Indigenous individuals possess human rights.[47] It proclaims, "Indigenous peoples have the right to the full enjoyment, as a collective or as individuals, of all human rights and fundamental freedoms as recognized in the Charter of the United Nations, the Universal Declaration of Human Rights and international human rights law."[48] Under this view, it would not be contrary to the spirit of UNDRIP to recognize that Indigenous governments have obligations in relation to individuals who fall within their jurisdictions.[49] The adoption of UNDRIP by First Nations, Metis and Inuit communities would reinforce this view. It would be tragically ironic if nation-states began recognizing and protecting the rights of Indigenous individuals, while Indigenous governments did not take the same action.[50]

It is instructive to itemize UNDRIP provisions that could apply to individuals within Indigenous nations. UNDRIP lists the following rights and freedoms for Indigenous peoples: religion,

43 Lillian Aponte Miranda, "Indigenous Peoples as International Lawmakers" (2010) 32 U Pa J Intl L 210.

44 This argument is made in the Charter context in David Milward, *Aboriginal Justice and the Charter: Realizing a Culturally Sensitive Interpretation of Legal Rights in Canada* (Vancouver, BC: UBC Press, 2012).

45 In the United States, tribal courts generally deal with human rights issues, see *Santa Clara Pueblo v Martinez*, 436 US 49, 98 S Ct 1670 (1978). For further discussion of the development of human rights perspectives in US tribal forums, see Angela Riley & Kristen Carpenter, "Indigenous Peoples and the Jurisgenerative Moment in Human Rights" (2014) 102 Cal L Rev 173.

46 *UNDRIP*, *supra* note 4 ("Recognizing and reaffirming that indigenous individuals are entitled without discrimination to all human rights recognized in international law", Preamble; "Indigenous peoples have the right to the full enjoyment, as a collective or as individuals, of all human rights and fundamental freedoms as recognized in the Charter of the United Nations, the Universal Declaration of Human Rights and international human rights law", art 1).

47 *Ibid*, art 1.

48 *Ibid.*

49 In fact, under article 35 of UNDRIP, the countries of the world proclaimed that "Indigenous peoples have the right to determine the responsibilities of individuals to their communities." While rights are not necessarily equivalent to obligations, such statements signal recognition of the importance of healthy international relationships within Indigenous governments.

50 UNDRIP's Preamble welcomes "the fact that indigenous peoples are organizing themselves for political, economic, social and cultural enhancement…in order to bring to an end all forms of discrimination and oppression wherever they occur." As Indigenous nations further organize themselves to bring an end to discrimination within their communities, this presumably fits within the activities encouraged by UNDRIP.

spiritual beliefs and practices;[51] speech and expression;[52] association;[53] life, liberty and security;[54] property;[55] family togetherness;[56] a right not to be discriminated against by their governments;[57] the privileges and immunities of citizenship;[58] language;[59] education;[60] labour fairness;[61] administrative law (notice, fairness, hearing);[62] health care;[63] and gender equality.[64] These apply in accordance with limitations imposed by law and in accordance with international law.[65] Again, while it is important to recognize that these laws were enumerated to apply as against states recognized by the United Nations, there is no good reason for restricting their reach in this respect, particularly if self-determination is the lens through which Indigenous human rights are recognized and affirmed.[66] To repeat, the widespread support among Indigenous peoples in the drafting and ratification of UNDRIP, along with the now-unanimous acceptance of this document at the United Nations, signals expectations that human rights, not only of communities, but also of Indigenous individuals, must be respected. It is arguable that this is the case no matter the source of government authority that impacts upon those individuals.

51 *UNDRIP*, *supra* note 4 ("Indigenous peoples have the right to manifest, practice, develop and teach their spiritual and religious traditions, customs and ceremonies; the right to maintain, protect, and have access in privacy to their religious and cultural sites; the right to the use and control of their ceremonial objects; and the right to the repatriation of their human remains", art 12(1); "States shall seek to enable the access and/or repatriation of ceremonial objects and human remains in their possession through fair, transparent and effective mechanisms developed in conjunction with indigenous peoples concerned", art 12(2)). See also *ibid*, arts 25, 36.

52 *Ibid*, art 31.

53 *Ibid* ("Indigenous peoples have the right to maintain and strengthen their distinct political, legal, economic, social and cultural institutions, while retaining their right to participate fully, if they so choose, in the political, economic, social and cultural life of the State", art 5).

54 *Ibid* ("Indigenous individuals have the rights to life, physical and mental integrity, liberty and security of person", art 7(1)).

55 *Ibid* ("Indigenous peoples shall not be forcibly removed from their lands or territories. No relocation shall take place without the free, prior and informed consent of the indigenous peoples concerned and after agreement on just and fair compensation and, where possible, with the option of return", art 10). See also *ibid*, arts 26, 28–30.

56 *Ibid* ("Indigenous peoples have the collective right to live in freedom, peace and security as distinct peoples and shall not be subjected to any act of genocide or any other act of violence, including forcibly removing children of the group to another group", art 7(2)).

57 *Ibid* ("Indigenous peoples and individuals are free and equal to all other peoples and individuals and have the right to be free from any kind of discrimination, in the exercise of their rights, in particular that based on their indigenous origin or identity", art 2). See also *ibid*, art 15(2).

58 *Ibid* ("Indigenous peoples and individuals have the right to belong to an indigenous community or nation, in accordance with the traditions and customs of the community or nation concerned. No discrimination of any kind may arise from the exercise of such a right", art 9). See also *ibid*, art 33.

59 *Ibid*, arts 13, 16.

60 *Ibid*, arts 14, 21.

61 *Ibid*, art 17.

62 *Ibid*, arts 17–19, 21–23, 32.

63 *Ibid*, art 24.

64 *Ibid*, art 44.

65 *Ibid*, art 46 (a Canadian Charter, section 1, type of provision).

66 See *Report of the Working Group on Indigenous Populations on its Eleventh Session*, UNESCOR, 45th Sess, UN Doc E/CN.4/Sub.2/1993/29 (1993) paras 189–91. See also Frank Pommersheim, "At the Crossroads: A New and Unfortunate Paradigm of Tribal Sovereignty" (2010) 55 SDL Rev 48 at 65–66; Rebecca Tsosie, "Reconceptualizing Tribal Rights: Can Self-Determination Be Actualized Within the U.S. Constitutional Structure?" (2011) 15 Lewis & Clark L Rev 923.

Conclusion

The application of UNDRIP by both Canadian and Indigenous governments, through UNDRIP's commitment to self-determination, should help courts discard pre- and post-contact distinctions in Canadian constitutional law. UNDRIP's embrace by the Canadian government fundamentally changes the character of the debate surrounding Indigenous law and governance.[67] *Van der Peet* and *Pamajewon* should be overturned; *stare decisis* should not be a straitjacket that condemns the law to stasis,[68] particularly when such stasis continues to tear the fabric of constitutional reconciliation as it relates to Indigenous peoples.[69] Furthermore, Indigenous peoples' own law must grapple on its own terms — and in accordance with its own cultural worldview — with UNDRIP's provisions. This will strengthen Indigenous governance and protect Indigenous citizens from their own governments in ways that syncretically draw upon Indigenous peoples' own regulatory and dispute resolution structures.

67 *Carter v Canada (Attorney General)*, 2015 SCC 5 at para 43 *[Carter]*, citing *Canada (Attorney General) v Bedford*, 2013 SCC 72, [2013] 3 SCR 1101 ("Trial courts may reconsider settled rulings of higher courts in two situations: (1) where a new legal issue is raised; and (2) where there is a change in the circumstances or evidence that 'fundamentally shifts the parameters of the debate'" at para 42).

68 *Carter, supra* note 67 at para 44.

69 Truth and Reconciliation Commission of Canada, *Honouring the Truth, Reconciling for the Future: Summary of the Final Report of the Truth and Reconciliation Commission of Canada* (2015), online: <www.trc.ca/websites/trcinstitution/File/2015/Findings/Exec_Summary_2015_05_31_web_o.pdf>.

4

"We have never been domestic": State Legitimacy and the Indigenous Question

Joshua Nichols

The Canadian government is currently examining what it means to implement the United Nations Declaration on the Rights of Indigenous Peoples (UNDRIP).[1] The most likely approach is to adapt UNDRIP to the existing juridical framework for Aboriginal rights and title under section 25 of the Charter,[2] section 35 of the Constitution Act, 1982[3] and section 91(24) of the Constitution Act, 1867.[4] While this could well seem to be the best approach to take when adopting an international declaration into constitutional law, it is not advisable in this area. The standards of UNDRIP should instead be used as a means to expose the problems with the current framework and to change the law by removing the doctrine of discovery from Canadian law. In order to see why the existing framework for Aboriginal rights and title is so problematic, we need to consider the history of the struggle for Indigenous self-determination in Canada over the last 240 years. This offers us a different perspective on the nature of the constitutional relationship between the Crown and Aboriginal peoples. A more historically informed and circumspect approach to the question of implementation offers the Canadian government the

1 *United Nations Declaration on the Rights of Indigenous Peoples*, GA Res 295, UNGAOR, 61st Sess, Supp No 49, UN Doc A/RES/61/295, 46 ILM 1013 (2007) [*UNDRIP*].

2 *Canadian Charter of Rights and Freedoms*, Part 1 of the *Constitution Act, 1982*, being Schedule B to the *Canada Act 1982* (UK), 1982, c 11.

3 *Constitution Act, 1982*, being Schedule B to the *Canada Act 1982* (UK), 1982, c 11.

4 *Constitution Act, 1867* (UK), 30 & 31 Vict, c 3, reprinted in RSC 1985, Appendix 11, No 5.

rare opportunity to be a true world leader in the area of Indigenous rights. By using UNDRIP to revitalize the current body of law and remove the existing barriers to self-determination, it is possible to foster a real nation-to-nation relation and restart the currently stalled process of reconciliation.

The question of implementation may be unprecedented in Canadian law, and as such it extends before us as part of the vast and unexplored territory of reconciliation. It is tempting to cast our gaze to the horizon and try to anticipate the path ahead. Justice Ian Binnie's words from *Beckman v Little Salmon/Carmacks First Nation* provide us with some guidance on how the courts are currently finding their way: "the future is more important than the past. A canoeist who hopes to make progress faces forwards, not backwards."[5]

This approach captures what has become of reconciliation in the courts: they have, in effect, crafted it into a blank map of the future. The government has taken it as their framework and now seems poised to continue the 150-year-old push into a future that could somehow escape the realities of its past. But attempting to survey the future is a risky venture; more often than not, it is the province of prophets and fortune tellers. If the way forward has little to offer us, how are we to get our bearings? How can we bring reconciliation back from this peculiar holiday?

My response is that we begin by refusing the temptation to look toward blank maps of the future, with their endless promises of a reconciliation *to come* — whose reality in the present is always confined to being simply a reconciliation *to the status quo*. In order to achieve authentic reconciliation, we need to ask what reconciliation means by looking behind us: we need a reconciliation with recollection. This means that the question of implementation cannot be limited to the abstract and formal application of a domestic constitutional "framework" to an international declaration. This exercise simply uses one framework to determine the measure of the other, which is as pointless as holding something against its own shape and seeing that it fits.[6] If reconciliation is going to come back from holiday, the question of implementation has to begin from the context of settler colonialism. This means that it must begin by acknowledging that the relationship between the struggle for Aboriginal self-government and international law is by no means a new one. Nor is implementation merely a domestic issue. It is, as Sa'ke'j Henderson rightly states, "part of the unfinished business of decolonization."[7]

In order to address the question of implementation, I will provide a sketch of the various points of convergence and overlap that connect the struggle for Aboriginal self-government in Canada and the international project of decolonization beginning in the 1920s. This is a rough and very limited sketch of a vast territory.[8] Its purpose is to show that the struggle for Aboriginal self-government has never been simply a domestic matter. This shows that the stakes of the Indigenous question are not limited to Canadian reconciliation; rather, it extends to the very

5 *Beckman v Little Salmon/Carmacks First Nation*, 2010 SCC 53 at para 10, [2010] 3 SCR 103.

6 Ludwig Wittgenstein, *Philosophical Investigations*, 3rd ed (Oxford, UK: Blackwell, 2001), s 216.

7 James Sa'ke'j Youngblood Henderson, *Indigenous Diplomacy and the Rights of Peoples: Achieving UN Recognition* (Saskatoon: Purich, 2008) at 34.

8 A more adequate approach to it would be to adopt a comparative and international focus. This would begin by exploring the question of Indigenous self-determination in multiple settler colonial contexts and how these sets of laws, policies, practices and institutions (this family of Crown machines) related both to one another and to the development of international legal institutions in the twentieth century. It is, in my opinion, not simply chance that the mandate system of the League of Nations so strongly resembles the Crown machinery that we find preceding it in dominions such as Canada. Given the focus of my current investigation, this broader project can only be seen as a possible line of future inquiry.

future of popular sovereignty as the legitimating principle for political organization. In order to see these stakes, I argue that we must reject the simplistic vision of historicism that serves to ground the myth of the unitary state and its unified and singular people. This means coming to grips with the fact that the struggle for Aboriginal rights and title *was never merely a domestic matter*. The prospect of the implementation of UNDRIP is thus not akin to the sudden arrival of a stranger; rather, it is part of the 240-year-old tradition of Aboriginal constitutionalism and diplomacy.

Inter and Intra-national Struggles of Decolonization

There is a pattern of criss-crossing and overlapping lines that connects the struggle for Aboriginal self-government in Canada with the international process of decolonization. The Six Nations presenting their case at the League of Nations in the 1920s (a tactic that was also used by the Maori during the same period) and the *Lovelace* case in the 1970s clearly show that international law has always been part of the conversation in Canada.[9] It has been a part of each major shift in Canadian Indian policy. This should be no surprise. After all, the international legal institutions of the twentieth century were designed to restructure the colonial system of the preceding century.[10] From their inception, these institutions became avenues for all colonized peoples (those subjected to the external as well as the internal forms of colonization) to contest the legitimacy of the system created by the colonizing powers. This meant that the language and practices of colonial legitimation were being simultaneously contested and re-asserted at both the intra- and international stage. The arguments that Indigenous peoples in Canada have been continually asserting over the last 240 years (i.e., what James Tully refers to as the "prior and coexisting sovereignty argument" and many others — following Russel Lawrence Barsh and Henderson — have called "treaty federalism") were applied to the emerging field of international legal discourse.[11] They applied and adapted the historical and contextual resources of the "prior and coexisting sovereignty argument" to the concept of self-determination on the international stage. This means that the self-determination argument was never a separate and discrete line, but rather a related and parallel path.

This can be easily seen as soon as we begin to consider the course of the intra-national struggle in Canada in relation to the development of international law. The second wave of international Indigenous diplomacy (following the failure of the League of Nations) begins with the rise of international human rights in the 1960s.[12] In the mid-1960s, the Declaration on the Elimination of All Forms of Racial Discrimination[13] and, a few years later, the International Convention on the Elimination of All Forms of Racial Discrimination, provided a definition of "racial discrimination" that served to delegitimize the maintenance of separate rights for different

9 Henderson, *supra* note 7 at 24.

10 See Antony Anghie, *Imperialism, Sovereignty and the Making of International Law* (Cambridge, UK: Cambridge University Press, 2005); Marti Koskenniemi, *The Gentle Civilizer of Nations: The Rise and Fall of International Law 1870–1960* (Cambridge, UK: Cambridge University Press, 2001).

11 James Tully, *Public Philosophy in a New Key*, vol 1 (Cambridge, UK: Cambridge University Press, 2008) at 278 [Tully, *Public Philosophy*]; Russel Lawrence Barsh & James Youngblood Henderson, *The Road: Indian Tribes and Political Liberty* (Berkeley: University of California Press, 1980).

12 Henderson, *supra* note 7 at 24.

13 *Declaration on the Elimination of All Forms of Racial Discrimination*, GA Res 1904 (XVIII), UNGAOR, 18th Sess, UN Doc A/RES/18/1904 (20 November 1963).

racial groups.[14] While it did not mention Indigenous peoples, it was clear that it could be used to terminate their treaty rights and this is precisely what the White Paper set out to do in 1969.[15] This (unintentional) shift against the rights of Indigenous peoples was counterbalanced by the Human Rights Covenants in 1966 (the International Covenant on Economic, Social, and Cultural Rights and the International Covenant on Civil and Political Rights), as the first article of both asserts that "All peoples have the right of self-determination."[16] This brought a new wave of international diplomatic efforts on the part of Indigenous peoples. It was through their concerted efforts that in 1972 — a year before the court released its decision in *Calder* — the Sub-Commission on the Prevention of Discrimination and Protection of Minorities of the United Nations Commission on Human Rights appointed a special rapporteur to study "the problem of discrimination against Indigenous populations."[17] In 1975, the International Court of Justice (ICJ) released its advisory opinion in the *Western Sahara* case.[18] Tully provides a useful summary of the opinion:

> [T]he ICJ rejected the doctrine of discovery and asserted that the only way a foreign sovereign could acquire a right to enter into territory that is not *terra nullius* is with the consent of the inhabitants by means of a public agreement. The Court further advised that the structure and form of government and whether a people are said to be at a lower level of civilization are not valid criteria for determining if the inhabitants have rights, such as the right of self-determination. The relevant consideration is if they have social and political organization.[19]

This served as yet another blow to the nineteenth-century doctrines that had legitimated the European colonial projects. Its ramifications were not (and could not be) limited to those who experienced an external form of colonization. It added to the building international momentum on the question of Indigenous self-determination. In 1977, at the International NGO Conference on Discrimination Against Indigenous Populations in the Americas in Geneva, Indigenous leaders moved toward developing human rights standards appropriate for this concern. The result of this diplomatic effort was the Declaration of Principles for the Defense of Indigenous Nations and Peoples of the Western Hemisphere.[20] This was later followed in 1982 by the formation of a Working Group on Indigenous Populations. The group was established within the Sub-Commission on the Prevention of Discrimination and Protection of Minorities of the Commission on Human Rights. This was the beginning of the long and arduous process that resulted in UNDRIP in 2007.[21] While this constitutes a major advance in the Indigenous

14 *International Convention on the Elimination of All Forms of Racial Discrimination*, 21 December 1965, 660 UNTS 195 (entered into force 4 January 1969), online: <www.ohchr.org/EN/ProfessionalInterest/Pages/CERD.aspx>.

15 Ministry of Indian Affairs and Northern Development, *Statement of the Government of Canada on Indian Policy* (The White Paper), Queen's Printer Catalogue No R32-2469 (Ottawa: Ministry of Indian Affairs and Northern Development, 1969).

16 *International Covenant on Economic, Social and Cultural Rights*, 16 December 1966, 993 UNTS 3, 6 ILM 360 (entered into force 3 January 1976), online: <www.ohchr.org/EN/ProfessionalInterest/Pages/CESCR.aspx>; *International Covenant on Civil and Political Rights*, 16 December 1966, 999 UNTS 171 (entered into force 23 March 1976), online: <www.ohchr.org/en/professionalinterest/pages/ccpr.aspx>.

17 Sub-commission on Prevention of Discrimination and Protection of Minorities, José R Martinez Cobo, *Study of the Problem of Discrimination against Indigenous Populations*, E/CN.4/Sub.2/1986/7/Add.4 (1987).

18 *Western Sahara*, Advisory Opinion [1975] ICJ Rep 12.

19 Tully, *Public Philosophy*, *supra* note 11 at 281.

20 *Declaration of Principles for the Defense of Indigenous Nations and Peoples of the Western Hemisphere*, UN Doc E/CN.4/Sub.2/476/Add.5, Annex 4 (1981).

21 *UNDRIP*, *supra* note 1.

struggle for self-determination, it is also not without its limitations. As Tully notes, "under the 2007 Declaration, the transcendent priority of existing exclusive state jurisdiction and territorial integrity is reproduced rather than questioned by the way the distinction between internal and external self-determination can be interpreted."[22] The main issue to be decided concerns the conflict between territorial integrity (article 46) and self-determination (articles 3 and 4).[23] This conflict is not a new one. It has shaped the course from the intra- to the international legal stage.

The rejection of the Indigenous question at the League of Nations by the settler states and their colonial powers (via the concept of territorial integrity) was extended into the United Nations.[24] This extension can be seen in the General Assembly's Declaration on the Granting of Independence to Colonial Countries and Peoples, which legitimated the dismantling of the external colonial projects while excluding the internal ones.[25] The so-called "saltwater thesis" denied Indigenous peoples the right to self-determination. The basis of its denial was, once again, territorial integrity. It was attractive to the newly independent states that had inherited the deep social and cultural fractures left by the colonial powers and were concerned by the prospect of intra-national division.

The basic structure of the territorial integrity argument was by no means new to Aboriginal peoples. It exists within the 1888 decision of *St Catharine's Milling*, which positions them (without their consent) as already a part of a state.[26] It magically converts their claims to their lands and the pre-existing nation-to-nation treaties as being little more than gifts from the imperial Crown that become the burdens of the Dominion — burdens that, as we well know, can be unilaterally abandoned, or, to use the legal term "extinguished." This magical argument hides its presumptions by presenting itself as a simple application of the rules of formal legal interpretation. This enables Lord Watson to read section 91(24) as a complete and final grant of unilateral power over Indians and their lands.[27] What it ignores (and must always refuse) is any and all references to the context for this constitutional provision. In order to continue to serve as a foundation, it requires that either the British Crown be able to give what it did not have or that it be able to interpret (unilaterally) all pre-existing agreements in its favour. Once its foundations are laid bare, all that remains of it is that "might makes right." This absence of a foundation is propped up by the pernicious and absurd legal fiction known as the doctrine of

22 Tully, *Public Philosophy*, *supra* note 11 at 285.

23 *UNDRIP*, *supra* note 1. This conflict also necessarily concerns the phrase "free, prior and informed consent," as the concept of "consent" presumes self-governance and jurisdiction over territory (articles 10, 11, 19, 28 and 29).

24 I am referring to the Six Nations status case that Chief Deskaheh (also known as Hi-wyi-iss and Levi General) brought to the attention of the League of Nations in 1923. See Deskaheh, "The Redman's Appeal for Justice," cited in *Strange Visitors: Documents in Indigenous-Settler Relations in Canada from 1876*, Kevin D Smith, ed (Toronto: University of Toronto Press, 2014) at 143–48. While he was unable to get a formal hearing of the case (due in large part to British sabre rattling), his efforts generated significant international attention and prompted the Dominion of Canada to publish a formal response in the official journal of the League of Nations in 1924. See "Appeal of the 'Six Nations' to the League" (1924), *League of Nations Official Journal* vol 6 at 829.

25 *Declaration on the Granting of Independence to Colonial Countries and Peoples*, GA Res 1514, UNGAOR, 15th Sess, Supp No 16, UN Doc A/4684 (14 December 1960), online: <www.un.org/en/decolonization/declaration.shtml>. See also Tully, *Public Philosophy*, *supra* note 11 at 283.

26 *St Catharine's Milling and Lumber Co v R*, [1888] UKPC 70, 14 App Cas 46 [*St Catharine's Milling* cited to App Cas].

27 *Ibid* at 59.

discovery (a fiction based on what I have called "Bluebeard logic"[28]) and theatrical displays of violence (such as the use of police force to suppress the Six Nations in the 1920s, and Canada's use of the police and military power to respond to the resistance of the Mohawk of Kanesatake in the Oka Crisis in 1990).[29]

The fixed nature of this response can be seen in the similarity between the arguments used by Canada against the Six Nations in the 1920s and those used against the Mi'kmaw Nation in the 1980s. In 1980, the United Nations Human Rights Committee accepted a complaint from the Mi'kmaw Nation that alleged violations of their right of self-determination. Just one month after Canada received notice of the complaint from the Secretary-General, the Sûreté du Québec (provincial police) conducted a raid on the Mi'kmaw Reserve at Listuguj. Canada followed this action with a formal response to the Mi'kmaq. Their position was simple: self-determination "cannot affect the national unity and territorial integrity of Canada"; and the treaties "are merely considered to be nothing more than contracts between a sovereign and a group of its subjects."[30] Both the pattern of response and its conceptual basis are the same.

The conceptual basis of this position appeared again in 1993 at the World Conference on Human Rights in Vienna, during the drafting of the Vienna Declaration and Programme of Action.[31] Canada, along with Indonesia and India, took the position that Indigenous peoples should be described as a "people" and not "peoples." The basis of this absurd position is that the use of the singular term "people" would serve as a kind of formalistic bar to the application of human rights doctrines so that these states could continue treating Indigenous peoples as a minority.[32] Quite simply, Canada has continually maintained that Aboriginal peoples can only ever be a minority or a secessionist movement. The process of reconciliation has been constructed on this very basis; it is a reconciliation to the Crown's unilateral power over Aboriginal peoples and their lands via the "broad view" of section 91(24) of the Constitution Act, 1867. Aboriginal peoples have continually responded to this argument by reminding the Crown of their treaties and the nation-to-nation relationship that the Royal Proclamation of 1763 recognized.[33]

This context helps to frame exactly what is at stake in implementation. The stakes are, quite simply, the future of popular sovereignty as the legitimating principle for political organization. This could well strike some readers as little more than hyperbole, but I would ask those readers

28 Joshua Nichols, *Reconciliation and the Foundation of Aboriginal Law in Canada* (DCL, University of Victoria, 2017) at 18: "There is a kind of logic that is reminiscent of the folktale *Bluebeard* at play here: a castle is opened up for us as the reader and we are welcome to explore each and every room with the exception of one. This excluded room is an open secret. We are simply told not to use our key to go inside. Once we violate this prohibition and enter the room we see its simple truth: it conceals violence without measure or proportion. We also see that the violence and death that it hides (which is in a certain way, flat, or banal, as there is no real magic to be seen here) is, at least to my mind, the actual foundation of the castle and the explanation of the bizarre color that marks the owner of the castle. The name of the door within the castle is, for the purposes of my analogy, sovereignty. This *Bluebeard logic* can be found in any number of political thinkers who propose to offer a system of thought that explains away the foundations of law by marking off a 'state of nature' (or other open secret) in which the rules are paradoxically presented as both entirely a part of and entirely separate from the rest of the system."

29 For more on the Oka Crisis and its context, see Gerald R Alfred, *Heeding the Voices of Our Ancestors: Kahnawake Mohawk Politics and the Rise of Native Nationalism* (Oxford, UK: Oxford University Press, 1995) at 93–114.

30 "Response of the Government of Canada respecting Communication submitted by Mr. Alexander Denny on behalf of the people of the Mi'kmak tribal society on September 30, 1980 (date of initial letter)" (21 July 1981) at 2, 4, online: <www.usask.ca/nativelaw/unhrfn/mikmaqfiles/No4.pdf>. See also Henderson, *supra* note 7 at 38–39.

31 UN General Assembly, *Vienna Declaration and Programme of Action*, 12 July 1993, A/CONF.157/23.

32 Henderson, *supra* note 7 at 53, 122.

33 *Royal Proclamation, 1763* (3 Geo III), reprinted in RSC 1985, Appendix II, No 1.

to pause and consider the situation carefully. The conflict between the concepts of territorial integrity and self-determination is a foundational one. The question of Indigenous self-determination exposes this clearly. If the Westphalian model of the state is to be retained, then we must refuse to recognize Indigenous peoples as peoples. They must be nothing more than a minority within currently existing states.[34] The cost of this position is high; it must withstand the historical reality that Aboriginal peoples did not consent to this relationship. This means it must either simply draw a line that forbids inquiry into the historical warrant of sovereignty or judicially reinterpret each and every piece of historical evidence. Both of these options rely on unilateral power over Aboriginal peoples and neither of them are convincing. They are attempts to finesse rather than face the challenge of reconciliation. Tully draws out the consequences of this strategy: "*Unilateral* defence of the status quo, unilateral constitutional change and unilateral secession are all unjust in the sense that they violate with respect to other members the very principle that is invoked to justify the act. Moreover, such unilateral acts are unstable, for the disregarded members are seldom silenced for long. All the force of existing society or of the secessionist state cannot stabilize effectively the unjust situation or gain the recognition they need from others, as we have seen in many tragic cases."[35]

The implications are unavoidable; either find a way to finesse legitimation (and paint continued resistance as secessionist) or forgo legitimation altogether. In any case, what is clear at this point is that the Westphalian model of the state is caught in this dilemma. Simply put, the picture of the ship of state is no longer a sustainable one. Clifford Geertz captures the situation:

> The diffusionist notion that the modern world was made in northern and western Europe and then seeped out like an oil slick to cover the rest of the world has obscured the fact...that rather than converging toward a single pattern those entities called countries were ordering themselves in novel ways, ways that put European conceptions, not all that secure in any case, of what a country is, and what its basis is, under increasing pressure. The genuinely radical implications of the decolonization process are only just now coming to be recognized. For better or for worse, the dynamics of Western nation building are not being replicated. Something else is going on.[36]

It is precisely the "implications of the decolonization process" that are at stake in the question of implementation. If the Canadian government continues forward with the status quo and uses its framework to read down the right of self-determination to fit the municipal model of *St Catharine's Milling*, then reconciliation will continue its current holiday.[37] As Tully reminds us, "If the Constitution does not rest on the consent of the people or their representatives, or if there is not a procedure by which it can be so amended, then they are neither self-governing

34 Will Kymlicka's work on the meaning of the term "minority" is especially helpful on this point as he provides a clear distinction between an "ethnic minority" and a "national minority." As he so clearly puts it, "the basic claim underlying self-government rights is not simply that some groups are disadvantaged within the political community (representation rights), or that the political community is culturally diverse (polyethnic rights). Instead, the claim is that there is more than one political community, and that the authority of the larger state cannot be assumed to take precedence over the authority of the constituent national communities. If democracy is the rule of 'the people', national minorities claim that there is more than one people, each with a right to rule themselves." See Will Kymlicka, *Multicultural Citizenship: A Liberal Theory of Minority Rights* (Oxford, UK: Oxford University Press, 1995) at 182.

35 Tully, *Public Philosophy*, *supra* note 11 at 201 [emphasis in original].

36 Clifford Geertz, *Available Light: Anthropological Reflections on Philosophical Topics* (Princeton, NJ: Princeton University Press, 2000) at 230–31.

37 *St Catharine's Milling*, *supra* note 26.

nor self-determining but are governed and determined by a structure of laws that is imposed on them. They are unfree. This is the principle of popular sovereignty by which modern peoples and governments are said to be free and legitimate."[38]

The consequence is that Aboriginal peoples will effectively be left in a constitutional prison fashioned by the court and when they inquire why, the response will be that it is how power is reconciled with duty. This is not the only available course of action. It is also possible to use implementation to work through and remove the barricades of the past from the current framework. It is possible for Canada to lead the way toward a post-Westphalian model of the state that takes the open-ended plurality of contests over recognition as its starting point. This would replace the unitary model of the ship of state and its endless historical progress toward reconciliation — which has never been anything more than a theological mechanism of deferral — with the diverse and unmoving black canoe.[39] In other words, it is possible to use this moment as an opportunity to find a reconciliation with Aboriginal peoples and thereby shape future processes of internal self-determination.

38 Tully, *Public Philosophy*, *supra* note 11 at 286.

39 This is a reference to Bill Reid's iconic sculpture *The Spirit of Haida Gwaii* and, more particularly, to James Tully's reading of it. As Tully puts it, "the answer given by the black canoe is that, although the passengers vie and negotiate for recognition and power, they always do so in accord with the three conventions [viz. mutual recognition, consent and continuity]....we must listen to the description of each member of the crew, and indeed enter into conversation ourselves, in order to find the redescriptions acceptable to all which mediate the differences we wish each other to recognize." See James Tully, *Strange Multiplicity: Constitutionalism in an Age of Diversity* (Cambridge, UK: Cambridge University Press, 1995) at 111, 212.

5

Indigenous Legal Orders, Canadian Law and UNDRIP

Gordon Christie

"Indigenous law" refers not only to systems of rules or precepts but also to the authority of Indigenous communities and nations to craft their own understandings of law and the particular form and content their legal orders may take on. For the purpose of this chapter, I will focus attention on the presence of Indigenous legal and political authority over Indigenous lands and waters. Indigenous law refers to the authority of particular Indigenous communities, tied to particular lands and waters, to make decisions binding all in regard to how these lands and waters are approached. This authority extends to how people living on the land properly think of their relationships to these lands — for example, in base-level terms of rights, powers and exploitation or in terms of responsibilities and stewardship.

The question, then, is how Canadian authorities might respond to the challenges of implementing provisions of the United Nations Declaration on the Rights of Indigenous Peoples (UNDRIP)[1] in light of the existence of Indigenous legal and political authority over Indigenous territories. If one were to employ the metaphor of braiding laws together, the image would then be of separate parties — the Crown and numerous distinct Indigenous communities — each enjoying authority over some common territory, each coming to the exercise of braiding with their own

1 *United Nations Declaration on the Rights of Indigenous Peoples*, GA Res 295, UNGAOR, 61st Sess, Supp No 49, UN Doc A/RES/61/295, 46 ILM 1013 (2007) [*UNDRIP*].

strands of law, and together having to work out how state law and Indigenous law could be interwoven, with guidance from international law, to form a single, strong rope.

If we began this exercise by imagining that the Canadian state and its courts engage in braiding laws the way we might imagine a single person braids a rope out of materials on hand, we would then have to begin with the notion the state has control over Indigenous law.[2] To think of the state as having control over Indigenous law is, however, to think of Indigenous law as being bits and pieces, constituting no more than articulated rules and principles. This effectively removes Indigenous law from the landscape. There can only be such a thing as Indigenous law if there are Indigenous legal and political authorities, those entities that determine the nature and functioning of legal orders under contemplation. To cut away the possibility these legal and political authorities exist and exercise their authority through their laws and policies is to move directly into a world where the colonial project has been completed.

The challenge as posed is significantly more pronounced than some make it out to be. While Canadian authorities might believe the task ahead is simply to work out on their own how to implement UNDRIP (perhaps with "input" from the voices of Indigenous leaders), the real task as described (if UNDRIP and Indigenous legal orders are taken seriously) is to recognize and accept strong legal pluralism and to work from that initial point.

Recommendations made in this chapter incorporate principles and provisions contained in UNDRIP, as that instrument speaks clearly to the idea that Indigenous peoples possess the legal and political authority that accounts for this fact of strong legal pluralism.[3] Thus, while the thought is of a braiding exercise carried out by the Crown and Indigenous nations, as they go about discussing as partners how they might work together to implement UNDRIP, UNDRIP itself enters the discussion as support for the notion that this exercise must be carried out in this fashion.[4] One could say, then, that the reason I approach the question of braiding laws as I do is that I accept the general spirit and intent of UNDRIP. To the extent the Crown is serious in its pronouncements on implementing UNDRIP, it too would see the wisdom in approaching the task in this truly collaborative fashion.

2 That the Crown has control over international law must also be imagined, but only in the sense that the Crown is entirely at its leisure to decide what aspects of international law it might bring into the domestic scene, which reflects how the state and its courts overwhelmingly think of international law.

3 *UNDRIP, supra* note 1, arts 18, 20(1), 34, *inter alia*, speak to this authority:
article 18: *Indigenous peoples have the right to participate in decision-making in matters which would affect their rights, through representatives chosen by themselves in accordance with their own procedures, as well as to maintain and develop their own indigenous decision-making institutions*;
article 20(1): *Indigenous peoples have the right to maintain and develop their political, economic and social systems or institutions*, to be secure in the enjoyment of their own means of subsistence and development, and to engage freely in all their traditional and other economic activities; and
article 34: *Indigenous peoples have the right to promote, develop and maintain their institutional structures* and their distinctive customs, spirituality, traditions, procedures, practices *and,* in the cases where they exist, *juridical systems* or customs, in accordance with international human rights standards [emphasis added].

4 The Preamble, for example, recognizes "the urgent need to respect and promote the inherent rights of indigenous peoples which derive from their political, economic and social structures and from their cultures, spiritual traditions, histories and philosophies, especially their rights to their lands, territories and resources," while articles 18 and 19 hold that "Indigenous peoples have the right to participate in decision-making in matters which would affect their rights, through representatives chosen by themselves in accordance with their own procedures, as well as to maintain and develop their own indigenous decision-making institutions" and that "States shall consult and cooperate in good faith with the indigenous peoples concerned through their own representative institutions in order to obtain their free, prior and informed consent before adopting and implementing legislative or administrative measures that may affect them." *Ibid*, Preamble, arts 18, 19.

And so we begin where we must, with multiple parties wielding authority over the same territory. How might the braiding of law unfold in this situation? Recognition and acceptance of strong forms of legal pluralism require that matters unfold through dialogue, as each source of legal and political authority must be persuaded to act, since *ex hypothesi* no one source of authority enjoys binding authority over all others.[5] Much, then, would depend on how conversations between the Crown and Indigenous communities unfold. Nevertheless, there are historical, social and political factors that determine certain conditions and that speak to matters the Crown must attend to in order that meaningful dialogue can emerge. These factors indicate where energies of the state should be immediately directed (as we build toward a world in which meaningful dialogue can take place).

One central matter demanding attention from the state is the fact (and ongoing legacy) of colonialism.[6] One cannot reasonably expect dialogue to spring forth between the Crown and Indigenous communities around how UNDRIP should be meaningfully implemented without attention first being focused on the long and difficult shadow cast by a century and a half of settler colonialism. Indigenous legal and political authority has been under relentless assault since the middle of the nineteenth century, and troubling indications are that the Crown persists in thinking it can move forward today while the effects of this assault remain unresolved. Indeed, arguably the assault itself continues, as the Crown aggressively acts as though it is the sole sovereign authority over Canadian territory, all of which is also Indigenous territory.

Those few places where Indigenous legal and political authority are meaningfully exercised in the context of a relationship with the Crown must be carefully unpacked, as the more meaningful and substantial one finds the exercise of Indigenous authority, the more one simultaneously finds this is the result of relentless resistance by an Indigenous nation. Scratch the surface and

5 This stands in contrast to most instances of "co-management" and land use planning exercises one has found emerging over the last few decades. In most cases, the Crown dictated terms of the ensuing "dialogue" concerning co-management, allowing discussion only about certain carefully defined topics. There are notable exceptions, such as the Kunst'aa guu – Kunst'aayah Reconciliation Protocol, an agreement reached in 2009 between the Haida Nation and the province of British Columbia. The Preamble is key in framing the agreement, as it sets out parallel understandings of the nature of the situation vis-à-vis jurisdiction and ownership of Haida Gwaii. The Haida assert that "Haida Gwaii is Haida lands, including the waters and resources, subject to the rights, sovereignty, ownership, jurisdiction and collective Title of the Haida Nation who will manage Haida Gwaii in accordance with its laws, policies, customs and traditions," while the province asserts that "Haida Gwaii is Crown land, subject to certain private rights or interests, and subject to the sovereignty of her Majesty the Queen and the legislative jurisdiction of the Parliament of Canada and the Legislature of the Province of British Columbia." The two parties essentially agree to disagree over this fundamental matter, so they can progress to attempting to reach agreements around land use planning and the like. This is not a process we see unfolding in most other Crown-Indigenous contexts. See "Kunst'aa guu – Kunst'aayah Reconciliation Protocol" (2009), online: Council of the Haida Nation <www.haidanation.ca/Pages/Agreements/pdfs/Kunstaa%20guu_Kunstaayah_Agreement.pdf>.

6 Much of UNDRIP is built in light of the history of colonialism and the effects of this history on the abilities of Indigenous peoples to manage their own lands and waters. For example, articles 25 and 26 speak to the rights Indigenous communities have in relation to traditional territories and difficulties they face in fulfilling responsibilities to lands and waters, while articles 20(2) and 28 contemplate "just and fair redress" for historical deprivations. *UNDRIP*, *supra* note 1: article 25: Indigenous peoples have the right to maintain and strengthen their distinctive spiritual relationship with their traditionally owned or otherwise occupied and used lands, territories, waters and coastal seas and other resources and to uphold their responsibilities to future generations in this regard; article 26: (1) Indigenous peoples have the right to the lands, territories and resources which they have traditionally owned, occupied or otherwise used or acquired;
(2) Indigenous peoples have the right to own, use, develop and control the lands, territories and resources that they possess by reason of traditional ownership or other traditional occupation or use, as well as those which they have otherwise acquired; article 20(2): Indigenous peoples deprived of their means of subsistence and development are entitled to just and fair redress; and article 28(1): Indigenous peoples have the right to redress, by means that can include restitution or, when this is not possible, of a just, fair and equitable compensation, for the lands, territories and resources which they have traditionally owned or otherwise occupied or used, and which have been confiscated, taken, occupied, used or damaged without their free, prior and informed consent.

one will inevitably find this resistance had to be fuelled and sustained by resources, energies and fortuitous surrounding circumstances, all in the service of a decades-long, continuous, back-breaking struggle to stand up to the force of Crown pressure and intimidation.

The Truth and Reconciliation Commission of Canada noted the background tension responsible for this seemingly endless struggle in the executive summary of its final report: "What is clear to this Commission is that Aboriginal peoples and the Crown have very different and conflicting views on what reconciliation is and how it is best achieved. The Government of Canada appears to believe that reconciliation entails Aboriginal peoples' acceptance of the reality and validity of Crown sovereignty and parliamentary supremacy, in order to allow the government to get on with business. Aboriginal people, on the other hand, see reconciliation as an opportunity to affirm their own sovereignty and return to the 'partnership' ambitions they held after Confederation."[7]

Twenty years earlier, the same background tension was noted by the commissioners of the Royal Commission on Aboriginal Peoples: "But governments have so far refused to recognize the continuity of Aboriginal nations and the need to permit their decolonization at last. By their actions, if not their words, governments continue to block Aboriginal nations from assuming the broad powers of governance that would permit them to fashion their own institutions and work out their own solutions to social, economic and political problems. It is this refusal that effectively blocks the way forward."[8]

There are at least three activities the Crown can engage in over the next few years (and decades), each of which would undo some of the harms inflicted on Indigenous communities and nations, in particular in relation to the communities' and nations' abilities to meet responsibilities to lands and waters to which they have been connected for many generations.

Internal Crown Activities

One focus for immediate attention is dealing with matters internal to the Crown. At least two matters require attention, one directed toward ensuring the Crown can meaningfully and productively work with Indigenous peoples concerning land and water issues and the other directed toward effecting the massive shift in direction envisioned under strong legal pluralism.

For Indigenous communities to engage with the authority of the Crown over their traditional territories, the communities will, for the most part, need to dialogue with both the federal government and whichever provincial or territorial regime makes most decisions relating to their lands and waters. In both *Tsilhqot'in Nation*[9] and *Grassy Narrows*,[10] the Supreme Court of Canada noted a recent shift to a stronger focus on "cooperative federalism," in particular in relation to Crown-Indigenous relations. Historically, federal-provincial cooperation regarding Indigenous issues was absent or fleeting, and usually only arose when the aim was to further negatively affect independent Indigenous legal and political authority. A tremendous amount

7 Truth and Reconciliation Commission of Canada, *Honouring the Truth, Reconciling for the Future: Summary of the Final Report of the Truth and Reconciliation Commission of Canada* (2015) at 241, online: <www.trc.ca/websites/trcinstitution/File/2015/Findings/Exec_Summary_2015_05_31_web_o.pdf>.

8 Canada, Indigenous and Northern Affairs Canada, *Highlights from the Report of the Royal Commission on Aboriginal Peoples* (1996) [*Royal Commission*], online: <www.aadnc-aandc.gc.ca/eng/1100100014597/1100100014637>.

9 *Tsilhqot'in Nation v British Columbia*, 2014 SCC 44.

10 *Grassy Narrows First Nation v Ontario (Natural Resources)*, [2014] 2 SCR 447.

of effort needs to go into determining how federalism can respond to the need to work within a world structured by strong legal pluralism. The onus is on the Crown to begin immediately to carry the language of cooperative federalism into new territory, where both levels of Crown authority work together with the ultimate objective of enabling cooperative relations with Indigenous authorities.

The second internal movement has to be toward adjusting the culture that infuses life within federal and provincial governments. The focus must be on coming to terms with the fact of strong legal pluralism and on effecting concomitant shifts away from current efforts to either ignore (or deny) Indigenous legal and political authority, or to attempt to tame this authority by pulling it into the orbit of state power. Adjusting culture requires several interlocking movements, as this culture affects all levels of government. Change should be initiated through top-down movement, with the highest levels of government — the prime minister or premier, Cabinet, ministers, deputy ministers and the like — leading the way, directed perhaps by either legislation or proclamations (although executive action seems sufficient for this particular movement, on both federal and provincial/territorial levels).

In concert with direction from the highest levels, education and training efforts should unfold at all levels of government. The history of colonialism — and, in the context of this discussion, specifically the history of Crown efforts to suppress and erase independent Indigenous legal and political authority in relation to lands and waters — should be made visible to all government actors, alongside discussions of theories of legitimate exercise of power in a liberal democracy. This would serve to highlight the fundamental problem facing the Crown as it attempts to exercise its authority over the geography of Canada and to make clear to all government actors that strong legal pluralism is not something to be worked toward but rather something that has always existed across this one expanse of lands and waters.

External Crown Activities

The second set of actions lies in interaction with Indigenous communities and nations. Tremendous care needs to be taken in this regard, in full light of the fact the Crown has been the protagonist in the Crown-Indigenous relationship. Enormous problems — some seemingly intractable — plague Indigenous communities and nations as they attempt to maintain, rebuild and exercise their legal and political authority. The primary reason behind all their struggles is the history and legacy of colonial activity by the Crown.

The first move on the part of the Crown is not difficult to imagine, although it may be challenging to implement fully. The Crown must cease its aggressive activities, pulling back from the varied techniques it has employed over the years to subvert and destroy Indigenous legal and political authority. In recent decades, these techniques have become covert, as the era of open and overt colonial activity is now long past. The act of selectively choosing representatives from fractured Indigenous communities (those individuals who agree with government positions) to speak with, to fund and to elevate to positions of power must cease. All other related activities meant to further fracture communities, and to widen divisions that already exist, must likewise cease.

A challenge for the Crown, beyond these obvious moves, is in the business of repairing damage caused. The Crown cannot simply act to repair fractures or bring people together. That is essentially the business of Indigenous peoples. In many cases, however, Indigenous communities or nations cannot make significant headway without the cessation of destructive activities by the Crown. Besides renouncing and ceasing destructive activities, the Crown can also do two things. First, it can listen to Indigenous communities, stepping in when assistance is requested (and when it seems appropriate, which would likely be difficult to measure in cases where communities have been riven by generations of assault by the Crown). Second, the Crown can help provide conditions favourable to internal healing within Indigenous communities. Resources can be provided, some capacity building could take place (carefully arranged and managed), and advisers willing to collaborate with Indigenous communities could travel the country, providing outside guidance. It cannot be stressed enough how delicate all these matters would be, given the history of outside interference that indelibly marks the history of Crown-Indigenous relations.

Education

Finally, much can be done by the state and its institutions to educate the larger Canadian population.[11] This includes, essentially, work within the educational structures of the country (requiring in many instances, again, strengthening cooperative federalism). It also entails use of other varied tools available to the Crown — the funding of public forms of media to promote programming that speaks to the history of colonialism and its effects on Indigenous legal and political authority, the funding of research endeavours aimed at further enriching our collective understanding of the history of Crown-Indigenous relations and so forth.

While educational endeavours aimed at telling the truth about Canada's origins and troubling history would go a long way toward enriching the environment in which strong legal pluralism can flourish, focus can also be on telling the truth about the challenges facing the country, both Indigenous and non-Indigenous populations. The most pressing challenges are global in nature, but, as with all global matters, how regional decision-making bodies act is fundamentally important. The Crown should be turning its attention to the vast ecological problems we seem determined to bequeath to our children and grandchildren. Working in an environment accepting of strong legal pluralism can move us all toward possible solutions to these problems. As we make difficult multi-party decisions over shared lands and waters, stewardship responsibilities can move into the centre of discussions, displacing the frantic rush to resource exploitation and capitalist accumulation that is the sole source of these threats to the entire planetary ecology.

It should be appreciated this entails not just matters such as the appearance within existing environmental assessment processes of Indigenous knowledge or perspectives. For the necessary forms of braiding to occur, entire legal regimes need to be reworked from the ground up; they need to be infused with principles and values that move us all in a direction away from the neo-liberal policies and models that have come to animate so much of what passes for environmental law and natural resource management.

11 This was called for in *Royal Commission*, *supra* note 8 ("We were told many times during our mandate that most Canadians know little of Aboriginal life and less of Aboriginal history. Information in school curriculums is limited. Media coverage is often unsatisfactory. Few governments, agencies and organizations promote awareness of Aboriginal issues among members, employees and colleagues.... Part of the answer is information. We recommend a number of steps to increase and improve the quality of information about Aboriginal people and their concerns.... We urge Canadians to become involved in a broad and creative campaign of public education").

This chapter is written in full awareness of the unlikely nature of the premise that the Crown might think seriously about engaging in braiding laws in line with principles informing UNDRIP and in light of the fact of strong legal pluralism. Nevertheless, the fact remains that only if the Crown were to make the changes recommended could we imagine a world unfolding in which Indigenous law and Canadian law are interwoven in light of principles and provisions contained in UNDRIP. Moving forward with the assumption that the Crown controls Indigenous law violates fundamental facts at play in the world around us and would signal further attempts on the part of the state to complete the project of colonialism.

6

Bringing a Gendered Lens to Implementing the UN Declaration on the Rights of Indigenous Peoples

Brenda L. Gunn

The role of Indigenous women is an issue that exists in many Indigenous communities today, given the amount of colonial interference, including interference with gender roles, within these societies. When working toward implementing the United Nations Declaration on the Rights of Indigenous Peoples (UN Declaration)[1] in Canada and, in particular, when bringing together Indigenous and constitutional law, it is important to bring a gendered lens to ensure that Indigenous women benefit equally from the implementation. Another issue related to the role of Indigenous women is whether the movement toward realizing Indigenous peoples' right to self-determination, as recognized in the UN Declaration, "will promote the ability of indigenous groups to violate the rights of vulnerable members, particularly women."[2]

Women have a special role in many Indigenous societies, including special responsibilities. These roles often include leadership aspects that were critical for the nation.[3] An often cited example is the Haudenosaunee: "During the formation of the Five Nations Confederacy, a woman was the

1 *United Nations Declaration on the Rights of Indigenous Peoples*, GA Res 295, UNGAOR, 61st Sess, Supp No 49, UN Doc A/RES/61/295, 46 ILM 1013 (2007) [*UN Declaration*].

2 Rebecca Tsosie, "Indigenous Women and International Human Rights Law: The Challenges of Colonialism, Cultural Survival, and Self-Determination" (2010) 15 UCLA J Intl L & Foreign Aff 187 at 187.

3 See Maria Campbell's introduction for her discussion on the role of Métis women: Nicole St-Onge, Carolyn Podruchny & Brenda Macdougall, eds, *Contours of a People: Metis Family, Mobility and History* (Norman, OK: University of Oklahoma Press, 2012) at xiii.

first person to accept the Peacemaker's message of peace and unity. This woman was given the name Jikonsahseh, the 'Mother of Nations', by the Peacemaker, who explained that all women would have an important role in this peace."[4]

Beyond the writing about the prototypical example of the matriarchal and matrilineal Haudenosaunee clan system, much has been written about the particular roles of Indigenous women.[5] Val Napoleon is critical of written history, which portrays Indigenous women's role as limited to dealing with the meat men bring home from the hunt.[6] In many Indigenous societies, Indigenous women were revered and played key roles in politics and leadership. Sharon Venne speaks about Indigenous women's authority in entering into Treaty 6: "The Creator gave women the power to create. The man is the helper to the woman, not the other way around. Women are linked to Mother Earth by their ability to bring forth life. The women sit beside the Creator as a recognition of their role and position."[7]

Métis women also play an important role in the development and maintenance of the Métis nation: "[I]t was indigenous women who carried the history of the land and identity of the people, which they then shared with their families. An individual's connection to place was made through family, but those connections were derived from their maternal ancestry."[8] Brenda Macdougall notes that, historically, one's Métis identity arose from one's "maternal connection to home, land and family."[9] Generally, Métis children took their fathers' last names but resided in the homelands of their mothers' families.[10]

The Royal Commission on Aboriginal Peoples' (RCAP's) final report considers the roles of Indigenous women, including Inuit women: "There is agreement that women were traditionally responsible for decisions about children, food preparation and the running of the camp. While clear divisions of labour along gender lines existed, women's and men's work was equally valued."[11] The work of the RCAP highlights that, despite their different roles, men and women are to be equally respected and valued. While colonialism may have interfered with the internal workings of some Indigenous communities, Indigenous women continue to play key roles within their societies.

These different roles also mean that Indigenous women have different knowledge, including regarding Indigenous laws: "This means that, for the most part, women's knowledge of the land

4 Royal Commission on Aboriginal Peoples (RCAP), *Report of the Royal Commission on Aboriginal Peoples: Volume 4, Perspectives and Realities* (Ottawa: Supply and Services, 1996) at 7, online: Library and Archives Canada <http://data2.archives.ca/e/e448/e011188230-04.pdf>. See also Robert A Williams Jr, "Gendered Checks and Balances: Understanding the Legacy of White Patriarchy in an American Indian Cultural Context" (1989–1990) 24 Ga L Rev 1019.

5 See e.g. Megan Davis, "Aboriginal Women and the Right to Self-Determination" (2012) 16:1 AILR 78. See also Kiera L Ladner, "Gendering Decolonisation, Decolonising Gender" (2009) 13:1 AILR 62; Emma LaRocque, "Metis and Feminist: Ethical Reflections on Feminism, Human Rights, and Decolonization" in Joyce Green, ed, *Making Space for Indigenous Feminism* (Winnipeg: Fernwood, 2007) 53; Nathalie Kermoal & Isabel Altamirano-Jimenez, *Living on the Land: Indigenous Women's Understanding of Place* (Edmonton: Athabasca University Press, 2016).

6 Val Napoleon, "Aboriginal Discourse: Gender, Identity and Community" in Benjamin J Richardson, Shin Imai & Kent McNeil, eds, *Indigenous Peoples and the Law: Comparative and Critical Perspectives* (Oxford, UK: Hart, 2009) 233 at 241.

7 Sharon Venne, "Understanding Treaty 6: An Indigenous Perspective" in Michael Asch, ed, *Aboriginal and Treaty Rights in Canada: Essays on Law, Equity, and Respect for Difference* (Vancouver: UBC Press, 1997) 173 at 191.

8 Brenda Macdougall, *One of the Family: Metis Culture in Nineteenth-century Northwestern Saskatchewan* (Vancouver: UBC Press, 2010) at 344–45.

9 *Ibid* at 343.

10 *Ibid.*

11 RCAP, *supra* note 4 at 22.

and resources remains unacknowledged politically and legally. Since men and women often have different traditional knowledge of natural resources in relation to 'habitat, conservation, management, use, storing, and processing', women's knowledge can, and will disappear. This includes knowledge relating to access to, and control and use of, natural resources, which are basic elements of indigenous law. Without the thoughtful and deliberate inclusion of aboriginal women, the aboriginal discourse will continue to be impoverished, incomplete, and therefore profoundly flawed."[12]

Scholars have noted that Indigenous women's rights have failed to be included within the political and legal agendas. Rauna Kuokkanen notes, "Indigenous women's rights remain a contentious and often neglected issue both at international and local levels."[13] This failing to address and include Indigenous women's issues or to take a gendered analysis is perpetuated in the existing literature on Indigenous rights.[14] As noted by Nathalie Kermoal and Isabel Altamirano-Jimenez, "to ignore the specific ways in which Indigenous women know is to undermine them as active producers of knowledge that participate in complex socio-environmental community processes."[15] And, so, this chapter considers the need to bring a gendered perspective to implementing the UN Declaration in Canada.

Indigenous Rights Movements and the UN Declaration

The UN Declaration makes few references to women. Where the UN Declaration does reference Indigenous women, it has been criticized for its deficit approach. For example, article 21, which recognizes the right to the improvement of economic and social conditions, includes a need for states to take special measures, paying particular attention to the special needs of Indigenous women. The other specific reference to Indigenous women is in article 22(2), which notes the need for states to take measures to prevent violence against Indigenous women.

Despite this deficit approach in the UN Declaration, this article argues that greater attention needs to be paid to the requirement for states to pay particular attention to the special needs of Indigenous women when implementing the UN Declaration.[16] As well, article 44 recognizes that all the rights guaranteed in the UN Declaration are guaranteed equally to Indigenous men and women. In light of this provision, it is important that states undertake a gendered approach when implementing the UN Declaration. However, I argue that a gendered approach is necessary not only because Indigenous women have special needs, but also because Indigenous women have particular knowledges that contribute to Indigenous nations and laws, and that need recognition and protection.

Where the literature does address Indigenous women, the focus tends to be on experiences of violence. This literature too often portrays Indigenous women as victims in need of special

12 Napoleon, *supra* note 6 at 243.

13 Rauna Kuokkanen, "Self-Determination and Indigenous Women's Rights at the Intersection of International Human Rights" (2012) 34 Hum Rts Q 225 at 231.

14 Napoleon, *supra* note 6 at 235.

15 Kermoal & Altamirano-Jimenez, *supra* note 5 at 4.

16 *UN Declaration*, *supra* note 1, art 22.

assistance, thus perpetuating the deficit model in which Indigenous women are found lacking the ability to help themselves and in need of state assistance. However, this approach fails to support Indigenous women's agency and fails to identify the problem as the gendered impacts of colonialism. It further fails to address the broad range of human rights violations that Indigenous women experience:

> Indigenous women face violations of their civil and political rights when they are marginalized or excluded from their communities and when their membership is denied. They encounter abuses of their economic and social rights in the intersections of racism, sexism, poverty, and discrimination, which lead to a lack of employment opportunities, and access to health care and social services. They are confronted with violations of their personal integrity and human dignity in the form of sometimes extreme physical and sexual violence. Failure to recognize that indigenous women's rights are violated not only as indigenous people but also as women ultimately leads to a failure in promoting and protecting indigenous rights in general.[17]

Given that Canada's colonial project engaged in gendered attacks, including the various provisions in the Indian Act that removed power and representation from Indian women (for example, the prohibition against voting and running in band council elections and the provisions that caused many women and their descendants to lose status), a gendered analysis is necessary to ensure that implementation of the UN Declaration addresses these harms of colonization as well. Taking a gendered approach is particularly important to reveal the structures of power that "create hierarchical and differential access to resources, representation, political influence, and to being 'heard' in indigenous societies."[18]

Despite the recognition that colonization had a gendered impact, both Indigenous rights movements and women's rights movements have failed to address Indigenous women's issues and participation: "both rights movements often require Indigenous women to make trade-offs (either as women or as Indigenous peoples) rather than make space for the more fully intersectional frameworks that Indigenous women have been lobbying for."[19]

As efforts are made to implement the UN Declaration, the different ways Indigenous women experience human rights violations, including the intersectional discrimination based on race, gender, ability and sexuality that impacts both their individual and collective rights, must be recognized and addressed.[20] One example of the particular ways in which Indigenous women experience violations of their rights is their experience of environmental pollution resulting from large resource extraction projects, as such pollution not only limits access and control over traditional lands, but can also "compromise women's ability to take care of their children and families due to health problems, contamination, displacement, and increased violence."[21]

17 Kuokkanen, *supra* note 13 at 249.

18 *Ibid* at 226.

19 Laura Parisi & Jeff Corntassel, "In Pursuit of Self-determination: Indigenous Women's Challenges to Traditional Diplomatic Spaces" (2007) 13:3 Can Foreign Pol'y 81 at 81.

20 Mairin Iwanka Raya, "Indigenous Women Stand Against Violence: A Companion Report to the United Nations Secretary-General's Study on Violence Against Women" (Presented at the United Nations 16 October 2006) at 8.

21 Kuokkanen, *supra* note 13 at 231–32.

Moving Forward

A couple of key issues must be addressed moving forward, including the recognition that implementation of the UN Declaration must consider gender in order to ensure that Indigenous women's rights are protected. This requires understanding how Indigenous women experience violations of their rights. Unfortunately, Indigenous women experience violations of their rights both from the state and from within their own nations and communities. Regardless of whether the oppression that Indigenous women face is the result of the colonial process, or existed prior to contact, "gender imbalances exist in Indigenous communities today, [and] so must be addressed."[22]

While one of the aims of a gendered lens approach to implementing the UN Declaration is to ensure that Indigenous women's roles within Indigenous societies are protected and respected, it is important that we not romanticize traditions. This approach may also require working against fundamentalism, especially where the invocation of tradition aims "to silence multiple truths, experiences, and knowledges."[23] Rebecca Tsosie asks the following questions: "There is a strong sense in the Declaration that indigenous peoples ought to have the right to practice and revitalize their cultural traditions and customs. But what if these customs and traditions are not gender neutral? What if they are perceived as discriminatory toward Native women? It is a fact that the traditional governmental systems of some tribes do not allow direct participation by women. In some tribes, membership policies may be gender-based."[24]

As we engage a gendered lens, it is important to draw on Indigenous understandings of gender. Tracey Lindberg provides an example of such an understanding: "Maybe the reason that our languages seldom differentiate between gender and sex is because we are supposed to stand as one. In Cree, as Neheyiwak we are people. As Iskwew (women), we have specific stories, ceremonies, dances, and traditions but Iskwew are not a segment of Neheyiwak. We are the people; womanhood is our obligation and gift. That gendered line, as I mentioned at the outset, is not clear, and it zigs, zags, and becomes invisible depending on who we are with, what we are doing, and when we are doing it."[25]

When working to implement the UN Declaration, we must remember that human rights are indivisible, interdependent and interrelated. This means that the realization of Indigenous women's rights cannot be achieved by prioritizing certain rights over others. For example, one cannot prioritize self-government and land rights at the expense of rights to clean water, housing, health care and to be free from violence. There is no hierarchy of human rights. The denial of any human right impacts other human rights. The interrelatedness of human rights is particularly important for Indigenous women's rights. This means that when developing processes for implementing Indigenous peoples' right to participate in decision making, including free, prior and informed consent, to include Indigenous women is critical. Indigenous women's inclusion provides an opportunity not only to fully appreciate the scope of potential impact of any proposed measure, but also to benefit from Indigenous women's knowledge. Including

22 Emily Snyder, "Indigenous Feminist Legal Theory" (2014) 26 CJWL 365 at 367.

23 *Ibid* at 368.

24 Tsosie, *supra* note 2 at 217.

25 Tracey Lindberg, "Not My Sister: What Feminists Can Learn about Sisterhood from Indigenous Women" (2004) 16 CJWL 342 at 351.

Indigenous women and their knowledge in these processes broadens the available information, as "Indigenous women's ways of knowing are shaped by their livelihoods and shared experiences of racism, colonialism, and by their experiences as leaders, mothers, sisters, and grandmothers," which may not be known otherwise.[26] Including the recognition that "Indigenous women's experiences are integral to decolonizing knowledge production"[27] will ensure that Indigenous women benefit equally from implementation of the UN Declaration.

Conclusion

Given that the colonial project had particular gendered aspects, and that Indigenous women continue to experience violations of their human rights in particular fashions, it is critical that the implementation of the UN Declaration includes a gendered analysis to ensure that Indigenous women and Indigenous men benefit equally from its implementation.

Engaging in a gendered approach that aims to ensure Indigenous men and Indigenous women benefit equally requires governments to engage directly with the rights holders, including Indigenous women, to ensure that women's rights, knowledges and roles are specifically considered. This requires moving beyond the national Indigenous organizations (the Assembly of First Nations, Inuit Tapiriit Kanatami, the Métis National Council, the Native Women's Association of Canada and the Congress of Aboriginal Peoples) and, potentially, even political/territorial organizations, such as the Chiefs of Ontario, the Assembly of Manitoba Chiefs, the Federation of Sovereign Indigenous Nations and so on. While these various political organizations have great expertise on Indigenous women's concerns and particular violations of rights, the negotiation of rights must occur directly with the rights holders. Engaging with rights holders, including traditional knowledge holders, ensures that Indigenous women's rights and knowledges are protected. Additionally, many of the negotiations will require engaging at a local level on specific issues, unless women specifically delegate negotiating authority to political organizations.

Taking a gendered analysis in the implementation of the UN Declaration will also require the working group on the review of laws and policies to take a gendered analysis of existing Canadian laws and policies to determine how these different laws and policies impact Indigenous men and women differently. This requires going beyond the obvious directly gendered policies, such as the Indian Act provisions that caused Indigenous women to lose their status when they married non-status men. There may be general laws, such as environmental legislation, that have a different impact on Indigenous men and women.

A gendered analysis also requires implementing economic, social and cultural rights with the same priority as civil and political rights.[28] This means that Canada must stop thinking about education, social housing, health care and so on as policy issues and must start with a rights-based approach to these issues. For example, the lack of affordable housing has contributed to

26 Kermoal & Altamirano-Jimenez, *supra* note 5 at 9.

27 *Ibid* at 4.

28 Sarah Morales, "How can Canada's economic, cultural and social human rights obligations inform the National Inquiry?" (Paper delivered at Planning for Change: Towards a National Inquiry and an Effective National Action Plan, Symposium on Murders and Disappearances of Indigenous Women and Girls, Ottawa, 31 January 2016) [unpublished]. Copy on file with author.

an increased rate of child apprehension (often experienced as another form of violence).[29] Other government policies, including forced sterilization programs and the forced removal of children, have had negative impacts on Indigenous women.[30] As part of the process of implementing the UN Declaration with a gendered lens, Canada should ensure that other instruments that protect Indigenous women's rights, such as the International Covenant on Economic, Social and Cultural Rights,[31] are also fully implemented.

A final step that will be important in taking a gendered approach to implementing the UN Declaration is to continue to interpret the UN Declaration in light of (and in conjunction with) other international human rights instruments. While the Convention on the Elimination of All Forms of Discrimination Against Women[32] is an obvious relevant international human rights treaty, there are others as well, including the Inter-American Convention on the Prevention, Punishment, and Eradication of Violence Against Women.[33]

29 M Celeste McKay & Craig Benjamin, "A Vision for Fulfilling the Indivisible Rights of Indigenous Women" in Jackie Hartley, Paul Joffe & Jennifer Preston, eds, *Realizing the UN Declaration on the Rights of Indigenous Peoples: Triumph, Hope and Action* (Saskatoon: Purich, 2010) 156 at 167.

30 See Yvonne Boyer, "First Nations, Métis and Inuit Women's Health" (2006) National Aboriginal Health Organization Discussion Paper Series in Aboriginal Health: Legal Issues No 4.

31 *International Covenant on Economic, Social and Cultural Rights*, 16 December 1966, 993 UNTS 3, 6 ILM 360 (entered into force 3 January 1976).

32 *Convention on the Elimination of All Forms of Discrimination Against Women*, 18 December 1979, 1249 UNTS 3 (entered into force 3 September 1981).

33 *Inter-American Convention on the Prevention, Punishment, and Eradication of Violence Against Women*, 9 June 1994, OAS A-61 (entered into force 5 March 1995).

PART II

Indigenous Law Perspectives

Previous page:

Douglas in Formal Wear (part of the *Romancing Stanley* series)
Kim Hunter

2016, digital vector painting

7

Braiding the Incommensurable: Indigenous Legal Traditions and the Duty to Consult

Sarah Morales

On May 10, 2016, the federal Minister of Indigenous and Northern Affairs, Carolyn Bennett, announced Canada's latest position on the United Nations Declaration on the Rights of Indigenous Peoples (UNDRIP).[1] She confirmed that Canada is now a full supporter of UNDRIP, without qualification, and that Canada intends to adopt and implement UNDRIP in accordance with the Canadian Constitution. At the United Nations Permanent Forum on Indigenous Issues, she recognized that "Canada has a long history of multilateralism and respect for the values of internationalism and pluralism."[2] The minister also stated, "through Section 35 of its Constitution, Canada has a robust framework for the protection of indigenous rights.... Canada believes that our constitutional obligations serve to fulfill all of the principles of the declaration, including 'free, prior and informed consent.' We see modern treaties and self-government agreements as the ultimate expression of free, prior and informed consent among

1 *United Nations Declaration on the Rights of Indigenous Peoples*, GA Res 295, UNGAOR, 61st Sess, Supp No 49, UN Doc A/RES/61/295, 46 ILM 1013 (2007) [*UNDRIP*].

2 Minister of Indigenous and Northern Affairs Carolyn Bennett, "Announcement of Canada's Support for the United Nations Declaration on the Rights of Indigenous Peoples" (Statement delivered at the 15th Session of the United Nations Permanent Forum on Indigenous Issues, 10 May 2016).

partners."[3] Arguably, some Indigenous peoples may question that understanding of free, prior and informed consent (FPIC).[4]

Over the last decade, the federal government has repeatedly approved large-scale resource development projects — such as the Trans Mountain Expansion Project (often referred to as the Kinder Morgan Pipeline), the Northern Gateway Pipeline and the Site C dam in British Columbia — over the objections of Indigenous communities, many that are currently engaged in modern treaty and self-government negotiations or have already entered into treaty relationships with the Canadian state.[5] Approval of these projects is not sitting well with Indigenous peoples, who argue that their existing Aboriginal rights and title, which are supposed to be protected by section 35 of the Constitution Act, 1982,[6] are being infringed by these development projects. As stated by Chief Ian Campbell of the Squamish Nation, "Ottawa and Victoria need to hear loud and clear that they can't just run roughshod over aboriginal rights and title. That era has come and gone."[7] Drawing on the Supreme Court of Canada's (SCC's) judgment in *Haida Nation v British Columbia (Minister of Forests)*,[8] Chief Campbell and other Indigenous leaders are voicing their frustrated concerns that, with the recognition by Canada's highest court, "[t]he Crown, acting honourably, cannot cavalierly run roughshod over Aboriginal interests where claims affecting these interests are being seriously pursued in the process of treaty negotiation and proof."[9]

Indigenous peoples still do not feel that they are being consulted adequately during these types of decision-making processes. Indigenous peoples do not feel that their own laws or decision-making processes are being taken into consideration, or relied upon, throughout these engagement processes. Chief Maureen Thomas of the Tsleil-Waututh Nation stated the following about the Trans Mountain Expansion Project consultation process: "The federal government's consultation process was disappointingly flawed. The economic information they relied on was outdated. The oil spill risks and health impacts were significantly understated. We have done our own independent assessment and made a decision based on Tsleil-Waututh law. We do not consent to the Kinder Morgan pipeline project in our territory. We are asking the Court to overturn the federal cabinet's decision to approve this project."[10]

The SCC has stated that "the doctrine of aboriginal rights exists, and is recognized and affirmed by section 35(1), because of one simple fact: when Europeans arrived in North America,

3 *Ibid.*

4 See Christopher Alcantara, "To Treaty or Not to Treaty? Aboriginal Peoples and Comprehensive Land Claims Negotiations in Canada" (2007) 38:2 Publius: J Federalism 343; Richard Day & Tonio Sadik, "The BC Land Question, Liberal Multiculturalism and the Spectre of Aboriginal Nationhood" (Summer 2002) 134 BC Studs 5; Sarah Morales, "(Re)Defining 'Good Faith' through *Snuw'uyulh*" in John Borrows & Michael Coyle, eds, *The Right Relationship: Reimagining the Implementation of Historical Treaties* (Toronto: University of Toronto Press, 2017).

5 For example, many Coast Salish First Nations, including the Squamish Nation and the Tsleil-Waututh First Nation, are actively involved in opposing the Trans Mountain Expansion Project. The Treaty 8 Tribal Association, in particular Prophet River and West Moberly First Nations, are currently defending their treaty rights, in opposition to the Site C dam, in courts across Canada.

6 *Constitution Act, 1982,* being Schedule B to the *Canada Act 1982* (UK), 1982, c 11, s 35 [*Constitution Act, 1982*].

7 "Advisory: New Legal Challenges Against the Kinder Morgan Pipeline from First Nations", *Tsleil-Waututh Nation Sacred Trust Initiative* (17 January 2017), online: <http://blog.twnsacredtrust.ca/blog/update-new-legal-challenges-against-the-kinder-morgan-pipeline-from-first-nations> [TWN, "Advisory"].

8 [2004] 3 SCR 511 at para 27 [*Haida*].

9 *Ibid.*

10 TWN, "Advisory", *supra* note 7.

aboriginal peoples were already here, living in communities on the land, and participating in distinctive cultures, as they had done for centuries."[11] However, despite this recognition, there is a failure to recognize that Indigenous legal traditions[12] are the sources of these rights[13] and, as a result, Indigenous peoples' own laws and legal processes have not played a prominent role in defining and interpreting the rights contained in section 35(1), such as the duty to consult. This error has had a negative effect on the process of reconciliation,[14] which the court has stated to be one of the overarching purposes of constitutional recognition of Aboriginal rights and title.

This chapter will discuss how the framework of FPIC, as recognized in UNDRIP, could be used to braid together the duty to consult and Indigenous legal traditions in a manner that comes closer to achieving the overarching constitutional goal of reconciliation. The chapter will first examine the duty to consult and accommodate, as recognized under section 35, and discuss why it has been unable to achieve reconciliation between Indigenous peoples and the Canadian state. Second, the doctrine of FPIC, as articulated in UNDRIP, will be examined as a useful interpretive framework for the duty to consult. Finally, the chapter will assess the importance of Indigenous legal traditions to the development of the duty to consult and consider whether UNDRIP could be used to make constitutional space for these legal traditions within section 35.

An Impediment to Reconciliation: Issues with the Implementation of the Duty to Consult

In 2004 and 2005, the SCC released a series of cases[15] that marked a shift from a focus by the court on static constitutional rights (whether or not a particular interest and/or activity could be recognized as an existing Aboriginal right within section 35[1]) to a dynamic proceduralism, a new approach that allows for the opportunity to recognize asserted Aboriginal rights and interests and protect them from unilateral Crown action, even before they have been proven to exist in court.[16] Although the duty to consult had been recognized in earlier jurisprudence,[17] the court had previously limited its discussion to requirements regarding the infringement of established Aboriginal rights.[18] It was not until the court's decision in *Haida* that the duty's foundational principles were explained and a framework for consultation was outlined.[19]

11 *R v Van der Peet*, [1996] 2 SCR 507 at para 30 [*Van der Peet*].

12 "A legal tradition…is a set of deeply rooted, historically conditioned attitudes about the nature of law, about the role of law in the society and the polity, about the proper organization and operation of a legal system, and about the ways law is or should be made, applied, studied, perfected, and taught." See JH Merryman, *The Civil Law Tradition: An Introduction to the Legal Systems of Western Europe and Latin America*, 2nd ed (Stanford: Stanford University Press, 1996) at 11. This term is used in this chapter to refer to not only Indigenous laws, but also Indigenous legal systems, methodologies and beliefs about the role of law in Indigenous societies.

13 Ghislain Otis, "Constitutional Recognition of Aboriginal and Treaty Rights: A New Framework for Managing Legal Pluralism in Canada?" (2014) 46:3 J Leg Pluralism & Unofficial L 320 at 322.

14 *Van der Peet*, *supra* note 11 at 548, 551.

15 *Haida*, *supra* note 8; *Taku River Tlingit First Nation v British Columbia (Project Assessment Director)*, 2004 SCC 74, [2004] 3 SCR 550; *Mikisew Cree First Nation v Canada (Minister of Canadian Heritage)*, 2005 SCC 69, [2005] 3 SCR 388 [*Mikisew Cree*].

16 Kaitlin Ritchie, "Issues Associated with the Implementation of the Duty to Consult and Accommodate Aboriginal Peoples: Threatening the Goals of Reconciliation and Meaningful Consultation" (2013) 36 UBC L Rev 397 at 398.

17 See e.g. *R v Sparrow*, [1990] 1 SCR 1075 at 1119, 70 DLR (4th) 385 [*Sparrow cited to SCR*]; *Delgamuukw v British Columbia*, [1997] 3 SCR 1010 at para 168, 153 DLR (4th) 193 [*Delgamuukw cited to SCR*].

18 *Sparrow*, *supra* note 17 at 1111.

19 See *Haida*, *supra* note 8.

In *Haida*, the SCC explained that the duty to consult and accommodate arises when there are established or asserted section 35 rights that the Crown is or should be aware of and those rights will likely be affected by the Crown's proposed decision or action.[20] However, the level of consultation required depends on the strength of the asserted claim to rights or land title and on the extent to which the proposed decision or activity will potentially harm those existing or asserted rights.[21] The duty exists on a spectrum, ranging from obligations of notice and disclosure in instances of minor breaches to "deep consultation, aimed at finding a satisfactory interim solution" in instances of significant breaches.[22] However, the court articulated that regardless of the level of consultation owed, in all circumstances, consultation must be meaningful and performed in good faith, with the intention of substantially addressing the concerns of the affected Indigenous group.[23] "However, there is no duty to agree; rather, the commitment is to a *meaningful* process of consultation."[24] The duty to consult also applies in the context of treaty rights; however, the content and scope of the consultation may be on the lower end of the spectrum, as a treaty itself is the product of negotiation.[25]

Arguably, the framework described above does not offer much certainty to the process of consultation; in *Haida*, Chief Justice Beverley McLachlin provided some statements about the nature of meaningful negotiation and consultation. First, she stated that meaningful consultation prohibits the Crown from engaging in "sharp dealings" and requires the Crown to act "in good faith."[26] In the most basic sense, this means that the Crown must act fairly in its negotiations with Indigenous peoples and ensure, to the greatest extent possible, that negotiations are the product of a balanced and equitable conversation.[27] This process is guided by the doctrine of the honour of the Crown, the underlying source of the duty to consult,[28] which requires that the Crown must act in an honourable manner in all its dealings with Aboriginal people.

Second, meaningful consultation requires that negotiations be initiated at an early stage in the process, that is, at the strategic planning level, because decisions at this level have the potential to have significant impacts on Aboriginal rights and interests.[29] In *Haida*, the court determined that the duty to consult was owed when considering the transfer of tree farm licences that would have permitted the cutting of old-growth forests within the traditional territory of the Haida Nation. In other duty to consult cases, strategic, higher-level decisions triggering the duty have included the approval of a multi-year forest management plan for a large geographic area[30] and the establishment of a review process for a major gas pipeline.[31]

20 *Ibid* at para 35.
21 *Ibid* at para 39.
22 *Ibid* at paras 43–44.
23 *Ibid* at para 42.
24 *Ibid* [emphasis added].
25 *Mikisew Cree, supra* note 15 at paras 63–64.
26 *Haida, supra* note 8 at paras 41–42.
27 Ritchie, *supra* note 16 at 399.
28 *Haida, supra* note 8 at para 16.
29 *Ibid* at para 76.
30 *Klahoose First Nation v Sunshine Coast Forest District (District Manager)*, 2008 BCSC 1642, [2009] 1 CNLR 110.
31 *Dene Tha' First Nation v Canada (Minister of Environment)*, 2008 FCA 20, 35 CELR (3d) 1.

Finally, *Haida* provided that "meaningful consultation" may require the Crown to "make changes to its proposed action based on information obtained through consultations."[32] Courts have elaborated on this requirement, suggesting that meaningful consultation requires the Crown to take the interests and concerns voiced by the affected Indigenous group seriously, to ensure they are considered and, wherever possible, to ensure they are integrated into the proposed plan of action.[33]

Despite these guidelines and guarantees, many Indigenous peoples continue to voice their frustrations with consultation processes in Canada, especially those involving the extractive industry (as illustrated by the comments of the chiefs in the introductory section of this chapter). Although the court in *Haida* explicitly stated that the objective of the duty to consult is "reconciliation…of Crown-Aboriginal relations,"[34] arguably the development of this doctrine has not yet led to this result. This chapter contends that this failure is a result of the power imbalance inherent within this framework and the failure of these consultative processes to adequately consider and rely upon Indigenous legal traditions.

The power imbalance inherent in the duty to consult framework is apparent when one considers the words of the court in *Haida* regarding the power to issue a veto. The duty to consult does not provide Indigenous peoples with the opportunity to say no to a Crown initiative that has the potential to adversely affect their rights and interests. As the SCC stated, "the duty to consult does not give Aboriginal groups a veto over what can be done with land pending final proof of the claim.… Aboriginal 'consent'…is appropriate only in cases of established rights, and then by no means in every case."[35] *Mikisew Cree*, a case dealing with treaty rights, alludes to the notion that there may be a case for a veto in circumstances in which an Indigenous community could be left with "no meaningful right to hunt";[36] however, the court is clear that, other than in this limited circumstance, the duty does not provide Indigenous peoples with the ability to stop or prevent outright a particular Crown initiative from occurring.[37] This results in a negotiation process whereby one party, the Crown, has the ability to outwardly reject Indigenous initiatives, but Indigenous peoples do not have the ability to stop the Crown's initiatives.

Although a notion of consent that does not include a veto is damaging enough to a relationship of reconciliation in and of itself, this damage is compounded further by the court's acknowledgement that the duty to consult does not include a duty to reach an agreement: "[T]here is no duty to agree; rather, the commitment is to a meaningful process of consultation."[38] This means that the Crown could proceed, even in the absence of an agreement, if it so chose. As discussed in the final section of this chapter, this notion that a good faith negotiation process is not dependent on reaching an agreement runs counter to several Indigenous legal principles.

Finally, the court has not precluded any hard bargaining on the part of the Crown: "Sharp dealing is not permitted.…Mere hard bargaining, however, will not offend an Aboriginal

32 *Haida, supra* note 8 at para 46.

33 *Halfway River First Nation v British Columbia (Minister of Forests)* (1999), 178 DLR (4th) 666, 64 BCLR (3d) 206 (CA), aff'g (1997), 39 BCLR (3d) 227 (SC).

34 *Haida, supra* note 8 at para 14.

35 *Ibid* at para 48.

36 *Mikisew Cree, supra* note 15 at para 48.

37 *Haida, supra* note 8 at para 48.

38 *Ibid* at para 42.

people's right to be consulted."[39] Combined with the factors mentioned above, and the vast disparity in resources that exist between the Crown and Indigenous nations, the right to hard bargaining creates a significant power imbalance that has the potential to seriously undermine the goal of reconciliation.

Reconciliation is also undermined by the failure to include Indigenous understandings, principles and laws around decision making in the consultation framework. Rather than making space for Indigenous concepts of engagement, negotiation and decision making, the court has dictated obligations, based on its own legal framework, to the Indigenous participants in these processes. The court has stated that "Aboriginal claimants...must not frustrate the Crown's reasonable good faith attempts, nor should they take unreasonable positions to thwart government from making decisions or acting in cases where, despite meaningful consultation, agreement is not reached."[40] This obligation not only suggests that the court has an expectation that Indigenous peoples will cooperate and agree, but also suggests that positions put forward by Indigenous peoples, based on their own legal traditions, will be considered unlawful if they hinder the government from making decisions. According to this understanding, it is not difficult to see why the duty to consult has not led to greater reconciliation in Canada. The next section of this chapter will examine whether the UNDRIP principles of FPIC can help to rectify this situation.

How Can the UNDRIP Principles of FPIC Meaningfully Inform the Duty to Consult?

As stated previously, the Government of Canada has recently expressed its commitment to implementing UNDRIP as part of its overall process of achieving a nation-to-nation relationship with its Indigenous peoples. This is significant, given that Canada was one of only four countries to vote against the adoption of UNDRIP on September 13, 2007. Even when the government reversed its position and endorsed UNDRIP in November 2010, it did so with qualifications, emphasizing that UNDRIP "does not reflect customary international law nor change Canadian laws" and further emphasizing Canada's objection to most of the major rights outlined in UNDRIP, including the right to FPIC when used as a veto.[41] Although Minister Bennett qualified her announcement by stating that section 35 provides a "robust"[42] framework for implementing UNDRIP, including FPIC, it is important to consider if and how the principles of FPIC can be implemented through section 35 of the Constitution.

39 *Ibid.*

40 *Ibid.*

41 Indigenous and Northern Affairs Canada, "Canada's Statement of Support on the United Nations Declaration on the Rights of Indigenous Peoples" (12 November 2010), online: <www.aadnc-aandc.gc.ca/eng/1309374239861/13093745461 42>.

42 Bennett, *supra* note 2.

FPIC as Derived from the Right to Self-determination

One of the major ongoing concerns for Indigenous peoples in Canada is that the government continues to make decisions that affect their lives with little or no input from them. The right to participate "in decision-making on the full spectrum of matters that affect their lives forms the fundamental basis for the enjoyment of the full range of human rights" for Indigenous peoples.[43] The right to participate in decision making is viewed as deriving from the right to self-determination, which is considered the founding principle of Indigenous peoples' rights and the central guiding principle of UNDRIP.[44] Accordingly, many provisions in UNDRIP relate to Indigenous peoples' right to participate in decision making, highlighting the importance of this principle. These provisions include articles 3–5, 10–12, 14, 15, 17–19, 22, 23, 26–28, 30–32, 36, 38, 40 and 41.[45]

The right to self-determination is clearly articulated in article 1 of the International Covenant on Civil and Political Rights[46] and of the International Covenant on Economic, Social and Cultural Rights, which both state: "All peoples have the right of self-determination. By virtue of that right they freely determine their political status and freely pursue their economic, social and cultural development."[47] UNDRIP closely mirrors this established language: "Indigenous peoples have the right to self-determination. By virtue of that right they freely determine their political status and freely pursue their economic, social and cultural development."[48] Accordingly, it is well established in international law that Indigenous peoples, as peoples, have the right to self-determination.[49] It could also be argued that in order to be meaningful, self-determination must include economic self-determination, which ultimately involves control over traditional lands, territories and resources.[50] Thus, it could be argued that Indigenous peoples have the right to be informed and to engage with, and grant or withhold consent, to certain development projects within their lands that impact their resources and ways of life.[51]

This understanding, that the right to FPIC flows from the recognition of a right to self-determination, could greatly influence the interpretation of the duty to consult in Canadian

43 UN Human Rights Council, *Progress Report on the Study on Indigenous Peoples and the Right to Participate in Decision-making*, UNGAOR, 15th Sess, UN Doc A/HRC/15/35 (23 August 2010) at para 2.

44 Bartolome Clavero, "The Indigenous Rights of Participation and International Development Policies" (2005) 22 Ariz J Intl & Comp L 41 at 42.

45 *UNDRIP*, *supra* note 1.

46 19 December 1966, 999 UNTS 171, art 1 (entered into force 23 March 1976).

47 16 December 1966, 993 UNTS 3, 6 ILM 360, art 1 (entered into force 3 January 1976).

48 *UNDRIP*, *supra* note 1, art 3.

49 This is significant because UNDRIP may be understood to embody or reflect customary international law. See S James Anaya, *International Human Rights and Indigenous Peoples* (New York: Aspen, 2009). Accordingly, it may be applied by Canadian courts without any need for an express legislative act, unless there is a clear conflict with statute law or common law, which, arguably, is not the case here. See Maxwell Cohen & Ann F Bayefsky, "The Canadian Charter of Rights and Freedoms and International Law" (1983) 61 Can Bar Rev 265 at 275.

50 UN Economic and Social Council, *Prevention of Discrimination and Protection of Indigenous Peoples: Indigenous Peoples' Permanent Sovereignty over Natural Resources: Final Report of the Special Rapporteur, Erica-Irene A Daes*, UNESCOR, 56th Sess, UN Doc E/CN.4/Sub.2/2004/30 (13 July 2004) at 17.

51 *Ibid* at 10.

law.[52] As previously stated, although reconciliation is an overarching purpose of the duty to consult, arguably the doctrine has not developed in a manner that recognizes the right to self-determination.[53] Instead, it assumes Crown sovereignty and attempts to reconcile Indigenous interests to the development interests of the Canadian state. This is made evident by the court's statements on consent, which clarify that consent does not include a right to say no, and its statement that Indigenous peoples "must not frustrate the Crown's reasonable good faith attempts, nor should they take unreasonable positions to thwart government from making decisions or acting in cases where, despite meaningful consultation, agreement is not reached."[54] Arguably, the recognition of a right to consultation, interpreted as deriving from an overarching right to self-determination, could greatly advance the project of reconciliation in Canada.

When Is FPIC Owed to Indigenous Peoples?

UNDRIP also offers guidance in terms of when an Indigenous community has the right of consultation. As stated previously, in Canada, the SCC has determined that the duty to consult and accommodate arises when there are established or asserted section 35 rights that the Crown is aware of, or should be aware of, and those rights will likely be affected by the Crown's proposed decision or action.[55] The right to FPIC is articulated in many provisions of UNDRIP and arises prior to the approval of any project affecting Indigenous peoples' lands or territories or other resources;[56] prior to the taking of any lands, territories and resources that Indigenous peoples have traditionally owned or otherwise occupied or used;[57] prior to the storage or disposal of hazardous materials in Indigenous peoples' lands or territories;[58] and prior to the taking of any cultural, intellectual, religious and spiritual property.[59]

Although at first glance it might seem that the standards within UNDRIP are captured by the court in *Haida*, these standards need to be considered in conjunction with the right to property in international human rights law. The United Nations Permanent Forum on Indigenous Issues has observed that "[l]and is the foundation of the lives and cultures of indigenous peoples all over the world. Without access to and respect for their rights over their lands, territories and natural resources, the survival of indigenous peoples' particular distinct culture is threatened."[60] It is a right that is essential for the maintenance of other human rights, including, for example,

52 It is well established in Canadian case law that "[t]he general principles of constitutional interpretation require that these international obligations be a relevant and persuasive factor in *Charter* interpretation." *Reference Re Public Service Employee Relations Act (Alberta),* [1987] 1 SCR 313, 51 Alta LR (2d) 97. See William A Schabas & Stephane Beaulac, *International Human Rights and Canadian Law: Legal Commitment, Implementation and the Charter* (Toronto: Thomson Carswell, 2007) at 84–102. A similar argument could be made that these international obligations should be considered relevant and persuasive in section 35 constitutional interpretation.

53 See *Reference Re Secession of Quebec*, [1998] 2 SCR 217 at para 126, where the court stated: "The recognized sources of international law establish that the right to self-determination of a people is normally fulfilled through internal self-determination — a people's pursuit of its political, economic, social and cultural development within the framework of the existing state" [emphasis in original]. This suggests that although the court has previously recognized economic self-determination as forming part of the right to self-determination in Canadian law, it has not been recognized in its duty to consult jurisprudence.

54 *Haida, supra* note 8 at para 42.

55 *Ibid* at para 35.

56 *UNDRIP, supra* note 1, art 32(2).

57 *Ibid*, art 28.

58 *Ibid*, art 29(2).

59 *Ibid*, art 11(2).

60 UN Economic and Social Council, *Permanent Forum on Indigenous Issues, Report on the Sixth Session (14-15 May 2007)*, UNESCOR, Supp No 23, UN Doc E/2007/43, E/C.19/2007/12 at para 4.

the right to self-determination or the right to culture. Although some might question the utility of relying on the international right to property in a Canadian legal context, given that a general right to property is not protected in Canada's Constitution[61] or the Charter,[62] Aboriginal title has been recognized and affirmed under section 35(1) of the Constitution Act, 1982[63] by the SCC in *Tsilhqot'in Nation v British Columbia.*[64] Therefore, Indigenous nations, such as the Tsilhqot'in Nation, with recognized Aboriginal title possess *constitutionally* protected rights to certain lands.[65] These are wide-ranging rights, "including: the right to decide how the land will be used; the right of enjoyment and occupancy of the land; the right to possess the land; the right to the economic benefits of the land; and the right to pro-actively use and manage the land."[66] International human rights law is of use in further defining and clarifying these rights, and the corresponding remedies[67] that exist to enforce these rights.

The Inter-American Human Rights System has developed an advanced and substantive body of jurisprudence on the rights of Indigenous peoples, drawing on UNDRIP. In particular, this system has recognized the collective rights of Indigenous peoples to land, to the natural resources traditionally used and found within Indigenous territories and, ultimately, to FPIC with regard to any large-scale development projects that impact their survival as Indigenous peoples. This body of jurisprudence has been developed around the rights to property and culture, as outlined by the American Declaration on the Rights and Duties of Man[68] (American Declaration) and the American Convention on Human Rights[69] (American Convention). It should be noted that although the American Declaration is not a legally binding document, it is interpreted by both the Inter-American Commission on Human Rights and the courts as a source of international legal obligations for member states of the Organization of American States, such as Canada. The American Convention, on the other hand, is a legally binding treaty; however, Canada is not a party to this treaty.

The case of *Mayagna (Sumo) Awas Tingni Community v Nicaragua* was the first internationally binding ruling that recognized that the right to property, in international human rights law, includes the communal property of Indigenous peoples.[70] The court ordered Nicaragua to adopt the necessary domestic legal measures to "create an effective mechanism for delimitation, demarcation, and titling of the property of indigenous communities, in accordance with their customary laws, values and mores."[71] The court also stated that until the delimitation and titling

61 John Borrows, "Aboriginal Title and Private Property" (2015) 71 SCLR Osgoode's Annual Constitutional Cases Conference 91 at 93 [Borrows, "Aboriginal Title"]. See also Richard Bauman, "Property Rights in the Canadian Constitutional Context" (1992) 8 SAJHR 344.

62 *Canadian Charter of Rights and Freedoms, Part I of the Constitution Act, 1982,* being Schedule B to the *Canada Act* (UK), 1982, c 11.

63 *Constitution Act, 1982, supra* note 6.

64 [2014] 2 SCR 257, [2014] SCJ No 44 (QL) [*Tsilhqot'in Nation*].

65 Borrows, "Aboriginal Title", *supra* note 61.

66 *Tsilhqot'in Nation, supra* note 64 at para 73, cited in Borrows, "Aboriginal Title", *supra* note 61.

67 *Tsilhqot'in Nation, supra* note 64 at paras 89, 90. These remedies include "injunctive relief, damages, or an order that consultation or accommodation be carried out" (at para 89).

68 OAS, Inter-American Commission on Human Rights, *American Declaration on the Rights and Duties of Man,* OR OEA/ Ser.L/V/I.4 Rev 9 (31 January 2003), 43 AJIL Supp 133 (1949).

69 OAS, Inter-American Specialized Conference on Human Rights, *American Convention on Human Rights,* OAS TS No 36, 1144 UNTS 123 (1969).

70 (2001), Merits, Reparations and Costs, Inter-Am Ct HR (Ser C) No 79 at paras 140–55 [*Awas Tingni v Nicaragua*].

71 *Ibid* at para 148.

of the Awas Tingni community's land was complete, Nicaragua must prevent agents of the state or third parties from acting in a way that affects the Awas Tingni community members' use, value or enjoyment of the property where they live and carry out their activities.[72] Accordingly, this seminal ruling affirmed the right of Indigenous peoples to their lands and resources without state interference and also asserted a positive obligation on the state to prevent interference with that right by third parties.[73] This goes beyond the SCC's requirements in Haida because it requires the state to recognize Indigenous customary rights according to the legal traditions of Indigenous peoples themselves and places a positive obligation on states to protect those rights prior to state recognition.

The case of *Saramaka People v Suriname*[74] also goes beyond the SCC's requirements in *Haida*. This case dealt specifically with the right of Indigenous peoples to FPIC and revolved around the fact that Suriname granted resource concessions to private companies within the territories of the Saramaka people without their consultation or consent. Drawing on articles 10 (relocation) and 29 (disposal of hazardous materials) of UNDRIP, the Inter-American Court held that measures that have a potentially substantial impact on the basic physical and/or cultural well-being of an Indigenous community should not proceed without the community's consent.[75] According to this interpretation, the right to FPIC would arise whenever an activity has the potential to significantly impact the physical and cultural well-being of an Indigenous community; this goes well beyond the rights requirement in *Haida*.

The Content of FPIC

While an in-depth analysis of the history and content of the principles of FPIC is beyond the scope of this chapter, a short overview of its content is provided for the purposes of comparison with the duty to consult. It is important to acknowledge that there is not one specific formula for carrying out consultations with Indigenous peoples that applies to all countries and in all circumstances.[76]

According to former UN Special Rapporteur James Anaya, the duty to consult directly with Indigenous peoples, through "special, differentiated procedures," applies only when a state decision has the potential to affect Indigenous peoples in ways not felt by other members of society.[77] This does not mean that the duty to consult and the principles of FPIC are limited in application to circumstances in which a proposed measure will or might affect an already recognized right or legal entitlement. Rather, FPIC is required whenever state action pertains to lands that Indigenous people occupy or otherwise use, whether or not they hold title to those lands.[78] This is due to the recognition that, commensurate with the right to self-determination and democratic principles, the duty arises whenever Indigenous peoples' particular interests are

72 *Ibid* at para 164.

73 S James Anaya, *Indigenous Peoples' Participatory Rights in Relation to Decisions about Natural Resource Extraction: The More Fundamental Issue of What Rights Indigenous Peoples Have in Lands and Resources* (2005) 22 Ariz J Intl & Comp L 7 at 16.

74 (2007), Preliminary Objections, Merits, Reparations & Costs, Inter-Am Ct HR (Ser C) No 174 [*Saramaka*].

75 *Ibid.*

76 James Anaya, *Promotion and Protection of All Human Rights, Civil, Political, Economic, Social and Cultural Rights, Including the Right to Development*, HRC Res 6/12, UNHRC, 12th Sess, UN Doc A/HRC/12/34 (2009) at para 37 [Anaya, "Promotion and Protection"].

77 *Ibid* at para 43.

78 *Ibid* at para 44.

at stake, even when those interests do not correspond to a recognized right to land or other legal entitlement.[79]

The character of the consultation procedure and its object are also determined by the nature of the right(s) or interest(s) at stake for the Indigenous peoples concerned and the anticipated impact of the proposed measure.[80] UNDRIP establishes that, in general, consultations with Indigenous peoples must be carried out in "good faith…in order to obtain their free, prior and informed consent."[81] James Anaya has noted the importance of adhering to these good faith consultation processes in order to create a climate of confidence with Indigenous peoples, which favours productive dialogue.[82] The first step is often to ensure that the consultation procedure itself is a product of consensus.[83] Further, states must ensure that Indigenous peoples have the financial, technical and other assistance they need, in order to address the imbalance of power. These provisions must be afforded freely, absent any type of coercion or attempt to use such assistance to leverage or influence positions in the consultations.[84]

FPIC also depends on a consultation procedure in which Indigenous peoples' own institutions of representation and decision making are fully respected.[85] James Anaya has stated that Indigenous peoples may need to develop or revise their own institutions, through their own decision-making procedures, in order to set up representative structures to facilitate the consultation process.[86] In noting that the failure of Indigenous groups to clarify their representative organization structures may confuse and slow down the process, he observed that it may be useful to bear in mind that UNDRIP states that the functioning of Indigenous institutions should be in accordance with the international human rights standards.[87]

In order for the Indigenous peoples concerned to make free and informed decisions about a potential project, it is necessary that they be provided with full and objective information about all aspects of the project that will affect them, including the impact of the project on their individual lives and the environment.[88] It is essential for the state to carry out environmental and social impact studies and present these studies to the Indigenous people concerned at the early stages of consultation, allowing them time to "understand the results of the impact studies and to present their observations and receive information addressing any concerns."[89] These impact assessments should be objective and the state should ensure the objectivity of impact assessments, either by subjecting them to independent review or by requiring that the assessments be performed free from the control of the promoters of the extractive projects.[90]

79 *Ibid.*

80 *Ibid* at para 46.

81 *UNDRIP, supra* note 1, art 19.

82 Anaya, "Promotion and Protection", *supra* note 76 at para 50. He noted that the creation of a climate of confidence is particularly important in relation to Indigenous peoples, given their lack of trust in state institutions, marginalization and histories of colonization.

83 *Ibid* at para 51.

84 *Ibid.*

85 *UNDRIP, supra* note 1, art 19.

86 Anaya, "Promotion and Protection", *supra* note 76 at para 52.

87 *Ibid.*

88 *Ibid* at para 53.

89 *Ibid.*

90 James Anaya, *Extractive Industries and Indigenous Peoples*, HRC Res 6/12 and 15/14, UNHRC, 24th Sess, UN Doc A/HRC/24/41 (2013) at para 65 [Anaya, *Extractive Industries*].

Additionally, a consensus-driven, good faith consultation process, in the context of extractive industry projects, should not only address measures to mitigate or compensate for adverse impacts of the project, but also explore and arrive at means of equitable benefit sharing in the spirit of "true partnership."[91]

In respect of timing, consultations and agreement with Indigenous peoples should happen "before the State authorizes or a company undertakes, or commits to undertake, any activity related to the project within an indigenous territory, including within areas of both exclusive and non-exclusive indigenous use."[92] As a result, consultation and consent may be required at various stages of a project, from exploration to production to project closure.[93]

Related to the statements above regarding timing, FPIC requires effective grievance mechanisms, spanning the entire project life cycle, including any post-project impacts, to be guaranteed. In situations in which a private company is the operator of the project, company grievance procedures should be established that complement the remedies provided by the state.[94] "The grievance procedures should be devised and implemented with *full respect for indigenous peoples' own justice and dispute resolution systems*."[95] FPIC not only works to establish the processes of consultation and negotiations that have to be followed, but also imposes a requirement that the outcome of these processes be recognized and upheld.[96]

As is evident from the descriptions above, FPIC builds safeguards into the consultative process and recognizes Indigenous authority throughout the decision-making process. This is a marked departure from the Canadian approach, which focuses its discussion on assessing the strength of the right involved and the level of infringement, rather than on the content of the right itself. This ambiguity, arguably, is one of the reasons why consultation cases continue to flood Canadian courts. If Canada is serious about its commitment to implement UNDRIP, these principles of FPIC should be used to interpret the duty to consult and breathe new life into these decision-making processes.

Veto or Consent?

Because the requirement to obtain consent implies respecting the right to say no, one of the contentious issues raised by Canada regarding UNDRIP revolved around the notion of a veto. Canada objected to the inclusion of FPIC in UNDRIP and argued that it "could be interpreted as a veto over development and other decisions made in the broader public interest."[97]

91 Anaya, "Promotion and Protection", *supra* note 76 at para 37.

92 Anaya, *Extractive Industries, supra* note 90 at para 67.

93 *Ibid.*

94 *Ibid* at para 78.

95 *Ibid* [emphasis added].

96 Jérémie Gilbert & Cathal Doyle, "A New Dawn over the Land: Shedding Light on Collective Ownership and Consent" in Stephen Allen & Alexandra Xanthaki, eds, *Reflections on the UN Declaration on the Rights of Indigenous Peoples* (Oxford, UK: Hart, 2011). See also *Awas Tingni v Nicaragua, supra* note 70; *Saramaka, supra* note 74; *Dann v US* (2002), Inter-Am Comm HR, No 11.140, Report No 75/02, OEA/Ser.L/V/II.117/doc 5; *Maya Indigenous Communities of the Toledo Dist v Belize* (2004), Inter-Am Comm HR, No 12.053, Report No 40/04, OEA/Ser.L/V/II.122/doc 5/rev 1; *Kichwa People of Sarayaka and its members v Ecuador* (2010), Inter-Am Comm HR, No 12.465, Application to the Inter-Am Ct HR.

97 Gloria Galloway, "Canada drops opposition to UN indigenous rights declaration" *The Globe and Mail* (9 May 2016), online: <www.theglobeandmail.com/news/politics/canada-drops-objector-status-on-un-indigenous-rights-declaration/article29946223/>.

Although the requirement to obtain Indigenous peoples' consent in relation to development projects in their territories is protected within the normative framework of Indigenous peoples' rights, at present there is some divergence of opinion within the human rights regime as to when this requirement arises.[98] While some would argue that Indigenous peoples have the right to say no for any project or activity affecting their lands, territories, resources or well-being, others would argue that the right to veto only arises when there is a potential for a profound or major impact on the property rights of an Indigenous people or where their physical or cultural survival may be endangered.[99] The first approach recognizes that consent is an integral part of the right to self-determination, whereas the second approach seems to suggest that the extent of the requirement to obtain consent is a function of the degree of impact of the proposed activity. As explained in the previous section of this chapter, in all cases in which an Indigenous peoples' particular interests are affected by a proposed measure, obtaining their consent should be an objective of the consultations. As stated, this requirement does not provide Indigenous peoples with a veto power; however, it does establish the need to frame the consultations in a manner that works to make every effort to build consensus on the part of all those concerned.[100]

As explained by Anaya, a project or decision that has a "significant, direct impact on indigenous peoples' lives or territories establishes a strong presumption that the proposed measure should not go forward without indigenous peoples' consent."[101] In some circumstances, this presumption may harden into a prohibition of the measure or project in the absence of Indigenous consent.[102] Articles 10 and 29(2) of UNDRIP recognize two situations in which the state is under an obligation to obtain the consent of the Indigenous peoples concerned, beyond the obligation to have consent as the objective of consultations. These situations include cases in which the project will result in the relocation of a group from its traditional lands and cases involving the storage or disposal of toxic waste within Indigenous territories.[103]

Whether or not Indigenous consent is a strict requirement, as previously stated, UNDRIP and other sources require that states engage in good faith negotiations in an effort to reach agreement or consent.[104] However, when a state determines that it is not necessary to obtain Indigenous consent and chooses to proceed with a project in the absence of consent, it remains "bound to respect and protect the rights of indigenous peoples and must ensure that other applicable safeguards are implemented, in particular steps to minimize or offset the limitation on the rights through impact assessments, measures of mitigation, compensation and benefit sharing."[105] The adequacy of these measures and the consultations about them will be factors in determining proportionality in regard to any limitations on rights.[106] Any decision by the state to proceed with or permit a measure or project without the consent of Indigenous peoples should be subject to review by an impartial judicial authority.[107] Any judicial review should ensure

98 Gilbert & Doyle, *supra* note 96 at 316–17.

99 *Ibid* at 317.

100 Anaya, "Promotion and Protection", *supra* note 76 at para 48.

101 *Ibid* at para 47.

102 *Ibid.*

103 *UNDRIP, supra* note 1, arts 10, 29(2).

104 *Ibid*, arts 19, 32(2).

105 Anaya, *Extractive Industries*, *supra* note 90 at para 38.

106 *Ibid.*

107 *Ibid* at para 39.

compliance with the applicable Indigenous human rights international standards and provide for an independent assessment of whether or not the state has met its burden of justifying any limitation on rights.[108]

In determining how UNDRIP, and international human rights law, should be used to frame the notion of consent in Canadian law, it is also important to look to domestic legal precedent. The SCC in *Delgamuukw* clarified that where Aboriginal people hold title to land, the government's duty to consult is "in most cases...significantly deeper than mere consultation" and can require the "full consent of an aboriginal nation."[109] This understanding was recently affirmed in the 2014 *Tsilhqot'in Nation*[110] decision of the SCC, which recognized the right to veto on Aboriginal title lands. Taken together with international human rights law, these cases support the argument that a proper understanding of FPIC, within Canada's constitutional framework, includes the right to say no, at least in some circumstances.

The Importance of Indigenous Legal Traditions in Implementing the Duty to Consult

As recognized in UNDRIP, FPIC is essential for the operationalization of the right to self-determination. Accordingly, if the purpose of FPIC is to give effect to the right to self-determination, then the right itself must be interpreted in a manner that makes space for Indigenous laws and practices regarding decision-making practices and dispute resolution. To do otherwise would run the risk of recognizing a procedural right that actually diminishes the substantive right to self-determination — similar to some of the criticisms surrounding the current section 35 jurisprudence on the duty to consult and accommodate.

The Liberal government of Canada has publicly stated that it is committed to resetting its relationship with Canada's Indigenous peoples. However, in order to give effect to this nation-to-nation relationship, Canada must recognize Indigenous nations as peoples who bring well-established legal traditions to the relationship. These laws and legal orders are capable of influencing not only Indigenous peoples' own internal decision-making practices, but also the external practices of the Canadian state.

Articles 18 and 19 of UNDRIP explicitly state that Indigenous peoples have the right to participate in decision-making processes according to their own legal traditions. Accordingly, if Canada is to implement UNDRIP in any meaningful way, it must make space for Indigenous laws and practices to be utilized within the creation of the process itself. This necessarily will require different processes for different Indigenous peoples; however, the result will be one more likely to achieve true reconciliation.

Indigenous peoples have developed systems to maintain and regulate their relations since time immemorial. Living in independent communities and nations across the land, they developed norms and practices to govern their societal relations, manage territories, regulate trade, resolve

108 *Ibid.*

109 *Delgamuukw, supra* note 17 at para 168.

110 *Tsilhqot'in Nation, supra* note 64.

disputes and govern the relationships between different nations.[111] Over time, the diverse norms and practices progressed into highly developed legal traditions that guided these peoples for centuries in the governance of community, the environment and relationships between people. Passed down through generations in stories, songs, ceremonies and practices, there are many Indigenous societies in Canada today that still rely on these legal traditions to guide their affairs.[112] However, currently these traditions have an indeterminate status before certain Canadian institutions. Our country's history of denial has resulted in a failure to recognize that Indigenous peoples have systems of law that governed, and still govern, our lives today.[113]

Working with my Coast Salish community, the Hul'qumi'num Mustimuhw[114] (Hul'qumi'num People), I have to understand some of our decision-making processes that may prove useful in determining what FPIC means according to our laws. While a full discussion is beyond the scope of this commentary, it is useful to consider a few examples relating to the principle of consent.

In my research on dispute resolution in the Coast Salish world, the importance of reaching consensus has been stressed to me many times by Elders.[115] "The leaders got together from the different communities and whatever time it took, one day, two days, three days, of deliberations and then they would decide. They decided, well, you can go...and my community will go...and someone else will sometimes volunteer, I will go....But the leaders deliberated and then the communities were brought together and this is what I'm talking about — reconciliation."[116]

Former Stz'uminus Elder Willie Seymour described one of the first times he witnessed such an event:

> Another one I remember clearly, I was just a little guy and there was a problem in the community that needed to be dealt with right away.
>
> All the big houses were on the waterfront in Kulleet Bay, and there was a point, a rock that went out...my grandfather went down there.
>
> I remember one summer day and somebody was there talking to him and it wasn't long and he grabbed his drum. He had a big drum — hand drum.
>
> We walked down to the big house, he unlocked the doors, opened up the doors, and someone saw him walking, I can't remember who it was, they went in and started the fire right away. And he beat on his drum. Beating on his drum for maybe five minutes so the whole community can hear it. And then five minutes later, he beat on his drum

111 Law Commission of Canada, "Justice Within: Indigenous Legal Traditions" (Ottawa: Law Commission of Canada, 2006) at 1.

112 *Ibid.*

113 See John Borrows, *Canada's Indigenous Constitution* (Toronto: University of Toronto Press, 2012).

114 Hul'qumi'num Mustimuhw refers to the five Coast Salish communities that comprise the Hul'qumi'num Treaty Group. They include Cowichan Tribes, Halalt First Nation, Penelakut Tribes, Lake Cowichan First Nation and Lyackson First Nation.

115 Sarah Morales, *Snuw'uyulh: Fostering an Understanding of the Hul'qumi'num Legal Tradition* (PhD Dissertation, University of Victoria, 2014) [unpublished] at 304 [Morales, *"Snuw'uyulh"*].

116 Interview of Willie Seymour (23 June 2010) in Morales, *"Snuw'uyulh", supra* note 115.

> again and that was his notice for the people to come; that there was business to be taken care of. And if it was an urgent matter, then there was a third time.
>
> The people rushed down, "We need to talk about whatever the concern was." And every family brought something. The women, they would go in the kitchen...the women would start cooking and the men would be down the other end discussing what had to be taken care of.

When the table was ready, they continued their discussion as they ate. And when the women were finished cleaning up, they came in and joined and they were invited to continue the discussion. It was open and sometimes they involved women if it was a husband and wife conflict or whatever.

> And they didn't leave until they came to a satisfied resolution. Sometimes they were there until real late at night. Really late at night they would stop and eat again.
>
> If there was somebody missing, they would send one of the young men. There was trails between the villages...so they would send a runner from Kulleet Bay to Shellbeach, from Kulleet Bay to Nelson Point — to call all the individuals that were knowledgeable on the issues they were discussing, or so that they could contribute to some solution.
>
> They asked everyone; they asked every individual, "*nil ow' sthuthi' ni' 'utun shqualuwun.*" "Is it okay with you, okay with you personally? Is our decision effective? Is our decision acceptable?" They go around asking each individual and then they say, "*tun' ni' 'utunu 'il kwet ch*" — from this day on we put this to rest. Then they will appoint a couple of Elders to go deal with the involved.[117]

Although it was acknowledged that this type of consensus-building process may, at times, be difficult and lengthy, the process was valued for its ability to foster harmony and relations within and between communities.[118] The process of dialoguing with individuals and taking the time to hear and understand their positions works not only to foster a shared understanding of the issues (which can, in turn, aid in a more timely resolution) but also to develop a mutual respect and relationship between the parties involved.

However, while developing consensus is definitely the high-water mark in dispute resolution practices, it is also acknowledged that reaching consensus is simply not possible in all cases.[119] Reaching consensus is contingent upon the parties to the dispute and the issue at hand; therefore, many dispute resolution practices in the Coast Salish world allow for an ultimate decision maker when appropriate; this may be an Elder, a respected leader within the community or chief and council.[120]

This understanding of the principle of consensus can work to inform the understanding of FPIC. It demonstrates that this right entails more than just a veto, but rather encompasses Indigenous

117 *Ibid.*

118 Morales, "*Snuw'uyulh*", *supra* note 115 at 270.

119 *Ibid* at 304.

120 *Ibid.*

perspectives around legitimacy, fairness and respect. These are the types of considerations that must be taken into account in working toward implementing UNDRIP in an effective manner.

Conclusion

UNDRIP provides a normative framework for engagement between Canada and its Indigenous peoples. If implemented in good faith, with the aim of realizing its overarching purpose of Indigenous self-determination, it will provide an opportunity to address historical power imbalances, which have led to illegal land takings and resource exploitation. In doing so, UNDRIP has the potential to strengthen the relationship between Canada and its Indigenous peoples as they work toward the national goal of reconciliation.

However, this project of implementation will involve a careful braiding together of Canadian law, international law and Indigenous legal traditions. Although all three of these systems of law contain principles and processes relating to decision making, at times they may be incommensurable. In such circumstances, it will be important to return to the overarching purpose of this right — Indigenous self-determination — to determine the best path forward. UNDRIP provides a useful framework for overcoming these obstacles and strengthening the ties between the Indigenous and Canadian strands of sovereignty.

Author's Note

I raise my hands to my teachers, my Elders, and thank them for their gift of time and their willingness to share their knowledge and wisdom with me.

8

Mapping the Meaning of Reconciliation in Canada: Implications for Métis-Canada Memoranda of Understanding on Reconciliation Negotiations

Larry Chartrand

The primary purpose of this chapter is to determine the understanding of reconciliation being applied to the recent Métis-Crown memoranda of understanding (MOUs) on reconciliation and to compare them with the different understandings of reconciliation, as understood from the perspective of the Truth and Reconciliation Commission (TRC) and as understood from the perspective of the courts.[1] This comparison necessarily involves a discussion of how the courts define reconciliation and how the TRC defines reconciliation. I argue that the courts take a decidedly narrow and impoverished understanding of reconciliation based on constitutional doctrine the courts have applied in relation to the interpretation of section 35 of

1 There are three similar agreements entered into between Canada and the Métis Nation of Ontario, the Métis Nation of Alberta and the Manitoba Metis Federation. See *Memorandum of Understanding on Advancing Reconciliation*, Manitoba Metis Federation and Canada, 27 May 2016, online: <www.mmf.mb.ca/land_claims_MOU.php>; *Memorandum of Understanding on Advancing Reconciliation*, Métis Nation of Ontario and Canada, 3 February 2017, online: <www.aadnc-aandc.gc.ca/eng/1500480929912/1500480979726>; *Memorandum of Understanding on Advancing Reconciliation*, Métis Nation of Alberta and Canada, 30 January 2017, online: <www.aadnc-aandc.gc.ca/eng/1500571091177/150057113793 6>. These agreements are anticipated and consistent with a Canada-Métis Nation Accord entered into between Canada and the Métis National Council and its provincial affiliates. See *Canada-Métis Nation Accord*, Canada and Métis National Council, 13 April 2017, online: <https://pm.gc.ca/eng/canada-Métis-nation-accord>.

the Constitution Act, 1982.[2] This understanding of reconciliation differs quite dramatically from the approach the TRC takes, due in large part to the TRC's grounding of reconciliation in the adoption of the United Nations Declaration on the Rights of Indigenous Peoples (UNDRIP).[3] The human rights principles adopted in UNDRIP are considerably more robust and fuller than Canada's domestic Aboriginal rights law at the present time.

Based on the comparison between the TRC/UNDRIP and the judicial understanding of reconciliation, I then turn specifically to concerns regarding the recent Métis-Crown "reconciliation" agreements. Perhaps surprisingly, it becomes quite evident that these agreements have chiefly adopted the impoverished doctrinal approach to reconciliation and not the TRC/UNDRIP approach. After demonstrating that this is the case through a primarily textual analysis of the agreements, I then raise preliminary questions about why these Métis provincial organizations are willing to accept this impoverished approach to reconciliation.[4] I provide some very tentative and speculative reasons as to why this might be the case, admitting that I have not undertaken a comprehensive study. At this stage, I only wish to raise a few questions. I then urge, by way of policy advice to both Métis and Canadian authorities and leadership, that the understanding of reconciliation flowing from the TRC/UNDRIP is what should be applied in guiding any agreements or treaties to be negotiated in the future between Canada and the Métis. Otherwise, we are seriously disadvantaging Métis interests and, indeed, violating Métis human rights.

Differing Understandings of Reconciliation

Legal commentators and lawyers often interpret the meaning of "reconciliation" as the successful resolution of a section 35 rights claim. This is not surprising, since the Supreme Court of Canada (SCC) has stated on more than one occasion that the purpose of section 35 is to achieve reconciliation between Aboriginal rights and British/Canadian Crown sovereignty. This is, however, a very impoverished understanding of "reconciliation" and not one that is at all consistent with critical Indigenous legal scholars or the TRC report and its understanding of reconciliation, which is much deeper and more profound.

From the TRC's and critical Indigenous legal scholars' perspectives, reconciliation cannot be achieved by simply resolving claims based on existing Aboriginal rights doctrine, since that very doctrine itself is viewed as a major source of the problem that has caused the inequitable and unjust relationship in the first place. Such perspectives maintain that one cannot achieve

2 *Constitution Act, 1982,* being Schedule B to the *Canada Act 1982* (UK), 1982, c 11. Section 35(1) states: "The existing aboriginal and treaty rights of the aboriginal people in Canada are hereby recognized and affirmed. (2) In this Act, 'Aboriginal Peoples of Canada' includes the Indian, Inuit, and Métis Peoples of Canada." This chapter assumes that the reader has some familiarity with Métis history, identity and politics. It is beyond the scope of the chapter to offer an account of who the Métis are. For a full discussion of the issues around Métis identity and recognition, see Chris Anderson, *"Métis": Race, Recognition, and the Struggle for Indigenous Peoplehood* (Vancouver: UBC Press, 2014).

3 *United Nations Declaration on the Rights of Indigenous Peoples*, GA Res 295, UNGAOR, 61st Sess, Supp No 49, UN Doc A/RES/61/295, 46 ILM 1013 (2007) [*UNDRIP*].

4 Evidence of the purpose and intent of the agreements can be found in the various preamble clauses and objectives sections of the agreements and national accord.

reconciliation by using tools that are tainted by racism and are founded on the belief that Indigenous peoples are inferior and uncivilized.[5]

What is needed are tools that view both sides with respect and dignity, while addressing past harms through meaningful decolonization and restoration of lands and governance authority. UNDRIP and the constitutional reforms advanced by the TRC are the alternative tools grounded in human rights discourse that are needed and should be applied instead of section 35 Aboriginal rights doctrine which, as one jurist remarked, is "rotten to the core."[6] After all, when one takes a section-by-section comparison of the principles of Aboriginal rights defined domestically by the Canadian courts and aligns them with the minimum human rights standards under UNDRIP, in every case the Canadian judicial understanding is weaker than the international human rights understanding.

Table 1 provides this comparison with respect to governance, lands and resources, and state relations.[7] As can be seen from, an understanding that reconciliation is to be achieved by compliance with section 35, as it is currently interpreted, is not what reconciliation looks like according to UNDRIP. As many know, there have been strong endorsements by the Government of Canada toward implementing the "Calls to Action" of the TRC,[8] which includes adopting UNDRIP as the framework for reconciliation in Canada.[9] Are we experiencing a true paradigm shift? Is Canada really committed to UNDRIP? If we examine some important reconciliation agreements, discussed below, between the Métis and Canada, there is serious reason to doubt Canada's positive claims.

5 Robert Williams, *Like a Loaded Weapon: The Rehnquist Court, Indian Rights, and the Legal History of Racism in America* (Minneapolis: University of Minnesota Press, 2005). For the purposes of this chapter, I define critical Indigenous scholars as those who recognize that the entirety of the doctrine of Aboriginal rights and the unilateral use of the common law itself (without reference to Indigenous peoples' own laws) is unjust and harmful in and of itself. This excludes non-Indigenous (or Indigenous scholars, for that matter) who simply study the doctrine in terms of reforms toward making sense of it, but within existing parameters. One can distinguish such scholars by asking whether the work is directly challenging the status quo (advocating for a paradigm shift in regard to Indigenous-Canada relations) or whether the work is validating or reinforcing the legitimacy of the doctrine indirectly by arguing to fix it by making it "fairer," more logical or clearer? Are the scholars working with the doctrine or challenging it directly as fundamentally flawed and based on racist principles of discovery and imposed sovereignty?

6 Harry Laforme, "Section 25 of the Charter; Section 35 of the Constitution Act, 1982: Aboriginal and Treaty Rights; 30 Years of Recognition and Affirmation" in Stéphane Beaulac & Errol Mendes, *Canadian Charter of Rights and Freedoms, 5th Edition / Charte canadienne des droits et libertés, 5e édition* (Toronto: LexisNexis, 2013).

7 See also Gordon Christie, "Implementation of UNDRIP within Canadian and Indigenous Law: Assessing Challenges" (this volume, ch 20) for another, but different, account of comparing UNDRIP with the common law of Aboriginal rights. I compiled the chart as an instruction aide for classes on Aboriginal rights. The idea for developing the chart came from the work of Justice Laforme, *supra* note 6.

8 TRC, "Calls to Action" (Winnipeg: TRC, 2015).

9 TRC, *The Final Report of the Truth and Reconciliation Commission of Canada: Reconciliation, Volume 6* (Montreal: McGill-Queen's University Press, 2015).

Table 1: Comparison between Aboriginal Rights Doctrine and UNDRIP Principles

Domestic Aboriginal Rights Doctrine	UNDRIP
Governance	*Governance*
• Governance claims are treated no differently conceptually than other *sui generis* Aboriginal rights claims. • Governance authorities must be proven on a piecemeal basis (as a broad claim to governance as a whole will not be considered by the SCC).[8] • These discrete piecemeal authority rights must have existed prior to European contact and have continuity to the present day. • These rights are treated like individual Charter rights (as opposed to political rights of an independent nation) and are therefore subject to unilateral justified infringement by federal or provincial authorities.[9] • In theory, the inherent right to self-government exists (no court in Canada has yet recognized such a right), but is understood by Canadian authorities as narrow and circumscribed.	• Preamble: "Affirming that indigenous peoples are equal to all other peoples, while recognizing the right of all peoples to be different, to consider themselves different, and to be respected as such." • Article 3: "Indigenous peoples have the right of self-determination. By virtue of that right, they freely determine their political status and freely pursue their economic, social and cultural development." • Article 4: "Indigenous peoples, in exercising their right to self-determination, have the right to autonomy or self-government in matters relating to internal and local affairs, as well as ways and means for financing their autonomous functions." • Article 5: "Indigenous peoples have the right to maintain and strengthen their distinct political, legal, economic, social and cultural institutions, while retaining their right to participate fully, if they so choose, in the political, economic, social and cultural life of the State."
Land and Resources	*Land and Resources*
• Although Aboriginal title is a *sui generis* protected right in section 35, it is conceptually inferior to fee simple and remains a mere burden on the Crown's underlying title acquired by the fiction of discovery. In 1990, the SCC stated that there was "never any doubt that sovereignty and legislative power, and indeed the underlying title, to such lands vested in the Crown."[10] • The Canadian Parliament retains ultimate jurisdiction and power and can, notwithstanding section 35, modify the exercise of rights without consent (albeit in a more restrictive manner). • Indigenous laws are relevant only as one source of possible evidence of occupation and are not considered as normative or legal in character.	• Article 26(1): "Indigenous peoples have the right to the lands, territories and resources which they have traditionally owned, occupied or otherwise used or acquired." • Article 26(2): "Indigenous peoples have the right to own, use, develop and control the lands, territories and resources that they possess by reason of traditional ownership or other traditional occupation or use, as well as those which they have otherwise acquired." • Article 26(3): "States shall give legal recognition and protection to these lands, territories and resources. Such recognition shall be conducted with due respect to the customs, traditions and land tenure systems of the indigenous peoples concerned."

10 *R v Pamajewon*, [1996] 2 SCR 821, 1996 CanLII 161.

11 *R v Sparrow*, [1990] 1 SCR 1075 [*Sparrow*]; *Delgamuukw v British Columbia*, [1997] 3 SCR 1010 [*Delgamuukw*].

12 *Sparrow*, *supra* note 9.

State Relations	State Relations
• Proven and established Aboriginal interests to lands, resources (and, theoretically, governing authority) can be interfered with by federal and provincial governments, provided the Crown can show that it engaged in meaningful consultation with the rights holder. Only in extreme cases is consent required (no court has yet required consent in Canada).[11] • If rights are asserted, but not yet proven, the obligation of the Crown is only to consult and, in some cases, accommodate, but no agreement is necessary.[12]	• Article 19: "States shall consult and cooperate in good faith with the indigenous peoples concerned through their own representative institutions in order to obtain their free, prior and informed consent before adopting and implementing legislative or administrative measures that may affect them."

Métis Peoples and the Negotiation of Reconciliation

When Canada decided to unconditionally endorse UNDRIP, there was considerable optimism that the status quo would finally change and that there is now a willingness on Canada's part to work toward reforming and changing the judicial doctrine of Aboriginal rights to conform with UNDRIP principles. When Minister of Indigenous and Northern Affairs Carolyn Bennett appeared before the United Nations to adopt UNDRIP unconditionally, she made the statement that "we intend nothing less than to adopt and implement the Declaration in accordance with the Canadian Constitution."[13]

There was considerable concern raised that if this was how Canada was going to implement UNDRIP, then not much could be achieved because the Canadian Constitution, as it is currently interpreted, is itself the most significant barrier to equality of nationhood. As the above table demonstrates, Aboriginal rights doctrine flows directly from section 35 of the Canadian Constitution and, on a principle-by-principle comparison between UNDRIP and the domestic judicial doctrine of Aboriginal rights, the domestic doctrine falls short on each count. A review of recent "reconciliation" agreements with the Métis seems to affirm these concerns as valid.

When I reviewed the agreements being made between political representatives of major Métis associations and the federal Crown, like the recent Memorandum of Understanding on Advancing Reconciliation entered into between the Métis Nation of Alberta and the federal Crown, there seemed to be blind acceptance by Métis political authorities of the impoverished meaning of reconciliation.

Very telling is the fact that in the Métis Nation of Alberta-Canada agreement's preamble, or in the substantive provisions themselves, there is no mention or reference at all to UNDRIP (or the TRC, for that matter). To be fair, however, there is reference to the idea of reconciliation, as the title of each memorandum says that it is for the purpose of "advancing reconciliation." In addition, all three memoranda contain a preamble that refers to Canada's commitment of working from a "nation to nation and government to government basis…to advance reconciliation." However, it

13 Minister of Indigenous and Northern Affairs Carolyn Bennett, "Announcement of Canada's Support for the United Nations Declaration on the Rights of Indigenous Peoples" (Statement delivered at the 15th Session of the United Nations Permanent Forum on Indigenous Issues, 10 May 2016).

would appear that neither the UNDRIP nor the TRC understanding of reconciliation is what the drafters of the memoranda had in mind. Instead, there are references to section 35 of the Canadian Constitution as embodying the purpose of reconciliation. Indeed, there is no shortage of references to section 35 in the preamble, and in one clause, reconciliation is understood as the concept that is applied under section 35 when asserting Aboriginal rights. In other words, it appears that these memoranda are based on the courts' understanding of reconciliation, which many legal experts and scholars have consistently criticized as unjustly narrowly defined and based on perceptions of Indigenous peoples as inferior.[14]

The Métis-Canada agreements are revealing of the government's understanding of reconciliation and they seem to affirm the view that it is the UNDRIP and the TRC legal standards that must defer to section 35 of the Canadian Constitution, not the other way around. For many, this stance differs markedly from the positive rhetoric of Prime Minister Justin Trudeau and federal officials who claim that Canada intends to adopt UNDRIP and to promote decolonization.

The positive rhetoric from federal officials is also characteristic of the recently released statement of "Principles Respecting the Government of Canada's Relationship with Indigenous Peoples."[15] It speaks of transformative change and adopting UNDRIP. Yet when one examines each of the 10 principles closely, they involve no fundamental change whatsoever and, in fact, are simply positively framed statements of the existing status quo of Aboriginal rights doctrine or Canadian policy on self-government through treaties. They do not challenge Canada's unilateral assertion of Crown sovereignty or the discovery doctrine in which this unilateral assertion is grounded. Nor do they question Canada's ability and right to unilaterally infringe Aboriginal rights in the broader interests of Canadian society.[16] It is apparent from a close reading of the statement that the Department of Justice sees reconciliation as that endorsed by the courts in their interpretation of the purpose behind section 35 of the Canadian Constitution and that all we need to do is ensure that the rights contained therein are implemented.[17]

Selling Out?

Although the comments I present here may be regarded as somewhat controversial, I wish to raise questions about why Métis polities are accepting a largely colonial understanding of reconciliation. I think we do have choices and I think we need to respond forcefully and critically against any affirmation of domestic Aboriginal rights doctrine in any discussions or agreements going forward.

---

14 Legal scholars include Felix Hoehn, Sa'ke'j Henderson, John Borrows, Justice Laforme, Gordon Christie, Joshua Nichols, Kent McNeil, June McCue, Angela Cameron, Aimée Craft, Brenda Gunn, Sarah Morales, Grace Woo, Karen Drake, Robert Hamilton, D'Arcy Vermette, Darren O'Toole, Brad Morse and many others.

15 Department of Justice Canada, "Principles Respecting the Government of Canada's Relationship with Indigenous Peoples", online: <www.justice.gc.ca/eng/csj-sjc/principles-principes.html>.

16 *Ibid,* principle 7 of the statement states: "The Government of Canada recognizes that respecting and implementing rights is essential and that any infringement of section 35 rights must by law meet a high threshold of justification which includes Indigenous perspectives and satisfies the Crown's fiduciary obligations."

17 There is no positive statement that Aboriginal self-government is a right. Nor is there any challenge to the judicial doctrine that Aboriginal rights are defined by racist tests limited to customs, practices and traditions integral to the distinctive cultures of Indigenous peoples prior to European contact and untainted by European influence. See *R v Van der Peet,* [1996] 2 SCR 507.

What is particularly puzzling about the Métis MOUs with Canada is that the Métis leadership did not seem to have objected to the limited understanding of reconciliation that is reflected in these agreements. I am not aware of any record in which the leadership expressed concern over agreeing to a process of reconciliation, where reconciliation is tied so directly to the colonial judicial understanding of reconciliation. One has to wonder if the leadership is more interested in looking like they are making progress on Métis rights recognition for their own political image instead of ensuring that the Métis they represent will actually benefit from a robust and decolonized understanding of reconciliation.[18] Or is it the negotiators or legal counsel that Métis leadership is relying on that are doing Métis peoples the disservice? There is some evidence from personal experience to suggest that the legal advice being offered is framed exclusively within the colonizer's Aboriginal rights framework and is accepting of this discriminatory framework without any acknowledgement of the enormous body of critical literature.

It is interesting to compare the Métis agreements with other agreements between Indigenous peoples and Canada. For instance, compare these with the agreement reached between the Haida Nation and Canada in 1993, called the Gwaii Haanas Agreement.[19] Essentially, the parties agree to disagree regarding the rights of the Haida Nation to sovereignty over Haida Gwaii, while at the same time setting up a structure to cooperatively manage the natural resources of the island. In section 1.1 of the agreement, the parties acknowledge that their views "diverge with respect to sovereignty, title or ownership" of the island.[20] In particular, regarding the Haida Nation, the agreement states: "The Haida Nation sees the Archipelago as Haida Lands, subject to the collective and individual rights of the Haida citizens, the sovereignty of the Hereditary Chiefs, and jurisdiction of the Council of the Haida Nation. The Haida Nation owns these lands and waters by virtue of heredity, subject to the laws of the Constitution of the Haida Nation, and the legislative jurisdiction of the Haida House of Assembly."[21]

In contrast, with regard to Canada, the agreement states: "The Government of Canada views the Archipelago as Crown land, subject to certain private rights or interests, and subject to the sovereignty of her Majesty the Queen and the legislative jurisdiction of the Parliament of Canada and the Legislature of the Province of British Columbia."[22]

I provide this illustration to show that it is possible to adopt a critical understanding of domestic Aboriginal rights and assert sovereignty and nationhood status, even if Canada is not prepared to do so. In contrast to the Métis MOUs, a more recent example of an agreement that does include language of self-determination and Crown-First Nation reconciliation is the Nenqay Deni Accord between the Crown (Province of British Columbia) and the Tsilhqot'in Nation

18 Similar concerns were stated by representatives of the British Columbia Métis Federation (BCMF), which was formed by discontented members of the Métis Nation British Columbia association that is affiliated with the umbrella Métis National Council organization. According to the BCMF, the "Métis Nation BC decisions are more about a preservation of the 'status' and a 'fear of loss.' This makes one wonder about their view of reconciliation, which appears as 'zero-sum politics' and 'competition for scarce resources' and 'handouts' by governments." See BCMF, "Métis Nation BC Builds Walls Instead of Bridges Between Métis" (29 January 2017), *BC Métis Federation News* (blog).

19 *Gwaii Haanas Agreement,* Government of Canada and Council of the Haida Nation, 30 January 1993, online: <www.haidanation.ca/wp-content/uploads/2017/03/GwaiiHaanasAgreement.pdf>.

20 *Ibid*, s 1.1.

21 *Ibid.*

22 *Ibid.*

regarding land management of Tsilhqot'in territory.[23] Importantly, the agreement acknowledges UNDRIP and the TRC principles of reconciliation in the preamble. Maybe the difference is due to the fact that the Tsilhqot'in have established Aboriginal title to the territory subject of the agreement and the Métis have yet to do so. However, that does not change the fact that the Nenqay Deni Accord references international law and UNDRIP as a basis for reconciliation and moving the agreement forward.

Perhaps the reasons I raise above regarding Métis complacency are not at all correct and the Métis leadership simply has no choice but to accept the colonial framework. Are federal officials insisting, then, that this is as far as they are willing to go? If so, it is a far cry from the positive rhetoric of political statements coming from Ottawa. Is it a "take it or leave it" approach? If so, then it is likely, perhaps, since Métis peoples have generally been without for so long, for the leadership to reluctantly accept limited and narrow rights recognition than nothing at all. More research is needed as to why First Nations agreements differ in this respect from Métis agreements.

Conclusion and Policy Recommendations

One option for section 35 of the Canadian Constitution, as it has been interpreted by the SCC, to become consistent with UNDRIP is to require the SCC to denounce past principles of Aboriginal title, including the various legal tests for the recognition of Aboriginal rights, as well as denouncing the findings it has rendered thus far regarding the legal nature of existing treaties and the rights contained therein. Because the existing doctrine and SCC pronouncements on the nature of those rights is a binding precedent on lower courts as a result of the doctrine of *stare decisis*, it is going to make it very difficult for Parliament or any other legislative body to change that constitutional doctrine, in particular as it provides for the means of provincial governments and the federal government to continue to interpret their relationship with Indigenous peoples in the manner the courts have provided thus far. Any changes by Parliament would not affect the constitutional ability of the provinces to infringe proven Aboriginal rights according to the Sparrow[24] or Badger[25] tests, unless the federal legislation was very clear that the provinces could not rely on the justification tests set out in those decisions.

Alternatively, we need to remember that the SCC is not immune from societal changes in values and has, on occasion, reversed itself or significantly modified existing precedent to accommodate changing values. There are especially compelling arguments these days for the court to change its position, not the least of which is that UNDRIP represents the minimum human rights standards in regard to state relations with Indigenous peoples and that the doctrine of Aboriginal rights violates many of those minimum human rights standards every day.

The federal government can, however, do much despite the SCC's definition of Aboriginal and treaty rights. The state can enact laws that uphold UNDRIP's articulation of Indigenous peoples' rights. Those laws would have to be followed by Canada and others, even if they are

23 *Nenqay Deni Accord*, Province of British Columbia and Tsilhqot'in Nation, 11 February 2016, online: <www.tsilhqotin.ca/Portals/0/PDFs/Nenqay_Deni_Accord.pdf>.

24 *Sparrow*, *supra* note 9.

25 *R v Badger*, [1996] 1 SCR 771.

far more progressive and richer than domestic judicial doctrine, as it is presently understood, is prepared to go. Despite Tsilhqot'in[26] and Grassy Narrows,[27] Parliament still has exclusive jurisdiction under section 91(24) to make the provinces subject to such federal legislation.[28] The doctrine of federal paramountcy would result in the federal law prevailing where provincial law is in an operational conflict with the federal law.

It is significant that Bill C-262 has recently passed second reading in the House of Commons. The intention behind the bill is to ensure consistency between the laws of UNDRIP and Canadian law.[29] The act requires the federal government, in consultation with Indigenous peoples, to "develop and implement a national action plan to achieve the objectives of the United Nations Declaration on the Rights of Indigenous Peoples."[30] This sounds very promising, but are we fooling ourselves into thinking that this process will result in the principles of UNDRIP being enacted into law? After all, the Department of Justice could have easily issued a statement of reconciliation that mirrored the principles and rights of UNDRIP or those of the TRC statement of principles. Instead, the Department of Justice simply reframed, albeit in a constructive manner, the existing colonial doctrine of Aboriginal rights as defined by the SCC.

There is a deep divide and inconsistency between embracing reconciliation as the full and respectful implementation of the doctrine of Aboriginal rights and embracing reconciliation as the full and respectful implementation of the UNDRIP principles. So far, little has been demonstrated, other than rhetoric, about adopting UNDRIP into Canadian law. Other countries have done so already.[31]

Regardless, Métis political organizations should not feel they are bound by the existing framing of reconciliation in future agreements arising under the MOUs or outside of them. Métis leadership needs to be much more open to the critical legal scholarship surrounding the entire doctrine of Aboriginal rights so they recognize how important UNDRIP is and why that framework should guide future negotiations instead of section 35 of the Canadian Constitution.

26 *Tsilhqot'in Nation v British Columbia,* [2014] 2 SCR 256.

27 *Grassy Narrows First Nation v Ontario (Natural Resources),* 2014 SCC 48, [2014] 2 SCR 447.

28 I make this point with hesitation because I have argued elsewhere that section 91(24) should not be seen as a plenary power, but a restricted negotiation power only. See Larry Chartrand, "The Failure of the *Daniels* Case: Blindly Entrenching a Colonial Legacy" (2013) 50:1 Alta L Rev 181.

29 Bill C-262, *An Act to ensure that the laws of Canada are in harmony with the United Nations Declaration on the Rights of Indigenous Peoples,* 1st Sess, 42nd Parl, 2016 (as passed by the House of Commons 30 May 2018), online: <www.parl.ca/DocumentViewer/en/42-1/bill/C-262/third-reading>.

30 *Ibid,* s 5.

31 The Philippines, for example, has enacted a national law mirroring UNDRIP that, in some respects, goes beyond the protections offered by UNDRIP. See WIPO, Philippines, *The Indigenous Peoples Rights Act of 1997,* Republic Act No 8371, online: <www.wipo.int/wipolex/en/text.jsp?file_id=225130>. It must be recognized that adopting human-rights-affirming legislation is one thing; implementing the principles and rights by the state that the legislation protects is, however, another matter. The experience in the Philippines shows that recognition is largely hollow unless followed by real on-the-ground implementation. Although the rights recognized in Canada by domestic Aboriginal rights doctrine are less generous, what is recognized is much more readily implemented, due to the relative values placed on the principle of the rule of law between the two countries — Canada and the Philippines.

9

Our Languages Are Sacred: Indigenous Language Rights in Canada

Lorena Sekwan Fontaine

Indigenous languages are the oldest languages of Canada. They contain a rich and diverse history that is intimately connected to the land, plants and living creatures. A significant part of the history of the country is embedded in Indigenous linguistic concepts that evolved as the peoples' relationship to the land developed. There are Indigenous laws and international laws that recognize the significance of these languages, in addition to Indigenous peoples' linguistic rights in areas such as education, government services and the translation of laws. Canada has not implemented Indigenous linguistic rights under domestic law.

In December 2016, Prime Minister Justin Trudeau announced that the federal government would introduce an Indigenous Languages Act to support the revitalization of Indigenous languages. The challenge for Canada is how it will incorporate international law and Indigenous law into the legislation. There are also a number of other factors that will have to be considered as the legislation is contemplated, such as the United Nations Declaration on the Rights of Indigenous Peoples (UNDRIP).[1]

1 *United Nations Declaration on the Rights of Indigenous Peoples,* GA Res 295, UNGAOR, 61st Sess, Supp No 49, UN Doc A/RES/61/295, 46 ILM 1013 (2007).

UNDRIP recognizes linguistic rights in a number of areas, such as the right to transmit languages to the next generation (article 13), the right to establish educational institutions that provide education in their own languages (article 14) and the right to be heard and understood in their own languages in a number of private and public settings. International human rights scholars have also recognized Indigenous language rights as a right of self-determination and cultural integrity.[2]

Recently, the Truth and Reconciliation Commission (TRC) of Canada called on governments to use UNDRIP as the framework for reconciliation (TRC Calls to Action 43 and 44).[3] The TRC also called on the federal government to acknowledge that Aboriginal rights under section 35(1) of Canada's Constitution Act, 1982[4] include Indigenous language rights (TRC Calls to Action 13).

In addition to their current backing of the TRC, Indigenous leaders have been attempting to advance Indigenous language rights in a number of contexts, but particularly in education, since the 1970s.[5] In light of discussions regarding Indigenous language rights, the objective of this chapter is to provide a survey of Indigenous customary law regarding Indigenous languages and international human rights, and examples of how other countries have implemented Indigenous language rights. This chapter also includes recommendations for promoting and advancing Indigenous language rights in proposed federal legislation.

Indigenous Customary Law

The basis for Indigenous language rights is derived from Indigenous customary law, where language is recognized as a sacred, inalienable right. For the Algonquian people, for example, according to the creation story, language is one of the sacred gifts given to people by the Creator. More specifically, language is a gift given in the spirit realm, during a sacred period described as the time before the beginning of time.

2 James Anaya, *Indigenous Peoples in International Law* (New York: Oxford University Press, 2004); Tove Skutnabb-Kangas, *Linguistic Genocide in Education — or Worldwide Diversity and Human Rights?* (Mahwah, NJ: Lawrence Erlbaum, 2000); Robert Dunbar & Tove Skutnabb-Kangas, "Forms of Education of Indigenous Children as Crimes Against Humanity?" (2008) Expert paper written for the United Nations Permanent Forum on Indigenous Issues [Dunbar & Skutnabb-Kangas, "Forms of Education"]; Tove Skutnaab-Kangas & Robert Dunbar, "Indigenous Children's Education as Linguistic Genocide and a Crime Against Humanity? A Global View" (2010) 1 Gáldu Čála – J Indigenous Peoples Rts [Skutnaab-Kangas & Dunbar, "Indigenous Children's Education"].

3 One of the TRC's conclusions is that "[i]f the preservation of Aboriginal languages does not become a priority both for governmental and for Aboriginal communities, then what the residential schools failed to accomplish will come about through a process of systematic neglect." TRC, *Canada's Residential Schools: The Legacy: The Final Report of the Truth and Reconciliation Commission of Canada*, vol 5 (Montreal: McGill-Queen's University Press, 2015) at 6.

4 *Constitution Act, 1982*, being Schedule B to the *Canada Act 1982* (UK), 1982, c 11, s 35(1).

5 Indigenous leaders have been advocating for the education of Indigenous languages since the 1970s in the following reports: Manitoba Indian Brotherhood/Assembly of Manitoba Chiefs, *Wahbung: Our Tomorrows* (Manitoba: Manitoba Indian Brotherhood, 1971); National Indian Brotherhood/Assembly of First Nations, "Indian Control of Indian Education" (1972) Policy Paper Presented to the Minister of Indian Affairs and Northern Development by the National Indian Brotherhood/Assembly of First Nations; Assembly of First Nations, *Tradition and Education: Towards a Vision of Our Future, A Declaration on First Nations Jurisdiction* (Ottawa: Assembly of First Nations, 1988); Assembly of First Nations, *Towards Linguistic Justice for First Nations* (Ottawa: Assembly of First Nations, 1991); Assembly of First Nations, *Towards Rebirth of First Nations Language* (Ottawa: Assembly of First Nations, First Nations Languages and Literacy Secretariat, 1992); Assembly of First Nations, *The National Strategy and Draft of First Nations Languages and Foundation Act* (Ottawa: Assembly of First Nations, 2000); Assembly of First Nations, *Submission of the Assembly of First Nations to the UN Committee on the Rights of the Child* (Ottawa: Assembly of First Nations, 2012).

The creation story indicates that before we travel from the spirit world to the physical world, the Creator speaks to us, prepares us for life in the physical world and gives us direction. These instructions, it is explained, are given in our ancestral languages.[6] This demonstrates that language is not only sacred but also a crucial part of our connection with the spiritual realm. Language is therefore more than just words and expression; it is recognized as a gift and responsibility received from the Creator, intended to teach principles of life and existence.[7]

Indigenous languages are also shaped by a number of aspects, such as geography and experience, that develop into cultural practices, needs and communicative systems that change over time.[8] This is demonstrated, for instance, in the multiple and different Indigenous languages spoken in specific areas in North America, among relations and communities, and in dialects within language families. Language is something crucial to the creation of Indigenous peoples. In addition to the views that characterize language as sacred, there are principles rooted within the language itself.

Cree customary law such as *iyiniw miyikowisowina*,[9] meaning "that which is given to the peoples," and *iyiniw saweyihtakosiwin* ("the peoples' sacred gifts") are derived from the peoples' unique relationship with the Creator.[10] These Cree principles stem from Indigenous customary law, which recognizes that languages are sacred.[11]

The basis for the constitutional status for Indigenous languages is also attributed to the inter-societal customs that initially governed the relationships between Europeans and Aboriginal peoples.[12] These customs would have been primarily derived from Indigenous customary law. Then, as time went on, communication exchanges flourished in a variety of ways, in areas such as trading practices, political and treaty negotiations, and diplomatic relationships. When gatherings occurred between Europeans and Indigenous peoples, not only was interpretation required, but there were also communication protocols to be observed. Over time, customary linguistic practices between Europeans and Indigenous peoples began to emerge that regulated communication exchanges.[13] These established inter-societal laws that came to regulate language practices in Canada.

Today, language practices translate into the right to maintain and develop languages, which includes the development of educational and cultural institutions that are required to maintain them.[14] It may also be important to self-government rights to pass language laws in addition to developing language education.[15] Language rights also fall under the umbrella of the "right

6 Harold Cardinal & Walter Hildebrandt, *Treaty Elders of Saskatchewan: Our Dream Is that Our Peoples Will One Day Be Clearly Recognized as Nations* (Calgary: University of Calgary Press, 2000) at 30.

7 *Ibid*; Task Force on Aboriginal Languages and Cultures, *Towards a New Beginning: A Foundational Report for a Strategy to Revitalize Indian, Inuit and Métis Languages and Cultures* (Ottawa: Department of Canadian Heritage, 2005) at 93.

8 Edward Benton-Banai, *The Mishomis Book: The Voice of the Ojibway* (Minneapolis: University of Minnesota Press, 2010).

9 These terms are in the Plains Cree dialect.

10 Cardinal & Hildebrandt, *supra* note 6 at 10.

11 Cardinal & Hildebrandt, *supra* note 6.

12 Brian Slattery, "Aboriginal Language Rights" in David Schneiderman, ed, *Language and the State: The Law and Politics of Identity* (Cowansville, QC: Éditions Yvon Blais, 1991) 119.

13 *Ibid.*

14 Brian Slattery, "A Taxonomy of Aboriginal Rights" in Hamar Foster, Heather Raven & Jeremy Webber, eds, *Let Right Be Done: Aboriginal Title, the Calder Case, and the Future of Aboriginal Rights* (Vancouver: UBC Press, 2007) 111 at 119.

15 *Ibid.*

to cultural integrity," under more current international and domestic norms. For Indigenous peoples, language is an integral feature of their ability to manifest, nurture and transmit culture.[16]

International Approaches

The international community has posited that past and present educational systems in which Indigenous children are taught in the dominant language — at the expense of their ancestral language — constitutes linguicide.[17] Studies have also demonstrated that the most effective methods of creating fluent speakers are immersion programs.[18]

Some Indigenous language education programs have been implemented in Bolivia, New Zealand, Norway, Finland and the United States.[19] Many of these countries also have legislation recognizing Indigenous language rights in a variety of areas.

Bolivia

The Bolivian Constitution declares 36 Indigenous languages, as well as Spanish, as official languages of the country.[20] The constitution also requires government representatives to use at least two official languages, including Spanish.[21] In 1994, education reform was implemented, resulting in intercultural bilingual education for Indigenous children.[22] Educational reforms include the inclusion of curriculum that has been developed based on the knowledge, values and cultures of Indigenous peoples in Bolivia. Indigenous teaching practices and methodologies are also integrated into teaching Indigenous languages.[23] Over the past few years, the social and political status of Indigenous languages has been strengthened because of the legislative and educational changes that have been introduced.[24]

New Zealand

The Maori Language Act 1987 declares the Maori language as the official language of New Zealand.[25] The Waitangi Tribunal has deemed the Maori language a national treasure, or *taonga*,

16 *Ibid* at 119.

17 Skutnabb-Kangas, *supra* note 2; Dunbar & Skutnabb-Kangas, "Forms of Education", *supra* note 2; Skutnaab-Kangas & Dunbar, "Indigenous Children's Education", *supra* note 2; Andrea Bear Nicholas, "Linguicide: Submersion Education and the Killing of Languages in Canada", *Briarpatch* (March/April 2011) 4.

18 Marka-Liisa Olthuis, Suvi Kivelä & Tove Skutnabb-Kangas, *Revitalising Indigenous Language: How to Recreate a Lost Generation* (Bristol: Multilingual Matters, 2013); Jim Cummins, "Total Immersion or Bilingual Education? Findings of International Research on Promoting Immigrant Children's Achievement in the Primary School" in J Ramseger & M Wagener, eds, *Chancenungleichheit in der grundschule: Ursachen und wege aus der krise* (Wiesbaden, Germany: CS Verlag fur Sozialwissenschaften, 2008) 44; Haley De Korne, "Indigenous Language Education Policy: Supporting Community-Controlled Immersion in Canada and the United States" (2008) 9:2 Language Pol'y 115; Jon Reyhner, "Indigenous Language Immersion Schools for Strong Indigenous Identities" (2010) 7:2 Heritage Language J 138.

19 Although Indigenous language rights have been recognized as a right to education in a number of countries, the legislation is not perfect. It is not within the scope of this chapter to provide a critique of the legislation; however, the challenges that Indigenous peoples face in advancing their languages should be considered as legislation is contemplated in Canada.

20 *Constitucion Politica del Estado Plurinacional de Bolivia* (2009), art 5.I.

21 *Ibid*, art 5.II.

22 Bolivia, *Education Reform Law, 1994* (Law 1565); Rosaleen Howard, "Language, Signs, and the Performance of Power: The Discursive Struggle over Decolonization in the Bolivia of Evo Morales" (2010) 37:3 Latin Am Persp 176.

23 Sonia Comboni Salinas & José Manuel Juárez Núñez, "Education, Culture and Indigenous Rights: The Case of Educational Reform in Bolivia" (2000) 30:1 Q Rev Comp Educ 105 at 110.

24 *Ibid* at 108.

25 *Maori Language Act 1987* (NZ), 1987/176 [*Maori Language Act*].

that the Crown must protect.[26] The Maori Language Act also established the Te Taura I Te Reo Maori, or the Maori Language Commission "to promote the Maori language, and, in particular, its use as a living language and as an ordinary means of communication."[27] Because of the commission's work, many Maori people have been empowered to learn Maori and take pride in their language.

United States

In 1978, the state legislature of Hawaii recognized Hawaiian as an official language, which generated a language revitalization program. Ten years later, a Hawaiian senator introduced a proposal in Congress, resulting in the adoption of the Native American Languages Act in October 1990.[28] This legislation acknowledges that the United States must act with Native Americans to help preserve Indigenous languages. It also establishes a federal policy to preserve, protect and promote the rights and freedom of Native Americans to use, practise and develop Native American languages and to encourage and support the use of Native American languages as a medium of instruction.[29]

Norway, Finland and Sweden

In the 1980s, all Scandinavian countries legislated legal guarantees and regulations for the right to use the Sami language. Norway adopted the first Sami language law in 1990.[30] In 1991, Finland established its law on the use of the Sami language before the authorities,[31] while Sweden, in contrast, has adopted some regulations on the use of Sami. All three states have directly elected Sami Parliaments.

Greenland

The Indigenous people in the Danish territory of Greenland have also made important gains with language rights. In 1979, Home Rule recognized Greenlandic as the main language of the country.[32] Since then, Greenlandic has become the medium of instruction in schools. Most inhabitants of Greenland acknowledge that children of Danish parents living in Greenland should learn Greenlandic.[33]

Canada

The federal government has made a commitment to deal with Indigenous rights on a nation-to-nation basis in Canada.[34] The Ministry of Indigenous and Northern Affairs as well as the Department of Justice have made commitments to implement UNDRIP according to the

26 Article 2 of the *Treaty of Waitangi* (1840) guarantees to Maori *hapu* (tribes) the control and enjoyment of those resources and *taonga* that it is their wish to retain. The preservation of a resource base, restoration of tribal self-management and the active protection of *taonga*, both material and cultural, are necessary elements of the Crown's policy of recognizing *rangatiratanga*.

27 *Maori Language Act, supra* note 25, s 7(b).

28 *Native American Languages Act of 1990*, Pub L No 101-477, 104 Stat 1152.

29 *Ibid.*

30 *Sami Language Act*, 1990, Norway.

31 *Sami Language Act 1991*, (516/1991) Finland (now replaced).

32 *The Greenland Home Rule Act*, No 577 (29 November 1978) s 9(1).

33 Lars S Vikør, *The Nordic Languages: Their Status and Interrelations* (Oslo: Novus Press, 1993) at 110.

34 Prime Minister Justin Trudeau, "Minister of Indigenous and Northern Affairs Mandate Letter" (2015), online: <http://pm.gc.ca/eng/minister-indigenous-and-northern-affairs-mandate-letter>: "No relationship is more important to me and to Canada than the one with Indigenous Peoples. It is time for a renewed, nation-to-nation relationship with Indigenous Peoples, based on recognition of rights, respect, cooperation, and partnership."

principles of free, prior and informed consent.[35] While the federal government is contemplating how it intends to fulfill its international and domestic responsibilities to Indigenous languages, other key players from across the country are contemplating Indigenous language revitalization strategies.

Two recent national events resulted in recommendations for the advancement of Indigenous language rights in Canada. Indigenous and non-Indigenous scholars gathered in Toronto to discuss the TRC Calls to Action on Indigenous Languages.[36] Subsequently, a national dialogue in Victoria with Indigenous language experts from across the country was held to discuss approaches to language revitalization in Canada.[37] Individuals at both events recommended implementing the TRC Calls to Action as well as UNDRIP.

Adding to these significant contributions, discussions at the community level have signalled that immersion and teacher training programs are essential for language revitalization efforts. Some of the barriers have been attributed to lack of guaranteed funding or institutional support. There are also jurisdictional issues among government departments regarding Indigenous languages and education. Heritage Canada is responsible for funding the Aboriginal Languages Initiative program and Indigenous and Northern Affairs is responsible for funding Indigenous education. The federal government has indicated that both departments will work together in advancing and promoting Indigenous languages.[38]

Canada has some internal legislative and educational models from which to draw. The Charter of Rights and Freedoms recognizes rights for minority languages under section 23.[39] As a result, Canadians have the right to have their children educated in their mother tongue, whether English or French. French language immersion encourages bilingualism for children with no constitutional right to education in French (that is, when their mother tongue is not French), and provides a model to consider for Indigenous language education.

35 Online Editor, "Justice Minister Jody Wilson-Raybould's Opening Address at UN Permanent Forum on Indigenous Issues" *Northern Public Affairs* (9 May 2016), online: <www.northernpublicaffairs.ca/index/justice-minister-jody-wilson-rayboulds-opening-address-at-un-permanent-forum-on-indigenous-issues/>; Online Editor, "Canada and UNDRIP: Indigenous Leaders Respond to the Announcement" *Northern Public Affairs* (11 May 2016), online: <www.northernpublicaffairs.ca/index/canada-undrip-indigenous-leaders-respond-to-announcement/>.

36 The event was held at Glendon College, York University, and was sponsored by the School of Public and International Affairs and the Centre for Research in Language and Culture Contact. The report was circulated across Canada. As well, a launch of a declaration on Indigenous languages was held in November 2016: "The Glendon Truth and Reconciliation Declaration on Indigenous Language Policy" (October 2016), online: <www.glendon.yorku.ca/crlcc/wp-content/uploads/sites/106/Glendon-declaration-Final-Draft-Oct-2016-public.pdf>.

37 The national dialogue was hosted by the First Peoples' Cultural Council on Indigenous Languages and was held in June 2016. The report focused on four areas: language rights, legislation and policy; community-based revitalization; education; and urban strategies. It was submitted to the Department of Canadian Heritage and to the Assembly of First Nations: "Indigenous Languages Recognition, Preservation and Revitalization" (30 September 2016), online: First Peoples' Cultural Council <www.fpcc.ca/files/PDF/General/FPCC__National_Dialogue_Session_Report_Final.pdf>.

38 Prime Minister Justin Trudeau, "Minister of Canadian Heritage Mandate Letter" (2015), online: <http://pm.gc.ca/eng/minister-canadian-heritage-mandate-letter>: "Work in collaboration with the Minister of Indigenous and Northern Affairs to provide new funding to promote, preserve and enhance Indigenous languages and cultures."

39 *Canadian Charter of Rights and Freedoms*, Part 1 of the *Constitution Act, 1982*, being Schedule B to the *Canada Act 1982* (UK), 1982, c 11, s 23: "23(1) Citizens of Canada (*a*) whose first language learned and still understood is that of the English or French linguistic minority population of the province in which they reside, or (*b*) who have received their primary school instruction in Canada in English or French and reside in a province where the language in which they received that instruction is the language of the English or French linguistic minority population of the province, have the right to have their children receive primary and secondary school instruction in that language in that province."

Certain Indigenous languages have also been granted regional quasi-constitutional status in the Northwest Territories, Nunavut, the Yukon and Manitoba.[40] A problem has been that the legislation does not guarantee the resources required for the revitalization and maintenance of Indigenous languages.[41]

Recommendations

Subject to further consultation with Indigenous peoples, it is recommended that the federal government do the following:

- Implement Indigenous language rights in accordance with the principles of Indigenous customary law, UNDRIP and the TRC's Calls to Action regarding Indigenous languages.
- Formally acknowledge that section 35 of the Constitution Act, 1982 recognizes and affirms Indigenous customary law as the right of Indigenous peoples to transmit their languages from generation to generation.
- Give effect to Indigenous customary law and inter-societal constitutional language rights by adopting legislation granting Indigenous parents the right to educate their children in their ancestral languages, through language courses or immersion programs made available in on-reserve and off-reserve schools, at the expense of the federal government.
- Authorize federal funding of such education through Heritage Canada, as is now done for minority language education under section 23 of the Charter.42
- Enter into legal and funding arrangements with provincial and territorial governments to ensure that such education is made available to parents whose children are not residing on reserve.

40 In 1984, the *Northwest Territories Official Languages Act*, RSNWT 1988, c 0-1, s 4 recognized nine Indigenous languages as official languages. In 2008, Nunavut implemented the *Official Languages Act*, SNu 2008, c 10 and the following year the *Inuit Language Protection Act*, SNu 2008, c 17 was introduced. In the Yukon, Indigenous languages have been granted official language status of the territory in the *Languages Act*, RSY 2002, c 133, ss 1(3), 3(1). In Manitoba, the *Aboriginal Languages Recognition Act*, CCSM c A1.5 recognizes the importance of the seven Indigenous languages.

41 Senator Murray Sinclair reported in a discussion regarding a bill on Aboriginal languages that, other than Heritage Canada's Aboriginal Languages Initiative, the only significant programs for language preservation are the Canada Territorial Language Accords, with a $4.1-million budget, which support territorial government-directed Aboriginal language services, as well as community projects in Nunavut and the Northwest Territories. In the Yukon, language revitalization and preservation projects are supported through transfer agreements, with 10 of the 11 self-governing Yukon First Nations becoming eligible. Compare that to the official languages program for English and French in Canada, which in recent years has been allotted funding as follows: in 2012-2013, $353.3 million; in 2013-2014, $348.2 million; in 2014-2015, $348.2 million. In Senator Sinclair's concluding remarks, he indicated that he had some concerns with the bill on Aboriginal languages but would "support [it] going on to committee in order to see if the committee members will support amendments to the bill…that…will make [it] stronger and consistent both with the TRC's calls to action as well as the principles espoused in the United Nations Declaration on the Rights of Indigenous Peoples." "Bill S-212, Aboriginal Languages of Canada Act", 2nd Reading, *Debates of the Senate*, 42nd Parl, 1st Sess, No 73 (17 November 2016) at 1510 (Hon Murray Sinclair).

42 Note that Heritage Canada's Aboriginal Languages Initiative does not currently provide funding for the development of regular accredited curriculum. See "eligible expenses" on the website of the Aboriginal Languages Initiative, online: <http://canada.pch.gc.ca/eng/1476991063660>.

- Create a national institute of Indigenous language education whose mandate should be as follows:
  - to collect and disseminate information about the teaching of Indigenous languages, whether in Canada or elsewhere;
  - to conduct and publish the results of research into the teaching of Indigenous languages;
  - to provide information to Indigenous parents and Indigenous communities about how and where Indigenous languages are currently taught and how to create new facilities or opportunities to learn Indigenous languages or be instructed in Indigenous languages;
  - to assist federal, provincial and territorial governments required to provide education in Indigenous languages; and
  - to train and certify teachers and teachers' aids to provide instruction in Indigenous languages.

Author's Note

The Recommendations section of this chapter was prepared with David G. Leitch.

10

Navigating Our Ongoing Sacred Legal Relationship with *Nibi* (Water)

Aimée Craft

"Indigenous peoples have the right to maintain and strengthen their distinctive spiritual relationship with their traditionally owned or otherwise occupied and used lands, territories, waters and coastal seas and other resources and to uphold their responsibilities to future generations in this regard."

United Nations Declaration on the Rights of Indigenous Peoples, article 25

I was in a boat with my Dad and Mishomis (grandfather) on the Winnipeg River. My Dad was steering and my Mishomis was giving directions because he knew all the spots along the river. At one point, my Mishomis pointed to one side. My Dad veered in that direction. We hit a rock and damaged the propeller on the motor. Later, when we arrived at our destination, my father asked "why did you lead me directly into the rock?" My Mishomis answered that he was pointing to the rock and explained that his role was to tell my father of the dangers, but not to tell him how to deal with them. "Your guide (teacher) will tell you what's there; he's not going to tell you what to do."

This is just like Anishinaabe law. It's a relationship of principles that are given to us by the Creator and modelled in our environment. What we do with it then as humans is up to us. It is based on our own willingness to comply with the will of the Creator and that of Creation itself.

Article 25 of the United Nations Declaration on the Rights of Indigenous Peoples (UNDRIP)[1] provides protection for the special relationship Indigenous people have with water.[2] It marries the concept of legally enforceable rights with Indigenous legal articulations of responsibilities to act, protect and think ahead to future generations. The question we must then ask is: how do we give effect to this international legal recognition in the domestic context? One mechanism is through overarching legislation that aims to adopt and implement UNDRIP, as proposed in Bill C-262.[3] However, as I suggest below, there is reason to reframe domestic application in the context of the exercise of Indigenous laws, *qua* Indigenous laws, reflecting on them both as the mechanism for recognition and the source of the spiritual relationships and responsibilities themselves.

The language and intent of article 25 is profoundly rich, not in the sense of material wealth (resource wealth being one of the Crown's primary concerns with the lands and territories clauses of UNDRIP), but rather in the article's inherent recognition of sacred spiritual relationships between Indigenous people and various parts of Creation (land, territories, water and resources). These sacred relationships with Creation have existed since the beginning of time and are the primary source of Indigenous legal understandings and Indigenous constitutionalisms throughout Turtle Island.[4] Thus, article 25 can be read as a recognition of Indigenous legal traditions, beginning from sacred sources of law that engage the relationships of Creation.

In its final report, the Truth and Reconciliation Commission of Canada (TRC) adopted UNDRIP as the framework for reconciliation. According to the TRC, reconciliation requires the "establishment and maintenance of mutually respectful relationships," which, in turn, "requires the revitalization of Indigenous law and legal traditions."[5] Giving effect to article 25 requires serious engagement with Indigenous legal traditions, on their own terms and utilizing their own Indigenous legal mechanisms.

For the purposes of this chapter, I will focus on the implications of UNDRIP in the context of Anishinaabe legal relationships with water. Many of the concepts and arguments may apply equally to the circumstances and laws of other Indigenous nations.

1 *United Nations Declaration on the Rights of Indigenous Peoples*, GA Res 295, UNGAOR, 61st Sess, Supp No 49, UN Doc A/RES/61/295, 46 ILM 1013 (2007), art 25.

2 Assembly of First Nations, "The United Nations Declaration on the Rights of Indigenous Peoples: What It Says and What It Means for First Nations in Canada" at 3–4, online: <www.afn.ca/uploads/files/07-12-4_un_declaration_flyer_fe.pdf>. The policy brief makes no direct mention of water. However, water issues have plagued Indigenous Canadians for years, from the need for safe drinking water, to navigation and to exploitation of water for hydroelectric generation, mineral extraction and oil and gas development.

3 Bill C-262, *An Act to ensure that the laws of Canada are in harmony with the United Nations Declaration on the Rights of Indigenous Peoples*, 1st Sess, 42nd Parl, 2016 (as passed by the House of Commons 30 May 2018), online: <www.parl.ca/DocumentViewer/en/42-1/bill/C-262/third-reading>.

4 John Borrows, *Canada's Indigenous Constitution* (Toronto: University of Toronto Press, 2010) at 23–58.

5 TRC, *Canada's Residential Schools: Reconciliation, The Final Report of the Truth and Reconciliation Commission of Canada*, vol 6 (Montreal: McGill-Queen's University Press, 2015) at 11–12.

Physicality: The Right to "Maintain and Strengthen"

UNDRIP article 25 entrenches the right to maintain and strengthen distinctive spiritual relationships with water. At its source, this is a recognition of an inherent right of Indigenous peoples to govern as self-determining peoples, in accordance with Indigenous systems of law. Article 25 enables our assertion of Indigenous legal jurisdictions over lands and territories, based on our own legal principles and values, as well as through our own legal mechanisms. It allows us to dismantle siloed jurisdictional approaches that consider water as a resource to be owned, managed and accessed, in favour of a spiritually based legal relationship with water.

The rights of water (in the forms of water bodies, waterways and nature as a whole) and/or the legal personhood of water have been recognized in various contexts internationally. Such recognition includes legislation, court rulings (and ongoing claims) and constitutional affirmations. While often generated out of and based in the premise of Indigenous peoples' sacred and spiritual relationships with lands and waters, this recognition rests in non-Indigenous legal mechanisms that are dependent on state recognition to be given full effect.

Examples of Western legal systems' claims and recognition of the rights of waters and lands and/or legal personhood include:

- Whanganui River, Aotearoa (New Zealand) — Act of Parliament (2017);
- Ganges and Yamuna Rivers (India) — High Court ruling (2017);
- Rights of Nature in Constitution (Ecuador) (2008);
- Rights of Mother Earth Law (Bolivia) (2010);
- Atrato River (Colombia) — Constitutional Court (2016);
- Colorado River — claim in Colorado District Court (US) (Fall 2017); and
- Colombian Amazon — Colombia Supreme Court (January 2018)

While pragmatically useful to contest state control over water, Western legal mechanisms can fall short of the legal relationships that currently exist between Indigenous peoples and water. The danger is that by using non-Indigenous legal mechanisms for the affirmation and framing of sacred relationships in non-Indigenous languages, we may lose the spirit of the relationship itself.

Many have argued that if corporations can have rights as legal persons, so can other non-human entities. However, a distinction should be drawn between corporations (as non-living beings) and water (as a living being with whom we are in relationship). Anishinaabe *inaakonigewin* (law) sees water as a living, spirited being. While this is not the case in Canadian domestic law, there is room to grow the law to include Indigenous legal concepts.

If we think back nearly a century ago to the Persons case (*Edwards v Canada (AG)*[6]), we see that the central question was whether or not women were "persons" in law.[7] The case explained the "living tree doctrine": our legal understandings grow and morph over time. As our social values grow, so must our constitutional understandings.[8] While no one would have disputed in the late 1920s that women were physical human beings, the recognition of women as persons in law required a shift in legal perceptions to recognize the rights that accompanied legal personhood. We are now at the precipice of understanding that water itself has and is life, and that it is an independent legal actor with whom we are in relationship.[9]

If given full effect, article 25 would support the full recognition of Indigenous legal mechanisms for the maintenance of spiritual relationships with water. In the context of Anishinaabe inaakonigewin, this would call for the support and maintenance of our sacred treaty relationships with nibi, water beings and all of Creation. In order to give effect to our legal relationships and exercise our responsibilities, we must define ourselves by the language of our law, the concepts that are understood through Indigenous languages.[10] This is essential for the reciprocal relationship with water, spirits, ourselves and all other beings in Creation. Any non-Indigenous language articulation or Western mechanism of law making will compromise Anishinaabe inaakonigewin.

Relationality (*Inendiwin*): Relationships and Responsibilities

Anishinaabe *nibi inaakonigewin* (water law) tells us that water is life — *nibi onje biimaadiiziiwin*. We are born of water, and we are primarily composed of water. Not only does it give and take life, it is also a living being in and of itself that relies on a larger web of relationships to be well and to bring wellness to other beings.

When we think about inaakonigewin through sacred creation stories, we are reminded that, as human beings, we were the last to be placed on the earth and the most dependent of all the beings in Creation. As humans, we depend on a complex web of relationships in order to live well, to live our mino-biimaadiiziiwin. Through the relationships that govern our interactions between beings, we develop a sense of our normative values and legal principles.[11] Relationships with land, water and other beings and among ourselves are equally sacred.[12]

6 *Edwards v Canada (AG)*, [1929] UKPC 86; [1930] AC 124; 1929 CanLII 438 [*Edwards*], online: <www.bailii.org/uk/cases/UKPC/1929/1929_86.html>.

7 Tabitha Marshall & David A Cruickshank, "Persons Case" (7 February 2006), online: Historica Canada <www.thecanadianencyclopedia.ca/en/article/persons-case/>.

8 *Edwards*, *supra* note 6.

9 Aimée Craft, "Giving and Receiving Life from Anishinaabe Nibi Inaakonigewin (Our Water Law) Research" in Jocelyn Thorpe, Stephanie Rutherford & L Anders Sandberg, eds, *Methodological Challenges in Nature-Culture and Environmental History Research* (New York: Routledge, 2016) at 109 [Craft, "Life"].

10 For example, the concept in article 25 that asserts the right over territories that are traditionally owned or otherwise occupied derives from concepts of common law where jurisdiction, akin to ownership, is recognized through consistent or continued land use. From an Anishinaabe perspective, one might refer to "the lands and waters that I belong to" or "akiin," which speaks to the place your family and ancestors are from, places where you maintain your sacred relationships and responsibilities, the place you were born or where your belly button is buried.

11 Craft, "Life", *supra* note 9 at 109.

12 Sean Wilson, *Research is Ceremony: Indigenous Research Methods* (Halifax: Fernwood, 2008) at 87.

Figure 1: Anishinaabe Legal Relationships[13]

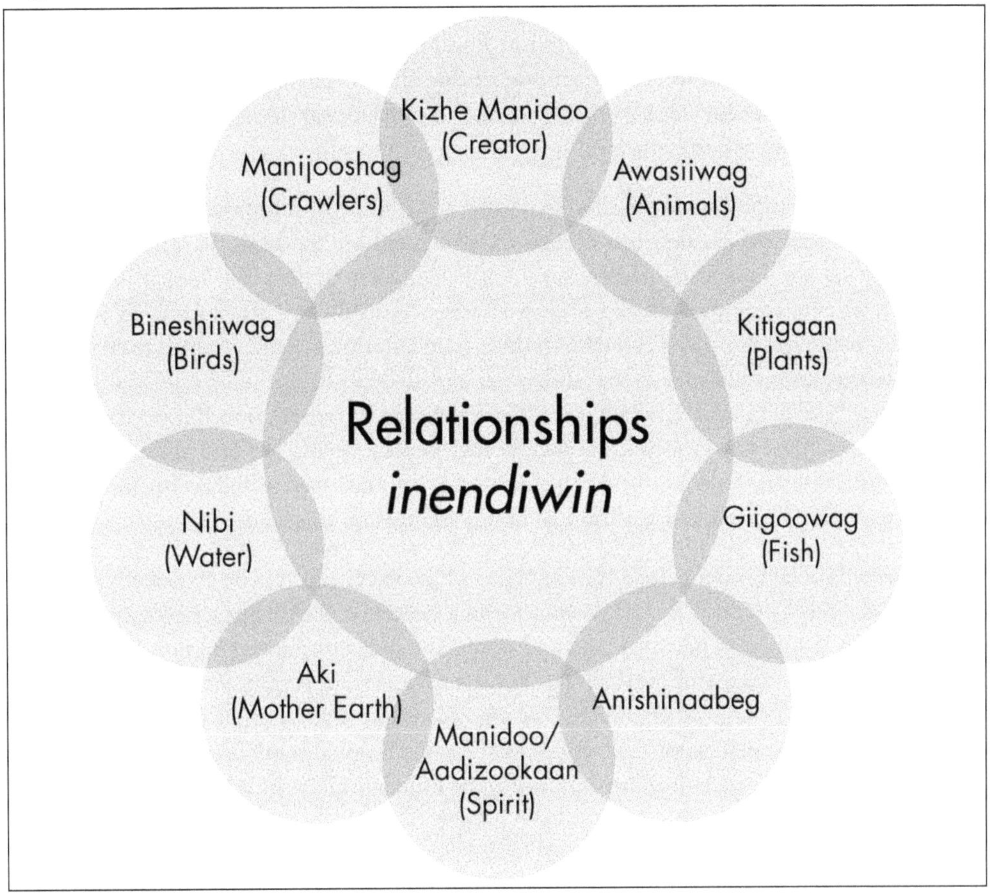

Source: Aimée Craft, "Neither Infringement nor Justification: The SCC's Mistaken Approach to Reconciliation", in Karen Drake & Brenda L Gunn, eds, *Renewing Relationships: Indigenous Peoples and Canada* (Saskatoon: Wiyasiwewin Mikiwahp Native Law Centre, University of Saskatchewan, 2019). Used with permission.

"The Great Spirit instructed us to honor all of life and to respect all of Creation. He gave us laws that govern all our relationships, to live in harmony with Creation and with humankind. We are spiritually and culturally obliged to have in our interest, the total well being of this Earth, this Creation, and the people."[14]

Anishinaabe law is centred in relationships.[13] These relationships exist between all beings that are part of Creation, in a variety of permutations and according to a system of generalized reciprocity.[14] Anishinaabe inaakonigewin is structured relationally, primarily in a realm of responsibilities (rather than the binary of rights and obligations). In some cases, one being has a responsibility toward another, not because there is an obligation that corresponds to a right,

13 Aimée Craft, "Anishinaabe Nibi Inaakonigewin Report" (Winnipeg: Centre for Human Rights Research, Public Interest Law Centre, 2014) [Craft, "Nibi"], online: <http://create-h2o.ca/pages/annual_conference/presentations/2014/ANI_Gathering_Report_-_June24.pdf> at 8.

14 Aimée Craft, *Breathing Life Into the Stone Fort Treaty* (Vancouver: UBC Press, 2013) at 71 [Craft, *Breathing Life*].

but rather because of a generalized responsibility to look after that relationship, potentially in relation to a variety of other relationships that are intrinsically connected. These legal relationships are multi-dimensional and reflect kinship structures. Therefore, in Anishinaabe law, when considering the impact of our actions, we do not think in terms of parties with a direct interest, but rather we evaluate the many combinations of relationships within a broader web of relationships that exist within Creation.

The multitude of relationships in inaakonigewin are not limited to those relationships between persons. Legal relationships between beings are structured on the basis of spirit. Spirit and life exist beyond the indicators of breathing entities and far beyond the human realm. For example, rocks, trees and water are all beings with whom Anishinaabe are in legal relationships. Responsibilities do not begin and end with the human relationships. Balance needs to be restored with recognizing responsibilities to the land, water and all other beings in Creation with whom we are related. "[W]hen we are talking about our relationship, our relationship to one another and our responsibilities as Anishinaabe people first because that's our first responsibility, to ourselves, our nations of people. And then we have another responsibility because we are responsible too for this land, our land and all of our relatives on this land."[15]

In other systems of law, water is treated as a subject or an object, often to be owned and used. In inaakonigewin, nibi (water) is treated as an actor in a relationship. Anishinaabe inaakonigewin does not starkly distinguish between land and water. The two are connected; their jurisdictions are complementary, mixed and overlapping. For example, we are taught through our creation stories that the land is our mother and the rivers are the veins of our mother. All of this belongs to and composes a spirited being that we personify as the original mother (in accordance with our creation stories). Our relationship with her is the foundation of our relationship with all of Creation. Bodies of water or waterways are also independent entities with spirits who look after them and who are acknowledged and named in ceremonies and prayer.

Elder Mary Deleary explains that the objective of reconciliation should be to restore balance to all relationships. She says, "Reconciliation must continue in ways that honour the ancestors, respect the land, and rebalance relationships."[16]

While the law in Canada considers water as an object or subject, Anishinaabe law considers water to be an independent (yet interconnected) agent in relationships of coexistence with other beings, all part of a larger web of Creation. Legislation therefore would be limited to the Canadian jurisdictional water context, which falls short of understanding or implementing Anishinaabe nibi inaakonigewin.

15 Elder Mary Deleary, Statement to the TRC (Winnipeg: TRC Forum on Reconciliation, Elders and Knowledge Keepers, 2014).

16 *Ibid.*

Sacredness: Our Spiritual Relationship with Water

Some Anishinaabe Elders share that there are four types of water: fresh water, salt water, rain water and birth water.[17] Water exists in many forms, with various spiritual entities that look after these types of water. Although this teaching has many permutations, all of which are true, the fact remains that Anishinaabe law sees water in its multiplicity. It recognizes water and all its guardians as living beings with whom we interact and to whom we must exercise responsibilities. We acknowledge that water is life — nibi onje biimaadiiziiwin. Anishinaabe *kweyag* (women), as keepers of sacred birth water, maintain a special relationship of care with water, somewhat akin to a fiduciary obligation. Prior to birth, and by being in water during our gestation period, we are imbued with an understanding of our living relationship with water. We are birthed from and through water. Our relationship with water is the most central and constant relationship of our human lifetime.

Through work with a faculty of Anishinaabe Elders from Treaty areas 1, 2 and 3, we were able to distill a set of primary legal principles relating to water.[18]

To understand Anishinaabe inaakonigewin, we are required to understand different levels of law, generated from different sources. This understanding and application of law requires a progression through levels, which might be described in a way that is similar to the teaching of progression from east to west during a lifetime, following the direction of the sun. It is a lifelong practice.

While some might assume that levels of law are hierarchical, that is not the intent of inaakonigewin. Each level of law represented below is part of a set of concentric circles dependent on each other for a complete legal understanding, all of it sourced in spiritual law. All beings have been gifted with the understanding of spiritual law. As humans, we observe the application of spiritual law in the natural environment, as applied by other beings in Creation. This basis of spiritual and natural law by which we are meant to model our human law has allowed us to develop our customs of interaction (customary law) over centuries of interaction among each other (and other beings). We then apply spiritual, natural and customary law to our current relational contexts, with a fuller understanding of our web of relationships and responsibilities.

Spiritual law is the first form of law from which we derive all other legal understandings. It is referred to differently in different regions and anishinaabemowin (language) dialects.[19] "The first law of our people is the Creator's law," the law which is given to us through ceremony, our creation stories and understanding the teachings about relationships to everything around us.[20]

In essence, spiritual laws are the instructions that the Creator provides to each being (human, animal, bird and so on) that journeys through four levels before arriving on the earth.[21] When we arrive on earth, we have this set of underlying normative values or principles that reveal themselves to us regularly throughout our lives and come to gather more meaning as our

17 Note that there are variations on the number and forms of water, which vary with teachings and among Elders and regions.

18 Craft, "Nibi", *supra* note 15 at 25–37.

19 It is sometimes referred to as the Great Binding Law, Creator's Law, *Kitchi Tibaakonigewin* and so on.

20 Personal communication from Harry Bone (5 August 2015).

21 Personal communication from Peter Atkinson (April 2012).

Figure 2: *Nibi Inaakonigewin* (Water Law Principles)

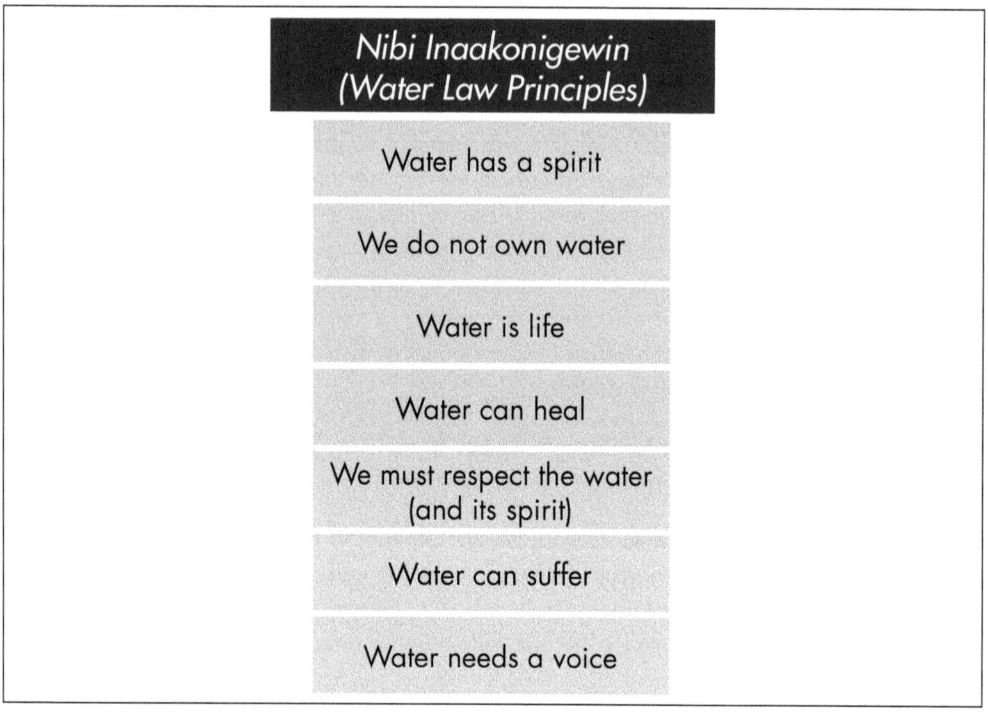

Source: Craft, "Nibi", *supra* note 15.

understanding of the other forms of law is enhanced. The essence of the spiritual instructions is love and kindness (for ourselves, others and all of Creation).[22]

Natural law is derived from spiritual law. With the basic spiritual instructions, we are able to connect to our original mother, the earth. From her and all other beings in Creation, we learn natural law. This is done primarily through observation of how the beings of the earth act and interact. From observing the earth and other beings that are placed on the earth, we are able to better understand the spiritual legal instructions that were given to us.

In the creation story, human beings were the last to be placed on the earth. We often refer to the other beings — animals, birds, fish, insects, plants, trees and rocks — as our older brothers and sisters, acknowledging that they were placed here before us and that we have something to learn from them, while also being dependent on them for our survival.[23]

From these older brothers and sisters (other non-human beings) and our mother (*akii* — the earth), we learn about our relationships and our responsibilities to one another. We discover that without the balance of those relationships, none of us would survive. We do this out of the love we have for each other (one of the Creator's spiritual instructions), as well as for the purpose of working toward mino-biimaadiziwin, our collective well-being.

22 Often we are told that children are the closest to the Creator and have a pure understanding of those spiritual laws. This is why young children are said to have the purest, most untainted understanding of those spiritual instructions.

23 Dumont, *supra* note 14 at 34.

Figure 3: Sources of Anishinaabe *Inaakonigewin* (Law)

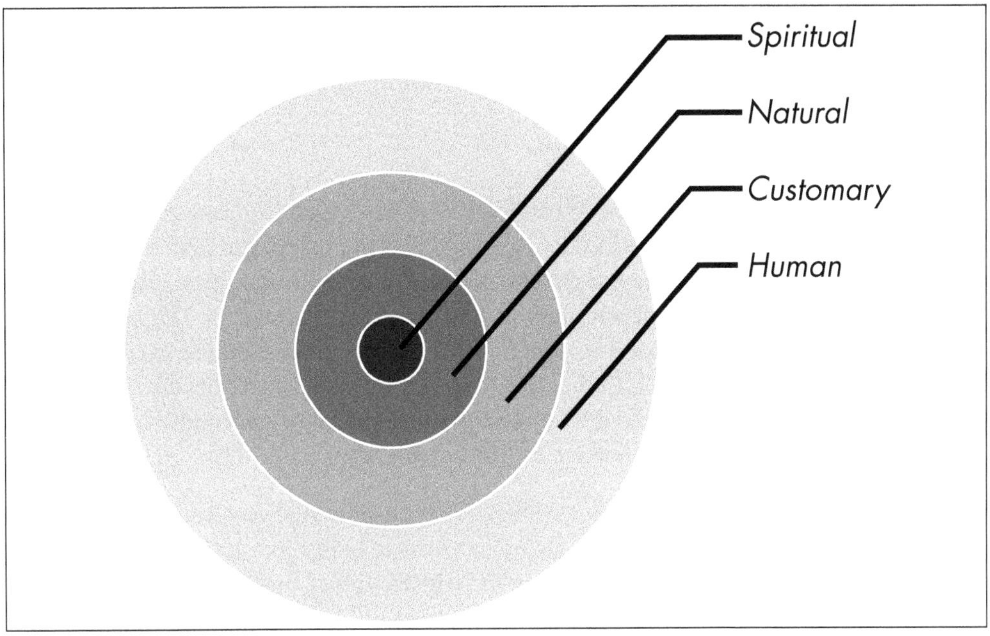

Source: Author.

Customary law is the application of spiritual and natural law in our ongoing human relationships. This entails accepting responsibility in relation to our relatives. Some explain customary law as the seven teachings of love, honesty, respect, courage, humility, wisdom and truth.[24]

All of these sources of law come together to make up the principles by which we govern our interactions among beings. In order to give effect to those legal principles and responsibilities, we must understand their sacred, natural and customary sources and maintain the sacred relationships that allow us to access and apply our Indigenous legal obligations throughout many generations. Federal and/or provincial legislation as a mechanism to give effect to these legal responsibilities would fall short of Anishinaabe legal mechanisms and their ability to engage in the complex web of legal relationships relating to water.

Temporality: "Uphold Responsibilities to Future Generations"

Anishinaabe inaakonigewin requires that we orient our decision making and actions toward mino-biimaadiiziwin. This foundational legal principle is aimed at the well-being of all parts of Creation, including those generations that come next. We accept that our well-being was considered and acted upon by previous generations. Article 25 confirms a right and an obligation to uphold responsibilities to lands and waters for future generations.

24 Deborah McGregor, "Indigenous Women, Water Justice and Zaagidowin (Love)" (2013) 30:2–3 Can Woman Stud 71 at 71–78; John Borrows, "Seven Generations, Seven Teachings: Ending the Indian Act" (Ottawa: National Centre for First Nations Governance, 2008) at 11–30.

This approach is distinct from much of existing Canadian law, which is not oriented to sustainability or actions based on the wellness of future generations. However, the language of article 25 provides a shift that reflects Indigenous laws and creates an opening for a different matrix of long-term and sustainable decision making.

Conclusion

The domestic implementation of article 25 of UNDRIP requires a shift from domestic legislation that recognizes and implements UNDRIP to a recognition and implementation of Indigenous legal traditions within individual Indigenous Nations and territories. This recognition of Indigenous laws and legal constructs is built into the language of article 25. The wording and intent of article 25 recognizes the two foundational pillars of Anishinaabe inaakonigewin, namely, collective well-being (mino-biimaadiiziiwin) and relationality (inendiwin). Further, article 25 makes individuals and the collective responsible for future generations, which is an essential temporal aspect of the application of Anishinaabe law.

The implementation of article 25 (and of UNDRIP, more generally) requires the recognition of self-determination, which includes the ability to revitalize Indigenous laws and to give them full force and effect. It also requires the ability to revitalize Indigenous languages that are the vessels for the transmission, interpretation and application of Indigenous laws. In Anishinaabe inaakonigewin, this would mean the ability to revitalize existing legal relationships with the water through the affirmation of treaties with water, water beings and water spirits.

Author's Note

With thanks to Rayanna Hourie and Alyssa Bird for their editing and footnoting assistance, and to Sherry Copenace with some of the translations. Thanks to the Faculty of Elders on the Anishinaabe nibi inaakonigewin project who have shared many teachings that inform this work.

11

Rebuilding Relationships and Nations: A Mi'kmaw Perspective of the Path to Reconciliation

Cheryl Knockwood

In light of the promises[1] aimed at improving the core relationship between Canadians and Indigenous peoples[2] being made by Canada, under the leadership of Prime Minister Justin Trudeau to the Indigenous peoples in Canada, it is important to take a moment to reflect on what potential next steps should be made by federal, provincial and Mi'kmaw governments in order to make those promises a reality. Canada has committed to reconciliation,[3] to honouring the nation-to-nation relationship, to endorsing the United Nations Declaration on the Rights of Indigenous Peoples (UN Declaration),[4] and to passing a law ensuring that the laws of Canada are in harmony with the UN Declaration.[5] This gives me, a Mi'kmaw person,

1 Canada, Department of Justice, "Principles respecting the Government of Canada's relationship with Indigenous peoples" (14 February 2018), online: <www.justice.gc.ca/eng/csj-sjc/principles-principes.html>.

2 Canada, Indigenous and Northern Affairs Canada, "Canada's Statement of Support on the United Nations Declaration on the Rights of Indigenous Peoples" (12 November 2010), online: <www.aadnc-aandc.gc.ca/eng/1309374239861/1309374546142>. Furthermore, Canada stated, "We are now confident that Canada can interpret the principles expressed in the Declaration in a manner that is consistent with our Constitution and legal framework."

3 Canada, Indigenous and Northern Affairs Canada, "Minister Bennett Announces Interim Board of Directors for the National Council for Reconciliation" (14 December 2017), online: <www.canada.ca/en/indigenous-northern-affairs/news/2017/12/minister_bennettannouncesinterimboardofdirectorsforthenationalco.html>.

4 The UN Declaration was adopted by the United Nations in 2007. *United Nations Declaration on the Rights of Indigenous Peoples*, GA Res 295, UNGAOR, 61st Sess, Supp No 49, UN Doc A/RES/61/295, 46 ILM 1013 (2007) [*UN Declaration*].

5 James Munson, "Liberals will back U.N. Indigenous rights bill", *iPolitics* (20 November 2017), online: <https://ipolitics.ca/2017/11/20/liberals-will-back-u-n-indigenous-rights-bill/>.

great hope for the future. In this chapter, I will outline what steps the federal, provincial[6] and Mi'kmaw governments[7] need to take to make those promises a reality and to start a legitimate reconciliation process based on the nation-to-nation approach.

Approach and Results

For reconciliation to succeed, the first step is for Canada and the provinces to understand and respect the Mi'kmaw worldview, in relation to Mother Earth. This knowledge is important, so that Canada and the provinces can understand why it is so vital for the Mi'kmaq to protect Mother Earth and therefore be involved in the decision making before any development occurs within Mi'kma'ki.[8] The second step involves Canada and the provinces taking responsibility for both the historical and ongoing injustices they inflicted upon the Mi'kmaw Nation and then taking steps to end those injustices. This includes compensating the Mi'kmaw Nation for these past harms and injustices. The third step involves Canada and the provinces taking immediate measures to implement existing Mi'kmaw Aboriginal and treaty rights and honouring Aboriginal title, as is currently practised by the Mi'kmaw Nation and already recognized by the Supreme Court of Canada and outlined in the UN Declaration. This step involves Canada and the provinces passing a Mi'kmaw Aboriginal and Treaty Rights Implementation Act (MATRIA) and harmonizing existing laws with successful Supreme Court of Canada Aboriginal and treaty decisions and with the UN Declaration. The final step involves the Mi'kmaw Nation hosting a Mi'kmaw Summit, where common issues will be discussed in order to come up with an action plan for nation rebuilding.

Mi'kmaw Teachings of Mother Earth

The Mi'kmaw legal tradition is rooted within the teachings from our ancestors that have been passed down to us from generation to generation. Albert Marshall, a Mi'kmaw Elder, shares that the Mi'kmaq have a knowledge base that has been evolving for thousands of years through our language and our belief systems.[9] The teachings are imparted in many ways, but a common way is through the oral tradition via the sharing of legends and storytelling. In this section, I would like to share Mi'kmaw teachings related to Mother Earth and our responsibility toward her. This responsibility of taking care of the lands and waters is embedded within the language and implicit within the oral tradition/stories that have been shared intergenerationally.

6 Newfoundland, New Brunswick, Nova Scotia, Prince Edward Island and Quebec.

7 Harold Franklin McGee Jr, "Mi'kmaq" in *The Canadian Encyclopedia*, revised by Michelle Filice (2017), online: <www.thecanadianencyclopedia.ca/en/article/micmac-mikmaq/>. The current status of Mi'kmaw communities is as follows: As of 2015, the number of people registered with Mi'kmaq First Nations was 58,763. Of that total, 23,997 were members of the Qalipu First Nation of Newfoundland, a landless community officially recognized by the Government of Canada in 2011. Excluding the landless Qalipu, 56 percent of Mi'kmaw people lived on reserves in 2015. Mi'kma'ki is home to 30 Mi'kmaq nations, 29 of which are located in Canada — the Aroostook Micmac Band of Presque Isle, Maine, has more than 1,200 members. All but two communities (the Qalipu Mi'kmaq First Nation and La Nation Micmac de Gespeg in Fontenelle, Quebec) possess reserve lands.

8 The traditional territory of the Mi'kmaq encompasses what is now known as the Gaspé region of Quebec, the eastern region of New Brunswick and Maine, Nova Scotia, Prince Edward Island and the island of Newfoundland.

9 Madeline Yakimchuk, "Netukulimk" (5 March 2010), online: YouTube <www.youtube.com/watch?v=wsNVewjgKxI>.

The Mi'kmaw legend, called the "American Marten Apistane'wj[10] & The First Pine Trees,"[11] teaches how the pine trees came to be. We learn how three warrior brothers, in their quest for greatness, approach Kluskap,[12] each with a wish. The first warrior wants to remain tall, the second warrior wants to sit and enjoy the beauty, and the third warrior — the oldest — wants wisdom and to be respected and to live longer than the others. Kluskap sees they are full of pride and grants their wishes, but turns them into pine saplings. He then asks Apistane'wj to plant them in the Unama'ki highlands. The warriors each got their wish: those pine saplings grew large and became the tallest, deeply and firmly rooted, and oldest living beings in the forest. The legend ends with a teaching: it is our job to take care of the forests so they can take care of us.

According to our legends, many animate beings can shape-change into different forms; for example, from a human to a pine tree or from a bear to the northern star.[13] The thunder, wind, and the change of seasons and directions are animate and can shape-change. Mountains, lakes and icebergs can also shape-change into persons. Boulders and cliffs are sometimes revealed in stories as shape-changers who choose these forms when they wish to hide or to rest.[14] Not only can they shape-change, but the sun, earth and moon are the ancestors of the Mi'kmaq.[15] Because the Mi'kmaq view the earth as family, as kin, this is why it is so important for the Mi'kmaq to honour and respect her.

Another important Mi'kmaw teaching is related to sustainability. According to Marshall, the Mi'kmaw concept of sustainability is also embedded within the Mi'kmaw language. He shares the Mi'kmaw word that captures the concept of sustainability, "*Netukulimk*," which means protecting the earth so as to not "compromise the future generations of their abilities, to sustain themselves but also to be able to appreciate and to maintain that connection to the source of life, which is our natural world."[16] *Netukulimk* has also been defined as "collective beliefs and behaviours in resource protection, procurement, and management to ensure and honour sustainability and prosperity for the ancestor, present and future generations."[17]

10 Mi'kmaw word for the animal commonly known as the marten.

11 UINRTV, "American Marten Apistane'wj & The First Pine Trees" (28 May 2015) ["American Marten"], online: YouTube <www.youtube.com/watch?v=RCoJzP7iAMI>.

12 Jennifer Reid in *Finding Kluskap: A Journey into Mi'kmaw Myth* (University Park, PA: Penn State University Press, 2013) describes Kluskap as being responsible for the creation of landscape features throughout Quebec, New Brunswick, Nova Scotia and Cape Breton Island. His kettle was an island; his canoe was a large rock; and his dogs, at his departure, were turned into stone. He created turtles, tadpoles, crabs and leeches, took the noses from porcupines and toads, gave beavers their tails, gave frogs and loons their distinctive voices, and reduced all of the animals to the size they are now. He left his footprints in stone, cleared rivers for navigation, carved channels with his paddle, gave names to the principal places along the shorelines of the Maritime provinces and, finally, named all the stars and constellations. The natural environment was a theatre in which Kluskap helped to create a world, and in that world, he gave the Mi'kmaq primordial rights to harvesting various types of plants and animals. He was, primarily, a teacher. As Reid put it, "All that the Indians knew of what was wise and good he taught them." Kluskap taught them the names of the stars and how to build canoes, but most often in the stories, he taught the Mi'kmaq how to hunt, fish and cure what they harvested, and how to find medicines to heal sickness.

13 Kowch, "Muin and the Seven Bird Hunters" (21 April 2009), online: YouTube <www.youtube.com/watch?v=3IYpP_pTF08>.

14 Ruth Holmes Whitehead, *Stories from the Six Worlds* (Halifax: Nimbus Limited, 1988) at 5. Whitehead also writes of the Mi'kmaq as "the People." In Mi'kmaq, we call ourselves "L'nu," which translates into "the people."

15 *Ibid* at 8.

16 "Netukulimk", *supra* note 9.

17 Kerry Prosper, L Jane McMillan, Anthony A Davis & Morgan Moffitt, "Returning to Netukulimk: Mi'kmaq cultural and spiritual connections with resource stewardship and self-governance" (2011) 2:4 Intl Indigenous Policy J.

Understanding that there is this familial relationship to Mother Earth and that Mi'kmaq have a responsibility to honour and take care of her for both current and future generations helps to enlighten others as to why it is so important to "defend" her and her rivers, her streams and her forests. It may help people to understand the motivation of Mi'kmaw individuals such as Amanda Polchies, who was photographed by Inuk photographer Ossie Michelin as she knelt before a line of police officers, her raised arm holding an eagle feather in defence of the water against exploratory shale gas drilling.[18] As a Mi'kmaw person, she had been taught to protect the forests and Mother Earth not only because the earth and forests can take care of us, but to protect them for future generations.[19]

Be Responsible

The Royal Commission on Aboriginal Peoples wrote:

> No segment of our research aroused more outrage and shame than the story of the residential schools...the incredible damage — loss of life, denigration of culture, destruction of self-respect and self-esteem, rupture of families, impact of these traumas on succeeding generations, and the enormity of the cultural triumphalism that lay behind the enterprise — will deeply disturb anyone who allows the story to seep into their consciousness and recognizes that these policies and deeds were perpetrated by Canadians no better or worse intentioned, no better or worse educated than we are today....It is also evident of the capacity of democratic populations to tolerate moral enormities in their midst.[20]

For reconciliation to be successful, Canada and the provinces need to take responsibility for past harms, as well as historic and current injustices inflicted through assimilationist policies and laws imposed upon the Mi'kmaw peoples. The intergenerational trauma that the Shubenacadie residential school system inflicted upon the Mi'kmaw children and the nation was devastating to the mental, emotional and spiritual health of Mi'kmaw people, and caused huge losses to the Mi'kmaw language and culture by disrupting the Mi'kmaw core family unit. Both levels of government should work with Mi'kmaw leaders to develop a Mi'kmaw Nation restitution process aimed at redressing historical and current injustices and support the healing programs of the Mi'kmaw nation and the renewal of the Mi'kmaw language and culture.

Be Honourable

Amnesty International Executive Director Craig Benjamin, who presented before the House of Commons Standing Committee on Indigenous and Northern Affairs on March 27, 2018, stated that "requiring Indigenous peoples to go to court if they want their rights respected imposes an onerous and unfair burden, and such processes are inherently adversarial, something that runs contrary to the intention of reconciliation."[21]

---

18 Ossie Michelin, photo of Amanda Polchies, APTN (17 October 2013), online: <http://osmich.ca/about/>.

19 "American Marten", *supra* note 11.

20 Royal Commission on Aboriginal Peoples, *Report of the Royal Commission on Aboriginal Peoples* (Ottawa: Supply and Services, 1996) at 601–02, online: <www.bac-lac.gc.ca/eng/discover/aboriginal-heritage/royal-commission-aboriginal-peoples/Pages/final-report.aspx>.

21 House of Commons, Standing Committee on Indigenous and Northern Affairs, *Minutes of Proceedings and Evidence*, 42nd Parl, 1st Sess, No 100 (27 March 2018) at 16:45.

For reconciliation to be successful, Canada and the provinces need to honour their legal obligations by implementing all Mi'kmaw treaties[22] and outstanding Supreme Court of Canada decisions.[23] To do so, the federal government and each respective provincial government operating within Mi'kma'ki should enact a MATRIA, legislating full implementation and protection of Mi'kmaw Aboriginal and treaty rights. This would eliminate the need for individuals within the Mi'kmaw Nation to continuously go to the courts to defend their Aboriginal and treaty rights, as well as their inherent rights to self-determination and their rights to lands, waters and resources as Indigenous peoples.

Be Wise

Engagement sessions with Indigenous nations have started within Canada to address what a Recognition and Implementation of Rights Framework[24] should look like. Instead of reinventing the wheel, Canada should refer to reports and recommendations made by the Royal Commission on Aboriginal Peoples in 1996. Canada, the provinces and the Mi'kmaw Nation need to re-examine the 440 recommendations and implement them, especially those related to nation building, land and resource sharing, public education, and implementation of treaty and Aboriginal rights. Mi'kmaw and other Indigenous law will play a critical role in the development of the Recognition and Implementation of Rights Framework.

Be Respectful

Indigenous legal scholar Val Napoleon, in her response to the House of Commons Standing Committee on Indigenous and Northern Affairs about implementing Bill C-262, states, "I believe it is a modest and positive step toward reconciliation. With its call for alignment and for an application of UNDRIP [the UN Declaration] to federal laws, it lays a solid foundation for the future of reconciliation."[25]

Not only should Canada harmonize Canadian law with the UN Declaration, but the provinces should do the same as well. To begin with, federal and provincial laws should be consistent with all articles from the UN Declaration, but priorities should be made to:

- honour the Mi'kmaw obligation for Netukulimk (sustainable development) (article 25);[26]

22 Treaties of 1725, 1726, 1749, 1752, 1760-61, 1779.

23 *Simon v The Queen*, [1985] 2 SCR 387; *R v Marshall*, [1999] 3 SCR 456.

24 Justin Trudeau, Prime Minister of Canada, "Government of Canada to create Recognition and Implementation of Rights Framework" (14 February 2018), online <https://pm.gc.ca/eng/news/2018/02/14/government-canada-create-recognition-and-implementation-rights-framework>.

25 House of Commons, Standing Committee on Indigenous and Northern Affairs, *Minutes of Proceedings and Evidence*, 42nd Parl, 1st Sess, No 100 (17 April 2018) at 16:45 [Standing Committee] (referencing Bill C-262, *An Act to ensure that the laws of Canada are in harmony with the United Nations Declaration on the Rights of Indigenous Peoples*, 1st Sess, 42nd Parl, 2016 [as passed by the House of Commons 30 May 2018], online: <www.parl.ca/DocumentViewer/en/42-1/bill/C-262/third-reading>).

26 *UN Declaration, supra* note 4, art 25, states: "Indigenous peoples have the right to maintain and strengthen their distinctive spiritual relationship with their traditionally owned or otherwise occupied and used lands, territories, waters and coastal seas and other resources and to uphold their responsibilities to future generations in this regard."

- recognize Mi'kmaw Aboriginal title to Mi'kma'ki (article 26);[27]
- compensate the Mi'kmaq for past injustices (article 28);[28]
- establish a process that seeks the free, prior and informed consent of the Mi'kmaw Nation for any current or future resource-based activities within their territory before any development occurs (article 32);[29] and
- enforce Mi'kmaw treaties (article 37).[30]

If Canada harmonized its laws with the UN Declaration, it would respect Mi'kmaw individuals such as Amanda Polchies and others like her who are fulfilling their duty to protect Mother Earth.

I echo the cautionary message of Ken Coates, Canada Research Chair in Regional Innovation at the University of Saskatchwen, in his statement to the House of Commons Standing Committee on Indigenous and Northern Affairs:

> When I think of what will actually make a difference for indigenous people, I see the re-empowerment of indigenous communities and nations with appropriate and equitable funding as being by far and away the most important thing we can have arise at the end of this, not necessarily more government programs....My concern, and I ask you to take it very seriously, is whether Canada will once again over-promise and underperform regarding indigenous rights and entitlements. We have done so over and over again, and we have not broken that cycle....Without the second part [the implementation of policy], without focusing on implementation, if this bill comes into effect, if we are going to harmonize these laws, how are we going to do it, what is the time period, and what are the funding allocations? Will real change actually occur at the other end of this? Without that second level of conversation and discussion, UNDRIP will lose its effectiveness and become yet another sort of failed promise to indigenous peoples.[31]

27 *Ibid*, art 26: "1. Indigenous peoples have the right to the lands, territories and resources which they have traditionally owned, occupied or otherwise used or acquired. 2. Indigenous peoples have the right to own, use, develop and control the lands, territories and resources that they possess by reason of traditional ownership or other traditional occupation or use, as well as those which they have otherwise acquired. 3. States shall give legal recognition and protection to these lands, territories and resources. Such recognition shall be conducted with due respect to the customs, traditions and land tenure systems of the indigenous peoples concerned."

28 *Ibid*, art 28: "1. Indigenous peoples have the right to redress, by means that can include restitution or, when this is not possible, just, fair and equitable compensation, for the lands, territories and resources which they have traditionally owned or otherwise occupied or used, and which have been confiscated, taken, occupied, used or damaged without their free, prior and informed consent. 2. Unless otherwise freely agreed upon by the peoples concerned, compensation shall take the form of lands, territories and resources equal in quality, size and legal status or of monetary compensation or other appropriate redress."

29 *Ibid*, art 32: "1. Indigenous peoples have the right to determine and develop priorities and strategies for the development or use of their lands or territories and other resources. 2. States shall consult and cooperate in good faith with the indigenous peoples concerned through their own representative institutions in order to obtain their free and informed consent prior to the approval of any project affecting their lands or territories and other resources, particularly in connection with the development, utilization or exploitation of mineral, water or other resources. 3. States shall provide effective mechanisms for just and fair redress for any such activities, and appropriate measures shall be taken to mitigate adverse environmental, economic, social, cultural or spiritual impact."

30 *Ibid*, art 37: "1. Indigenous peoples have the right to the recognition, observance and enforcement of treaties, agreements and other constructive arrangements concluded with States or their successors and to have States honour and respect such treaties, agreements and other constructive arrangements."

31 Standing Committee, *supra* note 25 at 16:60–17:00.

The recommendations shared in this chapter will focus on implementation. We do not need more broken promises — we need action.

Conclusion

Before governments can hope to start a reconciliation process and to renew the nation-to-nation relationship with the Mi'kmaq, they must first acknowledge the wrongs and injustices they committed against the Mi'kmaw Nation in relation to the dispossession of their lands, waters and resources, and the assault on their languages, culture and governance system. This acknowledgement must include a commitment from the federal and provincial governments to compensate the Mi'kmaw Nation for those injustices and wrongs. Restitution is a vital step toward reconciliation, as well as a vital element of international human rights law.

Reconciliation must then include actions from both the federal and provincial governments to give full meaning and effect to section 35(1) of the Constitution Act and to the implementation of the Mi'kmaw Aboriginal and treaty rights already confirmed by the Supreme Court of Canada. These actions would include Canada, Newfoundland, New Brunswick, Nova Scotia, Prince Edward Island and Quebec enacting Mi'kmaw Aboriginal and treaty rights implementation legislation. It would also include the harmonization of both federal and provincial laws with the UN Declaration. Canada and the provinces need to start respecting the Mi'kmaw Nation's fundamental sacred law to protect and respect Mother Earth. Therefore, the Mi'kmaw Nation must be included in all federal and provincial decisions that impact the lands, waters and resources within their traditional territory. Finally, the Mi'kmaw Nation needs to rebuild the nation. An important step toward this goal is hosting a Mi'kmaw Nation Summit.

The recommendations listed below will be helpful in renewing a nation-to-nation relationship. The first three recommendations are aimed at the Mi'kmaw Nation and involve internal work that would help us prepare for rebuilding the nation. The remaining recommendations are aimed at both the federal and provincial governments, and if implemented, will set the groundwork for reconciliation and the renewal of the nation-to-nation relationship between Canada and the Mi'kmaw Nation.

Recommendations for the Mi'kmaw Nation include:

- building the Mi'kmaw Nation by organizing a Mi'kmaw Nation Summit where the highest level of Mi'kmaw government decision makers (Mi'kmaw chiefs and Council, Mi'kmaw Grand Council members, Mi'kmaw band managers, Mi'kmaw executive directors and other senior band staff) meet to discuss and strategize on nation rebuilding; governance; treaty and Aboriginal rights protection and implementation; sustainable development and implementation of the UN Declaration;
- honouring and celebrating the Mi'kmaw legal tradition by hosting an event where Mi'kmaw Elders, storytellers, wampum-belt knowledge keepers, lawyers and language experts gather and reflect upon its application in modern times; and
- participating in international Indigenous fora such as the United Nations Permanent Forum on Indigenous Issues, the Expert Mechanism on the Rights of Indigenous Peoples and the

World Intellectual Property Organization, and celebrating the UN International Day of the World's Indigenous Peoples on August 9.

Recommendations for federal and provincial governments include:

- understanding that an integral part of the Mi'kmaw worldview is to respect Mother Earth and to ensure sustainability for future generations (article 25) and therefore include Mi'kmaw Nation representatives in all decision making related to lands and resources within their territory. Governments must cease to criminalize Mi'kmaw individuals who protect Mother Earth;
- establishing a Mi'kmaw Nation restitution process aimed at redressing historical and current injustices related to the dispossession of lands and resources, as well as assimilationist policies;
- honouring their international and national obligations by implementing all Mi'kmaw treaties. To do so, the federal and provincial governments operating within Mi'kma'ki should enact Mi'kmaw and Aboriginal treaty rights implementation legislation to fully implement and protect Mi'kmaw Aboriginal and treaty rights;
- supporting and implementing the Royal Commission on Aboriginal Peoples' recommendations related to nation building, land and resource sharing, public education, and implementation of treaty and Aboriginal rights; and
- ensuring all federal and provincial laws and policies are consistent with the UN Declaration by:
  - recognizing Mi'kmaw Aboriginal title to Mi'kma'ki (article 26);
  - compensating the Mi'kmaq for past injustices (article 28);
  - establishing a process that seeks the free, prior and informed consent of the Mi'kmaw Nation for any current or future resource-based activities within their territory before any development occurs (article 32); and
  - honouring and implementing Mi'kmaw treaties (article 37).

12

Canary in a Coal Mine: Indigenous Women and Extractive Industries in Canada

Sarah Morales

In Canada, and elsewhere in the world, the expansion of extractive industries into the traditional territories of Indigenous peoples is a continuing source of conflict and policy challenge for governments and industry and for Indigenous peoples themselves. While some individuals have highlighted the inroads made by industry with respect to changing corporate practices,[1] others point out that there is still a long way to go before Indigenous perspectives are appropriately integrated into decision making.[2] This view is largely influenced by the fact that although "Indigenous peoples are increasingly able to negotiate benefit agreements around projects approved by government, it is unlikely their voices will be heard if they believe a project should not proceed or should be substantially altered."[3] Federal and provincial governments have consistently denied that Indigenous consent to resource development is required, despite obligations under international law.

1 See Pamela Sloan & Roger Hill, *Corporate Aboriginal Relations: Best Practice Case Studies* (Toronto: Hill Sloan Associates, 1995); Fergus MacKay, "Indigenous Peoples' Rights to Free, Prior and Informed Consent and the World Bank's Extractive Industries Review" (2004) 4 Sustainable Dev L & Pol'y 43.

2 See Ciaran O'Faircheallaigh, "Indigenous Women and Mining Agreement Negotiations: Australia and Canada" in Kuntala Lahiri-Dutt, ed, *Gendering the Field* (Canberra, AU: ANU Press, 2011); Jacob Damstra, "Heroic or Hypocritical: Corporate Social Responsibility, Aboriginal Consultation, and Canada's Extractive Industries Strategy" (2015) 25 Transnat'l L & Contemp Probs 153.

3 Amnesty International, *Out of Sight, Out of Mind: Gender, Indigenous Rights, and Energy Development in Northeast British Columbia, Canada* (London, UK: Amnesty International, 2016) at 5 [Amnesty International, *Out of Sight*].

Given that a growing body of research in Canada and worldwide draws linkages between intensive resource development and negative social impacts in host communities,[4] Indigenous leaders and communities are adamant that recognition of their right to self-determination requires adequate consultation and, in some instances, consent.[5] Implicit in this recognition must also be an understanding that Indigenous women should play a major role in these consultative processes.

In Canada and around the world, research has revealed that the introduction of large-scale development adversely affects women in Indigenous communities to a greater extent than men.[6] In a KAIROS symposium held in the fall of 2014, entitled "Gendered Impacts: Indigenous Women and Resource Extraction," participants identified the following five impacts of increased extractive development on Indigenous women: first, Indigenous women experience the social, health and environmental impacts before others and most acutely; second, a correlation exists between resource extraction and violence against women; third, women derive little benefit from the positive impacts of mining, such as employment and increased income; fourth, Indigenous women are at the forefront of their communities' struggles for collective rights; and, fifth, Indigenous women are often excluded from the official consultation process and impact assessment.[7]

Arguably, the major factor that has contributed to the adverse impacts experienced by Indigenous women is that they have largely been excluded from negotiations concerning benefits from extractive industry development. International organizations such as the World Bank and Oxfam now recognize the potential disadvantage experienced by women with regard to extractive industries. These bodies now insist on the inclusion of gender aspects in impact assessments, and they promote gender equality as "smart economics."[8] Canada is adopting a Feminist International Assistance Policy that seeks to empower women and promote gender equality.[9] However, currently, this policy does not speak to extractive industry support at all.[10] In this period of increased extractive development, Canada must take a gendered approach to consultative processes if it is to uphold the rights of Indigenous women and girls and advance toward reconciliation.

This chapter will examine the gendered impacts of increased extractive development on Canada's Indigenous women and girls. It will then consider Canada's human rights obligations

4 See e.g. Amnesty International, *Out of Sight*, *supra* note 3; O'Faircheallaigh, *supra* note 2; Damstra, *supra* note 2; Victoria Sweet, "Extracting More than Resources: Human Security and Arctic Indigenous Women" (2014) 37 Seattle U L Rev 1157.

5 See Sarah Morales, "Braiding the Incommensurable: Indigenous Legal Traditions and the Duty to Consult" (this volume, ch 7).

6 See Sharmistha Bose, "Positioning Women within the Environmental Justice Framework: A Case for the Mining Sector" (2004) 8:3 Gender, Tech & Dev 407; Amnesty International, *supra* note 3; Joni Parmenter, "Experiences of Indigenous Women in the Australian Mining Industry" in Kuntala Lahiri-Dutt, ed, *Towards Sustainable Livelihoods for Mining Communities* (Canberra, AU: ANU Press, 2011).

7 KAIROS, *Gendered Impacts: Indigenous Women and Resource Extraction, Executive Summary* (Toronto: KAIROS, 2014) at 6–7, online: <www.kairoscanada.org/wp-content/uploads/2015/05/KAIROS_ExecutiveSummary_GenderedImpacts.pdf>.

8 World Bank, *Gender Equity as Smart Economics: A World Bank Group Gender Action Plan* (Washington, DC: World Bank, 2006), online: <http://siteresources.worldbank.org/INTGENDER/Resources/GAPNov2.pdf>.

9 Global Affairs Canada, "Canada's Feminist International Assistance Policy", online: <www.international.gc.ca/gac-amc/campaign-campagne/iap-pai/index.aspx?lang=eng>.

10 Craig Benjamin, "We can't afford to ignore indigenous women and girls with resource development plans", *The Globe and Mail* (4 November 2016).

to Indigenous women and girls and make recommendations on how both international law and Indigenous legal traditions can work to better protect the human rights of Indigenous women and girls in Canada. In particular, this chapter will examine how greater participation by Indigenous women in decision-making processes can work to reduce some of the potentially harmful impacts of extractive industry development. The impact of extractive industries on Indigenous women demands consideration because it raises issues of colonization, racism and sexism, and the dangerous interaction between these violations of human rights.

The Gendered Impacts of Extractive Industries

Public discourses (Indigenous and non-Indigenous) around resource development often focus on economic growth and employment; however, these considerations are often emphasized at the expense of appreciating the deep and lasting social and cultural effects on communities. Women and other marginalized populations, including Indigenous peoples, people with disabilities, seniors and immigrants, experience these and other negative effects disproportionately.[11] The issues are compounded when one considers those individuals at the intersection of these communities, such as Indigenous women; therefore, it is imperative that persons most deeply affected by these industries have a voice in the consultations leading up to the approval of such development agreements.

Personal Safety Impacts

In Canada, the workforce in the extractive industries is overwhelmingly young and male, and the majority of these workers come from outside the region, often on a temporary basis.[12] This has led to a number of social issues for the Indigenous women in the northern and remote communities where these developments take place.

In his report on the effects of the extractive industries on Indigenous peoples, former UN special rapporteur James Anaya noted that Indigenous women have reported that introduction of outside workers has led to increased sexual harassment and violence in these communities, including rape and assault.[13] Some Indigenous women reporting the violence are community members, and some are women working within the mining projects.[14]

Health Impacts

Resource development industries also pose direct and indirect health risks to Indigenous women. Direct health impacts can include injury, lung disease, increased rates of sexually transmitted infections and delayed intellectual development of children.[15] Anaya reported that Indigenous women living in communities near oil, gas and mining operations are vulnerable to sexually

11 Amnesty International, *Out of Sight*, *supra* note 3 at 2.

12 *Ibid* at 37.

13 James Anaya, *Statement by the United Nations Special Rapporteur on the Rights of Indigenous Peoples James Anaya to the International Expert Group Meeting on the Theme: Sexual Health and Reproductive Rights* (15 January 2014) [Anaya, *Statement*], online: <http://unsr.jamesanaya.org/statements/statement-to-the-international-expert-group-meeting-on-the-theme-sexual-health-and-reproductive-rights>.

14 *Ibid.*

15 Deborah Stienstra et al, *Gendered and Intersectional Implications of Energy and Resource Extraction in Resource-Based Communities in Canada's North* (Feminist Northern Network, 2016) at 10, online: <http://fnn.criaw-icref.ca/images/userfiles/files/SSHRC%20KS%20Report.pdf>.

transmitted diseases, including HIV/AIDS, which are often introduced by the outside workers brought into the territory.[16] Mental health risks, such as stress, addiction and depression, are also of concern. Research has documented that the arrival of resource development projects can also affect communities' substance abuse rates.[17]

Environmental Impacts

While extractive industries can foster growth and economic prosperity, they can also cause irreparable damage to the environment. When these operations result in the loss of lands and natural resources upon which Indigenous communities have traditionally relied, the effects can be devastating. Once projects are complete, they leave behind polluted and pillaged land that is no longer suitable for a subsistence lifestyle.[18] These projects can impact everything from water tables to soil fertility.[19] Further, the infrastructure associated with resource development projects, such as pipelines, dams, roads and airports, can also disrupt wildlife migration patterns, pollute land and drinking water, introduce mercury into waterways and create large reservoirs that change local microclimates.[20] These negative effects are often compounded by the fact that disruptions to, and subsequent decreases in, harvesting activities (such as berry picking and trapping) have been linked to a range of physical and mental health impacts.[21]

Women often experience the environmental impacts caused by extractive industries first and most acutely because of the roles and responsibilities they have in the domestic home.[22] Further, many Indigenous women are culturally connected to the land, and destroying the land destroys both their cultural and personal well-being. Indigenous women have said that they experience ecological and environmental destruction as violence: "So we're talking about territory body/land because it is not just about defending women's rights but also defending the land. This is because like it was said, it's not that men don't live the impacts of mining, but women live it in a different way, we think it's much more violent."[23]

Cultural Impacts

Anaya's 2011 report found that "several Indigenous and non-governmental organizations reported that the forced emigration of Indigenous peoples from their traditional lands — either because of the taking of those lands or environmental degradation caused by resource extraction projects — has had an overall negative impact on Indigenous cultures and social structures."[24] These forced migrations have been described as turning "ecosystem people" into "ecological refugees."[25] The migrations have been reported to have an especially negative effect on Indigenous

16 Anaya, *Statement*, *supra* note 13; Ginger Gibson & Jason Klinck, "Canada's Resilient North: The Impact of Mining on Aboriginal Communities" (2005) 3:1 Pimatisiwin: J Aboriginal & Indigenous Community Health 115, online: <http://caid.ca/JAICH2005v3n1p115.pdf>.

17 Stienstra et al, *supra* note 15 at 10.

18 Jill K Carino, "Women and Mining in the Cordillera and the International Women and Mining Network" in Ingrid Macdonald & Claire Rowland, eds, *Tunnel Vision: Women, Mining and Communities* (Victoria, AU: Oxfam, 2002) at 18.

19 *Ibid.*

20 Stienstra et al, *supra* note 15 at 11.

21 *Ibid.*

22 KAIROS, *supra* note 7 at 6.

23 *Ibid.*

24 James Anaya, *Extractive Industries Operating Within or Near Indigenous Territories*, UNHRC, 18th Sess, UN Doc A/HRC/18/35 (2011) at 10 [Anaya, *Extractive Industries*].

25 *Ibid.*

women, who often experience loss of social, economic and decision-making power when moved from their traditional territorial occupations.[26] The Royal Commission on Aboriginal Peoples looked at two examples of communities relocated to make way for hydroelectric developments: the Cheslatta Carrier Nation in northwestern British Columbia lost its communities when the Kemano dam was built on the Nechako River in the 1950s, and the communities of the Chemawawin Cree were relocated because of construction of the Grand Rapids hydro dam in Manitoba a few years later.[27]

Resource projects can also disrupt Indigenous traditions and cultural practices by blocking access to traditional land, affecting traplines, hunting grounds, family gathering sites and sacred sites. This has implications not only for the continuity of culture and traditions, but also for food security, well-being and many Indigenous peoples' identities.[28] Language maintenance is also affected.[29] Often, these projects lead to the destruction of places of cultural and spiritual significance for Indigenous peoples, including sacred sites.

Economic Impacts

Differing opinions exist with regard to the benefits of extractive industries, both within and outside of Indigenous communities. As previously stated, there is a tendency to stress the economic benefits to Indigenous peoples resulting from natural resource extraction projects, while often omitting the fact that some of the benefits are limited in scope and do not make up for the problems associated with these projects. This is especially true when one considers the effects of extractive industries on Indigenous women, who often face an increased risk of impoverishment when major extractive projects opening within their communities leave Indigenous women with little to no voice in how the projects proceed.[30]

Access to employment in extractive industries varies considerably between Indigenous and non-Indigenous people and between Indigenous men and Indigenous women. Often, Indigenous women endure the extra burden of experiencing racism as well as sexism within the work environment. For example, at a mine in Australia, Indigenous women perceived themselves as occupying the bottom position of the mine site hierarchy, where non-Indigenous men were at the top, followed by non-Indigenous women, Indigenous men and then Indigenous women.[31] This intersection of race and sex often results in Indigenous women occupying low service positions within the extractive industry, if they are able to secure a job at all. As stated by one Indigenous woman, "Mining has always been a men's thing. We are the cleaners, we never get anywhere else. Men can always get in before a woman because it's mining."[32] In addition to the challenges of accessibility, some Indigenous women choose not to participate in extractive industries because doing so would be counter to the customary laws regarding their relationship and responsibility to the natural world.

26 *Ibid.*

27 Royal Commission on Aboriginal Peoples, *Report of the Royal Commission on Aboriginal Peoples, Volume 1: Looking Forward and Looking Back* (Ottawa: Supply and Services, 1996), online: <http://caid.ca/DRepRoyCommAborigPple.html>.

28 Stienstra et al, *supra* note 15 at 11.

29 *Ibid.*

30 Margo Tatgenhorst Drakos, "The Corporate Human Rights Impact Assessment: Top-Down and Bottom Up" (2009) 18 Intl Affairs Rev 1.

31 Parmenter, *supra* note 6 at 76.

32 *Ibid.*

Indigenous women who are not able to or choose not to get service industry or mining jobs suffer when traditional livelihood opportunities are disrupted or lost as a result of the project. This most often occurs when the development projects damage the environment that was relied upon for traditional livelihoods, such as gathering and hunting activities.[33] When this occurs, Indigenous women have limited ability to provide for themselves and their families. Additionally, these economic challenges may be exacerbated after the development project has ended because often the local economy collapses, leaving workers dependent on a project that no longer exists and with fewer opportunities than originally existed in the area prior to the beginning of the project.[34]

Extractive industry projects impact all members of a community, but the unique issues that impact women are rarely acknowledged or addressed. As stated by representatives of one Indigenous non-governmental organization, "Only when mining companies acknowledge this and fundamentally change the way they engage with women and support their participating in decision-making processes, can they truly contribute to sustainable and equitable development."[35] The next section of this chapter will examine how we can rely on international human rights law and Indigenous legal traditions to ensure that Indigenous women's rights are recognized and acknowledged in extractive industry decision-making processes.

Moving Forward with International Human Rights Law and Indigenous Laws

In considering how international human rights law and Indigenous legal traditions can help to protect Indigenous women in a period of increased extractive industry, it is useful to consider Anaya's recommendation to utilize an approach that "comprehensively takes account of the rights that may be affected by extractive operations."[36] In his report, Anaya points out that when examining the issue of extractive industries affecting Indigenous peoples, the majority of the focus centres on the principles of consultation and free, prior and informed consent.[37] Anaya takes issue with this approach because it "is blurring understanding about the relevant human rights framework by which to discern the conditions under which extractive industries may legitimately operate within or near indigenous territories."[38] Rather, a better approach recognizes that consultation and consent are not stand-alone rights, but rather that "the principles of consultation and consent together constitute a special standard that safeguards and functions as a means for the exercise of indigenous peoples' substantive rights."[39] These substantive rights include rights to property, culture, religion and non-discrimination in relation to lands and natural resources, rights to health and physical well-being, and rights to

33 Carino, *supra* note 18 at 17.

34 Drakos, *supra* note 30 at 4.

35 *Ibid.* This depletion of opportunities can occur when the natural environment has been so altered as a result of the development activity that women can no longer return to their traditional modes of livelihood, for example, gathering and hunting.

36 James Anaya, *Report of the Special Rapporteur on the Rights of Indigenous Peoples*, UNHRC, 21st Sess, UN Doc A/HRC/21/47 (2012) at 12.

37 *Ibid.*

38 *Ibid.*

39 *Ibid* at 13.

set and pursue Indigenous peoples' own priorities for development, as part of their right to self-determination.[40]

However, as the previous section of this chapter demonstrated, the effects of extractive industries are not gender neutral, and so a comprehensive account of affected rights also requires one to consider the effects felt by Indigenous women alone. In fact, article 22 of the United Nations Declaration on the Rights of Indigenous Peoples (UNDRIP)[41] states that particular attention must be paid to the rights and special needs of Indigenous women and compels states to take positive measures to ensure that Indigenous women enjoy the full protection of UNDRIP.

Accordingly, human rights and Indigenous laws need to be considered and implemented in a manner that respects Indigenous women and their unique perspectives and needs. It is an approach that offers the most safeguards to Indigenous peoples and Indigenous women, if they choose to participate in, or even lead, resource extraction within their traditional territories.

Right to Culture

Article 11 of UNDRIP recognizes that "Indigenous peoples have the right to practise and revitalize their cultural traditions and customs."[42] Article 13 protects the right to transmit these cultural traditions to future generations.[43]

As demonstrated by the previous section, extractive industry development can have hugely detrimental effects on Indigenous cultures, many of which are specific to Indigenous women. For many Indigenous peoples, the connection between land and culture is paramount. As a result, the harmful effects of resource extraction on lands have serious consequences for many Indigenous cultural practices. For example, when traditional territories are contaminated to such a degree that they are no longer useable as a food source, this leads to a "loss of social and cultural capital," more specifically, "to an erosion of traditional ways."[44] Cultural knowledge about how to interact sustainably with the land and how to participate in traditional activities, such as hunting and gathering, may be lost.

---

40 See Rodolfo Stavenhagen, *Report of the Special Rapporteur on the Situation of Human Rights and Fundamental Freedoms of Indigenous People*, UNESC, 59th Sess, UN Doc E/CN.4/2003/90 (2003) at paras 6–30 (discussing the impact of large-scale development projects on Indigenous peoples' rights, including rights over lands and resources); Rodolfo Stavenhagen, *Report of the Special Rapporteur on the Situation of Human Rights and Fundamental Freedoms of Indigenous People*, UNESC, 58th Sess, UN Doc E/CN.4/2002/97 (2002) at paras 39–57 (a review of international and domestic law and practice upholding Indigenous rights over lands, territories and natural resources); James Anaya, *Report of the Special Rapporteur on the Situation of Human Rights and Fundamental Freedoms of Indigenous People*, UNHRC, 9th Sess, UN Doc A/HRC/9/9 (2008) at paras 20–30 (a review of the practice of human rights bodies under international instruments of general applicability); OAS, Inter-American Commission on Human Rights, *Report on the situation of human rights in Ecuador*, OR OEA/Ser.L/V/II.96/Doc. 10, rev. 1 (1997) at c VIII (discussing conditions of environmental pollution resulting from oil development as inconsistent with the rights to life and physical well-being); OAS, Inter-American Commission on Human Rights, *Indigenous and tribal peoples' rights over their ancestral lands and resources, norms and jurisprudence of the Inter-American Human Rights System*, OR OEA/Ser.L/V/II. Doc. 56/09 (2009) at paras 5–22 (reviewing the foundations of Indigenous rights over lands, territories and resources in international instruments, customary international law and the practice of treaty bodies).

41 *United Nations Declaration on the Rights of Indigenous Peoples*, GA Res 295, UNGAOR, 61st Sess, Supp No 49, UN Doc A/RES/61/295, 46 ILM 1013 (2007) [*UNDRIP*].

42 *Ibid*, art 11.

43 *Ibid*, art 13.

44 Raywat Deonandan, Kalowatie Deonandan & Brennan Field, "Mining the Gap: Aboriginal Women and the Mining Industry" at 13, online: <https://ruor.uottawa.ca/bitstream/10393/35187/1/deonandan%20-%20mining%20the%20gap%20SSHRC%20report.pdf>.

Cultural knowledge is gender specific. Accordingly, there is a danger in only considering Indigenous males' opinions about the permissibility of development in traditional territories. In speaking about the impact that privatization and development of land has had in the Coast Salish world, Charles Seymour shared: "Plants are used for spiritual preparation, cleansing and for medicinal purposes. I was raised by my grandmothers, so when I look back, I realize that I received quite a lot of ladies' teachings. Both of my grandmothers each taught me about different plants. So when I look back, I can see what side of my family held each particular knowledge."[45]

Further, many Indigenous customary laws are deeply connected to traditional territories. These laws and legal practices can also be gender specific:

> *Swuqus*, Mt. Prevost, is where one of our very first ancestors was dropped onto this earth....Later on, our people actually used each of the two butte areas on the mountain. One side was for male and one side was for female — during coming of age....There were ceremonies conducted on each side to help that person develop into a fully functioning adult in our society — to help bring them up properly.
>
> That is not an area where we can do that sacred work anymore because we have the general public accessing the mountain and our access to the mountain is actually cut off.
>
> Not having access to these areas, and not being able to continue these practices, is affecting the social health of our community.[46]

Accordingly, in order to protect Indigenous women's right to culture, it is necessary to consider the specific and unique ways in which extractive development can impact their cultural knowledge, practices and customary laws.

Right to Religion

Indigenous peoples' "right to maintain and strengthen their distinctive spiritual relationship with their traditionally owned or otherwise occupied and used lands, territories, waters and coastal seas and other resources and to uphold their responsibilities to future generations in this regard" is also recognized in UNDRIP.[47]

In much of the literature on Indigenous women and mining, Indigenous women point out that the harms caused to the environment by mining are having a direct and negative impact on Indigenous culture and spirituality.[48] As stated by one Indigenous woman, "Anything that I learned about water or hear about water as a child was always associated with the realm of matasawin (spirit). So when you think of the tar sands [development] or you see places where people are polluting water, it is pretty overwhelming. And you really think about what is going to happen to us."[49] This understanding, that land is sacred, and that the resources from the

45 Interview of William Charles Seymour by Sarah Morales (21 January 2010).

46 *Ibid.*

47 *UNDRIP*, *supra* note 41, art 25.

48 Deonandan, Deonandan & Field, *supra* note 44 at 12.

49 *Ibid.*

environment are to be respected because they are a gift from the Creator, is common to many Indigenous communities.[50]

For some Indigenous communities, the acknowledgement of their special and vital relationship to the lands and resources in their territories gives rise to specific legal principles. For example, the Tsleil-Waututh Nation describe their roles in maintaining their relationship to the land in the following way: "The Tsleil-Waututh Nation has a sacred, legal obligation to protect, defend and steward the water, land, air, and resources of our territory. Our stewardship obligation includes the responsibility to maintain and restore conditions that provide the environmental, cultural, spiritual and economic foundation for our nation and community to thrive."[51]

As well, in some instances, extractive development threatens specific spiritual locales, or sacred sites, within Indigenous traditional territories. Indigenous women, while suffering discrimination, marginalization, violence and a host of human rights violations as a result of industrial operations in their traditional territories, are often at the forefront of protecting these sites.[52] As described by Hul'qumi'num Elder Laura Sylvester: "There was a development, a sablefish hatchery, on Salt Spring Island at Walker's Hook. When they built it, the sewer from the sablefish ran right through one of our graves....I fought for that gravesite. I was prepared to go to jail to protect that gravesite. We went to court for two to three weeks in Victoria, fighting for Walker's Hook because that's where the Penelakut used to live."[53]

As a result, Indigenous women often face security issues as a result of their role as defenders of the sacred, the land and human rights.[54] This means that not only are Indigenous women fighting to protect their land, culture and spirituality, but also, often, they are struggling to maintain their right to physical safety and security at the same time.

Right to Health and Physical Well-being

UNDRIP also protects Indigenous peoples' right to health and physical well-being through article 24.

Not only does increased extractive industry destroy Indigenous peoples' traditional territories, it also destroys the resources they rely on to live a healthy life. Martina Joe, a young Coast Salish woman, described the effects in the following way:

> My grandma knows some stuff about different medicines, but the medicines are on private lands in our traditional territory. She can tell me and describe the sites to me but because someone else bought the land, we can't access it and I can't see the actual plants. This happens in different parts of the traditional territory with different medicines or even traditional foods.

50 *Ibid* at 13.

51 Tsleil-Waututh Nation, Treaty, Lands & Resources Department, *Assessment of the Trans Mountain Pipeline and Tanker Expansion Proposal* at 3, online: Sacred Trust Initiative <http://twnsacredtrust.ca/trans-mountain-assessment-report/>.

52 Judy Pasimio, "Mining and Violence against Rural and Indigenous Women in the Philippines" (Quezon City, Philippines: LILAK, Purple Action for Indigenous Women's Rights, 2013), online: <http://lilak.net/wp-content/uploads/2017/02/MiningVAW_online.pdf>.

53 Interview of Laura Sylvester by Sarah Morales (20 June 2010).

54 Inmaculada Barcia, "Women Human Rights Defenders Confronting Extractive Industries: An Overview of Critical Risks and Human Rights Obligations" (AWID and Women Human Rights Defenders International Coalition, 2017), online: <www.awid.org/sites/default/files/atoms/files/whrds-confronting_extractive_industries_report-eng.pdf>.

> I remember my grandparents going to get different plants and driving to different parts of the traditional territory to gather wild Indian celery or *yu'lu*....They used to tell me they were high in fibre and vitamins and natural enzymes that were good for you. Because of zoning and development, I don't have access to these areas anymore.
>
> Development is not considerate of other people's cultures.[55]

This inability to access, and the destruction of, traditional plants and medicines as a result of increased development is a violation of Indigenous women's right to health. It is well known that Indigenous women in Canada suffer from poor health as a result of "lower quality housing, poorer physical environment, lower educational levels, lower socioeconomic status, fewer employment opportunities, and weaker community infrastructure."[56] These socio-economic conditions are further exacerbated when extractive development encroaches on Indigenous territories.

As illustrated in the previous section, Indigenous women's right to physical health and safety is also compromised by increased extractive development in their communities. This is especially disconcerting when one considers that governments and law enforcement in Canada have acknowledged that Indigenous women and girls face more frequent violence, and more severe forms of violence, than other women and girls.[57] In describing the situation of Indigenous women in northern British Columbia (an area of increased extractive development), Helen Knott conveyed to Amnesty International that the risk to Indigenous women and girls in the area is increased by the large numbers of men who come to the region to work in the extractive industries and the way that their economic power emboldens them to express racist and sexist attitudes they might suppress elsewhere.[58] She said men use the racist and sexist stereotypes that Indigenous women and girls are "drunk, easy, and wanted it anyway" to justify harassment and violence.[59] In 2016, she told a reporter from a national newspaper that it is imperative to talk about the violence Indigenous women experience because the chaos created by resource development "really does create a dangerous place for our women and our young women coming up."[60] Therefore, if Canada is committed to implementing UNDRIP, it must consider the manner in which extractive industry development is negatively affecting the health and safety of Indigenous women and girls.

55 Interview of Martina Joe by Sarah Morales (9 April 2010).

56 Society of Obstetricians and Gynecologists of Canada, "SOGC Policy Statement: A Guide for Health Care Professionals Working with Aboriginal Peoples" (April 2001) 2 J SOGC 3.

57 See Amnesty International, *Canada: Stolen Sisters: A Human Rights Response to Discrimination and Violence against Indigenous Women in Canada* (2004), online: <www.amnesty.ca/sites/amnesty/files/amr200032004enstolensisters.pdf>.

58 Amnesty International, *Out of Sight*, *supra* note 3 at 51.

59 *Ibid.*

60 *Ibid* at 51 (interview of Helen Knott, Fort St. John, 16 October 2015).

Right to Participate in Decision Making

UNDRIP recognizes Indigenous peoples' "right to participate in decision-making in matters which would affect their rights, through representatives chosen by themselves in accordance with their own procedures, as well as to maintain and develop their own indigenous decision-making institutions."[61] Indigenous peoples also have the "right to determine and develop priorities and strategies for the development or use of their lands or territories and other resources."[62] Further, states are required to "consult and cooperate in good faith with the indigenous peoples concerned through their own representative institutions in order to obtain their free, prior and informed consent before adopting and implementing legislative or administrative measures that may affect them."[63]

The right of Indigenous peoples to participate in decision making in relation to extractive industries is interrelated with the right to self-determination, the right to autonomy, the right to be consulted and the duty of states to seek the free, prior and informed consent of Indigenous peoples. This right to participate in decision making in relation to extractive development activities is not confined to situations where Indigenous peoples have state-recognized title to the land where, or near to where, the extractive activity is to take place.[64] Rather, it extends to situations where Indigenous peoples own, use, develop and control land, territories and resources under their own Indigenous laws near to where, or on which, extractive activities take place or are proposed to take place.[65]

In its follow-up report on Indigenous peoples and the right to participate in decision making, with a focus on extractive industries, the Expert Mechanism on the Rights of Indigenous Peoples noted that there are several unique considerations in relation to Indigenous women and the right to participate in decision making in the area of extractive industries.[66] Participants at the expert group meeting "Combating violence against indigenous women and girls: article 22 of the United Nations Declaration on the Rights of Indigenous Peoples," identified violence against Indigenous women by state and non-state actors and corporate actors in the public domain as including: "militarization and the activities of multinational corporations and extractive industries that operate with impunity on Indigenous peoples' territories. Those actors and their activities have a detrimental impact on Indigenous women and girls, which manifests itself in sexual assault, sex trafficking, prostitution, bonded labour, the exploitation of overseas contract workers, the internal displacement of women and environmental violence."[67] The Expert Mechanism report also recognized, as discussed previously, that extractive industry development can have unique ecological, economic and spiritual impacts on Indigenous women in their role as traditional caretakers of the environment.[68] Accordingly, the Expert Mechanism

61 *UNDRIP, supra* note 41, art 18.

62 *Ibid*, art 32.

63 *Ibid*, art 19.

64 James Anaya, *Report of the Special Rapporteur on the Situation of Human Rights and Fundamental Freedoms of Indigenous People*, UNHRC, 12th Sess, UN Doc A/HRC/12/34 (2009) at para 44.

65 Anaya, *Extractive Industries, supra* note 24.

66 Expert Mechanism on the Rights of Indigenous Peoples, *Follow-up report on indigenous peoples and the right to participate in decision-making, with a focus on extractive industries*, UNHRC, 5th Sess, UN Doc A.HRC/EMRIP/2012/2 (2012).

67 Permanent Forum on Indigenous Issues, *Combating violence against indigenous women and girls: article 22 of the United Nations Declaration on the Rights of Indigenous Peoples*, UNESC, 11th Sess, UN Doc E/C.19/2012/6 (2012) at para 21. See also Expert Mechanism on the Rights of Indigenous Peoples, *supra* note 66 at 12.

68 Permanent Forum on Indigenous Issues, *supra* note 67 at para 27.

noted that these unique impacts and forms of violence against Indigenous women and girls must be resolved through an "understanding of the structural nature of violence against Indigenous women, through the full participation of Indigenous women in all aspects of decision-making and through consideration of this problem by Indigenous communities as an integral part of self-determination."[69]

This exercise of including women in decision-making processes is in keeping with many Indigenous legal traditions. For example, Willie Seymour, a Hul'qumi'num Elder, spoke of the importance of women participating in traditional consent-building processes:

> [H]e beat on his drum again and that was his notice for the people to come, that there was business to be taken care of.
>
> The people rushed down, "We need to talk about whatever the concern was."
>
> The women...they came in and joined and they were invited to continue the discussion. It was open and sometimes [the issues] involved women.
>
> And they didn't leave until they came to a satisfied resolution.
>
> They asked everyone; they asked every individual, "*nil ow' sthuthi' ni' 'utun shqualuwun.*" "Is it okay with you, okay with you personally? Is our decision effective? Is our decision acceptable?" They go around asking each individual and then they say, "*tun' ni' 'utunu 'il kwet ch*" — from this day on we put this to rest. Then they will appoint a couple of Elders to go deal with the people involved.[70]

As demonstrated by this account, women were always included in these processes and were asked for their input, especially when the issue to be resolved required a female perspective or dealt with an issue of which women had specialized knowledge.

Accordingly, if Canada is committed to implementing UNDRIP in a manner that addresses the rights of Indigenous women in relation to extractive industry development, it must ensure that Indigenous women's right to self-determination is respected by including them in all aspects of the decision-making processes and by actively seeking out their free, prior and informed consent to any development project taking place within or affecting their traditional territories.

Conclusion

Canada is rich in energy resources, but while some Canadians benefit immensely from the extraction of these resources, others are further marginalized and impoverished by development activities. As this chapter has illustrated, Indigenous peoples whose lands and resources provide the basis for the wealth generated by these activities are often excluded from a meaningful role in decision making and suffer significant adverse effects in relation to housing, health, culture, safety, transportation and other social services. Further, Indigenous women and girls experience these negative effects disproportionately. The issue of extractive resource development and

69 *Ibid* at paras 46, 50.

70 Interview of Willie Charles Seymour (23 June 2010) in Sarah Morales, *Snuw'uyulh: Fostering an Understanding of the Hul'qumi'num Legal Tradition* (PhD Dissertation, University of Victoria, 2014) [unpublished] at 306.

human rights involves a relationship between Indigenous peoples, governments and the private sector that must be based on the full recognition of Indigenous peoples' rights to lands, territories and natural resources, which in turn implies the exercise of their right to self-determination. Indigenous peoples' right to sustainable development means the right to determine their own pace of change, consistent with their own vision of development, including their right to say no. This right to self-determination must reflect the concerns and solutions of both Indigenous men and Indigenous women if Canada is to implement UNDRIP in a manner that seeks to achieve reconciliation and works to implement Indigenous legal traditions.[71]

71 Although I am not suggesting that it is solely the government's responsibility to determine the manner in which Indigenous women's voices are heard and considered during these decision-making processes (as every Indigenous legal tradition would have its own processes in place), I do believe that international human rights law places an onus on government to ensure that Indigenous women's views are considered in the decision-making process.

PART III

Domestic Law Perspectives

Previous page:

Guud
Ernest Swanson

2015, 14.5" x 22", serigraph edition (110)

13

Beyond *Van der Peet*: Bringing Together International, Indigenous and Constitutional Law

Brenda L. Gunn

Before Europeans arrived in North America, Indigenous peoples had thriving governments and legal systems. After many years of advocacy by a number of groups, the United Nations finally recognized that "Indigenous peoples are equal to all other peoples," while Indigenous peoples have the right to be respected for their difference as Indigenous peoples.[1] Indigenous peoples "contribute to the diversity and richness of civilizations and cultures, which constitute the common heritage of humankind."[2] Unfortunately, Indigenous peoples have been negatively impacted by colonization,[3] including the imposition of a foreign legal system that was used to undermine Indigenous peoples' own legal traditions.

Indigenous peoples have long fought against the negative impacts of colonization at both the domestic and international level, seeking to protect their fundamental human rights, according to their own legal traditions. Despite protecting Indigenous peoples' rights in the Constitution Act, 1982, section 35(1) failed to address the harms of colonialism, including recognizing the role of Indigenous laws when determining Indigenous peoples' rights.[4] There is much criticism

1 *United Nations Declaration on the Rights of Indigenous Peoples,* GA Res 295, UNGAOR, 61st Sess, Supp No 49, UN Doc A/RES/61/295, 46 ILM 1013 (2007), Preamble [*UNDRIP*].

2 *Ibid.*

3 *Ibid.*

4 *Constitution Act, 1982,* being Schedule B to the *Canada Act 1982* (UK), 1982, c 11.

on the scope of section 35(1). This chapter contributes to that body of literature by arguing that implementing UNDRIP provides an opportunity to move beyond the limited interpretations of section 35(1) to better recognize Indigenous peoples' rights according to their own legal traditions. In this way, the chapter argues that bringing together international human rights law, constitutional law and Indigenous law strengthens the protection of Indigenous peoples' rights. This process of using UNDRIP to make room for Indigenous peoples' laws within the broader Canadian legal landscape is critical for moving away from the colonial relationship toward a nation-to-nation relationship. In particular, it is important that section 35(1) be interpreted in line with UNDRIP, because UNDRIP grounds Indigenous peoples' rights in their own legal traditions.

Failings of Section 35

When the process to patriate the Canadian Constitution began, Indigenous peoples believed that the recognition and affirmation of Aboriginal and treaty rights would reset the relationship between Indigenous peoples and the Crown — moving beyond the colonial imposition of a new legal order back to a nation-to-nation relationship in which there is space for both Indigenous and Canadian laws to operate.[5] This section briefly discusses how the Supreme Court of Canada's (SCC's) interpretation of section 35(1) has failed to provide adequate scope to Indigenous peoples' rights, especially by failing to understand Indigenous peoples' rights according to their own legal traditions.

When the first case to consider the scope of section 35(1) came before the courts, it was an opportunity for the courts to define Aboriginal rights according to Indigenous peoples' own legal traditions and to provide protection against unchecked government power.[6] The SCC recognized that section 35(1) "represents the culmination of a long and difficult struggle in both the political forum and the courts for the constitutional recognition of aboriginal rights....It also affords aboriginal peoples constitutional protection against provincial legislative power."[7] This led Chief Justice Brian Dickson to conclude that section 35(1) requires the federal power under section 91(24) of the Constitution Act, 1867[8] to be reconciled with the federal fiduciary duty,[9] which should have restrained the government's power to limit Indigenous peoples' constitutionally recognized rights. However, for the court, it simply meant that the government would need to justify interferences with Aboriginal rights.[10] With this starting point, section 35(1) has not changed the colonial relationship between Indigenous people and the Crown — Canadian law still overruns Indigenous peoples' rights.

Judicial interpretations of section 35(1) have continued to limit the ability of section 35(1) to make space for Indigenous peoples' rights as understood in their own legal traditions. In *Van der Peet*, Chief Justice Antonio Lamer reiterated the *Sparrow* interpretive principles, including taking a purposive approach, upholding the fiduciary relationship, providing a generous and

5 James (Sa'ke'j) Youngblood Henderson, *First Nations Jurisprudence and Aboriginal Rights* (Saskatoon: Native Law Centre, 2006) at 34.

6 *R v Sparrow*, [1990] 1 SCR 1075 [*Sparrow*].

7 *Ibid.*

8 *Constitution Act, 1867* (UK), 30 & 31 Vict, c 3, reprinted in RSC 1985, Appendix II, No 5.

9 *Sparrow*, *supra* note 6.

10 *Ibid.*

liberal interpretation, and resolving ambiguities in favour of Aboriginal claimants.[11] Yet, Chief Justice Lamer failed to use the principles to guide his analysis. Now, section 35(1) only protects an activity if it is an "element of a practice, custom or tradition integral to the distinctive culture of the aboriginal group claiming the right."[12] Chief Justice Lamer's approach emphasizes the Aboriginal in Aboriginal peoples' rights, based on stereotypical ideas of indigeneity.[13] This approach undermines the recognition of Indigenous peoples as peoples who are equal to other peoples of the world. It further legitimizes the power of Canadian law over Indigenous laws.

In setting out the scope of section 35(1) rights, Chief Justice Lamer highlighted a new purpose of section 35(1): "what s. 35(1) does is provide the constitutional framework through which the fact that aboriginals lived on the land in distinctive societies, with their own practices, traditions and cultures, is acknowledged and reconciled with the sovereignty of the Crown....[T]he aboriginal rights recognized and affirmed by s. 35(1) must be directed towards the reconciliation of the pre-existence of aboriginal societies with the sovereignty of the Crown."[14]

According to Chief Justice Lamer, section 35(1) does not ensure space for Indigenous peoples' laws when defining Aboriginal rights. The purpose is to reconcile the Crown's assertion of sovereignty (and the right to impose a new legal order) with pre-existence of Aboriginal societies.[15] Chief Justice Lamer cites the US case *Johnson v M'Intosh*[16] to support his understanding of the purpose of section 35 rights: "aboriginal title is the right of aboriginal people to land arising from the intersection of their pre-existing occupation of the land with the assertion of sovereignty over that land by various European nations."[17] Chief Justice Lamer omits to mention that Chief Justice Marshall justified his decision on the basis that Indian tribes "were fierce savages whose occupation was war."[18] Reliance on the Marshall trilogy principles without acknowledging the basis of those principles allows Chief Justice Lamer to "adopt language and propose concepts that appear enlightened on their face but that actually are limited to formalizing the process of colonization."[19] As long as Chief Justice Lamer's approach to defining Aboriginal rights prevails, section 35(1) will fail to address the negative impacts of colonization on Indigenous peoples, including the imposition of a new legal system.

In *Van der Peet*, Chief Justice Lamer noted that the test for Aboriginal rights, which required protected activities to be traced back to the point of colonial contact, would not work for Métis people, one of the three constitutionally protected Aboriginal peoples.[20] This recognition that the test could not universally apply to all Aboriginal people, despite one common constitutional provision protecting rights of all Aboriginal people, is yet another indication of the flawed nature of Chief Justice Lamer's approach. When it came time to consider the scope of Métis

11 *R v Van der Peet*, [1996] 2 SCR 507 at paras 22–25 [*Van der Peet*].

12 *Ibid* at para 46.

13 John Borrows, "The Trickster: Integral to a Distinctive Culture" (2005) 8:2 Const Forum 27 at 28–29.

14 *Van der Peet*, *supra* note 11 at para 31.

15 *Ibid* at para 57.

16 *Johnson v M'Intosh*, 21 US (8 Wheat) 543 (1823) [*Johnson*].

17 *Van der Peet*, *supra* note 11 at para 36.

18 *Johnson*, *supra* note 16.

19 D'arcy Vermette, "Dizzying Dialogue: Canadian Courts and the Continuing Justification of the Dispossession of Aboriginal People" (2011) 29:1 Windsor YB Access Just 54 at 56.

20 *Van der Peet*, *supra* note 11 at paras 66–67.

peoples' rights, the court in R v Powley created a legal definition of Metis and modified the *Van der Peet* test to accommodate the post-contact ethnogenesis of the Metis peoples.[21]

R v Powley is yet another example in which the court placed itself in the position of defining Aboriginal people (Metis people specifically this time) and perpetuating the colonial relationship between Indigenous peoples and the state. Metis peoples' rights are also entrenched in backward-looking ideas of indigeneity, with Metis people having to trace their rights and identity back to a period post-contact but pre-Canadian control.[22] This again undermines the recognition of Metis people's right to self-define according to their own legal traditions and prioritizes the Canadian legal system. While there has been limited recognition of Indigenous legal traditions within section 35(1) jurisprudence, the court has failed to fully accept these legal traditions as the foundations for Indigenous peoples' rights protected under section 35(1).

Recently, Canada has expressed its full commitment to UNDRIP: "We intend nothing less than to adopt and implement the Declaration in accordance with the Canadian Constitution.... By adopting and implementing the Declaration, we are breathing life into section 35 and recognizing it as a full box of rights for Indigenous peoples. Canada believes that our constitutional obligations serve to fulfill all the principles of the Declaration, including 'free, prior and informed consent.'"[23]

To fully implement UNDRIP, the test to prove Aboriginal rights and the ability to justify infringements of those rights must be reconsidered. Implementing UNDRIP provides a framework for addressing the disconnect between Canadian law and Indigenous law, moving away from the current colonial relationship toward a nation-to-nation relationship, because UNDRIP recognizes that Indigenous peoples' rights are based in Indigenous peoples' own legal traditions.

UNDRIP

Canada's commitment to implement UNDRIP presents another moment to reconsider the relationship between the Crown and Indigenous peoples, including how Indigenous peoples' rights are defined and protected. At the international level, UNDRIP is necessary in part due to the failure of the general, existing human rights regimes to afford appropriate protection for Indigenous peoples' rights. As will be discussed in this section, domestically, UNDRIP is necessary to move beyond the interpretations of section 35 that perpetuate definitions of Indigenous peoples' rights based on a colonial understanding of those rights because UNDRIP grounds Indigenous peoples' rights in Indigenous legal traditions.

Some may attempt to limit the impact of UNDRIP by emphasizing the non-binding nature of declarations. While a declaration does not create directly enforceable, binding legal obligations on a state in and of itself, "soft law cannot be simply dismissed as non-law."[24] According to

---

21 *R v Powley*, 2003 SCC 43 at para 36, [2003] 2 SCR 207.

22 *Ibid* at para 37.

23 Minister of Indigenous and Northern Affairs Carolyn Bennett, "Announcement of Canada's Support for the United Nations Declaration on the Rights of Indigenous Peoples" (Statement delivered at the 15th Session of the United Nations Permanent Forum on Indigenous Issues, 10 May 2016).

24 Mauro Barelli, "The Role of Soft Law in the International Legal System: The Case of the United Nations Declaration on the Rights of Indigenous Peoples" (2009) 58 ICLQ 957 at 959.

the United Nations, "a 'declaration' is a solemn instrument resorted to only in very rare cases relating to matters of major and lasting importance where maximum compliance is expected."[25] There is a strong expectation and obligation for states to implement the rights set out in UNDRIP, which is, in part, demonstrated by the near consensus on the instrument.[26] Further, states and the United Nations recommitted to implementing UNDRIP at the World Conference on Indigenous Peoples in 2014, including through reaffirming their commitment "to consult and cooperate in good faith with the indigenous peoples concerned through their own representative institutions in order to obtain their free, prior and informed consent before adopting and implementing legislative or administrative measures that may affect them."[27] Much of the debate around the technical status of the international instrument has been a political manoeuvre to undermine its domestic application; hopefully, we can move beyond these debates, now that Canada has expressed its unconditional support, and begin the process of implementing UNDRIP in Canada.

The UNDRIP preamble tells a powerful story of the potential of UNDRIP to address the disconnect between Canadian law and Indigenous peoples' law on defining Indigenous peoples' rights. UNDRIP recognizes the essential humanity of Indigenous peoples: "*Affirming* that indigenous peoples are equal to all other peoples, while recognizing the right of all peoples to be different, to consider themselves different, and to be respected as such."[28] UNDRIP proclaims that Indigenous peoples can no longer be denied fundamental human rights based on imperialist/racist ideas that Indigenous peoples are "fierce savages whose occupation was war"[29] and resultant doctrines such as discovery and *terra nullius*.[30] The United Nations also recognized that Indigenous peoples have a right to be recognized as Indigenous and that special protections may be necessary to ensure their inherent rights are realized.[31] UNDRIP recognizes that colonization occurred and had a negative impact on Indigenous peoples, in particular the dispossession from their lands, territories and resources.[32] It further recognizes that colonization has led to the ongoing denial of basic human rights.

The path forward requires resetting the relationship between Indigenous peoples and Canada through recognizing and protecting Indigenous peoples' rights, according to their own legal traditions. The United Nations is "*convinced* that the recognition of the rights of indigenous peoples in this declaration will enhance harmonious and cooperative relations between the state and indigenous peoples, based on principles of justice, democracy, respect for human rights, non-discrimination and good faith."[33] A fundamental principle of UNDRIP is the need to

25 UN Economic and Social Council, *Commission on Human Rights: Report to the Economic and Social Council on the eighteenth session of the Commission, held at United Nations Headquarters from 19 March to 14 April 1962* inclusive, UNESCOR, 34th Sess, UN Doc E/CN.4/832 (26 April 1962) at para 105.

26 Siegfried Wiessner claims we have now "arrived at a global consensus on UNDRIP." Siegfried Wiessner, "Re-Enchanting the World: Indigenous Peoples' Rights as Essential Parts of a Holistic Human Rights Regime" (2010) 15:1 UCLA J Intl L & Foreign Aff 239 at 253.

27 UN General Assembly, *Outcome document of the high-level plenary meeting of the General Assembly known as the World Conference on Indigenous Peoples*, GA Res 69/2, UNGAOR, 69th Sess, UN Doc A/RES/69/2 (2014) at para 3 [*Outcome document*].

28 *UNDRIP*, *supra* note 1, Preamble [emphasis in original].

29 *Johnson*, *supra* note 16.

30 *UNDRIP*, *supra* note 1, Preamble.

31 *Ibid*, arts 1, 2.

32 *Ibid*, Preamble.

33 *Ibid*, Preamble [emphasis in original].

move from a colonial relationship in which Canada has control over all aspects of Indigenous peoples' lives toward self-determination of Indigenous peoples.[34] This is an important point because many people in Canada believe that recognizing special rights for Indigenous peoples will tear Canada apart. UNDRIP explains that the denial of Indigenous peoples' rights, and the assertion of colonial law and doctrines, is a cause of the current divisions between Indigenous peoples and the rest of Canadians.[35]

Finally, the United Nations "*solemnly proclaims* the following United Nations Declaration on the Rights of Indigenous Peoples as a standard of achievement to be pursued in a spirit of partnership and mutual respect."[36] This is an important reminder that achieving the ends of UNDRIP requires Indigenous peoples and Canada to work together. The Canadian federal and provincial governments cannot unilaterally implement UNDRIP. In fact, unilateral action would perpetuate the problems within the current system. Rather, implementation of UNDRIP requires Indigenous peoples and Canadian governments to work together "in a spirit of partnership and mutual respect."[37]

A critical distinction between rights protected under section 35(1) rights and UNDRIP is that the rights recognized in UNDRIP are defined according to Indigenous peoples' own laws, as a fundamental aspect of self-determination of peoples. This is the major difference from the section 35(1) articulation of Indigenous rights that legitimates defining these rights through Canadian common law, as described above. Many of the rights articulated in UNDRIP refer to Indigenous laws and institutions, including identification of and redress for violations of cultural rights,[38] land rights,[39] membership[40] and the many references to consultation and participation in decision making. Remedies for past violations are to be identified in relation to Indigenous peoples' laws[41] and consultation should be carried out in accordance with Indigenous peoples' own laws.

---

34 *Ibid*, art 3.

35 *Ibid*, Preamble.

36 *Ibid*, Preamble [emphasis in original].

37 *Ibid*.

38 *Ibid*, art 11 states:
11(1) "Indigenous peoples have the right to practise and revitalize their cultural traditions and customs. This includes the right to maintain, protect and develop the past, present and future manifestations of their cultures, such as archaeological and historical sites, artifacts, designs, ceremonies, technologies and visual and performing arts and literature."
11(2) "States shall provide redress through effective mechanisms, which may include restitution, developed in conjunction with indigenous peoples, with respect to their cultural, intellectual, religious and spiritual property taken without their free, prior and informed consent or in violation of their laws, traditions and customs."

39 *Ibid*, art 26(3) states: "States shall give legal recognition and protection to these lands, territories and resources. Such recognition shall be conducted with due respect to the customs, traditions and land tenure systems of the indigenous peoples concerned." *Ibid*, art 27 states: "States shall establish and implement, in conjunction with indigenous peoples concerned, a fair, independent, impartial, open and transparent process, giving due recognition to indigenous peoples' laws, traditions, customs and land tenure systems, to recognize and adjudicate the rights of indigenous peoples pertaining to their lands, territories and resources, including those which were traditionally owned or otherwise occupied or used. Indigenous peoples shall have the right to participate in this process."

40 *Ibid*, art 33(1) states: "Indigenous peoples have the right to determine their own identity or membership in accordance with their customs and traditions. This does not impair the right of indigenous individuals to obtain citizenship of the States in which they live." *Ibid*, art 33(2) states: "Indigenous peoples have the right to determine the structures and to select the membership of their institutions in accordance with their own procedures."

41 *Ibid*, art 40 states: "Indigenous peoples have the right to access to and prompt decision through just and fair procedures for the resolution of conflicts and disputes with States or other parties, as well as to effective remedies for all infringements of their individual and collective rights. Such a decision shall give due consideration to the customs, traditions, rules and legal systems of the indigenous peoples concerned and international human rights."

Indigenous legal institutions are also protected under UNDRIP,[42] including as appropriate venues for the expression or exercise of rights. Article 5 explicitly recognizes that "Indigenous peoples have the right to maintain and strengthen their distinct political, legal, economic, social and cultural institutions, while retaining their right to participate fully, if they so choose, in the political, economic, social and cultural life of the State." The flip side of the recognized role of Indigenous legal institutions is the need for Canadian legal institutions to exercise restraint when dealing with Indigenous peoples' rights. This is one of the greatest failures of the SCC when addressing rights under section 35(1). Rather than using Canadian law to define Indigenous rights, Canadian law should simply refer to Indigenous laws and institutions to articulate and protect the rights as indicated in UNDRIP.

Implementation is key to giving effect to UNDRIP and moving past the current colonial relationship. To implement UNDRIP, Canadian constitutional law must shift in its approach to defining Indigenous peoples' rights toward ensuring that the rights are defined according to Indigenous peoples' legal traditions. Ensuring that the rights protected under section 35(1) align with UNDRIP will mean that Indigenous peoples' rights will continue to be recognized in the highest law of the land.

States have reiterated their support for implementing UNDRIP or to "achieve the ends of the Declaration"[43] in the outcome document of the World Conference on Indigenous Peoples in September 2015. While Canada could be viewed as having broken international consensus when it registered its concerns with the outcome document at the World Conference, Canada has now expressed its unqualified support for UNDRIP. The question remains: how will Canada work toward implementing UNDRIP in Canada?

Moving Forward

Moving forward, beyond a colonial relationship toward a nation-to-nation relationship, requires working together to achieve the ends of UNDRIP. One of the best ways to achieve this in Canada is to reinterpret the scope of section 35(1)'s protection of Aboriginal and treaty rights to align with the standards set out in UNDRIP. This will require moving past the limited interpretation set out by the SCC in *Van der Peet* and ensuring the rights are defined according to Indigenous peoples' own legal traditions, as provided in UNDRIP.

This idea of revisiting an issue already decided is one that the SCC has recently confronted in the areas of assisted suicide and prostitution. When the SCC was faced with the constitutionality of the Criminal Code's prostitution provisions, the SCC held that an issue can be revisited when "new legal issues are raised as a consequence of significant developments in the law, or if there is a change in the circumstances or evidence that fundamentally shifts the parameters of the debate."[44] In *Carter*, the court recognized that it had already upheld a complete prohibition against physician-assisted suicide in *Rodriguez*.[45] After reviewing ongoing debate domestically and internationally, as well as several attempts to introduce legislation, the court concluded that

42 *Ibid*, Preamble.

43 *Outcome document*, *supra* note 27 at para 7.

44 *Canada (Attorney General) v Bedford*, 2013 SCC 72 at para 44, [2013] 3 SCR 1101.

45 *Rodriguez v British Columbia (Attorney General)*, [1993] 3 SCR 519, cited in *Carter v Canada (Attorney General)*, 2015 SCC 5, [2015] 1 SCR 331 [*Carter*].

these ongoing debates meant the issue was a live issue and ripe for reconsideration.[46] Based on these criteria, UNDRIP presents such a fundamental shift in the paradigm for recognizing Indigenous peoples' rights that it warrants moving past the *Van der Peet* approach and finding a new, more appropriate way to articulate the scope of section 35(1).

Moving past the "central and integral to the distinctive culture" test does not require setting aside all existing jurisprudence. Greater reliance on the approaches of Justices Claire L'Heureux-Dubé and Beverley McLachlin (now Chief Justice) in *Van der Peet* would help shift the law toward recognizing Indigenous peoples' rights as rights of peoples grounded in Indigenous peoples' laws. In *Van der Peet*, Justice L'Heureux-Dubé was critical of Chief Justice Lamer's approach because "an approach based on a dichotomy between aboriginal and non-aboriginal practices, traditions and customs literally amounts to defining aboriginal culture and aboriginal rights as that which is left over after features of non-aboriginal cultures have been taken away."[47] Justice L'Heureux-Dubé's approach focused on the significance of the activity to Aboriginal people, and not merely on the activity itself.[48] She focused on preserving Aboriginal peoples and proposed protecting "all practices, traditions and customs which are connected enough to the self-identity and self-preservation of organized aboriginal societies."[49] She would have extended protection to practices, traditions and customs that "maintain a continuing relevance to the aboriginal societies as these societies exist in the contemporary world."[50] Justice McLachlin's approach based the rights on the prior legal regime that gave rise to these rights.[51] Between these two approaches is the recognition of the need to protect the "peoples" in Indigenous peoples, based on their own legal traditions.

The SCC has recognized the ongoing role of Indigenous legal traditions in Canada. In *Mitchell*, Chief Justice McLachlin noted "the doctrine of continuity, which governed the absorption of aboriginal laws and customs into the new legal regime upon the assertion of Crown sovereignty over the region."[52] It is important to note that it is inappropriate for the Canadian common law to take over Indigenous law. Rather, Indigenous peoples have a right to continue their own legal traditions as a basis for their rights, as set out in UNDRIP. According to UNDRIP, Canadian law should simply be acknowledging or ensuring space for those legal traditions.

A starting point for the conversation on how to begin making space for Indigenous legal traditions is to accept that these conversations cannot occur on the global level, but need to happen at the national and local levels. Different Indigenous peoples may have different aspirations for the extent of the operation of their legal traditions within Canada. Different Indigenous peoples will have different understandings of their rights and responsibilities, as Indigenous legal systems vary across Canada. But, throughout central Canada, making space for Indigenous legal traditions includes a need to begin to uphold the original spirit and intent of Treaties 1 to 11. While the possibilities are endless, what follows are a couple of ideas to begin the conversations.

46 *Carter*, *supra* note 45 at paras 6–10.
47 *Van der Peet*, *supra* note 11 at para 154.
48 *Ibid* at para 157.
49 *Ibid* at para 162.
50 *Ibid* at para 173.
51 *Ibid* at para 230.
52 *Mitchell v Minister of National Revenue*, 2001 SCC 33 at para 62, [2001] 1 SCR 911.

International human rights standards, such as UNDRIP, provide guidance on how to begin the process of making space for Indigenous legal traditions. For example, a foundational aspect of UNDRIP is the right of Indigenous peoples to participate in decision making when their rights are impacted, according to their own traditional decision-making processes. If Canada were to begin to embrace this right of participation, then many more decisions (including resource development decisions) would take into consideration Indigenous laws on land and resource use.

According to UNDRIP, Indigenous peoples have the right to determine their own membership. The Canadian governments and courts must stop interfering with such internal membership decisions of Indigenous peoples, with the proviso that these internal decisions uphold fundamental human rights norms. Governments and Indigenous peoples can conclude agreements to recognize Indigenous peoples' right to control the legal systems within their own territories. This could include agreements that move beyond administering Canadian criminal law to agreements recognizing the right of Indigenous peoples to use their own criminal law within their territory.

Canadian judges need to recognize the limitations of their legal education and their ability to interpret Indigenous legal traditions. There should be continuing judicial training opportunities for learning more about Indigenous legal traditions in communities, on the land from Indigenous Elders. Another suggestion is to treat Indigenous law as foreign law in Canadian courts, which removes the need for Canadian judges to interpret Indigenous law.[53] The Federal Court Indigenous Bar Association — Aboriginal Law Bar Liaison Committee developed "Practice Guidelines for Aboriginal Law Proceedings," which include discussions on oral history and the role of Elders in Aboriginal law proceedings, as well as on other practical issues in actions, judicial reviews and dispute resolution options.[54] Lawyers who work with Indigenous peoples (either through section 35(1) claims or in other areas) must have an understanding of Indigenous legal traditions. Governments should also learn about Indigenous legal traditions by going to ceremonies and sitting with Indigenous Elders. To help this process of learning and using Indigenous law, Val Napoleon and Hadley Friedland have developed an approach for applying common law legal analysis and synthesis to Indigenous stories, narratives and oral histories.[55]

The inclusion of Indigenous legal traditions in Canada must allow for these systems to evolve and not be frozen in time. John Borrows maintains that "traditions can be positive forces in our communities if they exist as living, contemporary systems that are revised as we learn more about how we should live with one another."[56] In revitalizing Indigenous legal traditions, we must be careful to not romanticize Indigenous traditional legal systems by overstating traditional ideas of equality, as well as to be cautious when presented with fundamentalists' views of Indigenous

53 Karen Drake, "Decolonizing the Courtroom: A Trial Lawyer's Guide to Treating Indigenous Law as Law" (presented at Indigenous Bar Association, Academics Forum, Vancouver, 16 October 2016) [unpublished draft on file with author].

54 Federal Court Indigenous Bar Association — Aboriginal Law Bar Liaison Committee, "Practice Guidelines for Aboriginal Law Proceedings: April 2016", online: <http://cas-cdc-www02.cas-satj.gc.ca/fct-cf/pdf/Aboriginal%20Law%20Practice%20Guidelines%20April-2016%20(En).pdf>.

55 Val Napoleon & Hadley Friedland, "An Inside Job: Engaging with Indigenous Legal Traditions Through Stories" (2016) 61:4 McGill LJ 725 at 725.

56 John Borrows, *Canada's Indigenous Constitution* (Toronto: University of Toronto Press, 2010) at 8.

laws that purport to identify pure or true traditions.[57] Providing space for Indigenous legal traditions to evolve recognizes that "the teachings may be unchanging, but their application and sometimes even the interpretation changed over time."[58] Finally, where Indigenous legal traditions did not historically meet contemporary international human rights standards, the traditions must continue to evolve.

International human rights norms should continue to guide the development of both Canadian and Indigenous legal traditions. At the general and national level, the protection of Indigenous peoples' rights under section 35(1) should align with the broad range of international human rights, beyond just UNDRIP, for the scope of these rights to be fully appreciated. This includes the International Convention on the Elimination of All Forms of Racial Discrimination;[59] the International Covenant on Civil and Political Rights;[60] the International Covenant on Economic, Social and Cultural Rights;[61] the Convention on the Elimination of All Forms of Discrimination Against Women;[62] the Convention Against Torture and Other Cruel, Inhuman or Degrading Treatment or Punishment;[63] the Convention on the Rights of the Child;[64] and the Convention on the Rights of Persons with Disabilities.[65] At the local and practical implementation level, these general international standards must be implemented in accordance with Indigenous peoples' own legal traditions. Bringing constitutional law and the protections of section 35(1) together with international human rights law and Indigenous laws can reset the current relationship between Indigenous peoples and the Crown, moving it toward a nation-to-nation relationship.

57 Emily Snyder, "Indigenous Feminist Legal Theory" (2014) 26 CJWL 365 at 398.

58 Tracey Lindberg, "Critical Indigenous Legal Theory Part 1: The Dialogue Within" (2015) 27 CJWL 224 at 23.

59 21 December 1965, 660 UNTS 195 (entered into force 4 January 1969, ratified by Canada 14 October 1970).

60 16 December 1966, 999 UNTS 171 (entered into force 23 March 1976, accession by Canada 19 May 1976).

61 16 December 1966, 993 UNTS 3, 6 ILM 360 (entered into force 3 January 1976).

62 18 December 1979, 1249 UNTS 13 (entered into force 3 September 1981).

63 10 December 1984, 1465 UNTS 85 (entered into force 26 June 1987, ratified by Canada 24 June 1987).

64 20 November 1989, 1577 UNTS 3, 28 ILM 1456 (entered into force 2 September 1990).

65 13 December 2006, 2515 UNTS 3 (entered into force 3 May 2008, ratified by Canada 11 March 2010).

14

UNDRIP and the Move to the Nation-to-Nation Relationship

Joshua Nichols

On May 10, 2016, Indigenous and Northern Affairs Canada Minister Carolyn Bennett addressed the Permanent Forum on Indigenous Issues at the United Nations and officially endorsed the United Nations Declaration on the Rights of Indigenous Peoples (UNDRIP),[1] without the qualifications attached by the previous government. She further stated that Canada intends "nothing less than to adopt and implement the declaration in accordance with the Canadian Constitution."[2] This is a distinct shift away from the approach to UNDRIP of the previous government, which held UNDRIP to be aspirational. On September 21, 2017, Prime Minister Justin Trudeau addressed the United Nations General Assembly and reiterated this commitment. He took this opportunity to point to the many legacies of colonialism in Canada. As Trudeau put it, "The good news is that Canadians get it. They see the inequities. They're fed up with the excuses. And that impatience gives us a rare and precious opportunity to act. We now have before us an opportunity to deliver true, meaningful and lasting reconciliation."[3]

1 *United Nations Declaration on the Rights of Indigenous Peoples*, GA Res 295, UNGAOR, 61st Sess, Supp No 49, UN Doc A/RES/61/295, 46 ILM 1013 (2007).

2 Minister of Indigenous and Northern Affairs Carolyn Bennett, "Announcement of Canada's Support for the United Nations Declaration on the Rights of Indigenous Peoples" (Statement delivered at the 15th Session of the United Nations Permanent Forum on Indigenous Issues, 10 May 2016).

3 "Prime Minister Justin Trudeau's Address to the 72nd Session of the United Nations General Assembly" (21 September 2017), online: <https://pm.gc.ca/eng/news/2017/09/21/prime-minister-justin-trudeaus-address-72th-session-united-nations-general-assembly>.

While we could dismiss this statement on its own as a continuation of the status quo of the current judicially mediated process of reconciliation, this is not necessarily the case. In fact, this status quo interpretation is distinctly countered by the prime minister's insistence that the basic norms of UNDRIP are not aspirations, but rather will be used to guide the process of reconciliation. The basic norms of UNDRIP provide, in Trudeau's words, "a way forward."[4] As the prime minister noted in his speech, "There is no blueprint for this kind of change. There is no road map we can follow. But neither can we wait. The time has come to forge new paths together. To move beyond the limitations of old and outdated colonial structures, and to create in their place something new, something that respects the inherent right of Indigenous Peoples to self-govern, and to determine their own future."[5]

What this should clearly signal is that the language of law and policy relating to reconciliation in Canada is entering a period of sudden and dramatic change. The actual meaning of this apparent change in policy hinges on the question of what implementation in accordance with the Canadian Constitution looks like. At this point it seems that there are two possible approaches to implementation. My aim here will be to outline these two possible approaches, examine their underlying assumptions and suggest that the way forward is to stop seeing section 35 of the Constitution Act, 1982 as a set of Charter-like rights and start seeing it as jurisdictional in nature. I will then conclude by pointing to how this nation-to-nation approach to Canadian federalism is a more adequate reflection of the last 250 years of Indigenous-Crown relations.

Status Quo or Reconciliation via the *Sparrow* Framework

In the same 2016 speech, Minister Bennett also stated that section 35 provides a "robust framework" and a "full box of rights."[6] This could be read as a signal that the current *R v Sparrow*[7] framework (with all of its unilateral principles and doctrines) of section 35 and section 91(24) of the Constitution Act, 1867 will be used to restrict the application of the content of UNDRIP. If this is the case, it seems that, from the perspective of the federal government, the box of rights is already full and the change of policy is little more than a slight shift of emphasis. This approach is grounded on the Supreme Court of Canada's existing interpretation of the relationship between section 35(1) and section 91(24). What are the underlying assumptions of the court's current approach? In order to get a clear view of this, we will need to turn our attention to the first case to interpret the meaning of section 35(1), *Sparrow*.

In *Sparrow*, Chief Justice Brian Dickson and Justice Gérard La Forest acknowledge that section 35(1) is not a part of the Canadian Charter of Rights and Freedoms (Charter),[8] and so there is "no explicit language in the provision that authorizes this Court or any court to assess the legitimacy of any government legislation that restricts aboriginal rights."[9] It is easy to read over

4 *Ibid.*

5 *Ibid.*

6 Bennett, *supra* note 2.

7 *R v Sparrow*, [1990] 1 SCR 1075 [*Sparrow*].

8 *Canadian Charter of Rights and Freedoms*, Part I of the *Constitution Act, 1982*, being Schedule B to the *Canada Act 1982* (UK), 1982, c 11.

9 *Sparrow*, *supra* note 7 at 1109.

this as simply an acknowledgement of the basic structure of the Constitution Act, 1982, but had their analysis stopped there, Aboriginal and treaty rights would not be subject to unilateral infringement. In other words, Aboriginal and treaty rights would not have been interpreted as being a set of contingent rights within a sovereign-to-subjects relationship. Rather, Aboriginal and treaty rights would not be subject to unilateral infringement, and, thus, section 35 rights could be reimagined as a set of jurisdictional powers in a nation-to-nation relationship.

However, Chief Justice Dickson and Justice La Forest continued by stating that section 35(1) rights are "not absolute" (they are not jurisdictional in nature) because the federal legislative powers with respect to Indians pursuant to section 91(24) of the Constitution Act, 1867 "must...now be read together with s. 35(1)."[10] Chief Justice Dickson and Justice La Forest go on to state that "federal power must be reconciled with federal duty and the best way to achieve that reconciliation is to demand the justification of any government regulation that infringes upon or denies aboriginal rights."[11] The reasoning here seems to suggest that the court is protecting Aboriginal and treaty rights from government infringement by interpreting section 35(1) as a Charter-like limitation on the power of section 91(24). But that is simply not the case. In reality, the court is changing section 35(1) from being a jurisdictional provision that relates to the division of powers and Canadian federalism to being a set of Charter-like provisional rights. In other words, the court is moving away from the possibility of a nation-to-nation model of federalism and preserving the sovereign-to-subject model of rights whose sordid history extends back to early pre-Confederation colonial legislation such as the 1857 Gradual Civilization Act,[12] through to the Gradual Enfranchisement Act in 1869,[13] the Indian Act[14] in 1876 and Lord Watson's infamous characterization of Aboriginal rights as being a "mere burden" in *St Catharine's Milling*[15] in 1888.

The actual structure of the reasoning in *Sparrow* is thoroughly colonial. Let us reconsider it carefully: the court acknowledges that section 35(1) is outside of the Charter and thus not subject to the limitations of either section 1 or section 33, but this jurisdictional character can be negated by the court's absolute reading of section 91(24). The problem is that this reconciliation of constitutional terms is reliant on the notion that section 91(24) is an unlimited federal power over Indians and their lands. The court does not subject section 91(24) to any form of judicial inquiry. Rather, the court simply states that "there was from the outset never any doubt that sovereignty and legislative power, and indeed the underlying title, to such lands vested in the Crown."[16] And, in support of this absence of doubt, the court cites *Johnson v M'Intosh*,[17] the Royal Proclamation of 1763[18] and *Calder v Attorney-General of British Columbia*.[19] The citation of Chief Justice John Marshall's 1823 decision is particularly telling, as that decision is a *locus*

10 *Ibid.*

11 *Ibid.*

12 *An Act to Encourage the Gradual Civilization of the Indian Tribes in this Province, and to Amend the Laws respecting Indians* (UK), 1857, 20 Vict, c 26.

13 *An Act for the Gradual Enfranchisement of Indians, the Better Management of Indian Affairs, and to Extend the Provisions of the Act*, SC 1869 (31 Vict, c 42) c 6.

14 *An Act to amend and consolidate the laws respecting Indians*, SC 1876, c 18.

15 *St Catharine's Milling and Lumber Co v R*, [1888] UKPC 70, 14 App Cas 46 [*St Catharine's Milling*].

16 *Sparrow*, *supra* note 7 at 1103.

17 *Johnson v M'Intosh*, 21 US (8 Wheat) 543 (1823).

18 *Royal Proclamation, 1763* (3 Geo III), reprinted in RSC 1985, Appendix II, No 1.

19 *Calder v Attorney-General of British Columbia*, [1973] SCR 313.

classicus for the doctrine of discovery.[20] The court's reliance on the doctrine of discovery is made all the more obvious by the failure to cite Chief Justice Marshall's repudiation of it just a few years later in 1832 in *Worcester v Georgia*, where he characterized the doctrine as being an "extravagant and absurd idea."[21]

The court's unquestioning assumption of Crown sovereignty, legislative power and underlying title necessarily entails that the court is holding Indigenous peoples in a sovereign-to-subjects relationship on the basis of nothing more than unilateral proclamation. By interpreting section 91(24) as a "federal power" over Indians and their lands, the court magically transforms Indigenous peoples into subjects to a provision that they played no role whatsoever in legislating. The only possible basis for this reading is a pernicious and racist set of nineteenth-century European legal fictions (i.e., the doctrine of discovery, *terra nullius*, adverse possession, divine right and so on). We would do well to remember that the *Sparrow* court introduced the term "reconciliation" into the case law. What are they reconciling? They take two provisions of two constitutional documents separated by 115 years and, with the magical words "never any doubt," they manage to maintain section 91(24) as a federal power and convert section 35(1) into a paternalistic federal duty to be managed and mediated by the Crown itself.[22] This reasoning is a model that I imagine Lord Watson would immediately recognize as the one under which he characterized Aboriginal rights as a "mere burden."[23] This is the foundation of the so-called full box of rights.

Given these unstable foundations, what would occur if UNDRIP implementation was used as a way of maintaining the status quo? Naturally, any answer to this question at this time will be speculative, as we do not know the specific legislative approach that the government will take. Some scholars have already begun to raise questions about the compatibility of the basic principles of UNDRIP with the existing jurisprudence, and their conclusions point to significant problems. The example I have in mind here is Dwight Newman and Ken Coates's recent observations regarding the compatibility (or lack thereof) between the existing duty to consult and accommodate (DCA) case law and the principle of free, prior and informed consent (FPIC).[24] Their basic concern is that the duty to consult is well adapted to dealing with asserted rights (i.e., rights that are not yet proven via *Van der Peet*[25] litigation), whereas, if FPIC were introduced as the standard, the DCA could be restricted to dealing only with proven rights.

The only thing that we could say for certain is that if the government elects to take the status quo approach, the recondite complexity of the current section 35(1) jurisprudence will only increase.

20 *Ibid* at 320, 335, 346, 380–83, 387, 391–93, 416, 423.

21 *Worcester v Georgia*, 31 US (6 Pet) 515 (1832) at 544.

22 Ryan Beaton has recently written about the jurisprudential ambiguities that have grown out of the court's use of fiduciary law in this area. As he insightfully notes, "There is ambiguity and tension running through this judicial doctrine, revolving around the question: is the goal reconciliation across legal systems and the distinct societies in which they are grounded, or within a constitutional system grounded fundamentally in the Crown's assertion of sovereignty? The case law developed over the past three decades does not provide any clear or consistent answer." See Ryan Beaton, "The Crown Fiduciary Duty at the Supreme Court of Canada: Reaching Across Nations, or Held within the Grip of the Crown?" in Oonagh E Fitzgerald, Valerie Hughes & Mark Jewett, eds, *Reflections on Canada's Past, Present and Future in International Law* (Waterloo, ON: CIGI, 2018) at 161.

23 *St Catharine's Milling*, *supra* note 15.

24 Dwight Newman & Ken Coates, "Bill on implementing UNDRIP 'simplistic and laden with circular tension'", *The Hill Times* (14 December 2017), online: <www.hilltimes.com/2017/12/14/bill-implementing-undrip-simplistic-laden-circular-tensions/128903>.

25 *R v Van der Peet*, [1996] 2 SCR 507.

At the moment the so-called full box of rights subdivides roughly into rights, title, treaties and the duty to consult and accommodate. Each one of these areas is beset by thorny jurisprudential questions, ranging from the question of the possibility of commercial or unlimited rights (*Ahousaht*[26]), the problem of provincial jurisdiction (*Tsilhqot'in Nation*[27]), and the interpretation of treaties (*Grassy Narrows*[28] and *Chief Mountain*[29]) to cumulative effects and delegation (*Clyde River*[30] and *Chippewas of the Thames*[31]). The process of litigating claims via section 35(1) is costly, procedurally complex and uncertain. Even in cases in which the court seems to offer a clear decision, the actual on-the-ground results of that decision may well be marginal (*Gladstone*[32]) or so delayed that the actual value of the process itself is undermined (*Ktunaxa*[33]). It is difficult to see exactly who benefits from a process of litigation that takes decades to resolve any given conflict and then results in decisions whose jurisprudence is so dense and convoluted that the only certainty it can deliver is the promise of further litigation to work on the new legal knots it has tied.

This full box of rights does not offer the kind of procedural clarity and legal certainty that the government promises to third party proponents, nor does it serve the Indigenous peoples who struggle with dreadful environmental and socio-economic problems. The only real beneficiary of the existing byzantine system of multi-layered consultative processes, secretive memoranda of understanding and the production of voluminous expert reports are the experts, consultants and lawyers who operate it. I am not suggesting that these various professionals are unnecessary to the solution to the problem of the Indigenous-Crown relationship. I am, after all, included in their number. Rather, if the process itself is demonstrably failing to deliver on even its most basic aims (procedural clarity, legal certainty and the improvement of the everyday reality of Indigenous peoples), it is about as productive as an expedition guided by a blank map. As I see it, there is no need to bother asking whether this box is full or empty; it is simply the wrong kind of box altogether. The real path to reconciliation — the one that is not circular — is the one that leads to a nation-to-nation relationship. This is more than a change in language; it is a change in the legal-political paradigm from rights to jurisdiction, and this is precisely where UNDRIP implementation can offer a real way forward.

Nation-to-Nation Federalism

The first point that we need to be cognizant of is that UNDRIP does not introduce the possibility of a shift to an inherent jurisdictional approach to Indigenous-Crown relations. The roots of this approach extend back over 250 years to the Peace and Friendship Treaties in the early eighteenth century, the Royal Proclamation of 1763 and the Treaty of Niagara 1764[34] (we

26 *Ahousaht Indian Band and Nation v Canada (AG)*, 2009 BCSC 1494.

27 *Tsilhqot'in Nation v British Columbia*, [2014] 2 SCR 257.

28 *Grassy Narrows First Nation v Ontario (Natural Resources)*, [2014] 2 SCR 447.

29 *Sga'nism Sim'augit (Chief Mountain) v Canada (AG)*, 2013 BCCA 49.

30 *Clyde River (Hamlet) v Petroleum GeoServices Inc*, [2017] 1 SCR 1069.

31 *Chippewas of the Thames First Nation v Enbridge Pipelines Inc*, [2017] 1 SCR 1099.

32 *R v Gladstone*, [1996] 2 SCR 723.

33 *Ktunaxa Nation v British Columbia (Forests, Lands and Natural Resource Operations)*, [2017] 2 SCR 386.

34 *Treaty of Niagara* (1 August 1764).

can refer to this model as treaty federalism or, following John Borrows,[35] as Canada's Indigenous Constitution) and continue past Confederation even as the rights-based approach becomes the dominant model in the mid-nineteenth century. The practices of treaty federalism persist to this day in the practices of treaty making and negotiated settlements. The jurisdictional approach also surfaces in a number of key government reports. Immediately following the repatriation of the Constitution in 1982, the Penner Report recommended that the proper approach to section 35 was for the federal government to "occupy and vacate" section 91(24) to clear jurisdictional space for Indigenous self-government.[36] The report also clearly indicated that the rights-based solution of devolving powers to municipal-like Indigenous governments "fails to take account of the origins and rights of Indian First Nations in Canada," and the report presciently warned that litigation in the Supreme Court of Canada was not the best possible solution, as the procedure is "difficult to execute and uncertain in its outcome."[37]

This inherent-rights jurisdictional approach was also slated to be resolved in the constitutional conferences following 1982, but the failures of the Meech Lake and Charlottetown accords have left this as the unfinished business of the Canadian Constitution. This point is forcefully driven home by the recommendations in the Report of the Royal Commission on Aboriginal Peoples in 1996 and again in the Final Report and Calls to Action of the Truth and Reconciliation Commission (TRC) in 2015.[38] The point of this summary is that UNDRIP does not introduce the possibility of an inherent-rights-based jurisdictional approach; rather, it offers a set of tools that help us to see what has been taking place within Canada over the last 250 years.

This point is clearly emphasized by the TRC in the Final Report. The TRC recommended that Canada move beyond the old sovereign-to-subjects framework and adopt the current international norms expressed in UNDRIP. The TRC forcefully reminds us that "[t]he Doctrine of Discovery and the related concept of *terra nullius* underpin the requirement for Aboriginal peoples to prove their pre-existing occupation of the land in court cases in order to avoid having their land and resource rights extinguished in contemporary Treaty and land claims processes. Such a requirement does not conform to international law or contribute to reconciliation. Such concepts are a current manifestation of historical wrongs and should be formally repudiated by all levels of Canadian government."[39]

This is a clear and direct rejection of the absolute interpretation of section 91(24) and the framework of reconciliation that has been built upon it. It is a rejection of the racist fictions of international law that continue to inform the interpretation of Canada's constitutional order.

35 There is a wealth of excellent historical and constitutional scholarship in this area; see John Borrows, *Freedom and Indigenous Constitutionalism* (Toronto: University of Toronto Press, 2016); Colin G Calloway, *The Scratch of a Pen: 1763 and the Transformation of North America* (New York: Oxford University Press, 2006); Brian Slattery, "The Royal Proclamation of 1763 and the Aboriginal Constitution" in Terry Fenge & Jim Aldridge, eds, *Keeping Promises: The Royal Proclamation of 1763, Aboriginal Rights, and Treaties in Canada* (Montreal: McGill-Queen's University Press, 2015).

36 Parliament of Canada, Special Committee on Indian Self-Government, *Indian Self-Government in Canada* (Ottawa: Ministry of Supply and Services, 1983) at 3, 46.

37 *Ibid* at 45–47.

38 TRC, *Honouring the Truth, Reconciling for the Future: Summary of the Final Report of the Truth and Reconciliation Commission of Canada* (Winnipeg: TRC, 2015) [TRC, *Honouring the Truth*]; Report of the Royal Commission on Aboriginal Peoples, *Volume 1: Looking Forward Looking Back: Part Two: False Assumptions and a Failed Relationship* (Ottawa: Public Works and Government Services Canada, 1996).

39 TRC, *Honouring the Truth*, *supra* note 38 at vol 6, 32–33.

The TRC continues,

> We are not suggesting that the repudiation of the Doctrine of Discovery necessarily gives rise to the invalidation of Crown sovereignty. The Commission accepts that there are other means to establish the validity of Crown sovereignty without undermining the important principle established in the Royal Proclamation of 1763, which is that the sovereignty of the Crown requires that it recognize and deal with Aboriginal title in order to become perfected. It must not be forgotten that the terms of the Royal Proclamation were explained to, and accepted by, Indigenous leaders during the negotiation of the Treaty of Niagara of 1764.[40]

This constitutes a repositioning of the basis for the legitimacy of Crown sovereignty from the racist fictions of discovery and *terra nullius* to the processes of mutual agreement and consent that are found in the histories of treaty making. This also necessarily shifts Indigenous peoples from being wards who are subject to unlimited sovereign power to being *peoples* in a nation-to-nation relationship with the Crown. We can think of this as being a change from conceiving of Canada as a unitary nation-state with a rigid unilateral version of sovereignty to being a nation-to-nation federal state whose concept of sovereignty is, and has always been, *flexible and shared* (even if only honoured in the breach). The current Canadian government is making clear steps toward realizing this shift from a sovereign-to-subjects rights-based approach to a nation-to-nation inherent jurisdictional approach.[41]

---

40 *Ibid.*

41 The interpretation of the related concepts of "nation-to-nation" and "reconciliation" that I put forward here is indebted to John Borrows's work on Indigenous constitutionalism, Charles Taylor's work on deep diversity, James Tully's work on diverse constitutionalism and Sa'ke'j Henderson's work on treaty federalism (among others). For a small sample of the literature that I have found helpful in developing my own view of these concepts and the relationship between them, see Charles Taylor, *Reconciling the Solitudes: Essays on Canadian Federalism and Nationalism* (Montreal: McGill-Queen's University Press, 1993); James Tully, "Consent, Hegemony, and Dissent in Treaty Negotiations" in Jeremy Webber & Colin M Macleod, eds, *Between Consenting Peoples: Political Community and the Meaning of Consent* (Vancouver: UBC Press, 2010); John Borrows, "Wampum at Niagara: The Royal Proclamation, Canadian Legal History, and Self-government" in Michael Asch, ed, *Aboriginal and Treaty Rights in Canada* (Vancouver: UBC Press, 2000); Russel Lawrence Barsh & James Youngblood Henderson, *The Road: Indian Tribes and Political Liberty* (Berkeley: University of California Press, 1980); Michael Asch, *On Being Here to Stay: Treaties and Aboriginal Rights in Canada* (Toronto: University of Toronto Press, 2014).

15

Options for Implementing UNDRIP without Creating Another Empty Box

Jeffery G. Hewitt

From 2007 until its defeat in 2015, the Conservative Government of Canada of Stephen Harper steadfastly refused to adopt and implement the United Nations Declaration on the Rights of Indigenous Peoples (UNDRIP),[1] ultimately viewing it as aspirational. Conversely, in 2016, the Liberal government of Justin Trudeau stated an intention to adopt and implement UNDRIP in accordance with the Canadian Constitution.[2] Is this a sea change in the relationship between Canada and Indigenous peoples or simply a dressing up of Conservative aspirations in a Liberal constitutional robe?

Canada's International Conduct Regarding Indigenous Peoples

UNDRIP is an international declaration and therefore non-binding on Canadian courts. Canada has a long history of failing to implement non-binding matters from the United

1 *United Nations Declaration on the Rights of Indigenous Peoples,* GA Res 295, UNGAOR, 61st Sess, Supp No 49, UN Doc A/RES/61/295, 46 ILM 1013 (2007).

2 Minister of Indigenous and Northern Affairs Carolyn Bennett, "Announcement of Canada's Support for the United Nations Declaration on the Rights of Indigenous Peoples" (Statement delivered at the 15th Session of the United Nations Permanent Forum on Indigenous Issues, 10 May 2016).

Nations in relation to Indigenous peoples. Consider that, in 2004, Special Rapporteur on the Rights of Indigenous Peoples Rodolfo Stavenhagen visited Canada and reported "unacceptable gaps between [Indigenous] Canadians and the rest of the population in education attainment, employment and access to basic social services."[3] Although a number of recommendations were included in Stavenhagen's report, none were implemented, as evidenced in a 2013 follow-up report. In 2013, Special Rapporteur on the Rights of Indigenous Peoples James Anaya declared that Canada faces a crisis when it comes to Indigenous peoples.[4] Anaya repeated the serious concerns set out by Stavenhagen a decade earlier. Anaya also noted that the violations committed against Indigenous peoples ranged from disrespect for treaty and land rights and unaddressed violence against Indigenous women and girls to gaps regarding access to health care, housing, education, safe drinking water and the welfare and protection of Indigenous children.[5] In his 2013 report, Anaya expressed particular concern about the lack of sufficient and proper consultations by Canada with Indigenous peoples to obtain their free, prior and informed consent — in particular in relation to resource extraction — as required under UNDRIP.[6]

Following the Liberal government's election in November 2015, Prime Minister Justin Trudeau sent a mandate letter to the Minister of Indigenous and Northern Affairs[7] setting out 13 priorities for the minister. Among the priorities were the following: implementation of UNDRIP; a review of the laws and policies regarding the Crown's consultation and accommodation obligation that includes Indigenous peoples in the review process; and the amendment of environmental assessment legislation to enhance the inclusion of Indigenous peoples in the process as well as in the review and monitoring of major resource development in Canada.

However, in November 2016, the prime minister announced approval of pipelines to transport fossil fuels from Canada's western provinces to various parts of the continent[8] without having completed a review of law and policies related to consultation with Indigenous peoples and without any enhancements to environmental assessment legislation that would require consultation with Indigenous peoples. This conduct validates the concerns expressed by Anaya in 2013 relating to a lack of consultation and consent. In sum, Canada's behaviour of ignoring international concerns relating to Indigenous peoples persists in spite of changes in government. Canada's intention to implement UNDRIP through section 35 of the Constitution Act, 1982[9] may allow for the infringement of article 10 (which prohibits the relocation of Indigenous peoples without their free, prior and informed consent), in spite of international calls for meaningful change.

3 Paul Joffe, "UN Declaration on the Rights of Indigenous Peoples Not Merely 'Aspirational'" (22 June 2013), online: <http://rights.info.yorku.ca/files/2013/06/UN-Decl-Not-merely-aspirational-June-22-13.pdf>.

4 James Anaya, "Statement Upon Conclusion of the Visit to Canada" (15 October 2013), online: <http://unsr.jamesanaya.org/statements/statement-upon-conclusion-of-the-visit-to-canada>.

5 *Ibid.*

6 *Ibid.*

7 Justin Trudeau, Prime Minister of Canada, "Minister of Indigenous and Northern Affairs Mandate Letter", online: <http://pm.gc.ca/eng/minister-indigenous-and-northern-affairs-mandate-letter>.

8 Amy Minsky, "Fact Check: Did Justin Trudeau Break Promises Approving Pipelines?", *Global News* (30 November 2016), online: <http://globalnews.ca/news/3097871/fact-check-justin-trudeau-break-promise-approving-pipelines/>.

9 *Constitution Act, 1982*, being Schedule B to the *Canada Act 1982* (UK), 1982, c 11.

Infringement of UNDRIP through Section 35 of the Constitution Act, 1982

Section 35 forms part of Canada's Constitution, which includes the Charter of Rights and Freedoms.[10] Section 1 of the Charter "guarantees the rights and freedoms set out in it subject only to such reasonable limits prescribed by law as can be demonstrably justified in a free and democratic society." In the 1986 *R v Oakes*[11] decision (a case challenging certain assumptions within the Narcotic Control Act[12] that created a reverse onus on the accused to prove their innocence), the Supreme Court of Canada (SCC) rejected the burden of a reverse onus as unconstitutional and an unreasonable limit of law in a free and democratic society. *Oakes* established the test for addressing whether the government could justify Charter violations and thereby limit the rights and freedoms of Canadians.

Four years later, interpreting the meaning of section 35 of the Constitution Act, 1982 for the first time, the SCC rendered its judgment in *R v Sparrow*[13] (a challenge of fishing licence regulations that restricted Aboriginal fishing rights to "food purposes" only). In *Sparrow*, the court created a reverse onus burden on the Aboriginal claimants and established a legal test for infringing Aboriginal and treaty rights. In other words, the court in *Sparrow* applied a reverse onus test that it had rejected under the Charter in *Oakes*. This balancing of rights test, which was developed for and affirmed in the language of section 1 of the Charter, does not apply to section 35 of the Constitution Act, 1982 and should not have been incorporated therein. The result is that, while a reverse onus offends the principles of a free and democratic society under section 1 of the Charter, such principles are cast aside when Aboriginal claimants are entangled with Canadian law. *Sparrow* created powerful, severe and still-standing limitations on Aboriginal and treaty rights in favour of the settler-colonial narrative that assumes Aboriginal peoples were conquered and thereby subject to Crown sovereignty.[14] Such subjugation of Indigenous peoples allows section 35 to be used as a constitutional vehicle for infringement and to justify Crown intentions to extinguish Aboriginal and treaty rights.

But consider the wording of section 35(1), which states "existing aboriginal and treaty rights of the aboriginal peoples of Canada are hereby recognized and affirmed." There is no "reasonable limits" wording in section 35 as is plainly set out in section 1 of the Charter. The SCC's broad and liberal interpretation of section 1 in *Oakes* is in favour of protecting individual rights and places the burden on the Crown to justify its actions. On the other hand, the affirmative language of section 35 resulted in a restrictive and narrow constitutional interpretation, which placed the weight of proving an Aboriginal or treaty right on the Aboriginal claimant while protecting the Crown's asserted control over Indigenous peoples. Given this unsatisfactory judicial treatment of section 35, is it reasonable to expect the courts to do better in interpreting UNDRIP?

10 *Charter of Rights and Freedoms*, Part I of the *Constitution Act, 1982*, being Schedule B to the *Canada Act 1982* (UK), 1982, c 11.

11 [1986] 1 SCR 103.

12 *Narcotic Control Act*, RSC 1970, c N1.

13 [1990] 1 SCR 1075.

14 John Borrows, "With or Without You: First Nations Law (in Canada)"(1996) 41 McGill LJ 629.

Oakes and *Sparrow* are similar in their investigation into the infringement of a Charter right and an Aboriginal or treaty right, respectively. Both tests require the Crown to have a pressing and substantial objective to limit a right, but, according to *Sparrow*, the Crown might be liberated from having to further justify its actions if it can demonstrate the Aboriginal right was previously extinguished. Both require a rational connection, minimal impairment and proportionality.

In many ways, the *Sparrow* test defines section 35 and, more broadly, the means by which Canada will engage in a relationship with Indigenous peoples — exclusively on Canada's terms, favouring itself. It is among the means by which Canada continues to use Canadian law as lubricant for the machinery that sustains a settler-colonial narrative and upholds the country's long-standing legal mythology of sovereignty over lands, resources and Indigenous peoples. Therefore, implementing UNDRIP through section 35 allows Canada new ways to limit the rights of Indigenous peoples. It is not a "full box of rights"[15] for Indigenous peoples, as Canada's Minister of Indigenous and Northern Affairs has boldly declared, but may rather be viewed as a full access pass for Canada to the lands and resources of Indigenous peoples.

Using the *Sparrow* test, Canada is liberated from meaningfully adopting UNDRIP by continuing onward with its well-entrenched legal position that section 35 is an empty box.[16] Infringement and extinguishment of rights are inconsistent with the articles of UNDRIP. Section 35 potentially allows the Crown to hollow out the rights of Indigenous peoples found within UNDRIP — rights such as self-determination; entitlement to free, prior and informed consent; and control of lands and resources.[17] Thus, there is cause for concern regarding whether Canada's current position contributes to nation-to-nation relations or merely maintains the status quo, and whether such a position further restricts an already strained national reconciliation discussion. But there are means of implementing UNDRIP other than through section 35 that might meaningfully contribute to Canada's reconciliation discussion and advance the nation-to-nation relationship.

Accessing UNDRIP to Engage with Indigenous Legal Orders

Canada has options for implementation, including adopting UNDRIP wholesale by means of enabling legislation. If so adopted, the content of UNDRIP may be further developed and implemented without the restrictions built into section 35. This would allow the principles of each article to be meaningfully fulfilled through engagement on a level field between Indigenous peoples and Canada.

In a number of articles — although perhaps most directly in article 5 — UNDRIP makes room for Indigenous laws. UNDRIP asserts the necessity of creating institutions that support the social, political and legal infrastructure of Indigenous peoples. In addition, the Truth and Reconciliation Commission of Canada has called for the inclusion of Indigenous laws and the

15 Bennett, *supra* note 2.

16 For more, see John Borrows, "Frozen Rights in Canada: Constitutional Interpretation and the Trickster" (1997) 22:1 Am Indian L Rev 37 and Douglas Sanders, "The Supreme Court of Canada and the 'Legal and Political Struggle' Over Indigenous Rights" (1990) 22:3 Can Ethnic Stud 122.

17 *UNDRIP, supra* note 1, arts 3, 10, 26.

building of Indigenous legal institutions.[18] Therefore, rather than engaging with the potential limitations of section 35, Canada might opt to fund new institutions based on Indigenous legal orders[19] and ensure such institutions are mandated to interpret UNDRIP outside the confines of section 35.

The Trudeau government's drawing in of UNDRIP through section 35 is markedly different from the Harper government's resistance. But resistance comes in many forms. Sometimes what may appear to be change is merely resistance seen from a new perspective. Without careful consideration by the government, the implementation of UNDRIP through section 35 would mean that UNDRIP would ultimately become another empty box that refuses to include Indigenous legal orders.

Recommendations

Concerns that implementing UNDRIP through section 35 of the Constitution Act, 1982 will ultimately limit the potential impact of UNDRIP are reasonable. Consider that Canada has a history of ignoring international concerns relating to Indigenous peoples and that Canadian courts have developed jurisprudence in relation to section 35 that allows for the infringement of treaty and Aboriginal rights. Is the infringement of the rights set out in UNDRIP far behind? In *Sparrow*, in 1990, the court reversed the onus of proving a section 35 right, putting it on the Aboriginal claimant, although the same court had rejected the reverse onus in the Charter decision four years earlier in *Oakes*. While section 35 is not part of the Charter, it also does not have any of the limiting language found in section 1 of the Charter. Rather, section 35 recognizes and affirms Aboriginal and treaty rights. Filtering UNDRIP through section 35 will mean that the onus will be on Aboriginal claimants to prove the meaning of each article contained therein while allowing the Crown to infringe on such rights. Vigilance — not celebration — is required if Canada is insistent on using section 35 to implement UNDRIP. Implementing UNDRIP through section 35 is not inevitable. Canada has options, such as the following:

- Canada should reconsider its position on implementing UNDRIP through section 35, which, in light of the jurisprudence, is limiting and favours maintenance of the settler-colonial status quo.
- Canada should implement legislation mirroring each article of UNDRIP in order to fully implement UNDRIP into Canadian law, which will further the reconciliation dialogue between Canada and Indigenous peoples as one that takes place on a nation-to-nation basis. Moreover, Canadian legislation adopting UNDRIP would be binding on Canadian courts without necessarily forcing the courts to interpret such legislation through the limits of section 35.
- The creation of separate legislation adopting UNDRIP would further advance the legal framework for recognition of Indigenous laws through UNDRIP's articles and the Truth and Reconciliation Commission of Canada's Calls to Action for the building of Indigenous legal institutions.

18 Truth and Reconciliation Commission of Canada, "Calls to Action" (Winnipeg, MB: Truth and Reconciliation Commission of Canada, 2015) at Recommendation 50, online: <www.trc.ca/websites/trcinstitution/File/2015/Findings/Calls_to_Action_English2.pdf>.

19 For more on Indigenous legal orders, see Val Napoleon, "Thinking about Indigenous Legal Orders" in René Provost and Colleen Sheppard, eds, *Dialogues on Human Rights and Legal Pluralism* (Dordrecht, Netherlands: Springer, 2013) 229.

16

Asserted vs. Established Rights and the Promise of UNDRIP

Robert Hamilton

There is considerable debate about what implementation of the United Nations Declaration on the Rights of Indigenous Peoples (UNDRIP)[1] will look like in Canada and how the norms articulated in UNDRIP — notably self-determination and free, prior and informed consent (FPIC) — fit with existing state law in Canada. Statements from the federal government suggest a belief that UNDRIP can be implemented through the existing section 35 of the Constitution Act, 1982 Aboriginal rights framework.[2] However, incongruities between UNDRIP and the current Aboriginal rights regime present many challenges in this regard.[3] This chapter addresses one reason why the reliance on section 35 may in fact stall the process of implementation, arguing that the Aboriginal rights framework's reliance on categories of asserted and established rights is not compatible with UNDRIP implementation. The Supreme Court of Canada's (SCC's) assumed authority to unilaterally determine the rights of Indigenous peoples, while acceding

1 *United Nations Declaration on the Rights of Indigenous Peoples*, GA Res 295, UNGAOR, 61st Sess, Supp No 49, UN Doc A/RES/61/295, 46 ILM 1013 (2007) [*UNDRIP*].

2 Minister of Indigenous and Northern Affairs Carolyn Bennett, "Announcement of Canada's Support for the United Nations Declaration on the Rights of Indigenous Peoples" (Statement delivered at the 15th Session of the United Nations Permanent Forum on Indigenous Issues, 10 May 2016).

3 These incongruities have been raised both by those arguing for UNDRIP implementation (see e.g. Brenda L Gunn, "Beyond *Van der Peet*: Bringing Together International, Indigenous and Constitutional Law" (this volume, ch 13)) and those arguing against it (see e.g. Harry Swain & Jim Baillie, "The Trudeau government signs on to give Aboriginals veto rights nobody else has", *National Post* (26 January 2018)).

to asserted state authority, entrenches a power imbalance that undermines the meaningful implementation of UNDRIP's norms. Those norms support a model of legal pluralism and negotiated jurisdictional sharing that the domestic Aboriginal rights framework has difficulty accommodating.

This chapter first illustrates why the distinction between asserted and established rights must be re-thought in light of prospective UNDRIP implementation. It then argues that UNDRIP's provisions regarding FPIC are defined in relation to Indigenous powers of governance and that this fact requires that UNDRIP be understood through a lens of legal pluralism. The chapter concludes by offering examples of what Indigenous-Crown relations may look like with that distinction removed from the rights framework.

Asserted vs. Established Rights

Until such point as an Aboriginal right is proven in a domestic court, on the standards established by those courts, the rights remain merely asserted, thus receiving only the procedural protection — consultation — afforded at domestic law. This power asymmetry, cemented in the current section 35 framework, runs counter to the substantive norms articulated in UNDRIP. Dwight Newman has outlined the complications that the distinction between asserted and established rights causes for UNDRIP implementation when viewed from the perspective of domestic law. Newman has urged caution regarding UNDRIP implementation on the basis that UNDRIP does not necessarily exceed domestic Canadian law. He argues that consent already exists in Canadian law where Aboriginal rights have been established, and that the consultation and accommodation framework also applies to asserted rights.[4] Further, as Newman points out, the legal definition of consent is distinct from the colloquial definition, and the federal government has sought to define consent narrowly as an attempt to achieve consent.[5] The implication of Newman's first point is that UNDRIP's consent standard would not apply in relation to asserted rights, but only to those already established at Canadian law.[6] Accepting that the FPIC standard in UNDRIP applies only in relation to established rights, the twofold argument for why FPIC may not expand on Canadian law follows: first, consent already exists where rights are established; and, second, the duty to consult applies not only to established rights, but also to asserted rights. This argument can be addressed on its own terms and also by interrogating the presuppositions on which it relies.

What of consent in Canadian law? In *Tsilhqot'in Nation,* the SCC held that, where Aboriginal title is established, state incursions are permitted "only with the consent of the Aboriginal group or if they are justified by a compelling and substantial public purpose and are not inconsistent with the Crown's fiduciary duty to the Aboriginal group."[7] In *Haida Nation,* the court held that "Aboriginal 'consent'...is appropriate only in cases of established rights, and then by no means

4 Dwight Newman, *Political Rhetoric Meets Legal Reality: How to Move Forward on Free, Prior, and Informed Consent in Canada* (Ottawa: Macdonald-Laurier Institute, 2017) at 14.

5 *Ibid.*

6 Here I am speaking of rights at domestic law. FPIC indisputably applies to Indigenous rights recognized at international law: see James Anaya, *Report of the Special Rapporteur on the rights of indigenous peoples James Anaya: Extractive industries and indigenous peoples,* UNHRC, 24th Sess, UN Doc A/HRC/24/41 (2013) at 9, online: <http://unsr.jamesanaya.org/docs/annual/2013-hrc-annual-report-en.pdf>.

7 *Tsilhqot'in Nation v British Columbia,* 2014 SCC 44 at para 2 [*Tsilhqot'in Nation*].

in every case."[8] The qualifications attached to consent are important. Consent is required only where established rights are concerned. Rights must be established in court before the consent standard arises. Further, consent may not be required "in every case" of established rights, which may, for example, still be infringed pursuant to the justificatory standard.[9]

These qualifications must be taken into account when assessing where consent under section 35 sits in relation to FPIC. On its face, FPIC seems to sit well beyond current Canadian legal standards. Indeed, Canada's initial objection to UNDRIP concerned what Canada described as the veto power included in UNDRIP.[10] This concern has continued to animate opposition to the adoption of UNDRIP.[11] In an analysis of article 32 of UNDRIP, the Inter-American Court of Human Rights held that FPIC provided a basis for Indigenous peoples to reject large-scale intrusions into their traditional territories (large hydroelectric dams or mines, for instance).[12] Reporting on the relationship between Indigenous peoples and extractive industries, James Anaya wrote that there is a "general rule that extractive activities should not take place within the territories of indigenous peoples without their free, prior, and informed consent."[13] Yet Anaya also discusses "certain exceptions" to the general rule "within narrowly defined parameters."[14] That is, FPIC may not be an absolute requirement for all types of intrusion.[15] The exception applies when it "can be conclusively established" that the extractive activities in question "will not substantially affect indigenous peoples in the exercise of any of their substantive rights in relation to the lands and resources within their territories."[16] Where a limitation on a right is permitted absent Indigenous consent, Anaya argues that "standards of necessity and proportionality" must be met to justify such incursions.[17]

Even with these qualifications, however, the FPIC standard surpasses the consent standard in Canadian law for two reasons. First, even if FPIC incorporates a balancing standard that does not provide Indigenous peoples with a final say over all developments in their territories, this qualification would not seem to apply to serious incursions.[18] In domestic law, the inverse is true: serious incursions are precisely those the courts have identified as grounding justifiable infringement.[19] Second, section 35 rights are exceedingly difficult to prove in court. Litigation carries immense financial and human costs and considerable uncertainty as to outcome. This was recognized by the Inter-American Commission on Human Rights, when it held that there is

8 *Haida Nation v British Columbia (Minister of Forests)*, 2004 SCC 73 at para 48, [2004] 3 SCR 511 [*Haida Nation*].

9 *Tsilhqot'in Nation, supra* note 7 at para 2.

10 Brenda L Gunn, "Overcoming Obstacles to Implementing the UN Declaration on the Rights of Indigenous Peoples in Canada" (2013) 31:1 Windsor YB Access Just 147 at 151.

11 See Swain & Baillie, *supra* note 3.

12 *Case of the Saramaka People v Suriname* (2007), Inter-Am Ct HR (Ser C) No 82 at para 134 as cited in Michael Coyle, "From Consultation to Consent: Squaring the Circle?" (2016) 67 UNB LJ 235 at 242.

13 Anaya, *supra* note 6 at 9.

14 *Ibid* at 10–11.

15 Coyle, *supra* note 12 at 238. See also Shin Imai, "Consult, Consent and Veto: International Norms and Canadian Treaties" in Michael Coyle & John Borrows, eds, *The Right(s) Relationship: Reimagining the Implementation of Historical Treaties* (Toronto: University of Toronto Press, 2017) at 370–408.

16 Anaya, *supra* note 6 at 10.

17 *Ibid.*

18 Imai, *supra* note 15 at 384.

19 In *Delgamuukw*, for example, the SCC identified "the development of agriculture, forestry, mining, and hydroelectric power, the general economic development of the interior of British Columbia" as compelling legislative objectives that may support a justifiable infringement. *Delgamuukw v British Columbia*, [1997] 3 SCR 1010 at para 165 [*Delgamuukw*].

no effective remedy for Indigenous peoples seeking to resolve land rights disputes in Canada.[20] Both litigation and treaty negotiation are costly, lengthy and uncertain processes. Thus, consent exists as a standard at Canadian law largely at the conceptual level.

Where rights are asserted but not yet proven, the consultation framework applies.[21] To date, the courts have been clear that the duty to consult does not require Indigenous consent.[22] Consultation "guarantees a process, not a particular result."[23] The procedural requirements of the consultation framework do not ask whether Indigenous peoples want a development to occur, but rather for information about the impact of the proposed project on their asserted rights.[24] This has practical implications. As Michael Coyle writes, "If, in good faith, [the parties] seriously disagree about the strength of the community's rights claim or about the severity of a project's impacts, in a real sense the consultation process will fail. It will fail as a mechanism for consensus-building, it will fail as a reliable vehicle for facilitating decisions about resources on traditional lands, and it will fail as a process aimed at helping to achieve reconciliation between Indigenous peoples and the state."[25] That is, the duty to consult is limited in its ability to reconcile state and Indigenous interests because it ultimately permits unilateral action in the face of disagreement. The remaining question is whether the duty to consult provides greater protection of rights than UNDRIP does, by virtue of the protection the duty gives to asserted as well as established rights. Answering this question in the affirmative requires accepting the proposition that FPIC would apply only in relation to established rights.

As can be seen, there are reasons to question the proposition that the current Aboriginal rights and duty to consult frameworks provide protections equal to those that may be available under the FPIC regime envisioned in UNDRIP. Yet, it is a tenable argument. If UNDRIP implementation is pursued through section 35, as currently interpreted by the courts, Newman's analysis may well prove prescient. The problem with this framing is that it is based on foundational assumptions that must be challenged if UNDRIP is to be implemented. It is an interpretation that prima facie excludes implementation by maintaining the power of the state to unilaterally assess the validity of asserted Indigenous rights and decide what level of protection they should be afforded on the basis of that determination. It cannot be assumed that FPIC applies only in relation to established rights.

Overlapping Legal Regimes and *Sui Generis* Implementation

The distinction between asserted and established rights, as currently employed in Canadian law to determine the level of protection afforded Indigenous rights, is not tenable in light of UNDRIP. UNDRIP requires that the power of the state — and its courts — to unilaterally

20 *Admissibility: Hul'qumi'num Treaty Group — Canada* (2009) Inter-Am Comm HR, No 105/09, online: <www.sfu.ca/~palys/HulQumiNumPetitiontoIACHR.pdf>. Although this decision predated the SCC's recognition of title in *Tsilhqot'in Nation*, its reasoning would still seem applicable, given the enormous time and financial costs of that litigation.

21 *Haida Nation*, *supra* note 8.

22 *Ibid* at para 48; *Chippewas of the Thames First Nation v Enbridge Pipelines*, 2017 SCC 41 at para 59; *Ktunaxa Nation v British Columbia (Forests, Lands and Natural Resource Operations)*, 2017 SCC 54 at paras 80, 83, 119 [*Ktunaxa*].

23 *Ktunaxa*, *supra* note 22 at para 79.

24 Newman, *supra* note 4 at 9.

25 Coyle, *supra* note 12 at 238.

determine which rights are owed protection and which are merely asserted must no longer be assumed. The domestic Aboriginal rights framework as developed under section 35 accepts the Crown as holding a superior legal position to Indigenous peoples, a position that permits unilateral Crown action in the face of Indigenous opposition. A crucial tool in this regard is the ability to define rights as merely asserted and, therefore, as attracting only the lower standard of consultation. To implement UNDRIP means to understand that, in important respects, both Indigenous and Crown rights are asserted.[26] Drawing this equivalence puts Indigenous peoples on an even footing with the state when it comes to defining their respective rights and calls into question the assumption of unilateral Crown authority upon which the section 35 framework has been developed.

The relationship between FPIC and Indigenous governance is central in this regard. UNDRIP's provisions regarding FPIC are defined in relation to Indigenous powers of governance. The relationship between consent and governance is outlined in article 32.1, which provides that "Indigenous peoples have the right to determine and develop priorities and strategies for the development or use of their lands or territories and other resources," and article 32.2, which reads: "States shall consult and cooperate in good faith with the indigenous peoples concerned through their own representative institutions in order to obtain their free and informed consent."[27] Further, article 4 states: "Indigenous peoples, in exercising their right to self-determination, have the right to autonomy or self-government in matters relating to their internal and local affairs, as well as ways and means for financing their autonomous functions."[28] Through the recognition of Indigenous "representative institutions," the ability of those institutions to determine priorities in relation to development and the Indigenous nature of those institutions, these clauses not only require consent, but also protect Indigenous rights of governance and recognize Indigenous jurisdiction.[29] Self-determining peoples with representative institutions have legal orders. UNDRIP therefore envisions states as legally pluralistic, multi-juridical spheres. In this, UNDRIP recognizes "the fact of legal pluralism"[30] in a more robust manner than domestic law has been able or willing to do. FPIC should not be understood in the abstract, but rather as a manifestation of the right of self-determination.[31] What these articles on self-determination and FPIC envision is Indigenous jurisdiction in relation to Indigenous lands and resources, where Indigenous political and legal institutions are intimately involved in decision making about matters that impact Indigenous peoples. This is not consonant with a state of affairs where rights must be proven in domestic courts before UNDRIP standards apply.

What would it look like to reject a unilateral determination of asserted and established rights? To hold that Indigenous peoples should be able to establish rights that bind the Canadian state and impact citizens by merely asserting them would only invert the current problems. If unilateralism is the problem, it can hardly be the answer. But, if neither party can unilaterally define its rights

26 This is not meant to question the inherent nature of Indigenous rights, but only to point out that, from the Crown perspective, those inherent rights are asserted rights until such point as they have been established.

27 *UNDRIP*, *supra* note 1.

28 *Ibid*, art 4.

29 Walter R Echo-Hawk, *In the Light of Justice: The Rise of Human Rights in Native America and the UN Declaration on the Rights of Indigenous Peoples* (Golden, CO: Fulcrum, 2013) at 43–45.

30 See, int his volume, Gordon Christie, "Indigenous Legal Orders, Canadian Law and UNDRIP" (ch 5) at 49. Christie uses the phrase "fact of strong legal pluralism."

31 Gunn, *supra* note 10 at 153.

and obligations vis-à-vis the other, where do the parties stand? In the context of jurisdictional uncertainty created by competing claims to constitutional authority, negotiated settlements are required.[32] Where assertions of rights are made, those rights must be negotiated by the parties without one party having a cudgel of infringement or a judicial mandate to act unilaterally after satisfying judicially designed procedural requirements. FPIC is implemented not by requiring consent in relation to rights that colonial courts have recognized, but by requiring the negotiated settlement of contested terrain. When multiple forms of legal authority are functioning in the same space, pluralism requires that authority be negotiated through dialogue.[33]

Unless section 35 can be reimagined in a manner that excises its doctrinal unilateralism, it must be de-emphasized.[34] This is not to say it may not have strategic uses in its current iteration. The current logic of section 35, however, may not be amenable or helpful to the implementation of UNDRIP. Despite its emphasis on encouraging negotiation and its successes in compelling recalcitrant governments to give Indigenous peoples a voice at the table, it has not distributed the bargaining power of the parties evenly enough to ensure that negotiations can be a vehicle for consensus building and reconciliation. Thus, while the claim that implementation would "dismantle our courts' carefully constructed approach to reconciliation"[35] is true in one respect, it fails on another. Under its current judicial interpretation, section 35 proffers an impoverished conception of reconciliation — reconciling Aboriginal interest with underlying Crown sovereignty — which promotes unilateralism and fails to adequately balance the interests of the parties. UNDRIP undoubtedly challenges this approach to reconciliation. Seen another way, however, UNDRIP is a tool more suited than section 35 to achieving the SCC's often-stated aim of encouraging the negotiation of outstanding claims. The SCC has sought to encourage negotiation and has attempted to set conceptual and practical bounds on the exercise of Crown sovereign authority.[36] It has undoubtedly done much to advance Aboriginal rights in the process. Yet the SCC's own doctrine now seems to prevent it from laying the groundwork for a nation-to-nation relationship based on negotiated rights and jurisdiction. Until such time as section 35 doctrine can be divested of its reliance on unilateral Crown sovereign authority, the meaningful reconciliation the SCC gestures toward will not be achieved through section 35. UNDRIP offers the grounds for a more robust balancing of interests. Contrary to the concern of those who worry that UNDRIP gives Indigenous peoples a veto, UNDRIP does not seek to replace one unilateralism with another. As the preamble states, UNDRIP "will enhance harmonious and cooperative relations between the State and indigenous peoples, based on principles of justice, democracy, respect for human rights, non-discrimination and good faith."[37]

Thus, section 35 must be sidelined from this process. There are, fortunately, many examples of nations working outside the section 35 context to draw on. I will mention only two. While the Haida have used the judicial system, they have also taken other approaches. The Reconciliation Protocol signed between the Haida Nation and the Province of British Columbia acknowledges in its preamble that the parties hold different understandings of their rights, obligations and

32 Christie, *supra* note 30.

33 *Ibid* at 49.

34 As Jeffery G. Hewitt writes, "implementing UNDRIP through section 35 allows Canada new ways to limit the rights of Indigenous peoples" (this volume ch 15) at 140.

35 Swain & Baillie, *supra* note 3.

36 See e.g. *Delgamuukw*, *supra* note 19 at para 186; *Haida Nation*, *supra* note 8 at para 14.

37 *UNDRIP*, *supra* note 1, Preamble.

sovereign authority in relation to Haida Gwaii.[38] Such agreements represent one model for developing shared jurisdictions in relation to matters such as cultural heritage and co-management of wildlife, lands and resources.

A second example is tribal parks. Tribal parks are a *sui generis* form of property ownership and jurisdiction asserted by Indigenous peoples. They are not parks in the conventional sense or in the legal sense in Canadian law, but areas where Indigenous peoples assert authority and jurisdiction to manage the land.[39] While some of these parks are not recognized at Canadian law, provincial governments have entered into co-jurisdiction types of arrangements that recognize the status of some parks as protected areas under Indigenous law.[40]

What is pertinent about these examples in the context of UNDRIP implementation is that Indigenous peoples are involved in the processes through which the relative rights and obligations of the parties are negotiated. Unlike in the current section 35 framework, in which the rules of the game are crafted by the state's courts, in these examples, the terms through which the rights and obligations will be determined are themselves subject to negotiation. The "harmonious and cooperative relations between the State and indigenous peoples" spoken of in the preamble to UNDRIP must be worked toward on the basis of mutually agreed upon terms of engagement. Only then can self-determination and FPIC be put meaningfully into practice.

38 See "Kunst'aa Guu — Kunst'aayah Reconciliation Protocol" (2009), online: British Columbia <www2.gov.bc.ca/gov/content/environment/natural-resource-stewardship/consulting-with-first-nations/first-nations-negotiations/first-nations-a-z-listing/haida-nation-council-of>.

39 Grant Murray & Leslie King, "First Nations Values in Protected Area Governance: Tla-o-qui-aht Tribal Parks and Pacific Rim National Park Reserve" (2012) 40:3 Human Ecology 385 at 389.

40 On May 29, 2008, Bill 38 — 2008 (Bill 38 — 2008, *Protected Areas of British Columbia (Conservancies and Parks) Amendment Act, 2008*, 4th Sess, 38th Parl, British Columbia, 2008) established Duu Guusd park on Haida Gwaii. On December 17, 2008, the Province of British Columbia passed Order in Council No. 977/2008, which added 6,793 hectares and established revised boundaries for Duu Guusd that included Langara Island and an area of land in Rennell Sound. Online: <www.canlii.org/en/bc/laws/stat/sbc-2000-c-17/latest/part-8/sbc-2000-c-17-part-8.html#Eduuguusd>.

17

Articles 27 and 46(2): UNDRIP Signposts Pointing beyond the Justifiable-infringement Morass of Section 35

Ryan Beaton

In May 2016, Indigenous and Northern Affairs Minister Carolyn Bennett announced at the fifteenth session of the United Nations Permanent Forum on Indigenous Issues that Canada is "now a full supporter of the [United Nations] Declaration [on the Rights of Indigenous Peoples][1] without qualification."[2] She stated that Canada intends "nothing less than to adopt and implement the declaration in accordance with the Canadian Constitution." She also pointed to the constitutional provision that would be the focus of implementation: "By adopting and implementing the Declaration, we are excited that we are breathing life into Section 35 and recognizing it now as a full box of rights for Indigenous peoples in Canada."[3]

The minister is referring to section 35 of the Constitution Act, 1982.[4] Section 35(1) reads: "The existing aboriginal and treaty rights of the aboriginal peoples of Canada are hereby recognized and affirmed."[5]

1 *United Nations Declaration on the Rights of Indigenous Peoples*, GA Res 295, UNGAOR, 61st Sess, Supp No 49, UN Doc A/RES/61/295, 46 ILM 1013 (2007) [*UNDRIP*].

2 Minister of Indigenous and Northern Affairs Carolyn Bennett, "Announcement of Canada's Support for the United Nations Declaration on the Rights of Indigenous Peoples" (Statement delivered at the 15th Session of the United Nations Permanent Forum on Indigenous Issues, 10 May 2016).

3 *Ibid.*

4 *Constitution Act, 1982*, being Schedule B to the *Canada Act 1982* (UK), 1982, s 35.

5 *Ibid*, s 35(1).

The minister's statements raise both hopes for a newly vitalized section 35 and concerns that the United Nations Declaration on the Rights of Indigenous Peoples (UNDRIP) will be interpreted as consistent with, or even redundant to, the already existing section 35 framework developed by Canadian courts. This chapter notes one such major concern, raised in particular by the language of article 46(2) of UNDRIP, and points to a key component in addressing this concern, a component required by article 27.

In brief, article 46(2) allows for justified limits on the rights set out in UNDRIP. The justification analysis that currently exists in Canadian law under section 35 places the burden on section 35 rights holders to seek redress in the courts when the Crown infringes their rights in a manner that the rights holders believe cannot be justified. The fact that the Crown can act in the face of disagreement over the justifiability of infringements, subject only to subsequent review by the courts if the rights holders have the time, resources and willingness to pursue legal remedies, contributes greatly to the imbalance in bargaining power between the Crown and Indigenous peoples engaging in consultation and negotiation. It would be unfortunate, to say the least, if article 46(2) were interpreted to endorse the existing justification analysis and judicial procedure.

Indeed, such an interpretation of article 46(2) would be inconsistent with other provisions of UNDRIP (not to mention with the spirit of the declaration as a whole). In particular, article 27 requires states "in conjunction with indigenous peoples concerned" to establish "a fair, independent, impartial, open and transparent process...to recognize and adjudicate the rights of indigenous peoples pertaining to their lands, territories and resources." At a minimum, article 27 requires Canada to justify proposed infringements to section 35 rights before the infringements take place and to undertake this justification through a process jointly established by Indigenous peoples and the Crown. In other words, to the extent that article 46(2) provides for the possibility of justifying limits on the rights set out in UNDRIP, that justification must be provided in accordance with, among other things, the process required by article 27.

In the sections below, I first explain in greater detail the issue raised by article 46(2) in light of the section 35 framework as it currently exists in Canadian law. I then propose steps that the courts and, in broad strokes, Parliament and provincial legislatures could take toward implementing article 27 in a way that builds on existing Canadian law, while nonetheless transforming the current approach to justifying the infringements of rights under section 35.

Article 46(2) and the Current Justification Analysis under Section 35

Article 46(2) reads in part: "The exercise of the rights set forth in this Declaration shall be subject only to such limitations as are determined by law and in accordance with international human rights obligations. Any such limitations shall be non-discriminatory and strictly necessary solely for the purpose of securing due recognition and respect for the rights and freedoms of others and for meeting the just and most compelling requirements of a democratic society."[6]

6 *UNDRIP*, *supra* note 1, art 46(2).

The language of article 46(2) echoes section 1 of the Canadian Charter of Rights and Freedoms, which allows for "reasonable limits" on Charter rights and freedoms so long as these limits are "prescribed by law [and] can be demonstrably justified in a free and democratic society."[7] Section 1 does not apply directly to section 35, which is not part of the Charter. However, the Supreme Court of Canada (SCC) has held that a justification analysis, similar to that carried out under section 1, applies to section 35 and affords the Crown the opportunity to justify actions it takes that infringe section 35 rights. The court has interpreted this section 1 type analysis to impose a form of minimal impairment/proportionality test on infringements of section 35 rights, in accordance with which the Crown may justify infringements and potential adverse impacts of Crown action on section 35 rights.[8]

The concern I wish to highlight here with respect to article 46(2) of UNDRIP is that, whatever the substantive interpretation of terms such as "free, prior and informed consent" in other provisions of the declaration, article 46(2) opens the door to a line of argument that would replicate the current section 35 framework of "justified infringements." A great deal of commentary on UNDRIP focuses on the meaning of consent; equally important, however, is the process for resolving disagreements between the state and Indigenous peoples about any purported justification for infringing their rights. These "procedural"[9] aspects of any rights to free, prior and informed consent do not get the attention that their practical importance merits.

The most significant practical limitation on section 35 rights flowing from the court's imposition of a section 1 style justification test is the following "procedural" reality: in any given case where section 35 rights holders and the Crown disagree as to whether the Crown has fulfilled its constitutional obligations such that it can justify any infringements/adverse impacts on the rights in question, the Crown is allowed to act in the face of this disagreement. As a consequence, the section 35 rights holders carry the burden of bringing the matter to court if they wish to challenge the legality of the Crown's actions.

---

7 *Canadian Charter of Rights and Freedoms*, Part I of the *Constitution Act, 1982*, being Schedule B to the *Canada Act 1982* (UK), 1982, s 1. Section 1 of the Charter reads: "The *Canadian Charter of Rights and Freedoms* guarantees the rights and freedoms set out in it subject only to such reasonable limits prescribed by law as can be demonstrably justified in a free and democratic society." It is worth noting that, where section 1 of the Charter requires that "reasonable limits [be] prescribed by law," article 46(2) of UNDRIP requires that "limitations [be] determined by law *and in accordance with international human rights obligations*" [emphasis added]. However, the SCC has adopted the "interpretive presumption" that "the *Charter* be presumed to provide at least as great a level of protection as is found in Canada's international human rights obligations"; see *Ktunaxa Nation v British Columbia (Forests, Lands and Natural Resource Operations)*, 2017 SCC 54, [2017] 2 SCR 386 at para 65. This suggests that section 1, like article 46(2), cannot be used to justify limits on rights if those limits are not in accordance with Canada's international human rights obligations. While this chapter will not address the issue any further, the intent is not to discount the possibility that the explicit reference to international human rights obligations in article 46(2) might prove significant in protecting Declaration rights in certain contexts, notably where section 35 rights are not engaged.

8 See e.g. *R v Sparrow*, [1990] 1 SCR 1075 at 1109; *Tsilhqot'in Nation v British Columbia*, 2014 SCC 44, [2014] 2 SCR 256 [*Tsilhqot'in Nation*] at paras 76–88. There is a good deal of uncertainty in the case law as to what qualifies as an infringement, as opposed to a potential adverse impact, on a section 35 right. Arguably, the case law holds that an infringement triggers Crown fiduciary obligations, while a potential adverse impact triggers the Crown duty to consult. Certainly, different legal consequences may flow from a court concluding that the Crown has infringed section 35 rights, as opposed to potentially adversely impacting them. See, for instance, discussion of the different legal consequences throughout *Mikisew Cree First Nation v Canada (Governor General in Council)*, 2018 SCC 40. However, to repeat, the line between what constitutes an infringement and an adverse impact is not particularly clear. For the purposes of this chapter, I will consider together both infringements and potential adverse impacts.

9 I place quotation marks around "procedural" here because the process for resolving disputes over the justifiability of infringements on rights plays a central role in determining the substantive scope of those rights; the substance of the rights cannot be disentangled from the process established for justifying limits on them.

This feature of the existing section 35 framework contributes greatly to the bargaining imbalance between the Crown and Indigenous nations, and, thus, also to the vulnerability of section 35 rights. The Crown often proposes actions that may infringe or adversely impact Aboriginal or treaty rights. Very commonly, such actions involve economic development in the form of resource extraction or related activities, for example, permits related to mining, oil and gas resources, timber, hydroelectric dams, construction of roads and railways, and so forth. Often the rights holders and the Crown disagree as to whether the proposed infringements or potential adverse impacts violate the Crown's constitutional obligations under section 35.

Under current Canadian law, the Crown has the power to act unilaterally in the face of such disagreement, subject only to subsequent review by the courts if the rights holders (or other interested parties) have the time, resources and willingness to bring the dispute before the courts. Prior to pursuing its proposed course of action, the Crown is under no legal obligation to satisfy any person, tribunal, court, or entity other than itself that it has fulfilled the constitutional obligations it owes to the rights holders whose Aboriginal or treaty rights will be infringed or adversely affected.

To be clear, the Crown has various legal obligations under section 35 to consult, accommodate and otherwise engage Aboriginal and treaty rights holders prior to taking a course of action that may infringe or adversely impact their rights. The issue addressed here is that once the Crown satisfies *itself* that it has fulfilled these obligations, the Crown faces no legal barrier to pursuing its preferred course of action. If the rights holders (or any other interested parties) disagree with the Crown's self-assessment, the burden is on them to bring a legal challenge. As explained below, this procedural burden applies to all section 35 rights, including established Aboriginal title.

The fact that the Crown may act in the face of disagreement over fulfillment of its constitutional obligations places a heavy burden on rights holders who believe the Crown has violated constitutional obligations it owes them in respect of those rights. This is especially true in the case of Indigenous peoples who hold rights over land that the Crown has targeted for economic development. In such cases, a First Nation might receive a steady stream of "referrals" from the Crown approving various forms of industrial activity affecting its territory and section 35 rights. If the First Nation believes that the Crown is failing to live up to its constitutional obligations in approving these projects, its legal options and bargaining power are severely constrained by the fact that it, rather than the Crown, carries the burden of bringing the matter to court, case by case, if it wishes to have the issue adjudicated by a body whose authority the Crown recognizes.

In practical terms, then, even established section 35 rights may be severely eroded over time, as economic development projects chip away at the meaningful exercise of such rights.[10] (At the same time, a dense body of case law has now developed that provides tools for groups that do have the time and resources to challenge project approvals to block, or significantly delay, proposed projects *subsequent* to various forms of Crown approval. Thus, in many "high-

10 To take just one example recently highlighted in the media, the Blueberry River First Nation argues that exercise of its treaty rights has been irreparably harmed by extensive economic development on its territory. According to a 2016 report, across 73 percent of the nation's territory, any given location is within 250 metres of an industrial disturbance; see Yvette Brend, "Collision between Indigenous hunting and oil development rights set for legal showdown in B.C. court", *CBC News* (10 June 2017), online: <www.cbc.ca/news/canada/british-columbia/bc-treaty-rights-law-blueberry-river-first-nation-oil-and-gas-development-court-1.4151779>.

profile projects" in which parties with considerable resources take interest on all sides, costly and lengthy litigation is to be expected within the current section 35 framework. The situation in such cases is thus far from ideal for all parties involved — Indigenous nations, the Crown and industry proponents.)

The Proposal

Canada's commitment to fully implementing UNDRIP provides a chance to reconsider the power of the Crown to act unilaterally in the face of disagreement as to whether it has, in any given situation, fulfilled its constitutional obligations under section 35. This chapter proposes one modest, but important, step that is already implicit, if not fully stated, in the SCC's existing case law.

The proposal is that, where the Crown wishes to pursue a course of action that may infringe or adversely impact Aboriginal or treaty rights, and the rights holders dispute the Crown's self-assessment that it has fulfilled its constitutional obligations, the Crown should not be permitted to pursue its preferred course of action prior to resolution of the disagreement.

This proposal does not amount to giving the rights holders a "veto" over project approval. Indeed, it likely does not even go so far as to fully implement the free, prior, and informed consent standard set in several provisions of UNDRIP. (As explained below, it would, however, be a step in that direction and might open a path toward full implementation.) Rather, this proposal would simply see the burden shift to the Crown *either* to secure the actual consent of rights holders *or* to establish — *prior* to pursuing its proposed course of action — that it has fulfilled its constitutional obligations.

This proposal fits comfortably with — indeed, would bring greater coherence to — the SCC's landmark (and unanimous) rulings in *Haida Nation* and *Tsilhqot'in Nation*. In *Haida Nation*, the court stressed that in the case of *claimed but unproven* section 35 rights, the Crown could act in the face of disagreement as to whether it had fulfilled its duty of consultation and accommodation relating to proposed action that could adversely impact those asserted rights.[11] The court's statements, arguably, implied that the Crown would *not* have this power to act unilaterally in the case of *established* section 35 rights. In *Tsilhqot'in Nation*, the court went further in stressing that the Crown's obligations were distinct in cases of established rights from those that applied in cases of asserted but unproven rights. Yet the court refrained from explicitly prohibiting the Crown from acting unilaterally in the face of disagreement in cases of established rights. In particular, the court stated the following:

> At the claims stage, prior to establishment of Aboriginal title, the Crown owes a good faith duty to consult with the group concerned and, if appropriate, accommodate its interests. As the claim strength increases, the required level of consultation and accommodation correspondingly increases. Where a claim is particularly strong — for example, shortly before a court declaration of title — appropriate care must be taken

11 *Haida Nation v British Columbia (Minister of Forests)*, 2004 SCC 73, [2004] 3 SCR 511 [*Haida Nation*] at para 45. Focusing on rights claims that had yet to be settled, the court stated: "Pending settlement, the Crown is bound by its honour to balance societal and Aboriginal interests in making decisions that may affect Aboriginal claims. The Crown may be required to make decisions in the face of disagreement as to the adequacy of its response to Aboriginal concerns."

> to preserve the Aboriginal interest pending final resolution of the claim. *Finally, once title is established, the Crown cannot proceed with development of title land not consented to by the title-holding group unless it has discharged its duty to consult and the development is justified pursuant s. 35 of the Constitution Act, 1982.*[12]

The court's reasons in *Tsilhqot'in Nation* leave entirely unaddressed the crucial procedural point highlighted in the present policy proposal: the Crown remains free to act in the face of disagreement as to whether it has, in fact, discharged its duty to consult and can justify its proposed course of action. In the face of disagreement, the Crown may consider its proposed course of conduct justified and, with this self-assessment in hand, choose to pursue that course of conduct. The Aboriginal title holders are left with the burden of bringing the matter to court if they have the time, resources and willingness to do so.

It is unfortunate that the court has not explicitly addressed this important procedural issue in the case of established Aboriginal title and established section 35 rights more generally. The court's own distinctions between the nature of asserted and established rights, respectively, suggest that the Crown should not enjoy the same unilateral power to act in the case of established rights. The proposal made here would simply take the modest step of drawing out a conclusion that is, arguably, already implicit in the court's existing case law, and place the burden on the Crown to justify proposed action that would infringe established section 35 rights *before* the Crown is allowed to pursue that action. The courts could impose this requirement today as an incremental development of the interpretation of section 35.[13]

Of course, if the courts alone were to take this incremental step, they would remain the forum in which purported justifications of infringements of section 35 rights are adjudicated. The difference would be that the Crown would bear the burden of going to court when faced with a dispute as to whether it can justify proposed infringements of section 35 rights. The Crown would have to seek court approval for the infringements it proposes, rather than leaving the burden on rights holders to seek court disapproval of such infringements. That might not sound like much. After all, if Canada is truly committed to nation-with-nation relationships with Indigenous peoples and to upholding treaties it has concluded with them, it seems absurd (if taking a step back to look at the situation) that one party to a treaty can unilaterally propose to infringe the promises it made in the treaty and to have the question of justification adjudicated in its own courts. Although an incremental and rational step, simply shifting the burden to the Crown to have the question of justification adjudicated prior to infringement might bring substantially greater balance to bargaining power in the context of consultation and negotiations between Indigenous peoples and the Crown.

It might be objected that, if the courts adopted the incremental step proposed here, the result might well be an enormous backlog in the courts. Every permit issued by the Crown for industrial activity on Aboriginal title land, and many, if not most, such permits issued on treaty land, would require either Indigenous consent or adjudicating the disputed justifiability

12 *Tsilhqot'in Nation, supra* note 8 at para 91 [emphasis added].

13 Precisely this issue will likely be put to the British Columbia Supreme Court in the Blueberry River First Nation case on the cumulative effect of treaty infringements, if the case proceeds to trial (see Brend, *supra* note 10).

of the proposed infringement before any activity could be undertaken pursuant to the permit.[14] There can be no denying or minimizing the enormity of the disputes between the Crown and Indigenous peoples over the use of, and control over, lands and natural resources. That harsh reality belongs to the legacy and ongoing nature of colonialism. As explained above, the current procedural framework for adjudicating the justifiability of infringements on section 35 rights places a tremendous burden on section 35 rights holders themselves, by allowing the Crown to act in the face of disagreements about the justifiability of proposed Crown action. To the extent the policy proposal made here would create any backlog in the courts, the result would be to make that burden visible and put pressure on federal and provincial governments to work with Indigenous peoples to develop more balanced and collaborative solutions.

The most effective path forward would be for Parliament and the provincial legislatures to develop a legislative framework (either of their own initiative, or in response to further judicial elaboration of section 35 along the lines noted above) for the resolution of Indigenous-Crown disagreements over the justifiability of proposed infringements. The legislative framework should allow for some forum or body composed of both Indigenous and Crown representation to resolve, negotiate, or, if necessary, adjudicate the justifiability of proposed infringements before the Crown is allowed to undertake any infringing action. Perhaps, as discussed below, existing co-management boards could provide an institutional foundation around which to build or design these independent bodies. Naturally, there are many details to consider; these details will matter a great deal and require a certain amount of flexibility and experimentation. The essential point of this policy proposal is that the Crown must be required to go through some such independent body *prior* to pursuing any course of action that would infringe section 35 rights against the wishes of the rights holders.

Moreover, this is a step called for in article 27 of UNDRIP: "States shall establish and implement, in conjunction with indigenous peoples concerned, a fair, independent, impartial, open and transparent process, giving due recognition to indigenous peoples' laws, traditions, customs and land tenure systems, to recognize and adjudicate the rights of indigenous peoples pertaining to their lands, territories and resources, including those which were traditionally owned or otherwise occupied or used. Indigenous peoples shall have the right to participate in this process."

Article 27 requires the Crown to work with Indigenous peoples to establish a process, as described in that article, that could take the institutional form of co-management fora, reconciliation tables, independent tribunals or some other body composed of both Indigenous and Crown representatives empowered to resolve cases of disagreement between section 35 rights holders and the Crown relating to proposed activity that could infringe or adversely impact section 35 rights. For ease of reference, I refer to these proposed bodies simply as "co-management fora."

14 Disputes would surely arise as to whether certain Crown actions even engaged section 35 rights and, therefore, whether there was any infringement needing to be justified. However, those kinds of disputes already arise in the context, for instance, of determining whether a given Crown action triggers a duty to consult. The courts are already developing case law around such questions, and I do not address them any further.

These co-management fora[15] could allow for the interpretation and application of different bodies of law — Indigenous legal traditions, federal and provincial law, and international law, including UNDRIP itself. Establishing these fora within the existing Canadian constitutional framework would require some attention, notably to issues of superior court jurisdiction under section 96 of the Constitution Act, 1867. However, these issues seem inherently manageable.

These co-management fora could also begin to flesh out principles already announced in the section 35 case law, in particular decisions of the SCC, in accordance with both Indigenous legal systems and federal and provincial laws. For instance, in *Tsilhqot'in Nation*, the SCC explained that both Aboriginal title holders and the Crown have an obligation to sustainably manage land held under Aboriginal title.[16] This sustainability principle ought to be developed in accordance with both Indigenous legal orders and federal and provincial law; perhaps it could help form a basis for rethinking the Indigenous-Crown fiduciary relationship along the lines of an equal partnership, rather than on the outdated and offensive model of a guardian-ward relationship.

If article 27 were implemented along the broad lines proposed here, the resulting co-management fora could also play a crucial institutional role in implementing other articles contained in UNDRIP. Most obviously, these co-management fora could be the institutional locus of discussion, negotiation and, if necessary, adjudication of issues relating to articles 26 and 28 to 32, which spell out principal protections for Indigenous lands and resources, including, for example, that "Indigenous peoples have the right to determine and develop priorities and strategies for the development or use of their lands or territories and other resources."[17] Clearly, such co-management fora would also provide an appropriate institutional setting to implement article 37, including "the right to the recognition, observance and enforcement of treaties, agreements and other constructive arrangements."[18]

Finally, implementation of article 27 along the lines proposed here would also support Indigenous involvement in decisions that affect them and their territories and resources, helping to fulfill rights of self-determination, autonomy and self-government, as provided in articles 3, 4, 18, 23, 38 and 40.

---

15 Note that in two recent cases, the Supreme Court of Canada held that an "independent regulatory agency" such as the National Energy Board (NEB) is empowered to carry out the Crown duty of consultation owed to Indigenous peoples under section 35, and to then make a determination as to whether the Crown has fulfilled its duty of consultation; see *Clyde River (Hamlet) v Petroleum Geo-Services Inc*, 2017 SCC 40 [*Clyde River*]; *Chippewas of the Thames First Nation v Enbridge Pipelines Inc*, 2017 SCC 41 [*Chippewas*]. Unfortunately, the result of *Clyde River* and *Chippewas* is, for all practical purposes, that the Crown (in the form of the NEB) still needs only to satisfy *itself* that it has fulfilled its constitutional obligations before pursuing its proposed course of action. In this respect, *Clyde River* and *Chippewas* simply entrench the Crown's self-assessment problem identified in this chapter — a situation that is inconsistent with the letter and spirit of UNDRIP and the proposal offered here. The independent bodies (for example, co-management fora recommended in this chapter) must be independent in more than name only if they are to contribute meaningfully to healthier Indigenous-Crown relations.

16 *Tsilhqot'in Nation*, *supra* note 8 at paras 86, 105, 121.

17 *UNDRIP*, *supra* note 1, art 32(1).

18 *Ibid*, art 37(1).

Conclusion

In sum, proper implementation of article 27 of UNDRIP has the potential to serve as a linchpin for successful implementation of a significant portion of the declaration. As explained above, the proper implementation of article 27 is particularly important in light of the concern that article 46(2) might suggest a basis for maintaining the procedural status quo in assessing the justifiability of infringements of section 35 rights. Article 27 establishes important conditions on the process that must be followed in adjudicating or otherwise resolving Crown claims that it can justify proposed infringements. These conditions are inconsistent with the current state of Canadian law, for the reasons spelled out in this chapter. Thus, proper regard for article 27 should pre-empt any argument that article 46(2) renders Canada's existing section 35 framework consistent with UNDRIP as a whole.

Fortunately, Canadian law as it currently exists already offers a bridge toward implementing article 27. Incremental development of the existing section 35 framework could shift the burden to the Crown to seek judicial approval of its proposed infringements on established section 35 rights *before* it proceeds with any action that will cause such infringements. The courts could move the case law forward in this direction by drawing on existing precedent, as explained above. Building on such a step (or, preferably, without waiting for such prompting by the courts), federal and provincial governments in dialogue and partnership with Indigenous peoples could, in accordance with the requirements of article 27, establish co-management fora to resolve disputes relating to infringements of section 35 rights. It is hard to see how any path to genuine nation-with-nation treaty relationships can avoid this relatively modest, yet significant, step.

18

Strategizing UNDRIP Implementation: Some Fundamentals

Kerry Wilkins

If it is to fulfill its stated objectives, the United Nations Declaration on the Rights of Indigenous Peoples (UNDRIP)[1] must govern, in some meaningful way, relations between Indigenous peoples and Canada's federal, provincial and territorial governments. The rights and obligations it articulates need to be enforceable. This is a task for domestic Canadian law. UNDRIP itself vests no international forum with jurisdiction to adjudicate states parties' infringements of it. Instead, it instructs participating states to provide for its enforcement.[2]

In Canada, international instruments such as UNDRIP are not self-executing. The Government of Canada describes UNDRIP as a political commitment, not legally binding.[3] And the Supreme Court of Canada (SCC) has held repeatedly that international instruments have no domestic legal effect except pursuant to competent domestic legislation[4] (or, most probably, valid treaties

1 *United Nations Declaration on the Rights of Indigenous Peoples*, GA Res 295, UNGAOR, 61st Sess, Supp No 49, UN Doc A/RES/61/295, 46 ILM 1013 (2007) [*UNDRIP*].

2 *Ibid*, arts 27, 38, 40.

3 Indigenous and Northern Affairs Canada, "United Nations Declaration on the Rights of Indigenous Peoples", online: <www.aadnc-aandc.gc.ca/eng/1309374407406/1309374458958>.

4 *Baker v Canada (Minister of Citizenship and Immigration)*, [1999] 2 SCR 817 at paras 69, 79 [*Baker*]; *Capital Cities Communications Inc v Canadian Radio-Television Commission*, [1978] 2 SCR 141 at 172–73; *Francis v The Queen*, [1956] SCR 618 at 621.

made with Indigenous peoples).[5] This means, in brief, that UNDRIP will be enforceable against the Crown in Canada only if, and only when, the Crown and/or relevant legislative bodies agree — by statute, by treaty or conceivably by constitutional amendment — to be bound by it. In the meantime, UNDRIP can, at most, influence judicial interpretation of some domestic legislation.[6]

The federal government has expressed unqualified public support for UNDRIP; it intends, it says, "nothing less than to adopt and implement the declaration in accordance with the Canadian Constitution."[7] This is welcome news. To date, however, the federal government's public efforts at implementation consist entirely of government caucus support for a private member's bill about UNDRIP,[8] which received third reading in the House of Commons on May 30, 2018,[9] and first reading in the Senate the next day.[10] The bill, if it becomes law, will affirm UNDRIP "as a universal international human rights instrument with application in Canadian law" (section 3), will commit the federal government, "in consultation and cooperation with indigenous peoples," to taking "all measures necessary to ensure that the laws of Canada are consistent with" UNDRIP (section 4) and to developing and implementing "a national action plan to achieve the objectives of" UNDRIP (section 5), and will require the relevant federal minister to report to Parliament annually until 2037 on the implementation of these measures (section 6). These provisions contemplate, and arguably obligate, eventual federal implementation of UNDRIP,[11] but even the bill's proponents do not suggest that it would suffice alone, if enacted, to render UNDRIP's provisions enforceable.[12]

UNDRIP, therefore, still awaits implementation in Canada. Successful implementation is by no means assured; the political risks for Crown and Indigenous leaders alike are extremely high. For the Justin Trudeau Liberals, UNDRIP implementation is a legacy initiative, undertaken not for the short-term political gain, but because it is "the right thing to do." It is at least as likely to

5 The *Constitution Act, 1982*, being Schedule B to the *Canada Act 1982* (UK) (1982), c 11, which is "the supreme law of Canada" (s 52(1)), recognizes and affirms the "existing...treaty rights of the aboriginal peoples of Canada" (s 35(1)), including such "rights that now exist by way of land claims agreements or may be so acquired" (s 35(3)).

6 Other things being equal, courts are to assume that domestic legislation is meant to be consistent with recognized international norms: *114957 Canada Ltée (Spraytech, Société d'Arrosage) v Hudson (Town)*, 2001 SCC 40 at para 30, [2001] 2 SCR 241; *Baker, supra* note 4 at paras 70–71; *R v Hape*, 2007 SCC 26 at para 53, [2007] 2 SCR 292.

7 Minister of Indigenous and Northern Affairs Carolyn Bennett, "Announcement of Canada's Support for the United Nations Declaration on the Rights of Indigenous Peoples" (Statement delivered at the 15th Session of the United Nations Permanent Forum on Indigenous Issues, 10 May 2016).

8 Bill C-262, *An Act to ensure that the laws of Canada are in harmony with the United Nations Declaration on the Rights of Indigenous Peoples*, 1st Sess, 42nd Parl, 2016 (as passed by the House of Commons 30 May 2018), online: <www.parl.ca/DocumentViewer/en/42-1/bill/C-262/third-reading>.

9 *House of Commons Debates*, 42nd Parl, 1st Sess, No 304 (30 May 2018) at 1555, online: <www.ourcommons.ca/DocumentViewer/en/42-1/house/sitting-304/hansard>. Liberal, NDP and Green members of Parliament supported the motion; Conservative members of Parliament opposed.

10 See *Debates of the Senate*, 42nd Parl, 1st Sess, No 212 (31 May 2018), online: <https://sencanada.ca/en/content/sen/chamber/421/debates/212db_2018-05-31-e?language=e#37>.

11 This said, it is far from clear to what extent these obligations would be enforceable or, if they were, what the remedy for their breach would be.

12 In the second reading debate on Bill C-262, neither its sponsor, Romeo Saganash (NDP, Abitibi–Baie-James–Nunavik–Eeyou), nor the Liberal Party respondent, Yvonne Jones (Labrador, Parliamentary Secretary to the Minister of Indigenous and Northern Affairs), characterized the bill as achieving domestic implementation of UNDRIP; see *House of Commons Debates*, 42nd Parl, 1st Sess, No 245 (5 December 2017) at 1745–1815, online: <www.ourcommons.ca/DocumentViewer/en/42-1/house/sitting-245/hansard#9866873>; *House of Commons Debates*, 42nd Parl, 1st Sess, No 245 (5 December 2017) at 1805–15, online: <www.ourcommons.ca/DocumentViewer/en/42-1/house/sitting-245/hansard#9866993>, respectively. According to Jones, in fact, the shift to full UNDRIP implementation "cannot be achieved through just one piece of legislation alone" (*ibid* at 1810).

cost the Liberals votes and campaign contributions in forthcoming elections as to yield them.[13] And the government knows that. UNDRIP implementation will entail substantial change to the conduct of mainstream governance and of business, especially in the energy and resource sectors. Change on this scale is not, as a general rule, welcome in mainstream experience. From the federal government perspective, therefore, it will seem imperative that UNDRIP implementation proceed in a smooth and orderly way, that it improve Indigenous peoples' lives without unduly inconveniencing non-Indigenous peoples, that it trigger no unpleasant surprises and, not least, that it not cost too much. The federal government will want certainty about what will happen after implementation and will want to avoid outcomes that cause alarm. There is always a risk that the government will conclude, perhaps with real regret, that UNDRIP implementation (like electoral reform?)[14] is just too arduous or too expensive to achieve, at least within a foreseeable period.

For Indigenous peoples to whom UNDRIP implementation matters, the stakes are similarly high. In the best case, they will have one real chance to render UNDRIP meaningfully enforceable against the Crown. It is extremely important that implementation achieve the results Indigenous peoples require of it; they will have to live for quite some time in the world that UNDRIP implementation creates. But from a strategic standpoint, it is no less important that Indigenous peoples do what they can to deprive the federal government of excuses to delay or abandon the implementation effort.

This chapter discusses, from the perspective of mainstream Canadian law, what needs to happen for UNDRIP to become an enforceable part of that law, binding on the Crown. (I have neither permission nor sufficient expertise to discuss UNDRIP from within Indigenous law.) The chapter identifies four questions on whose resolution, at a minimum, successful UNDRIP implementation (as mainstream law) will depend: specifying the Indigenous peoples to whom, and the lands and waters to which, UNDRIP, once in force, would apply; choosing among imperfect available implementation mechanisms; and clarifying the Crown's post-implementation responsibilities. Fresh, constructive Indigenous engagement with these questions may very well be a prerequisite to success.[15]

13 In a recent Angus Reid poll, only 34 percent of Canadians surveyed said that Indigenous communities should be "[m]oving toward more independence and control of their own affairs." Sixty-six percent said they should be "[g]overned by the same systems and rules as other Canadians." Fifty-three percent of those surveyed said that Indigenous peoples should have no special status that other Canadians do not have: Aaron Hutchins, "First Nations: New Solitudes", *Maclean's* (1 July 2018) 28 at 29, 31.

14 See e.g. Laura Stone, "Trudeau abandons electoral reform, breaking key campaign promise", *The Globe and Mail* (1 February 2017), online: <www.theglobeandmail.com/news/politics/trudeau-abandons-electoral-reform/article33855925/>.

15 It will not suffice for this purpose simply to point at the excellent work already done — by the Royal Commission on Aboriginal Peoples (RCAP) and the Truth and Reconciliation Commission (TRC), for instance — in documenting the plight of Indigenous peoples in (what is now) Canada and calling for appropriate change. Those studies were not undertaken with UNDRIP implementation in mind and do not purport to represent the views of any particular Indigenous constituencies. It would be perfectly appropriate for Indigenous peoples wishing to do so to endorse and present as their own the relevant RCAP recommendations or TRC Calls to Action, but it would not do for Canada just to assume, in the absence of some such endorsement, that the RCAP or TRC proposals, developed at a different time and for a somewhat different purpose, were definitive answers to the relevant questions. Federal assumptions about Indigenous peoples have not, as a general rule, been sound.

The Who

Apart from articles 6, 22 and 43, which speak only of "indigenous individuals," and articles 41, 42 and 46, which are institutional and procedural, every UNDRIP provision articulates rights of, or states' obligations to, "indigenous peoples." Nowhere, though, does UNDRIP tell us what makes "indigenous peoples" Indigenous, or what makes them "peoples."[16] Answering these questions — identifying the bearers of these rights and the beneficiaries of these obligations — is a crucial early step in UNDRIP implementation. Overlooking them invites inconvenient dispute and unpleasant surprise.

Given Canada's recent setbacks with the Indian status rules,[17] it might very well be pleased to get out of the business of deciding — or, at least, deciding unilaterally — who counts as an Indian or what makes someone Indigenous, as long as Canada is not held responsible for what happens when Indigenous peoples make those determinations themselves.[18] The more difficult issue will be how — and at what level of generality — to individuate Indigenous "peoples"[19]: the nominate bearers of the UNDRIP rights. No sensible mainstream government would implement UNDRIP without prior identification of the entities deemed to have the right of self-determination (UNDRIP, article 3), whose "free, prior and informed consent" would have to precede "adopting and implementing legislative or administrative measures that may affect them" (article 19), placing hazardous materials on their lands or territories (article 29(2)) or approving "any project affecting their lands or territories and other resources" (article 32(2)).

This issue of denomination has significant operational implications. The proliferation of federally constituted "bands" that has suited Canada for decades might well not seem so suitable within a regime that assures Indigenous peoples of robust rights of informed consent and self-determination. Mainstream politicians and bureaucrats already find burdensome the transaction costs incurred in resolving issues of jurisdiction, financial transfers and essential service provision with a single federal entity and 13 provincial and territorial governments. Including more than 600 self-determining reserve communities and several more Métis and Inuit groups would increase the shared administrative inconvenience exponentially. Canada, therefore, might very well welcome, post-UNDRIP, adoption of something like the RCAP's recommendation that it acknowledge rights of self-determination in somewhere between 50 and (not more than) 80

16 Given the diversity of Indigenous peoples throughout the world, and the variety of the circumstances in which they find themselves (see *UNDRIP*, *supra* note 1, Preamble, recital 23), such silence is understandable.

17 *McIvor v Canada (Registrar of Indian and Northern Affairs)*, 2009 BCCA 153, 91 BCLR (4th) 1 and *Descheneaux c Canada (Procureur général)*, 2015 QCCS 3555, [2016] 2 CNLR 175 each required amendments to the status and band membership rules in the *Indian Act*, RSC 1985, c I-5, ss 6, 11 to correct for unjustified gender discrimination, contrary to section 15 of the *Canadian Charter of Rights and Freedoms*, Part I of the *Constitution Act, 1982* (*supra* note 5) [*Charter*]. Those amendments — *Gender Equity in Indian Registration Act*, SC 2010, c 18, ss 2–3 and *An Act to amend the Indian Act in response to the Superior Court of Quebec decision in Descheneaux c Canada (Procureur général)*, SC 2017, c 25, ss 1–3 [*An Act to Amend the Indian Act*] — have made those schemes almost impenetrably complicated, sufficiently so that the 2017 statute requires the federal government to consult First Nations and interested others about, among other things, "the continued federal government role in determining Indian status and band membership" (*An Act to Amend the Indian Act*, s 11(1)(f)).

18 See generally the section in this chapter titled "And Then What?"

19 In *Reference re Secession of Quebec*, [1998] 2 SCR 217, the SCC acknowledged that "the precise meaning of the term 'people' remains somewhat uncertain" in international law (at para 123). It added "that 'a people' may include only the portion of the population of an existing state" (at para 124): that "the reference to 'people' does not necessarily mean the entirety of a state's population," but declined to be more specific, or even to opine on whether the people of Quebec comprise a "people" (at para 125).

Indigenous nations,[20] or even Roger Gibbins' suggestion, several years earlier, that "[a]t the very least we are talking about a province-wide Indian government, one that would have the power to enforce its decisions with respect to its constituent bands or communities."[21]

Even so, credible instruction on this issue can come only from the Indigenous side. Such expertise as there is about the constitution, recognition and denomination of discrete Indigenous peoples resides where it always has, with Indigenous Elders and leaders. It would be both utterly inconsistent with the spirit of UNDRIP and colossally stupid for Canada now to presume once again — as it has so often — to decide unilaterally how to denominate Indigenous peoples.

This leaves Indigenous peoples with the challenging task of deciding how to reconstitute themselves after generations of unfortunate colonial fragmentation. It is a task fraught with political consequence, but there is no obvious, credible alternative. The most that mainstream governments can contribute to this process is sufficient financial support to sustain it and sufficient patience to await its outcome.[22] One excellent way of testing Canada's seriousness about UNDRIP implementation would be to present the federal government with a carefully considered proposal (from a sufficiently representative group of First Nation, non-status, Métis and Inuit peoples) seeking sufficient funding to undertake and complete this surpassingly difficult work within a finite but reasonable time.

The Where

No fewer than nine UNDRIP articles concern rights that relate to Indigenous peoples' lands, waters, territories or resources.[23] Such rights, once fully in force, will exist throughout the whole of Canada. Their successful implementation, however, will require identification and attribution of the territories to which they pertain and those territories' locations. Prudent mainstream governments seem unlikely to agree to the rigours of the UNDRIP territorial rights regime without first knowing, or knowing how to ascertain for UNDRIP purposes, which lands, waters and resources are or were traditionally whose. These are not matters about which the Crown has any business making assumptions or guessing, let alone deciding unilaterally. The stakes, for everyone, are simply too high. Treaties, existing comprehensive and treaty land entitlement claims and even some judicial decisions may offer helpful clues in mapping traditional Indigenous territories, but they each occurred at a different time for a purpose different from that of UNDRIP implementation, and they may or may not align with the collectives demarcated for UNDRIP purposes as Indigenous peoples.

20 RCAP, *Report of the Royal Commission on Aboriginal Peoples, Volume 2: Restructuring the Relationship* (Ottawa: Supply and Services, 1996) at 177–84. According to the RCAP, eligibility to exercise self-determination rights should require, first, a shared sense of collective identity; second, sufficient critical mass to assume the powers and responsibilities that self-determination entails; and, third, a territorial base on which it comprises the predominant population.

21 Roger Gibbins, "Citizenship, Political and Intergovernmental Problems with Indian Self-Government" in J Rick Ponting, ed, *Arduous Journey: Canadian Indians and Decolonization* (Toronto: McClelland and Stewart, 1986) 369 at 372.

22 The RCAP, for example, recommended that the "federal government put in place a neutral and transparent process for identifying Aboriginal groups entitled to exercise the right of self-determination as nations": RCAP, *supra* note 20 at 184.

23 *UNDRIP*, *supra* note 1, arts 8(2)(b) (right to redress for dispossession), 10 (protection against involuntary relocation), 25 (right to maintain and strengthen spiritual and stewardship relationship with traditional lands and waters), 26 (right to state recognition of traditional lands, territories and resources), 27 ("fair, independent, impartial, open and transparent process" to adjudicate Indigenous territorial rights), 28 (right to restitution or compensation for lands taken, used or damaged without consent), 29 (right to environmental protection and conservation), 30 (protecting traditional lands from military activities), 32(2) (protection from development or resource exploitation without Indigenous consent).

It would be sound strategy, therefore, for Indigenous peoples to take the lead on the crucial issue of territorial identification: addressing it transparently, estimating its likely duration and seeking such support with it from the Crown as they may require. Indigenous peoples are the ones best placed to identify their own traditional lands and waters. Theirs are the stories, the oral histories and the traditional and local knowledge constitutive of their relationships with their respective ancestral territories. The proper course for non-Indigenous governments in this conversation is to begin by listening, learning and providing the time and resources required to complete this task.

The results of such activity are almost certain to be controversial. Some lands and waters may lie within the traditional territories of more than one Indigenous people,[24] requiring governments, under UNDRIP, to obtain required consents from each. Complications could ensue.[25] More frequent, and more difficult, will be contestation about the relative merits of competing non-Indigenous claims to some of those same territories and resources, including, probably, claims derived from surrender provisions in English versions of treaties.[26] When such disputes arise, a resolution will, of course, be necessary; UNDRIP article 27 requires that there be an impartial process for adjudicating Indigenous claims to territories. But knowing early in the UNDRIP implementation effort which resources, waters and territories are going to be in play alerts the parties to the locations and the magnitude of the challenges that await and creates space in which to address those challenges thoughtfully and cooperatively. Ignoring the territorial issue is simply not an option.

The How

Since its adoption by the UN General Assembly in 2007, UNDRIP has been available to Indigenous peoples as a source of norms they might use as appropriate, in accordance with their own laws, in their relations with one another. Using UNDRIP themselves is one way Indigenous peoples can demonstrate their commitment to its principles. As discussed above,[27] however, UNDRIP will constrain or compel the conduct of the Crown only if mainstream lawmakers do something to bring it into domestic law. Canada could make that happen unilaterally, but unilateral federal assumptions are, again, unlikely to yield optimal results. Successful UNDRIP implementation requires, among other things, deeper understanding of what Indigenous peoples in present-day Canada require from UNDRIP and what, to them, would count as implementation that binds mainstream governments. To encourage that conversation, this section considers some options relating to the mechanics of UNDRIP implementation.

24 In *Delgamuukw v British Columbia*, [1997] 3 SCR 1010 [*Delgamuukw*], the SCC specifically left room for jointly held Aboriginal title in circumstances where more than one Indigenous community occupied particular lands at the relevant time to the exclusion of all others (at paras 158, Lamer CJC, 196, La Forest J).

25 One recent instance concerned a development proposal for an area in southeastern British Columbia that the Shuswap and the Ktunaxa had each used traditionally. After consultations, the Shuswap agreed to the proposal for the benefits it would bring them; the Ktunaxa opposed it resolutely. See *Ktunaxa Nation v British Columbia (Forest, Lands and Natural Resource Operations)*, 2017 SCC 54, [2017] 2 SCR 386.

26 It is helpful to remember here, first, that provincial grants to settlers of fee simple interests in lands cannot suffice to extinguish Aboriginal title to those lands because the provincial Crown's own interest in those lands is subject to the pre-existing Indigenous interest (*Delgamuukw*, *supra* note 24 at para 175) and, second, that certain UNDRIP rights (those in articles 25 to 28) pertain to territories and resources that Indigenous peoples "have traditionally owned" or occupied, irrespective, apparently, of those territories' current ownership status.

27 See *supra* notes 2–6 and accompanying text.

If a goal is eventual enforceability within domestic Canadian law, at least three issues need attention: the pace and scale of implementation; the means to be used to introduce UNDRIP into Canadian law; and the choice of enforcement mechanism.

Pace and Scale

There are good reasons to consider giving enforceable effect to the whole of UNDRIP throughout Canada all at once. Uniform implementation reduces the risks of inconsistency, strategic behaviour, invidious comparison and unnecessary competition that could beset a phased implementation. But Canada is notoriously diverse, as are Indigenous peoples' predicaments here; postponing domestic reception of UNDRIP until every relevant difference has been acknowledged and accommodated could, in the worst case, closely resemble stalling. In the meantime, UNDRIP would remain, for mainstream governments, at most a political commitment and an interpretive aid for courts to use in construing legislation.[28]

Alternative approaches include: implementing across Canada the UNDRIP provisions that are easiest or most important to implement, then learning from that experience while phasing in implementation of the others; phasing in all or part of UNDRIP community by community, or willing province by willing province (again, potentially, learning as we go); or making UNDRIP's provisions, like some recent federal legislation,[29] available to Indigenous peoples exclusively on an opt-in basis.

Implementation Options

There are three possible ways of giving UNDRIP fully enforceable domestic legal effect: constitutional entrenchment, treaties and legislation.

Constitutional amendment proposals require, at a minimum, approval, within a three-year period, from both houses of Parliament and from the legislatures of seven provinces housing at least 50 percent of Canada's population.[30] Appealing though it may be to consider entrenching UNDRIP's rights and obligations in the Constitution, the likelihood today that any mainstream government would seriously consider proposing such an amendment seems vanishingly small, especially without concerted support from mainstream voters.[31]

Provided that it qualified as a "land claims agreement" under section 35(3) of the Constitution Act, 1982,[32] a treaty with Indigenous peoples implementing UNDRIP would give rise to treaty rights: constitutional rights for the signatory peoples protected under section 35(1)[33] against

28 See *supra* notes 3, 6 and accompanying text.

29 See e.g. *First Nations Land Management Act*, SC 1999, c 24; *First Nations Fiscal Management Act*, SC 2005, c 9.

30 *Constitution Act, 1982*, *supra* note 5, ss 38(1), 39(2).

31 See Hutchins, *supra* note 13.

32 Section 35(1) of the *Constitution Act, 1982*, *supra* note 5, recognizes and affirms only "existing" treaty and Aboriginal rights, that is, those already in existence when section 35 took effect in 1982: *R v Sparrow*, [1990] 1 SCR 1075 at 1091. Section 35(3) creates an exception for rights that "may be so acquired" "by way of land claims agreements." The courts have not yet said what must be true for a post-1982 instrument to qualify as a land claims agreement.

33 Might UNDRIP itself already be a treaty whose rights are entitled, under Canadian law, to this constitutional protection? Under current standards, "what characterizes a treaty is the intention to create obligations, the presence of mutually binding obligations and a certain measure of solemnity" as among the parties to the candidate arrangement: *R v Sioui*, [1990] 1 SCR 1025 at 1044. And because the federal government gave full approval to UNDRIP only after 1982, UNDRIP would also need to qualify as a "land claims agreement" for the purposes of section 35(3): see *supra* note 32.

unjustified federal or provincial infringement,[34] irrespective of whether any province were involved in its negotiation.[35] Treaties could be an attractive option for piecemeal or phased UNDRIP implementation; implementation schedules could be tailored specifically to the circumstances of each party to a given agreement. This, of course, would probably be easiest to achieve in those parts of Canada not already subject to existing treaties that feature contested surrender provisions. Even there, though, modern treaties have typically required years, if not decades, of very expensive negotiations. A nationwide treaty with all Indigenous peoples in Canada is not impossible, but would be unprecedented.[36]

Federal legislation, on the other hand, need not take so long and is typically countrywide in scope. We now know that "all Aboriginal peoples" are "Indians" within federal legislative authority;[37] Parliament, therefore, probably has sufficient constitutional capacity to enact laws implementing UNDRIP nationwide. Even so, there are important constraints.

First, the rights in UNDRIP, if enacted in legislation, will have the force of only statutory, not constitutional, rights. (The Charter of Rights, therefore, will almost certainly apply to the exercise of any authority deemed to derive from such legislation.) As such, they are subject to repeal at any time. And under the usual canons of statutory interpretation, federal (or provincial) legislation that is newer or more specific supersedes, other things being equal,[38] older, generic federal (or provincial) legislation in case of conflict. Even if left unrepealed, therefore, federal legislation incorporating UNDRIP rights could be susceptible to gradual erosion by subsequent conflicting legislation.[39]

Second, federal legislation does not bind the Crown unless it says it does or unless its purpose would be wholly frustrated unless the Crown were bound.[40] Domestic legislation, therefore, may not render UNDRIP's affirmative obligations[41] enforceable unless it says expressly that it binds the federal Crown.

34 See e.g. *R v Badger*, [1996] 1 SCR 771 (justification of federal treaty right infringements); *Grassy Narrows First Nation v Ontario (Natural Resources)*, 2014 SCC 48 at para 53, [2014] 2 SCR 447 [*Grassy Narrows*] (justification of provincial treaty right infringements).

35 *Grassy Narrows*, *supra* note 34 at paras 32–35, 50, 51.

36 Twenty-four different Indigenous nations from several different geographic areas took part in the meetings described as comprising the Treaty of Niagara, 1764, incorporating into a consensual arrangement the relevant provisions of the Royal Proclamation, 1763 and extending the reach of the Two-Row Wampum. See e.g. John Borrows, "Wampum at Niagara: The Royal Proclamation, Canadian Legal History, and Self-Government" in Michael Asch, ed, *Aboriginal and Treaty Rights in Canada: Essays on Law, Equity, and Respect for Difference* (Vancouver: UBC Press, 1997) 155. According to the Ontario Court of Appeal, the Treaty of Niagara "established friendly relations with many First Nations who had supported the French in the previous war. It also gave treaty recognition to the nation-to-nation relationship between the First Nations and the British Crown, Indian rights in their lands and the process to be followed when Indian lands were surrendered": *Chippewas of Sarnia Band v Canada (AG)* (2000), 51 OR (3d) 641 (CA) at para 56. I am not aware of another more inclusive Crown treaty with Indigenous peoples. Treaties with smaller numbers of Indigenous communities located in geographic proximity to one another have been much more common.

37 *Constitution Act, 1867* (UK), 30 & 31 Vict, c 3, reprinted in RSC 1985, Appendix II, No 5, s 91(24); *Daniels v Canada (Indian Affairs and Northern Development)*, 2016 SCC 12 at para 46, [2016] 1 SCR 99.

38 It is possible to draft a statute to give it priority over subsequent conflicting coordinate legislation. According to section 47(2) of the *Ontario Human Rights Code*, RSO 1990, c H 19, for example, "Where a provision in an Act or regulation purports to require or authorize conduct that is a contravention of Part I [of the *Code*], this Act applies and prevails unless the Act or regulation specifically provides that it is to apply despite this Act."

39 If Bill C-262, *supra* note 8, becomes law, it may bind the Government of Canada to harmonize federal laws with UNDRIP (see *supra* notes 8–12 and accompanying text), but it would not bind Parliament.

40 *Interpretation Act*, RSC 1985, c I-21, s 17; *Canada (AG) v Thouin*, 2017 SCC 46 at paras 1, 19–21, [2017] 2 SCR 184.

41 *UNDRIP*, *supra* note 1, arts 8(2), 11(2), 12(2), 13(2), 14(3), 15(2), 16(2), 17(2), 19, 22(2), 26(3), 27, 29(2–3), 30(2), 32(2–3), 36(2), 38, 40.

Finally, one cannot overlook the provinces. Certain matters UNDRIP addresses — labour practices,[42] education,[43] health professions[44] and natural resource extraction[45] among them — are, under Canadian law, presumptively within provincial, not federal, legislative authority.[46] Valid federal legislation can bind provincial Crowns,[47] but unwilling provinces may very well challenge provisions in federal legislation that seem to encroach on exclusively provincial matters. Some provinces may even insist that UNDRIP, which makes no mention of subnational units, has nothing to do with them. Constitutional doctrines exist that could support the federal position in such disputes,[48] but the outcome of litigation is never assured.

Different implementation options, therefore, have different strengths and weaknesses. Understanding these differences will help Indigenous peoples determine and indicate which domestic mechanism would best suit their purposes.

Enforcement

Unless specified otherwise, the task of enforcing UNDRIP's rights or obligations against mainstream governments would fall to Canadian courts. It might very well be impossible (without constitutional amendment) to deprive Canadian courts of supervisory jurisdiction altogether over such enforcement decisions.[49] But there is room at least to consider appropriate alternative forms of dispute resolution, including arrangements that draw on both Indigenous and mainstream authority and expertise. UNDRIP itself expressly requires attention to Indigenous law in some circumstances,[50] so domestic enforcement mechanisms should, at a minimum, provide for its reception, proof and consideration. Indigenous peoples are uniquely well situated to offer productive options for doing so.

42 *Ibid*, art 17.

43 *Ibid*, art 14.

44 *Ibid*, art 24.

45 *Ibid*, art 32.

46 Canada does not acquire legislative authority over a subject matter otherwise within exclusive provincial authority by ratifying an international instrument concerning that subject matter. As a result, it can implement domestically only those aspects of the international agreement that otherwise come within federal legislative authority: *Canada (AG) v Ontario (AG)*, [1937] AC 326 (PC).

47 *Alberta v Canadian Transport Commission*, [1978] 1 SCR 61 at 72, Laskin CJC for the majority; *Ontario v Board of Transport Commissioners*, [1968] SCR 118 at 124.

48 Under the so-called "ancillary powers" doctrine, a provision in federal (or provincial) legislation that, considered in isolation, would be invalid may nonetheless be valid if it is "sufficiently integrated" into a federal (or provincial) scheme that is known to be valid. The test for sufficient integration depends on the severity of the provision's encroachment on the exclusive legislative authority of the other order of government. Where the encroachment is less serious, a "rational, functional connection" with the parent scheme will suffice. When the encroachment is more severe, the impugned provisions must be "necessarily incidental" to the parent scheme as a whole. See *General Motors of Canada Ltd v City National Leasing*, [1989] 1 SCR 641 at 665–72; *Kitkatla Band v British Columbia (Minister of Small Business, Tourism and Culture)*, 2002 SCC 31 at paras 56–58, [2002] 2 SCR 146; *Quebec (Attorney General) v Lacombe*, 2010 SCC 38 at paras 32–46, [2010] 2 SCR 453.

49 See e.g. *Crevier v Quebec (AG)*, [1981] 2 SCR 220.

50 *UNDRIP*, *supra* note 1, arts 11(2) (redress for property taken without Indigenous consent or in violation of Indigenous law), 27 (taking account of Indigenous laws in recognizing and adjudicating Indigenous peoples' land rights), 40 (due consideration to Indigenous peoples' customs, traditions, rules and legal systems in resolving their conflicts with states and other parties).

And Then What?

UNDRIP does subject states to some affirmative obligations,[51] but it also instructs them to get out of the way to make room for Indigenous peoples' own ways of doing things. The right of self-determination (articles 3 and 4) is the clearest indication of this, although not the only one.[52] But what if something goes wrong while Indigenous peoples are doing things their own way? Suppose, for example, that a self-determining Indigenous community suffered a serious financial loss because of an unlucky or improvident investment or that some members of such a community felt marginalized by rogue Indigenous leadership. How much authority and responsibility would the Crown retain to mitigate?

The fate of UNDRIP implementation could depend upon the answer to this question. The Crown's worst nightmare would be to retain exposure for the harm in such a circumstance, without sufficient residual control to prevent or contain the harm.[53] The SCC has held, for example, that the federal Crown, as fiduciary, may not transfer to First Nations property it currently manages on their behalf, surrendering both control of and responsibility for the property, unless it is "satisfied that any transfer is in the best interest of the bands."[54] The First Nations' own wishes are not sufficient warrant for the transfer. How should this law translate post-UNDRIP?

Here is a different example. UNDRIP includes a right to full enjoyment of all human rights recognized in international human rights law (article 1) and guarantees all the rights it contains "equally...to male and female indigenous individuals" (article 44). Compliance with UNDRIP requires compliance with these provisions. In the early 1990s, when there was serious talk of entrenching inherent rights of Indigenous self-government in the Constitution, several Indigenous commentators urged the federal government not to abandon Indigenous women to the authority of predominantly male community leadership.[55] The Native Women's Association of Canada famously went to court to try to ensure that the Charter would police any constitutional right of self-government,[56] fearing what might happen to Indigenous women if it did not.

How should mainstream governments respond if similar fears emerge in the course of UNDRIP implementation? According to UNDRIP article 46(2), the exercise of UNDRIP rights "shall be subject only to such limitations as are determined by law and in accordance with international

51 See *supra* note 41 and accompanying text.

52 See e.g. *UNDRIP*, *supra* note 1, arts 5, 11–14, 16, 23–25, 31–36.

53 "In circumstances where Aboriginal groups wish the Crown to have certain ongoing obligations, self-government jurisdiction or authority will, correspondingly, be limited....There is no justifiable basis for the Government to retain fiduciary obligations in relation to subject matters over which it has relinquished its control and over which an Aboriginal government or institution has, correspondingly, assumed control": *Aboriginal Self-Government: The Government of Canada's Approach to Implementation of the Inherent Right and the Negotiation of Aboriginal Self-Government*, online: <www.rcaanc-cirnac.gc.ca/eng/1100100031843/1539869205136>.

54 *Ermineskin Nation and Band v Canada*, 2009 SCC 9 at para 152, [2009] 1 SCR 222. The court added that the Crown could require a release from future liability in respect of such property before executing any such transfer (*ibid* at paras 180–81).

55 See e.g. Thomas Isaac & Mary Sue Maloughney, "Dually Disadvantaged and Historically Forgotten? Aboriginal Women and the Inherent Right of Aboriginal Self-Government" (1992) 21 Manitoba LJ 453; Joyce Green, "Constitutionalizing the Patriarchy: Aboriginal Women and Aboriginal Government" (1993) 4 Const Forum Const 112; Emma LaRocque, "Re-examining Culturally Appropriate Models in Criminal Justice Applications" in Asch, *supra* note 36 at 75–96.

56 *Native Women's Association of Canada v Canada*, [1994] 3 SCR 627.

human rights obligations" and are "strictly necessary solely for the purpose of securing due recognition and respect for the rights and freedoms of others and for meeting the just and most compelling requirements of a democratic society." But who should get to decide what limitations satisfy these exacting criteria or who may impose them? And what are the consequences if mainstream governments choose not to impose them?

Each of these questions has several possible answers, with different possible outcomes, in a post-UNDRIP world. Successful UNDRIP implementation is going to require reasonable certainty, and reasonable consensus between the Crown and Indigenous peoples, about which answers to these questions are most appropriate. That, in turn, is going to require clarification and discussion of the expectations Indigenous peoples will have of the Crown, in circumstances not governed by affirmative UNDRIP obligations, once UNDRIP takes effect. Anticipating and addressing the need for such clarification and being ready to offer it proactively will demonstrate Indigenous commitment to UNDRIP implementation and reduce, if not eliminate, one potential barrier to its realization.

Conclusion

UNDRIP implementation in Canada has been a hope and a dream for Indigenous peoples here since at least 2007, the year of UNDRIP's adoption. There is at last a realistic chance of making that happen. No one knows yet when or if there will be another such opportunity if the current federal implementation initiative fails.

The purpose of this chapter has been to help make the most of the current opportunity. It has identified four key issues that must be resolved for UNDRIP implementation to be successful: identification and denomination in Canada of the Indigenous peoples that are to benefit from UNDRIP rights and obligations; identification of the territorial spaces traditional to each, to which UNDRIP's land regime would apply; consideration of the means by which UNDRIP might be rendered enforceable against the Crown in Canadian courts; and consideration of what powers and responsibilities mainstream governments should retain in a post-UNDRIP Canada that features robust rights of Indigenous self-determination. And it has encouraged Indigenous proponents of UNDRIP implementation to address these issues early and proactively. At least two of these issues — called here "the who" and "the where" issues — *require* Indigenous leadership to be brought to resolution. Taking the initiative has the strategic advantages of demonstrating Indigenous peoples' commitment to, and facility at, the task of UNDRIP implementation, of helping to shape the implementation agenda and of depriving Canada of some of the reasons or excuses it might otherwise have to delay or defer implementation if it were expected to drive the process unilaterally. Proactive Indigenous engagement with UNDRIP puts Canada, and other mainstream governments, to the proof of their own intentions for UNDRIP implementation. And, at an absolute minimum, it ensures that Indigenous perspectives are front and centre in UNDRIP deliberations.

19

UNDRIP Implementation, Intercultural Learning and Substantive Engagement with Indigenous Legal Orders

Hannah Askew

Anishinaabe legal scholar John Borrows suggests that recent commitments made by both federal and provincial governments to implement the United Nations Declaration on the Rights of Indigenous Peoples (UNDRIP)[1] offer an opportunity to reset the relationship between settler and Indigenous peoples on an improved basis of mutual respect and equality.[2] Crucial to this project is respect for and engagement with Indigenous legal orders. UNDRIP recognizes that Indigenous peoples' rights are rooted in Indigenous peoples' own legal traditions, rather than a colonially imposed legal regime that defines Aboriginal rights according to European understandings of law.[3] Settlers and settler governments committed to implementation of UNDRIP, and to the broader project of reconciliation, must therefore be prepared to invest significant amounts of time and resources into substantive engagement with Indigenous legal orders.

1 *United Nations Declaration on the Rights of Indigenous Peoples*, GA Res 295, UNGAOR, 61st Sess, Supp No 49, UN Doc A/RES/61/295, 46 ILM 1013 (2007).

2 John Borrows, "Revitalizing Canada's Indigenous Constitution: Two Challenges" (this volume, ch 3).

3 Sarah Morales, "Braiding the Incommensurable: Indigenous Legal Traditions and the Duty to Consult" (this volume, ch 7).

A "Duty to Learn"[4] Indigenous Law

There is simply no shortcut away from the humility, patience, time and effort that is required for settlers to learn in a meaningful way about Indigenous law and governance. As former chief justice Lance Finch of the British Columbia Supreme Court eloquently put it: "How can we make space within the legal landscape for Indigenous legal orders? The answer depends, at least in part, on an inversion of the question: a crucial part of this process must be to find space for ourselves, as strangers and newcomers, within the Indigenous legal orders themselves."[5]

A particular Indigenous legal order is intimately connected to the culture and worldview of the nation to which it belongs. As Borrows states, "The underpinnings of Indigenous law are entwined with the social, historical, political, biological, economic, and spiritual circumstances of each group. They are based on many sources, including sacred teachings, naturalistic observations, positivistic proclamations, deliberative practices, and local and national customs."[6]

As with all immigrants, settler Canadians (including their government representatives) must make the effort to seek out opportunities to learn about the laws of their adopted homelands. An obligation for settlers to learn about Indigenous legal orders does not imply a corresponding obligation for Indigenous peoples to teach settlers about their laws. This obligation would not exist in any event, but in particular in a context where the past and ongoing violence of colonialism is an open wound, Indigenous peoples are likely to have other more urgent priorities connected to healing and rebuilding their own communities. In circumstances where Indigenous peoples are willing and able to teach settlers, their time, knowledge and expertise should be valued and appropriately compensated.

It is important to note that Indigenous legal orders across Canada are diverse and unique, so that learning about the legal order of one nation does not guarantee, or even make likely, enhanced proficiency in understanding another. For settlers embarking on learning about the Indigenous laws governing the territories on which they live and work, there are many publicly available resources that can serve as a starting place to become familiar with Indigenous worldviews, values and understandings of place. Self-educating with publicly available sources can initiate a foundation from which, over time, a deeper and more sophisticated understanding of Indigenous law and legal process may be built.

Some Resources for Learning Indigenous Law

While it is beyond the scope of this chapter to thoroughly canvass the diverse resources that exist for learning Indigenous law, some relatively accessible examples that may be drawn on include: published traditional stories; online audio recordings of storytellers and speakers; language lexicons; nation and band council websites; cross-disciplinary Indigenous scholarship, including graduate theses; anthropological writing, past and present (treated with caution, as it

4 This phrase was coined by former chief justice of the British Columbia Supreme Court, the Honourable Justice Lance Finch; see Lance Finch, "The Duty to Learn: Taking Account of Indigenous Legal Orders in Practice" (Paper delivered at the Indigenous Legal Orders and the Common Law Conference, Continuing Legal Education Society of British Columbia, Vancouver, November 2012).

5 *Ibid* at 20.

6 John Borrows, *Canada's Indigenous Constitution* (Toronto: University of Toronto Press, 2010) at 23–24 [Borrows, *Canada's Indigenous Constitution*].

is often authored by non-members); public lectures; and visual art such as carvings, poles and weaving, as well as dance, music and film.[7] It is critical that newcomers to a culture and legal order approach these sources with humility and open-mindedness, in particular if they have not been trained on how to interpret or contextualize them. However, engaging with these sources can be done without burdening an Indigenous teacher and can help the learner to become aware of some of the basic values and structures of a specific Indigenous legal order.

Perhaps the richest opportunities to learn about a particular Indigenous legal order come from invitations to join the web of relations that structure Indigenous law by participating in land-based learning from knowledgeable community members, as well as the land itself. These precious learning opportunities are sometimes extended to individuals or groups by communities. One example is the Anishinaabe law camps led by John Borrows, co-taught by community members and invited instructors, and hosted by various Anishinaabe communities several times annually. Participants at these law camps have the opportunity to internalize Anishinaabe legal teachings by participating in relationships mediated by stories, ceremonies, shared meals and time spent on the land.[8] The Tsilhqot'in Nation also hosts an annual culture camp, where various aspects of Nenqayni law and culture are shared through hands-on activities such as fishing and tanning hides. This camp is mainly for members of the nation, but outsiders who are willing and able to conduct themselves in a respectful way are also welcome.

In terms of universities serving as sites to access knowledge about Indigenous law, as increasing numbers of Indigenous peoples join academia as undergraduate and graduate students, professors, visiting Elders and in other roles, there is also a growing body of Indigenous legal scholarship being generated. Michael Coyle did a synthesis and review of this body of work in the fall of 2017.[9] In summarizing this literature, he wrote: "The past two decades have witnessed an explosion of writing about Indigenous legal traditions in Canada. Those writings will be a valuable tool for Indigenous communities, government policy-makers, judges, and scholars. They offer important insights into questions like how to identify and interpret Indigenous laws, what

7 See e.g. the Accessing Justice and Reconciliation Project, "Project Documents", online: <www.indigenousbar.ca/indigenouslaw/project-documents/>; *ibid*, "Video", "Audio", online: <www.indigenousbar.ca/indigenouslaw/audiovideo/>; Indigenous Law Research Unit, University of Victoria, online: <www.uvic.ca/law/about/indigenous/indigenouslawresearchunit/index.php>.

8 For reflections on participants' experiences of these law camps, see Osgoode Hall Law School, York University, "The Anishinaabe Law Camp", online: <www.osgoode.yorku.ca/programs/jd-program/anishinaabe-law-camp/>; Lorne Sossin, "Anishinaabe Law Camp" (25 September 2017) *Dean Sossin's Blog* (blog), online: <https://deansblog.osgoode.yorku.ca/2017/09/anishinaabe-law-camp/>; Lorraine Land, "Rethinking legal education: the Anishinaabe Law Camp", online: <http://oktlaw.com/rethinking-legal-education-anishnaabe-law-camp/>; Hannah Askew, "Learning from the land: Anishinaabe law camp at Walpole Island First Nation" (15 May 2016), online: <www.wcel.org/blog/learning-land-anishinaabe-law-camp-walpole-island-first-nation>; Serena Dykstra, Zachary Donofrio & Jasleen Johal, "Anishinaabe Law Camp" (29 September 2014), online: <http://obiter-dicta.ca/2014/09/29/anishinaabe-law-camp/>; Allison Grandish, "Anishinaabe Law Camp 2015" (13 October 2015), online: <http://obiter-dicta.ca/2015/10/13/anishinaabe-law-camp-2015/>; Windsor Law, University of Windsor, "Anishinaabe Student Law Camp, March 29–April 1, 2018 Student Application Form", online: <www.uwindsor.ca/law/aboriginal/sites/uwindsor.ca.law.aboriginal/files/pii_ki_giigidod_2018_student_law_camp.pdf>; Faculty of Law, McGill University, "Anishinaabe Law Class: Law as a Human Experience" (1 November 2017), online: <http://publications.mcgill.ca/droit/2017/11/01/anishinaabe-law/>; Western Law, Western University, "Indigenous law camp imparts valuable lessons" (2017), online: <https://law.uwo.ca/news/2017/indigenous_law_camp_imparts_valuable_lessons.html>; Gemma Smyth, "Reflections on the Anishinabe Law Camp (Bkejwanong Territory)" (25 October 2016), online: <https://reconciliationsyllabus.wordpress.com/2016/10/25/reflections-on-the-anishinabe-law-camp-bkejwanong-territory/>; John Borrows, "An emphasis on indigenous law could help shape a future that's brighter than our past", *The Hill Times* (28 June 2017), online: <www.hilltimes.com/2017/06/28/emphasis-indigenous-law-help-shape-future-thats-brighter-past/111748>.

9 Michael Coyle, "Indigenous Legal Orders in Canada: A literature review" (2017) Western University Law Publications.

are their sources, and how to understand Indigenous legal reasoning."[10] Some of the work being produced by Indigenous scholars is explicitly designed for audiences outside the university. For example, the Indigenous Law Research Unit at the University of Victoria has an entire website with resources on Indigenous law, including a graphic novel and their popular "Indigenous Law on Demand" short video series.

The Indigenous Law Research Unit has also designed a methodology to access Indigenous legal principles through stories and commentary on stories, and regularly runs training sessions on request to teach this methodology to groups around the country and sometimes internationally. Val Napoleon and Hadley Friedland, the creators of the methodology, articulate their motivation as follows: "Interest in serious and sustained engagement with Indigenous legal traditions is building within Canada, across professional, academic and Indigenous communities. If the momentum is going to be sustained and grow productively, then we need shared frameworks for engaging with Indigenous legal traditions within and across these same Indigenous, professional and academic communities."[11]

As UNDRIP is implemented in Canada, with the accompanying requirements for the Canadian state to recognize Indigenous law, decision makers, legal institutions and process, the need for shared frameworks for engaging with Indigenous legal orders will become more acute.

The Dynamic and Evolving Nature of Indigenous Law

In Canadian case law, courts have taken a "frozen in time" approach to Aboriginal rights, recognizing only those aspects of the culture that evidence supports existing at the time of contact with early European settlers.[12] This line of reasoning in the jurisprudence has been heavily criticized for denying Indigenous peoples the inherent rights to grow, evolve and adapt over time, as all human societies necessarily do.[13]

Like Canadian law, Indigenous legal orders are dynamic and change over time to adapt to new circumstances and needs. As Borrows states: "Indigenous law as practised today may have connections to ancient history — or it may not. Law is fluid; it changes over time.... Indigenous legal traditions exist to address current and future needs."[14] This implies that the legal principles applicable to a conflict, and interpretation and application of those principles, must be open to community debate and capable of evolving through deliberative processes that are themselves integral to the legal order.[15]

10 *Ibid* at iv.

11 Val Napoleon & Hadley Friedland, "The Inside Job: Engaging with Indigenous Legal Traditions through Stories" in Tony Lucero & Dale Turner, eds, *Oxford Handbook of Indigenous Peoples' Politics* (Oxford, UK: Oxford University Press, 2014).

12 See *R v Van der Peet*, [1996] 2 SCR 507.

13 See e.g. Brenda L Gunn, "Beyond *Van der Peet*: Bringing Together International, Indigenous and Constitutional Law" (this volume, ch 13); Borrows, *Canada's Indigenous Constitution*, *supra* note 6 at 8; John Borrows, *Recovering Canada: The Resurgence of Indigenous Law* (Toronto: University of Toronto Press, 2002) at 60.

14 John Borrows, "Heroes, Tricksters, Monsters, and Caretakers: Indigenous Law and Legal Education" (2016) 61:4 McGill LJ 795.

15 Coyle, *supra* note 9.

For settlers seeking to understand and learn from contemporary applications of Indigenous law to vital current issues, Indigenous peoples' use of social media, Twitter in particular, has become a rich forum of discussion that is frequently public. A powerful recent example of this is a Twitter exchange that occurred on February 10, 2018, between Peter Sankoff, a University of Alberta law professor and criminal lawyer, and Kris Statnyk, a Gwich'in lawyer, over a point of Cree law following the killing of Cree youth Colten Boushie and the subsequent acquittal of Boushie's killer by the Canadian criminal justice system. In the exchange, Sankoff misinterpreted a statement delivered by Bobby Cameron, chief of the Federation of Sovereign Indigenous Nations, as a threat of revenge and was corrected by Statnyk over a series of tweets. The statement Sankoff misinterpreted as an "outright threat of revenge" was as follows: "Gerald Stanley, you've not got away with this yet. Don't think for a second that you've got away with this, because somewhere down the line you're going to pay. Your children will pay or your grandchildren will pay."[16]

The Twitter exchange between Sankoff and Statnyk then proceeded as follows:

> @PeterSankoff: This article shows a range of reaction to Stanley/Boushie case. Emotions are high in Saskatchewan.
>
> @PeterSankoff: And when I say "a range" I mean, ranging from "sad, but hoping this brings needed legislative change" to outright "threats of revenge".
>
> @gwichinkris: Hi Peter. Not one Indigenous person in this article makes "outright 'threats of revenge'". It does not help anyone to perpetuate the violent savage mythology that continues to kill us.
>
> @gwichinkris: This is not a threat of revenge. It's a statement truly rooted in Nehiyaw law (not that you would know). See for example the Principle of Natural and Spiritual Consequences to harm discussed here (at p. 27): http://indigenousbar.ca/indigenouslaw/wp-content/uploads/2012/12/cree_summary.pdf ...
>
> @gwichinkris: I'm not a Cree person so won't pretend to speak with authority but it is understood as a spiritual or natural consequence (i.e. it is enacted by natural or spiritual forces). It can serve a deterrence function. Don't harm someone or it will come back on your family.
>
> @PeterSankoff: OK - I think that is a different way to look at it. You're absolutely right - I wouldn't know. Neither would others without the context explained. Thanks for that, but it would help to have it in the article, for it sure sounds like a threat. But I stand corrected.
>
> @gwichinkris: But why is it that this is just a different way to look at it? Why are you unfamiliar with Nehiyaw law while living and working in Treaty 6? Why does this *sound* threatening to you? I think this is what this case [ought] to prompt from the white legal community.

16 Joe Friesen, "'Unacceptable': Boushie family vows to seek justice after jury acquits Stanley", *The Globe and Mail* (10 February 2018), online: <www.theglobeandmail.com/news/national/unacceptable-boushie-family-vows-to-seek-justice-after-jury-acquits-stanley/article37931731/>.

Other Cree people following this exchange on Twitter then entered the conversation to share examples of how the spiritual debt that accrues from taking a life can play out in a person's life. I include this as one example of the powerful Indigenous legal debates occurring in public places, such as Twitter, that are accessible to settlers who wish to follow and learn from Indigenous thinkers who are reflecting on, debating and applying Indigenous legal principles to contemporary conflicts and issues as they arise.

Rebuilding Work

As settler people and governments begin to do the work of learning about and engaging with Indigenous legal orders, many Indigenous nations are engaged in the labour-intensive process of rebuilding and revitalizing their Indigenous legal orders and governance systems.

Napoleon and Friedland caution that mere readiness on behalf of settler society to recognize Indigenous law is insufficient, as the violence that has been wrought against Indigenous peoples by colonialism has caused damage and loss that must be acknowledged, as a precondition to the healing and rebuilding work that must occur:

> [T]he ground of Indigenous law is uneven — Indigenous law exists, it has not gone anywhere — and we saw this, but there are also serious gaps where some Indigenous laws have been undermined, distorted, or lost. Given this, simply arguing for the recognition of Indigenous law is inadequate because we cannot just assume that there are complete and intact legal orders that can spring to life through recognition. This means that engagement with Indigenous law must move to thoughtful rebuilding, and this generates two questions: (1) What are the terms for this thoughtful rebuilding process with communities? and (2) What are the intellectual processes in each Indigenous society that historically enabled people to deal with and account for change?[17]

The late Anishinaabe linguist and storyteller Basil Johnston argued, in an essay entitled "One Generation from Extinction," that the federal government, which is directly responsible for Indigenous language loss due to its explicit past policies of cultural assimilation, should be responsible for providing funding to Indigenous community-led language revitalization efforts.[18] The same logic extends to funding revitalization efforts around Indigenous law. The residential school system, with its notorious agenda to "kill the Indian in the child," and colonial laws banning potlatches, sun dances and other important Indigenous legal institutions caused damage to Indigenous legal orders. It is therefore unjust that the entire burden of revitalizing Indigenous legal orders should be borne by Indigenous peoples, who bear no responsibility for causing the violence that led to the loss in the first place. Indigenous peoples must lead the work of rebuilding if it is to happen, but the federal government should provide financial support

17 Napoleon & Friedland, *supra* note 11.

18 Basil H Johnston, "One Generation from Extinction" (1990), online: <canlitweb.arts.ubc.ca/canlitmedia/pdfs/articles/canlit124-Generation(Johnston).pdf>.

to ensure that Indigenous communities can enlist, educate and compensate people to do the labour-intensive work of revitalization.[19]

Proceeding with Caution

The current unacceptable state of Crown-Indigenous relations demands urgent action. At the same time, 150 years of harm and violence against Indigenous peoples and their governance systems cannot be undone overnight, and actions undertaken too quickly and without sufficient reflection could easily result in more harm than good. Valine Crist, a member of the Haida Nation, counsels that the work of settler engagement with Indigenous law should "move at the speed of trust."[20] This means listening to and abiding by the pace and terms of rebuilding set by Indigenous communities according to their own decision-making processes. In many communities, where trauma caused by settler violence continues to cause intense pain, the work of rebuilding trust between settlers and Indigenous peoples must proceed slowly. As Nenqayni writer Linda Smith states:

> Among Tsilhqot'in, historic experiences overshadow present relationships with midugh.[21] Unfamiliar midugh are seen through the lens of previous encounters, many of whom have harmed the people. Practically everyone is known in Tsilhqot'in communities. When a stranger arrives, everyone hears of it. Midugh immediately "step into the spaces" left by previous midugh, in a sense, not to be trusted until they prove themselves to be trustworthy. They are closely watched. There is extreme poverty, oppression, physical and emotional suffering, grief, and intense anger. The stranger is seen as having an advantage. Midugh become heirs to the legacy of past murder, greed, exploitation, injustices, and racism left by others."[22]

As settlers step into the work of UNDRIP implementation, alongside Indigenous peoples, they must be cognizant of the continued pain caused by colonization and respect the pace determined to be appropriate by Indigenous communities for rebuilding and healing.

Increased Recognition of Indigenous Legal Orders Is Not a Zero-sum Game

A harmful belief that should be addressed as part of the national conversation on UNDRIP implementation is the notion that the growing recognition of Indigenous legal orders is a zero-sum game that can result only in diminished well-being for non-Indigenous peoples. Chief

19 As a starting point, publicly available examples include: Dean Billy et al, *Revitalizing Indigenous Law for Land, Air and Water: St'át'imc Legal Traditions Report* (2018), online: <www.wcel.org/publication/revitalizing-indigenous-law-land-air-and-water-statimc-legal-traditions-report>; Accessing Justice and Reconciliation Project, *Cree Legal Summary* (2012), online: <www.indigenousbar.ca/indigenouslaw/wp-content/uploads/2017/10/cree_legal_summary.pdf>; Hannah Askew & Lindsay Borrows, *Anishinabek Legal Summary*, online: <http://indigenousbar.ca/indigenouslaw/wp-content/uploads/2012/12/anishinabek_summary.pdf>; Indigenous Law Research Unit, University of Victoria & Shuswap Nation Tribal Council, *Secwépemc Lands and Resources Law Analysis Project Summary* (2016), online: <http://shuswapnation.org/wp-content/blogs.dir/124/files/2017/08/Secwepemc-Lands-and-Resources-Law-Analysis-Summary.pdf>. For a literature review on the topic, see Coyle, *supra* note 9.

20 Personal conversation with Valine Crist, September 2017.

21 Meaning "whiteman"; see FirstVoices, "midugh", online: <www.firstvoices.com/explore/FV/sections/Data/Athabascan/Tsilhqot'in%20(Xeni%20Gwet'in)/Tsilhqot'in%20(Xeni%20Gwet'in)/learn/words/80251>.

22 Linda Smith, unpublished paper, shared with the author, 11 February 2018.

Roger William of Xeni Gwet'in, whose community won the landmark title case at the Supreme Court of Canada in 2014,[23] has stated on a number of occasions that it is his goal that non-Tsilhqot'in people living on Tsilhqot'in title land will have a better experience living under Tsilhqot'in governance than they did under Crown governance.[24] This stated intention is as kind and generous as it is politically astute. With increased exposure to Indigenous law and governance, settlers may be able to better understand that they also may have the opportunity to flourish in an inter-societal political context where Indigenous legal orders are strong and respected.

Settlers stand to be transformed by the profound gift of learning about specific Indigenous legal orders. The continued generosity and willingness of many Indigenous peoples to share knowledge of their legal orders, in spite of the acute violence and disrespect that settler society has inflicted on them, should be met by settlers with gratitude and good-faith efforts to learn.

Conclusion

The violence that has been perpetrated against Indigenous systems of law and governance by the colonial state has not only caused grievous harm to Indigenous peoples but has also impoverished settlers by denying them access to rich and diverse Indigenous traditions of governance that could nourish a healthier, more just and more generative society. It is commonplace today for Canadian politicians to speak of a nation-to-nation relationship, but the meaning of this statement typically remains vague and ill-defined. UNDRIP provides insight into how this concept might be put into living practice, as many of the rights it articulates explicitly refer to Indigenous governance institutions, laws and legal processes. As Inuit law professor Gordon Christie suggests, UNDRIP provides a framework for addressing the disconnect between Canadian law and Indigenous legal orders, and moving from ongoing colonial dynamics toward a nation-to-nation relationship.[25] Serious, substantive engagement between the settler state and Indigenous legal orders will require hard and sustained work by both parties. The great difficulty of this work promises to be surpassed only by its rewards.

Author's Note

I thank and acknowledge John Borrows, Lindsay Keegitah Borrows, James (Sa'ke'j) Youngblood Henderson, Britton Jacob-Schram, Linda Smith, Carson Smith, Kris Statnyk, Mark Worthing and Kat Zimmer, for their shared knowledge, illuminating discussion and review of this chapter; Alisa Koebel for her assistance with editing and citations; and the two anonymous reviewers for their helpful feedback.

23 *Tsilhqot'in Nation v British Columbia*, 2014 SCC 44.

24 Personal conversation with then chief Roger William, June 2016.

25 Gordon Christie, "Indigenous Legal Orders, Canadian Law and UNDRIP" (this volume, ch 5).

PART IV

Concluding Thoughts

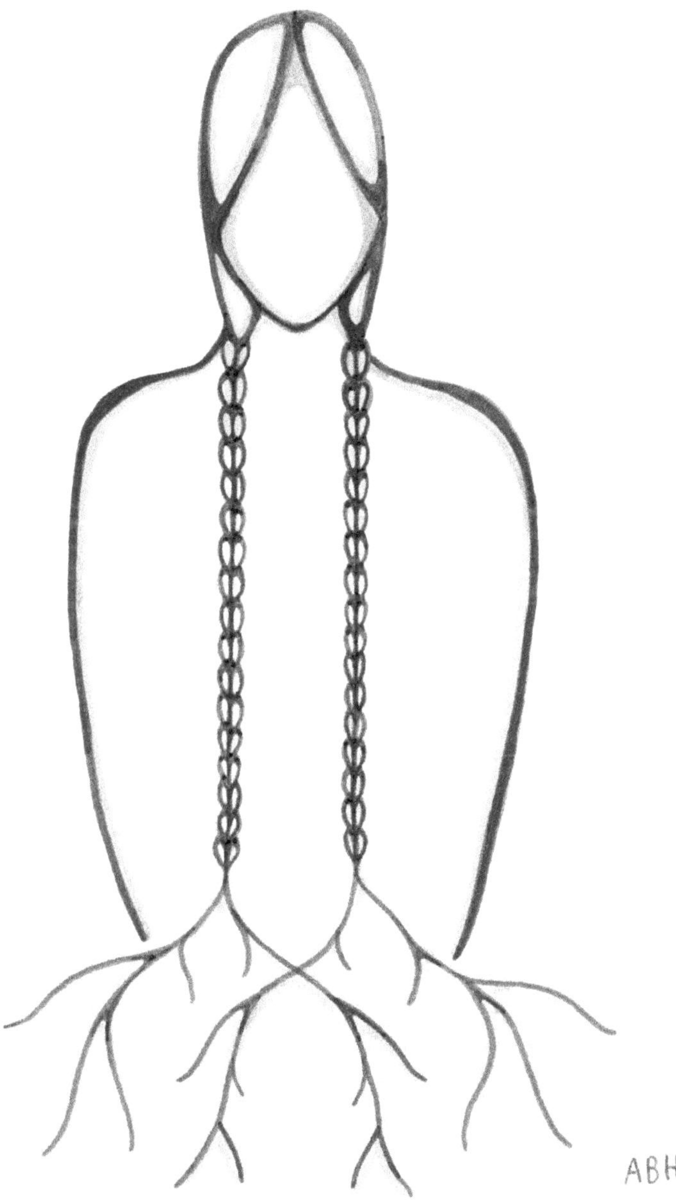

Previous page:

Ojiibikaawi (She Has Roots)
Anna Heffernan

2018, 8" x 10", marker and ink drawing

20

Implementation of UNDRIP within Canadian and Indigenous Law: Assessing Challenges

Gordon Christie

Shortly after the last federal election, Canada signalled its intent to implement the United Nations Declaration on the Rights of Indigenous Peoples (UNDRIP).[1] At that time, conservative commentators — Blaine Favel and Ken Coates — raised concerns they argued should lead us to prefer caution over hasty moves.[2] As, shortly after, the federal government also signalled its support for a private member's bill that essentially calls for adopting UNDRIP into Canadian law,[3] these voices — now joined by Dwight Newman, Arend Hoekstra, Harry Swain and Jim Baillie — have been re-energized, claiming such a move "verges on the simplistic" and

1 *United Nations Declaration on the Rights of Indigenous Peoples*, GA Res 295, UNGAOR, 61st Sess, Supp No 49, UN Doc A/RES/61/295, 46 ILM 1013 (2007) [*UNDRIP*].

2 Blaine Favel & Ken S Coates, *Understanding UNDRIP* (Ottawa: Macdonald-Laurier Institute, 2016) [Favel & Coates, *Understanding UNDRIP*], online: <www.macdonaldlaurier.ca/files/pdf/MLI-10-UNDRIPCoates-Flavel05-16-WebReadyV4.pdf>; Ken S Coates & Blaine Favel, *Understanding FPIC* (Ottawa: Macdonald-Laurier Institute, 2016) [Coates & Favel, *Understanding FPIC*], online: <https://macdonaldlaurier.ca/files/pdf/MLINumber9-FPICCoates-Flavel04-29-WebReady.pdf>.

3 Bill C-262, *An Act to ensure that the laws of Canada are in harmony with the United Nations Declaration on the Rights of Indigenous Peoples*, 1st Sess, 42nd Parl, 2016 (as passed by the House of Commons 30 May 2018), online: <www.parl.ca/DocumentViewer/en/42-1/bill/C-262/third-reading>. As of summer 2018, the bill was before the Senate, having passed through third reading in Parliament.

is "laden with circular tension."[4] Swain and Baillie called for the legislation to be withdrawn, while Newman called for reconsideration and redrafting.[5]

At the same time, although less prominently displayed in the dominant media, Indigenous peoples and nations have expressed concerns about the implementation of UNDRIP.[6] These are very different sorts of concerns, given that UNDRIP is the product of decades of Indigenous solidarity at the global level and promises a shift in Canada to a decolonizing discourse. Nevertheless, these concerns are as pressing and substantial as concerns raised by the voices of caution, and the two sets of concerns should be carefully examined to enhance the chances of adopting a strategy that would be most productive.

My intent is to examine the strongest arguments for caution raised by conservative commentators, placing these against concerns held by Indigenous peoples. Much of what conservative critics present is clearly meant to spread fear among the general Canadian public and to pander to powerful interests, but woven in and among their claims (some of which are simply absurd[7]) are arguments that those who welcome a generous implementation of UNDRIP should consider carefully. This is not simply a matter of knowing arguments that arise on the other side, but also of being aware of how those who raise such arguments hope to frame or contain the discourse. The danger is that even just in the act of responding in certain ways to some of these arguments, the battle is lost, as the terms of the debate are thereby set in ways that preclude meaningful reconciliation. Much of the concern on the Indigenous side is about how such voices of caution may play into a mode of implementation that strips from UNDRIP the very promise it holds out as a decolonizing instrument.

Voices of Caution

While I label the most vocal commentators "conservatives," at the core of their common ideology lies a strong liberal philosophy. They wish to conserve the world of liberalism. Terms of discourse set by these commentators are set down by allegiance to an individualistic, liberal conception of Canadian society, one that assumes Indigenous peoples are already contained within this ideological world. Coates and Favel, for example, caution us of the likelihood that implementing UNDRIP will undermine ongoing efforts to improve the lives and social

4 Dwight Newman & Ken Coates, "Bill on implementing UNDRIP 'simplistic and laden with circular tension'", *The Hill Times* (14 December 2017), online: <www.hilltimes.com/2017/12/14/bill-implementing-undrip-simplistic-laden-circular-tensions/128903>; Thomas Isaac & Arend JA Hoekstra, "Implementing UNDRIP in Canada: Challenges with Bill C-262", online: Cassels Brock Lawyers <www.casselsbrock.com/CBNewsletter/Implementing_UNDRIP_in_Canada__Challenges_with_Bill_C_262>; Harry Swain & Jim Baillie, "The Trudeau government signs on to give Aboriginals veto rights nobody else has", *Financial Post* (26 January 2018), online: <http://business.financialpost.com/opinion/the-trudeau-government-signs-on-to-give-aboriginals-veto-rights-nobody-else-has>.

5 Dwight Newman, "Written Brief to House of Commons Standing Committee on Indigenous and Northern Affairs re Bill C-262", online: <www.ourcommons.ca/Content/Committee/421/INAN/Brief/BR9762671/br-external/NewmanDwight-e.pdf<; Dwight Newman's oral presentation to the House of Commons Standing Committee on Indigenous and Northern Affairs, online: <www.ourcommons.ca/DocumentViewer/en/42-1/INAN/meeting-101/evidence>.

6 Many of these concerns were presented in evidence before the House of Commons Standing Committee on Indigenous and Northern Affairs re Bill C-262 at meetings held from April 17 to May 8, 2018 [Standing Committee on Bill C-262], online: <www.ourcommons.ca/Committees/en/INAN/StudyActivity?studyActivityId=9965131#DT20180508INANMEE107ID9965131>.

7 A number of the oddities contained in Isaac and Hoekstra's piece, *supra* note 4, are detailed by Paul Joffe; see "Commentary — UN Declaration on the Rights of Indigenous Peoples", online: Quaker Friends Service Committee <https://quakerservice.ca/news/commentary-un-declaration/>.

conditions of the Aboriginal peoples of Canada. In this sense, they argue, UNDRIP might turn out to be "counterproductive" and cost-prohibitive.[8]

This focus — on the suffering of peoples as individuals — shifts attention away from centuries of colonialism, dispossession, oppression, loss of self-determination and cultural genocide. Indigenous peoples resist this framing not because working to improve the lives of Indigenous peoples is somehow improper, but because *that* objective has its proper place in Canada in *other, separate* discussions. If Canada were to live up to its own self-description (as a liberal democracy), Aboriginal citizens would not have to fight for non-discriminatory levels of supply of basic services. We should not have to call upon UNDRIP when it comes to concerns in Canada over how Indigenous peoples should have access to equal measures of basic services meant to relieve poverty, provide clean drinking water, address suicide and addictions, and other related or similar matters. In other countries around the world, parts of UNDRIP might have to be called upon to prod states to begin delivering meaningful levels of basic social, economic and cultural support, but we should not have to think of UNDRIP playing this role in the Canadian context. Rather, its primary function in the Canadian context should be clear, given Canada's deep colonial nightmare — it can play a substantial role in our domestic context in working to address Canada's colonial history.

Let us move on, then, to arguments that do intersect with those aspects of UNDRIP's discourse that make sense in the Canadian context. Canada's original reservations about UNDRIP (raised when Canada voted against the General Assembly resolution to adopt UNDRIP and echoed a few years later when it equivocally signed on[9]) focused on three sorts of issues, each reflected in more recent conservative commentary. While the current Liberal government distances itself from earlier positions taken by Conservative governments, this is presently only at the level of rhetoric, and so whether these concerns still animate policies and actions of the current government remains an open question.

First, there was concern with those articles (such as 3 and 19) that Canada argued would require a fundamental restructuring of Canada's legal and political landscape (the "fundamental restructuring" concern). Article 3 recognizes an Indigenous right to self-determination, while article 19 requires that a state "consult and cooperate in good faith with the indigenous peoples concerned...in order to obtain their free, prior and informed consent before adopting and implementing legislative or administrative measures that may affect them."[10]

8 Coates & Favel, *Understanding FPIC*, *supra* note 2.

9 In 2010, when Canada first expressed support for UNDRIP (as an "aspirational" document), the federal government stated:

> In 2007, at the time of the vote during the United Nations General Assembly, and since, Canada placed on record its concerns with various provisions of the Declaration, including provisions dealing with lands, territories and resources; free, prior and informed consent when used as a veto; self-government without recognition of the importance of negotiations; intellectual property; military issues; and the need to achieve an appropriate balance between the rights and obligations of Indigenous peoples, States and third parties. Aboriginal and treaty rights are protected in Canada through a unique framework. These rights are enshrined in our Constitution, including our Charter of Rights and Freedoms, and are complemented by practical policies that adapt to our evolving reality. This framework will continue to be the cornerstone of our efforts to promote and protect the rights of Aboriginal Canadians.

See "Canada's Statement of Support on the United Nations Declaration on the Rights of Indigenous Peoples", online: Indigenous and Northern Affairs Canada <www.aadnc-aandc.gc.ca/eng/1309374239861/1309374546142>.

10 *UNDRIP*, *supra* note 1.

Second, article 26 speaks of Indigenous rights to lands and resources, holding, in particular, that "Indigenous peoples have the right to own, use, develop and control the lands, territories and resources that they possess by reason of traditional ownership or other traditional occupation or use."[11] This is a right that — Canada argued — is far too broad in application and does not line up with Canadian jurisprudence on Aboriginal title (the "Indigenous territory" concern).

Finally, there was the argument that UNDRIP would provide Indigenous peoples with a veto power not enjoyed by other Canadians, a power over such matters as resource development projects on their lands or waters. This power presumably arises through the application of the requirement that free, prior and informed consent (FPIC) be obtained, a requirement that we noted earlier appears in article 19, but that is also present in article 32[12] (the "FPIC as veto" concern).

As we will see, while recent critics seem to add to these three sorts of concerns, all their explicit concerns do fit into the three categories. By examining what is said, we can dig down to the critics' actual concerns (underlying what they seem to spell out).

Analyzing Stated Concerns

What sort of fundamental restructuring is being imagined, and how does it arise as an argument against fully implementing UNDRIP? We need to examine carefully how it might be that implementing UNDRIP would require fundamental changes to the domestic legal and political landscape.

Those voicing this concern all note the way UNDRIP came into being, as it was the product of many years of intense negotiations marked by remarkable, global Indigenous solidarity.[13] Less prominently noted, however, is a key part of that story, revolving around its last chapter, when states took over what had been a more open and mutually respectful process.[14] Behind closed doors, out of sight of Indigenous representatives, a number of powerful alterations were made to the text, most notably with the addition of article 46. Subsection 3 states: "The provisions set forth in this *Declaration* shall be interpreted in accordance with the principles of justice, democracy, respect for human rights, equality, non-discrimination, good governance and good faith."

Implementing UNDRIP means, of course, implementing the instrument as a whole, and so article 46 will play a key role in how this process unfolds. This is even if — or, more accurately, this is particularly so if — UNDRIP should be imported into Canada by way of a legislative framework. What, then, can this first concern amount to, if implementation of the instrument must be in accord with principles of justice, democracy, respect for human rights, equality, non-

11 *Ibid.*

12 *Ibid*, art 32(2): "States shall consult and cooperate in good faith with the indigenous peoples concerned through their own representative institutions in order to obtain their free and informed consent prior to the approval of any project affecting their lands or territories and other resources, particularly in connection with the development, utilization or exploitation of their mineral, water or other resources."

13 See e.g. Favel & Coates, *Understanding UNDRIP, supra* note 2, and evidence tendered by several witnesses at sessions of the Standing Committee on Bill C-262, *supra* note 6, such as that tendered by Miles Richardson and Paul Chartrand at the April 17 session.

14 For example, this is buried in Favel & Coates, *Understanding UNDRIP, supra* note 2, n 6.

discrimination, good governance and good faith? Are commentators wilfully ignoring this clear circumscription, or do they think UNDRIP might somehow be implemented in disregard of these constraints?

We need to consider another alternative, one that admits of a breakdown into two sub-concerns. We might wonder whether perhaps these commentators recognize that the current Canadian legal and political structure violates these constraints, and that implementing UNDRIP calls, then, for an injection of justice, non-discrimination and so forth into the Canadian landscape. This might be because established "classic" understandings of justice, non-discrimination, equality and human rights are such that Canadian law and policy cannot stand up when measured against them. Alternatively, it may be because emerging progressive understandings of justice, non-discrimination, equality and human rights clearly indicate that current Canadian law and policy are far outside what is just now coming to be understood to be just and fair.[15]

This third general option is the only reasonable one available (assuming the commentators read the entire UNDRIP and assuming they know that the governments of Canada — overseen by Canadian courts — will be in a vastly stronger position to dictate how the instrument actually unfolds in Canada, ensuring nothing is slipped somehow into new structures that emerge). It must be, then, that conservative concerns with possible changes to Canada's legal and political landscape have to do with the fact that critics know the current landscape either does not accord with established principles of justice, non-discrimination and so forth or that these principles are themselves in flux, and that progressive developments promise an expanded world of justice to Indigenous peoples. The first concern, then, can be reframed quite accurately as a concern that implementing UNDRIP might lead to Canada having to abide by such things as principles of justice, non-discrimination, good faith, respect for human rights, equality, good governance and democracy.

A similar line of attack deflects concerns about article 26 and Indigenous land interests. Over the last few decades, the Supreme Court of Canada has been developing substantive doctrine concerning Aboriginal title, and in 2014 the first instance of this Canadian legal instrument appeared in full form, with the Tsilhqot'in Nation being found to possess Aboriginal title over about 1,900 km^2 of their traditional territory.[16] But what does this legal instrument and its development rest upon? Before Canada asserted sovereignty and came to believe its unilateral acts could slip Crown title under Indigenous claims, all lands and territories in what is now Canada were tied to Indigenous peoples.[17] Purportedly acting under a "doctrine of discovery" (that even in its more benign forms holds that European powers, simply by being more "civilized," could "discover" Indigenous lands and thereby mysteriously gain powers over these territories[18]), the Crown pushed aside Indigenous peoples, disregarding their legal orders and systems of

15 It is most likely a mix of the two — commentators are aware that Canadian law and policy continues to offend established notions of justice, while they fret about expanded notions on the horizon (those that accord responsible weight to collective rights and interests, in particular as these relate to self-determination), where these notions even more deeply challenge the status quo of colonial law and policy.

16 *Tsilhqot'in Nation v British Columbia*, 2014 SCC 44 [*Tsilhqot'in Nation*].

17 I use the locution "tied to" to leave open the varied ways different Indigenous peoples would describe their own specific relations to the lands and waters they have lived with for countless generations. Each Indigenous nation would have to fill in what sorts of relationships they enjoy, and how they are to be understood within their own legal orders.

18 In its more malignant form, the doctrine holds that a European power, on "discovering" Indigenous lands, would find there no authority, claim or right that would need to be considered in its actions. Whatever positive action such a European power might take toward Indigenous peoples living in these lands would be only through its generosity.

authority. Indigenous relationships to their lands were not like those that mark nation-state concepts of title and jurisdictional authority, but to say they did not on their own amount to connections able to authoritatively stand up to foreign intrusion is clearly and unequivocally racist.

The fact is that UNDRIP speaks directly of Indigenous lands and territories in ways that do not import Western notions of property or jurisdiction to delimit this language of Indigenous land interests. When we speak of implementing UNDRIP in the Canadian context, what we witness, then, is a spotlight being shone directly on failures that lie at the heart of Canadian jurisprudence. The nature of Aboriginal title as it has developed within Canadian law (as non-territorial, tied to non-Indigenous tests of use and occupation, with little or no measure of jurisdictional authority attached[19]) might have been acceptable if it were the product of negotiations between Indigenous and non-Indigenous authorities, but that is not the case. It has been developed entirely by non-Indigenous jurists, working within a narrow and parochial understanding of justice (one that attempts to mask racism at the core of standing precedent).

Once again, for commentators to raise these sorts of concerns — this time about differences between land interests as articulated under UNDRIP and Aboriginal title as developed by Canadian courts — is for them essentially to agree with Canada's failure to live up to broad and substantive principles of justice and non-discrimination. Non-Indigenous judges, with no input at all from Indigenous peoples connected to their territories, continue to build on the racist doctrine of discovery that lies at the very foundation of Canadian law concerning Aboriginal rights and title. Critics of importing UNDRIP are standing behind this, arguing that nevertheless, somehow, the "arc of history is bending toward justice."[20] The tree of Canadian jurisprudence is firmly planted in a racist doctrine, so any bending it is doing is merely some swaying in the breeze.

Which brings us to the third concern (FPIC as veto), one that arguably moves us closer to the actual fears of Canadian governments (Liberal and Conservative), their courts and those who voice caution about UNDRIP. This third concern seems to connect most closely with the notion that implementing UNDRIP would provide Indigenous peoples in Canada with special rights not enjoyed by other Canadians. The first response to this should be fairly obvious by this point: when one reads the declaration in its entirety and thinks about how article 46 is meant to function, it is not clear how articles 19 and 32 could emerge in the Canadian landscape in a way that somehow violates principles of justice and non-discrimination. Non-discrimination on its own would seem to ensure that, whatever emerges from the implementation of UNDRIP, Indigenous peoples in Canada will not enjoy special rights. Having substantial input into what happens on their lands and waters is, however, another matter.

The real challenge here is with what is clearly a brazen attempt to frame the discourse, the point of concern of Indigenous peoples raised earlier. Conservative commentators hope to have the matter of UNDRIP's implementation be captured within liberal discourse, within the language of rights (where any citizen's access to rights must reflect rights equally accessible — at least in principle — to all). But consider the question of a veto with this in mind. A private property

19 *Tsilhqot'in Nation*, *supra* note 16 at paras 67–76.

20 Swain & Baillie, *supra* note 4 (paraphrasing a quotation by Theodore Parker, but most often attributed to Martin Luther King Jr).

holder in Canada with fee simple title enjoys the largest estate known in the common law world. Nevertheless, the Crown — possessed of sovereignty and underlying radical title — can infringe upon, and indeed expropriate, this property. Note, however, that a key point underlying the sense of this is that all property interests held by non-Indigenous parties in Canada issue originally (at least in principle) from grants by the Crown. What the Crown originally granted, the Crown can later interfere with (or take away). What UNDRIP acknowledges in law is the fact that Indigenous peoples do not hold their property interests as a result of original grants from the Crown. Indigenous peoples in Canada do not hold special rights in relation to jurisdictional authority and ownership of lands — rather, they enjoy original, pre-Crown interests. If any other citizen of the state were (somehow) in the same position, that citizen, too, would enjoy the sorts of interests UNDRIP speaks to. Once again, what UNDRIP is expressing is clear — it is built on broad notions of justice, equality, human rights and non-discrimination, the sorts of notions that can promise a new dialogue of decolonization and meaningful reconciliation.

Actual Concerns and Appropriate Responses

We arrive, then, at the nature of concerns recent conservative commentators must actually have in mind. They would rather have Canada continue on its slow track toward parochially defined justice, as this pulls us further and further away from substantive forms of justice, and preserves the status quo, built on racism and colonialism. In clearly seeing things this way, we simultaneously arrive at the deep concerns of Indigenous peoples in Canada — that the implementation of UNDRIP will be hijacked by conservative liberals, those who are devoted, knowingly or not, to the special interests that the Canadian state is built around and that it protects, those of a neoliberal-capitalist-extractive complex.

The principal concern with recent movement toward creating a legislative framework within which UNDRIP becomes a legal domestic instrument is clear when this core concern with UNDRIP is laid bare — conservative-liberal forces would rather all these matters be left to the political arena (where the appropriate "balancing" of interests can be managed), with the law playing a secondary role. Should UNDRIP come to be part of Canadian law, it would set hard legal standards, could form the basis for legal arguments, would suggest legal remedies, would be legally binding and, in particular, would generate enforceable legal obligations. Given that UNDRIP is suffused with principles and processes that point toward decolonization, married with a commitment to broad principles of justice, democracy, human rights, non-discrimination, good faith and good governance, the result would be a shift in Canada's legal and political landscape, one that redistributes power from the sole sovereign (power currently wielded by those who answer to special moneyed interests) to two sources of authority inhabiting a post-colonial world.

When conservative commentators speak of slowly evolving relations that could be derailed by the sudden importation of UNDRIP into the mix, what they are principally referring to are agreements — primarily economic in nature — that stand as the latest efforts to subvert shifts to decolonizing strategies. Governments and industries now frequently resort to negotiating local, one-off agreements (outside the treaty context), holding out financial and other incentives to impoverished communities and playing off factions within these communities, all to produce buy-in to the neoliberal-capitalist-extractive program. In the face of this, UNDRIP does, in fact, promise uncertainty. Injecting broad forms of justice into a system resting on racism and colonialism will be fraught with challenges, and it is impossible to foresee how many of the most difficult matters will play out.

The troubling form of uncertainty, however, is in relation to how the federal government will act over the next few years. It is currently sending mixed signals, occasionally offering indications it is willing to move the country in the direction of a full embrace of the spirit and intent of UNDRIP, but also on occasion sending strong signals that it hopes to "embrace" UNDRIP in a way that would sap UNDRIP of its decolonizing strength in the Canadian context.[21] We have seen that concerns of conservative critics are principally about decolonization and an aversion to the notion Canada should relinquish absolute power over lands and resources unjustly taken from Indigenous peoples. The most pressing concern, however, is that held by Indigenous peoples, as they wait to see whether the promise of decolonization translates into a fitting response to the persistent core of racism infecting Canada's legal and political environment.

21 In July 2016, at a meeting of the Assembly of First Nations, Attorney-General Jody Wilson-Raybould stated: "Simplistic approaches such as adopting the United Nations declaration as being Canadian law are unworkable and, respectfully, a political distraction to undertaking the hard work actually required to implement it back home in communities." See "Justice Minister Jody Wilson-Raybould says adopting UNDRIP into Canadian law 'unworkable'", *APTN National News* (12 July 2016), online: <http://aptnnews.ca/2016/07/12/justice-minister-jody-wilson-raybould-says-adopting-undrip-into-canadian-law-unworkable/>.

21

Conflicts or Complementarity with Domestic Systems? UNDRIP, Aboriginal Law and the Future of International Norms in Canada

Joshua Nichols and Robert Hamilton

The United Nations Declaration on the Rights of Indigenous Peoples (UNDRIP)[1] has the potential to prompt new ways of understanding both state obligations under international law and domestic frameworks governing state-Indigenous relations. Implementation of the Nagoya Protocol on Access to Genetic Resources and the Fair and Equitable Sharing of Benefits Arising from their Utilization to the Convention on Biological Diversity (Nagoya Protocol),[2] adopted as a supplementary agreement to the 1992 Convention on Biological Diversity (CBD)[3] in 2010, serves as a useful example of UNDRIP's potential in both these arenas. While the Nagoya Protocol has not been adopted or ratified by Canada, the tensions created by its potential adoption, as well as tensions within the Nagoya Protocol itself, illustrate how the implementation of UNDRIP in settler-colonial contexts will shape the interaction between domestic regimes and international instruments concerning Indigenous peoples.

1 *United Nations Declaration on the Rights of Indigenous Peoples*, GA Res 295, UNGAOR, 61st Sess, Supp No 49, UN Doc A/RES/61/295, 46 ILM 1013 (2007) [*UNDRIP*].

2 *2010 Nagoya Protocol on Access to Genetic Resources and the Fair and Equitable Sharing of Benefits Arising from their Utilization to the 1992 Convention on Biological Diversity*, 29 October 2010 (Montreal: Secretariat of the Convention on Biological Diversity, 2011) (entered into force 12 October 2014) [*Nagoya Protocol*], online: <www.cbd.int/abs/doc/protocol/nagoya-protocol-en.pdf>.

3 *Convention on Biological Diversity*, 5 June 1992, 1760 UNTS 79, 31 ILM 818 (entered into force 29 December 1993) [*CBD*].

This chapter focuses on the incongruities between international consent-based norms, such as those articulated in UNDRIP, and Canada's domestic consultation framework, which continues to allow the Crown to supersede Indigenous interests on the basis of unilaterally asserted sovereign claims. These incongruities are illustrated clearly in the Nagoya Protocol, which purports to meet the standards of UNDRIP while giving prominence to domestic legal standards. A consideration of the implications of implementing the Nagoya Protocol in Canada brings these complications to the fore. In our view, the ideal legal structures supporting the Nagoya Protocol come into conflict with pre-existing systems of domestic law and the legal orders of Indigenous peoples, which are themselves often in extended conflict with domestic state legal systems. Our aim in this chapter is to show, first, the tension between the domestic Canadian Aboriginal law framework and the emerging international consent-based standards and, second, to argue that the implementation of UNDRIP provides an avenue to address this tension. UNDRIP offers a possible way forward to implementing an access and benefit sharing (ABS) system, such as that envisioned in the Nagoya Protocol, that balances the rights of self-determination and free, prior and informed consent (FPIC) with Canadian territorial integrity. While we recognize that a distinct body of strictly international law rules is relevant, as are the legal traditions of Indigenous peoples themselves, space requires that we constrain ourselves to a discussion of the extent to which the current domestic framework is compatible with international law and how international norms may be difficult to meet if international instruments continue to give prominence to domestic legal regimes.

Indigenous Rights in International Law

As has been covered elsewhere in this report, UNDRIP recognizes a range of Indigenous rights, including, most importantly, the right of self-determination and an FPIC regime. UNDRIP represents the most substantive and comprehensive articulation of Indigenous rights at the international level, as it builds on rights previously recognized in international law under instruments such as the International Labour Organization Convention No. 169.[4] The aim of the Nagoya Protocol is to provide a transparent legal framework for the fair and equitable distribution of benefits arising from the use of genetic resources (GR) and traditional knowledge (TK) associated with GR. In other words, this is a system for ABS. This ABS mechanism was one of the three objectives of the CBD.[5] In addition to the GR covered in the CBD, the Nagoya Protocol also protects the use of Indigenous TK associated with GR. The overarching aim of the Nagoya Protocol is to establish clear, binding rules and procedures for obtaining prior and informed consent and establishing mutually agreed terms for the use of GR and associated TK.[6] The Nagoya Protocol recognizes the importance of Indigenous rights in these areas, stating in its preamble that "nothing in this Protocol shall be construed as diminishing or extinguishing the rights of indigenous and local communities."[7] The Nagoya Protocol draws on UNDRIP, specifically in seeking to ensure that "the prior informed consent or approval and involvement of

4 *Convention concerning Indigenous and Tribal Peoples in Independent Countries* (27 June 1989) (ILO No 169), 72 ILO Official Bull 59, 28 ILM 1382 (entered into force 5 September 1991). See e.g. Jérémie Gilbert, *Indigenous Peoples' Land Rights under International Law: From Victims to Actors* (New York: Transnational, 2006).

5 The other two being "the conservation of biological diversity" and "the sustainable use of its components." *CBD*, *supra* note 3.

6 *Nagoya Protocol*, *supra* note 2, arts 6, 7, 12. See also Maria Yolanda Teran, "The Nagoya Protocol and Indigenous Peoples" (2016) 7:2 Intl Indigenous Pol J 1.

7 *Nagoya Protocol*, *supra* note 2, Preamble.

indigenous and local communities"[8] is attained. The Nagoya Protocol also notes the importance of UNDRIP[9] and states that the Nagoya Protocol implementation is to be done in "a mutually supportive manner with other international instruments relevant to this Protocol."[10] Thus, in addition to recognizing Indigenous ownership of GR, the Nagoya Protocol adopts UNDRIP's consent-based standards.

There is, however, a tension in the Nagoya Protocol's approach to Indigenous rights. The consent-based standard and recognition of Indigenous rights is qualified in two ways. First, the protocol recognizes state "sovereign rights over natural resources." As will be discussed below, the domestic interpretation of the content of "sovereign rights" can significantly limit Indigenous rights. Second, rights are to be understood "in accordance with domestic law." Article 6 reads: "In accordance with domestic law, each Party shall take measures, as appropriate, with the aim of ensuring that the prior informed consent or approval and involvement of indigenous and local communities is obtained"[11] where access to GR is concerned. Articles 7 and 12 qualify protection of TK and Indigenous laws, respectively, in the same manner.[12] This subordination to domestic law risks undermining the very principles of consent articulated in UNDRIP if domestic regimes fall short of the consent standard. This brings to the fore an inherent tension in the Nagoya Protocol, as it recognizes UNDRIP while seeming to prioritize domestic standards that are less robust. As we will argue, however, meaningful domestic implementation of UNDRIP will require domestic regimes to shift to standards that can accommodate these more robust international norms, thus providing an avenue for resolving the tension inherent in the Nagoya Protocol and the tension between domestic and international law concerning Indigenous peoples.

TK and Rights to GR in Canadian Law

In Canada, the existing written constitutional framework relating to Indigenous peoples consists of two constitutional provisions. First, section 91(24) of the Constitution Act, 1867 vests the federal government with power in relation to "Indians and lands reserved for Indians." This has been consistently interpreted as a power over Indigenous peoples. Second, section 35(1) of the Constitution Act, 1982 states that "[t]he existing aboriginal and treaty rights of the aboriginal peoples of Canada are hereby recognized and affirmed." The meaning of this provision has been subjected to almost 30

8 *Ibid*, art 6(2).
9 *Ibid*, Preamble.
10 *Ibid*, art 4(3).
11 *Ibid*, art 6 [emphasis added].
12 *Ibid*, arts 7, 12.

years of litigation and has given rise to a complicated and contested body of jurisprudence. No constitutional right to GR or associated TK has been recognized in Canadian law.[13]

Unless a political solution could be found — more on that below — any attempt to have rights to GR or TK recognized would have to move through the litigation process that has developed around section 35(1). The existing Aboriginal rights and title frameworks, and the duty to consult and accommodate (DCA), would play an important role. An Indigenous nation could choose, for example, to attempt to have a novel right to GR recognized, or to lay claim to such resources through a conventional rights claim — by asserting exclusive use and occupation rights through an Aboriginal title claim, for example. In either instance, the clash between a government activity and the asserted right would raise the strong possibility of duty to consult litigation.

The existing case law makes the recognition of a new section 35 right a difficult proposition. Under the *Van der Peet* analysis, an activity must have been "integral to the distinctive culture" of the group in question at the time of first European contact in order to be protected.[14] This requires the marshalling of extensive historical evidence to demonstrate not only that an activity — say, the use of a given resource — took place, but also that such a use "made the society what it was."[15] This burden is then compounded at the so-called characterization stage of the analysis. At this stage, the court characterizes the claim to determine what right, precisely, is being sought, requiring evidence of increasingly specific historic activities to be adduced. In this analysis, a GR claim would face a significant hurdle. In self-government claims, for instance, this stage of the analysis has been employed to restrict the nature of the claim by requiring proof not of governance in itself but of governance in relation to a specific matter, such as high-stakes gaming.[16] This requirement creates an evidentiary burden that is almost impossible to satisfy. Such a judicial approach could foreclose the recognition of a right to GR.

The DCA presents what at first glance seems a more favourable approach. The DCA provides a level of procedural protection not only for established claims, but also for asserted rights. While this has, to date, been applied only to asserted rights that have been recognized in other contexts (for example, hunting, fishing and title rights), there is nothing in principle to prevent Indigenous peoples from claiming consultation is owed on the basis of an asserted novel claim.[17]

13 We recognize that TK is protected in some ways in Canada. What is protected, however, is the role for TK in decision-making processes. This role is found in several regulatory regimes. As David Laidlaw notes, "Statutes referencing ATK [Aboriginal TK] fall into several categories: environmental protection, environmental assessment, oceans, land and marine conservation areas, wildlife, forest conservation, species protection including migratory birds, surface and water rights in the North, land planning in Northern Ontario, Nunavut and Eastern Manitoba, nuclear waste disposal, and game conservation plans under Modern Land Claim Agreements that include the British Columbia governments as well as Canada"; David Laidlaw, "Aboriginal Traditional Knowledge in the Courtroom" in Allan E Ingleson, ed, *Environment in the Courtroom* (Calgary: University of Calgary Press, 2018). Bill C-69, with proposed amendments to a range of important environmental laws, also includes mention of TK. The preamble seeks to integrate scientific knowledge with "the traditional knowledge of Indigenous peoples"; Bill C-69, *An Act to enact the Impact Assessment Act and the Canadian Energy Regulator Act, to amend the Navigation Protection Act and to make consequential amendments to other Acts*, 1st Sess, 42nd Parl, 2018 (as passed by the House of Commons 20 June 2018). For a detailed analysis, see David V Wright, "Indigenous Engagement and Consideration in the Newly Proposed *Impact Assessment Act*: The Fog Persists" (27 February 2018), *AbLawg.ca* (blog), online: <https://ablawg.ca/2018/02/27/indigenous-engagement-and-consideration-in-the-newly-proposed-impact-assessment-act-the-fog-persists/>.

14 *R v Van der Peet*, [1996] 2 SCR 507, 1996 CanLII 216 at paras 45–67.

15 *Ibid* at para 55.

16 *R v Pamajewon*, [1996] 2 SCR 821, 1996 CanLII 161 at paras 26–27.

17 See e.g. *Ka'a'Gee Tu First Nation v Canada (AG)*, 2007 FC 763, 2007 CarswellNat 2067 ("*Haida* teaches that the Aboriginal group need not prove that an asserted right exists before the obligation is triggered" at para 102).

The DCA has undoubtedly done much to further Indigenous interests. The DCA establishes a constitutional requirement that governments consult and, in some instances, accommodate Indigenous peoples not only where recognized section 35(1) rights are subject to infringement but also where asserted title,[18] Aboriginal rights[19] or treaty rights[20] are potentially impacted. This has had a transformative effect, as Indigenous peoples gained a voice in development projects that, before the DCA, they could have opposed only through direct action or by litigating rights claims.

Yet, the structure of the DCA suggests this path, as well, is likely to provide protections short of those Indigenous peoples may hope for. With international norms trending toward consent, the age-old claims of Indigenous peoples to a right to determine what happens in their traditional territories have been given a new legal language — that of self-determination and FPIC. This new language sits in tension with the DCA framework. Under the DCA framework, courts determine the significance of asserted rights on a spectrum. They then determine the appropriate level of consultation, ranging from mere notice to accommodation, before determining whether consultation was adequate in the case at hand. The outcomes of this process are unpredictable and ultimately skew in favour of the Crown by ensuring that the final say rests with the Crown so long as certain procedural benchmarks are met. As the Supreme Court of Canada has repeatedly stated, consultation does not give Indigenous peoples a veto. Rather, it "is a right to a process, not to a particular outcome."[21] Undergirding the DCA framework is the notion that the Crown may act unilaterally in the name of the public interest despite Indigenous opposition. This raises the question of whether the current DCA framework sufficiently motivates governments to come to the negotiating table to resolve claims in the way the court seems to envision. On this point, there should be some doubt.[22] Thus, while offering procedural protection for asserted claims and judicial oversight of discretionary Crown action, the DCA framework fits awkwardly with Indigenous understandings of international norms and Indigenous peoples' own inherent jurisdiction.

This awkward fit exposes the foundational presumptions of the section 35 and DCA framework: first, Indigenous peoples exist within a sovereign-to-subjects relationship to the Crown; and, second, Indigenous peoples' claims are only cognizable within a contingent rights/duties context. The unilateral assertion of Crown sovereignty could have vested legal powers supporting these presuppositions in the Crown only if Europeans brought to North America a system of law superior to the systems of law that already existed or if Europeans had found a legally vacant landscape.[23] In other words, while the DCA framework does open up the possibility of Indigenous participation, it relies on a foundational logic that can only be supported by the doctrines of discovery and *terra nullius*. Although attenuating some of the more damaging features of these doctrines, the DCA incorporates these notions of European legal superiority, thereby relying on a racist ideology and pernicious legal fiction that is widely considered illegitimate.

18 *Haida Nation v British Columbia (Minister of Forests)*, [2004] 3 SCR 511 [*Haida Nation*].

19 *Taku River Tlingit First Nation v British Columbia (Project Assessment Director)*, [2004] 3 SCR 550.

20 For historic treaty rights, see *Mikisew Cree First Nation v Canada (Minister of Canadian Heritage)*, [2005] 3 SCR 388; for modern, see *Beckman v Little Salmon/Carmacks First Nation*, [2010] 3 SCR 103.

21 See *Ktunaxa Nation v British Columbia (Forests, Lands and Natural Resource Operations)*, 2017 SCC 54 at para 83.

22 We have elaborated on these points elsewhere — see Robert Hamilton & Joshua Nichols, "Reassessing the Reconciliation Basket: *Ktunaxa Nation* and the Foundation of the Duty to Consult" (2019) [forthcoming].

23 See John Borrows, "The Durability of Terra Nullius: *Tsilhqot'in Nation v British Columbia*" (2015) 48:3 UBC L Rev 701.

The Supreme Court of Canada seems aware of this. In *Haida Nation*, the court made the unusual decision to bring Crown sovereignty into question, labelling Crown sovereignty as de facto.[24] This labelling is evidently meant to draw a distinction between de facto and de jure (that is, factual and legal) sovereignty. The implication seems to be that the Crown lacks legal sovereignty. This could only stem from an acknowledgement that the Crown's claims to legal sovereignty on the basis of discovery are insufficient in themselves to establish legal sovereignty. As Ryan Beaton helpfully points out, however, there seems to be a logic to the court's move here, suggesting that the issue for the court may be one of legitimating Crown sovereignty through judicial oversight. Beaton calls this framework "judicially mediated sovereignty."[25] Although this description is apt, the issue of legitimacy remains. A Canadian court upholding the unilateral authority of the state must also uphold the continuing effects of the doctrine of discovery and, in doing so, undermine the court's own claims regarding constitutional legitimacy.

This tension highlights the cost of retaining a sovereign-to-subjects model of contingent rights. The existing process allows the courts to determine what rights are owed protections and where accommodation is required. This process, in turn, encourages the Crown to adopt a strategy of continual litigation, as governments have typically been hesitant to give away more than the courts have required them to. The problem is that the DCA framework does not provide certainty and offers the Crown little incentive to come to the negotiating table. Indigenous peoples often do not see the process to be fair and equitable and, as a result, have no motivation to accept decisions. Despite its success in some instances, in many others, this expansive system of procedural legitimation is little more than a recipe for extending conflict between the parties, thereby propagating an environment of uncertainty.

This resulting uncertainty has a direct bearing on any prospective ABS system, as such a system would need to offer parties procedural clarity and legal certainty in order to be seen as a legitimate way to resolve issues involving GR. As it currently stands, claims to GR could be subject to litigation through the existing DCA framework where Indigenous rights are at issue in the domestic context. As outlined above, the DCA framework is ill-suited to the task for two reasons: first, if protection for TK and GR were framed through the lens of currently recognized section 35(1) rights (for example, title, harvesting rights and so on), these rights would be subject to consultation standards that may fall short of international norms and may provide little by way of certainty; and, second, the extension of the DCA to novel rights (i.e., GR are not articulated as one of the groups of rights recognized to date) is speculative at best. The spectrum analysis would presumptively frame such novel claims as having a low likelihood of success, thereby requiring the bare minimum level of consultation (i.e., notice).

Can the domestic Aboriginal rights system be amended to resolve these problems? One response is that, yes, it can, but this requires a foundational change of the DCA framework to reflect Indigenous aspirations for greater self-determination and to create a greater motivation for state governments to negotiate jurisdiction with Indigenous peoples. The vision, then, would be one that moves away from the sovereign-to-subjects model of contingent rights and replaces it with a nation-to-nation model of negotiated jurisdiction. This, we argue, is what is required

24 *Haida Nation, supra* note 18.

25 Ryan Beaton, "De facto and de jure Crown sovereignty: Reconciliation and Legitimation at the Supreme Court of Canada" [unpublished draft paper].

if UNDRIP is to be meaningfully implemented and if the domestic system is to align with international norms.

UNDRIP and a Nation-to-Nation Framework for Negotiation

The existing section 35 framework is predicated on the notion that Indigenous peoples are subjects of the Crown and so can only lay claim to a set of residual rights. This seems to fit into the usual narrative of consent and contract that undergirds liberal democracy, which lumps the various individuals and groups within a defined territory into the curious amalgam referred to as "the people." This picture of state formation is what informs the court's repeated concern that Indigenous peoples should not be given a veto. In other words, the fear of Indigenous peoples having a veto is a bugbear that is produced by the assumption that the nation-state is the only model of political association. The problem with this picture is, as Stephen Tierney notes, "Mistaken assumptions about the unitary nature of 'the people' can generate constitutional models which fail to accommodate the specific political needs of different peoples within the state."[26] Tierney's analysis highlights a background assumption concerning the basic structure of a state that is responsible for much of the conflict with Indigenous peoples: the only possible form of the state is the unitary nation-state. Once this proposition is set in place, it drives the compulsion to fit Indigenous peoples into a sovereign-to-subjects framework.

The problem in settler states is that the relationship between the ideal model of the liberal democratic nation-state and the historical reality of settler colonialism cannot be bridged. There is no plausible account of Indigenous peoples consenting to enter into a sovereign-to-subjects relationship. By recognizing Indigenous self-determination and the principles of FPIC, and by rewriting the role of Indigenous peoples as actors in the international arena, UNDRIP challenges these legal relationships.[27] But, can the domestic system be reformed so as to reflect UNDRIP's substantive rights, thereby resolving the tension apparent in documents such as the Nagoya Protocol? Our view is that the single most important step to giving life to the legal pluralism envisioned in UNDRIP is to ensure that contested claims between the parties are subject to negotiation.[28] Domestic courts can facilitate this by ensuring that their doctrines effectively compel negotiated solutions. While the Supreme Court of Canada has often identified negotiation as the highest goal, its assumption of the sovereign legitimacy of the state and the sovereign-to-subjects model as the only possibility has undermined that possibility. If, instead, the court followed its own reasoning in the Secession Reference, which acknowledged the limitations of the court's jurisdiction and offered the parties a legal procedure for negotiating their dispute, negotiated solutions that reflect the self-determination of both parties would become the reality.[29] This would ultimately lead to legal certainty while bridging the gap between Canada's international obligations and domestic law.

26 Stephen Tierney, *Constitutional Law and National Pluralism* (Oxford, UK: Oxford University Press, 2004) at 13.

27 See e.g. Matthew Gonnella, "If You Are Not at the Table, Then You Are Probably on the Menu: Indigenous Peoples' Participatory Status at the United Nations" (2018) 41 Suffolk Transnat'l L Rev 145.

28 For legal pluralism in UNDRIP, see Gordon Christie, "Indigenous Legal Orders, Canadian Law and UNDRIP" (this volume, ch 5).

29 *Reference re Secession of Quebec*, [1998] 2 SCR 217.

A shift is necessarily required in the court's interpretation of Canada's Constitution as the court can no longer base its interpretation of section 35(1) on either a unilateral model of federal power grounded in section 91(24) or a generalized claim to the Crown (in all of its various manifestations) possessing underlying sovereignty. Rather, section 91(24) must be limited to embodying a federal power to negotiate with Indigenous peoples, which, in turn, means that section 35(1) must be read as being jurisdictional in nature. Section 35(1) is outside of the Charter and so should not be interpreted as a species of rights subject to the limitations of either section 1 or section 33. This interpretation is otherwise known as the third order of government interpretation of section 35, a model that Indigenous leaders negotiated toward in the 1992 Charlottetown Accord.[30] In effect, this model amounts to the removal of one set of international legal norms (i.e., discovery, *terra nullius*, divine right and so on) and its replacement with a set that is predicated on consent.

This shift in constitutional interpretation necessarily alters the DCA framework as the court can no longer determine when unilateral Crown infringements are justified. The duty is then reworked in order to compel negotiation on the basis of jurisdiction. Compelling negotiation on the basis of jurisdiction requires removing discrete rights as the basis of the claims and reframing the claims as jurisdictional issues. In effect, the duty to consult is converted into a duty to negotiate.[31] This model takes advantage of the strengths of the previous DCA framework, as it can still respond to issues of asserted jurisdiction and so can quickly and flexibly respond to conflicts, but the remedies available are limited to retaining good faith negotiations between the parties. Bargaining power would be more evenly distributed among the parties, thereby providing more impetus toward negotiated settlements than in the current framework. While constitutional reinterpretation may seem a daunting task, we should note that negotiated jurisdictional settlements are already common in Canada. While not all of these agreements fully dispense with the harmful residues of unilateral sovereign authority, many represent the kinds of negotiated jurisdiction advocated for in this chapter. Our purpose here is to suggest an avenue for judicial doctrine to support the further development of the kinds of solutions that are already being explored in some circumstances.

Conclusion

In sum, the tensions apparent in the Nagoya Protocol, which calls for a consent-based model while requiring consistency with domestic law, could undermine attempts to implement the substantive vision the protocol espouses. In contrast, the decolonized version of Canada's constitutional machinery that we outline here provides a complementary legal environment for an ABS system. It does this by clarifying the identity of the stakeholders and thereby offering the possibility of clear legal procedures and dependable legal certainty. UNDRIP implementation can guide the shifts in domestic law required to bring about these changes. Other contexts, those in settler-colonial states in particular, will face similar types of challenges. The task of re-articulating the role of Indigenous peoples in the constitutional structure of federated liberal democracies might follow a logic similar to that outlined here.

30 The Charlottetown Accord was, of course, rejected by public referendum. See Philip Resnick, "The Crisis of Multi-National Federations: Post-Charlottetown Reflections" (1994) 1 Rev Const Stud 189.

31 We expanded on the shift to a duty to negotiate in Hamilton & Nichols, *supra* note 22.

22

UNDRIP as a Catalyst for Aboriginal and Treaty Rights Implementation and Reconciliation

Cheryl Knockwood

For many decades, Indigenous nations from all over Mother Earth drafted and advocated for the adoption of the United Nations Declaration on the Rights of Indigenous Peoples (UNDRIP).[1] Many years were spent crafting the wording of each of the 46 articles of UNDRIP before it was finally adopted at the United Nations General Assembly on September 13, 2007.[2]

Indigenous nations held high hopes that, with the adoption of UNDRIP, many of their rights would be recognized, including, for example, Indigenous rights to self-determination (articles 3 and 4), to own and control their lands and resources within their traditional territories (article 26) and to establish and control culture and education (article 14) within their home states. Furthermore, Indigenous nations hoped that their home states would consult and cooperate in good faith with Indigenous nations to obtain their free, prior and informed consent (article 32) for any projects that concern their lands and resources within their traditional territories.

It has been nearly 10 years since UNDRIP was adopted by the United Nations in 2007. Canada only endorsed UNDRIP in 2010 and adopted it in 2016. Minister of Indigenous and Northern

1 GA Res 295, UNGAOR, 61st Sess, Supp No 49, UN Doc A/RES/61/295, 46 ILM 1013 (2007).

2 Lillian Aponte Miranda, "Indigenous Peoples as International Lawmakers" (2010) 32 U Pa J Intl L 210.

Affairs Carolyn Bennett stated that implementing UNDRIP is about righting historical wrongs and that what is needed is fundamental and foundational change.[3]

In July 2016, Canadian Justice Minister Jody Wilson-Raybould called the full adoption of UNDRIP into Canadian law "unworkable" in a statement to the Assembly of First Nations. Wilson-Raybould stated that hard work was required by Indigenous nations to implement UNDRIP in First Nation communities. She also stated that the Canadian government needs Indigenous nations to step forward with ideas for legislation and policy that will eventually wipe out laws such as the Indian Act.[4]

For Indigenous nations, the adoption of UNDRIP means the full implementation of self-determination and of Aboriginal and treaty rights. Indigenous nations, such as the Mi'kmaq, have been doing the hard work to ensure rights recognition and implementation since before Confederation. For the Mi'kmaq, treaty negotiations began in the 1700s,[5] and the Mi'kmaq have been advocating for, negotiating and litigating their rights ever since. The Mi'kmaq are ready to continue doing the hard work to ensure UNDRIP is recognized and implemented in Canada.

In the 150 years since Canada's Confederation, the Mi'kmaw Nation has gone from being an independent, self-sufficient and self-governing nation to one subjected to dispossessing laws and policies aimed at eliminating and assimilating the Mi'kmaq. This forced the Mi'kmaw Nation to depend upon Canada to recognize its legal and ethical obligations. Sadly, Canada has often failed in meeting its obligations to the Mi'kmaq; Mi'kmaw Aboriginal and treaty rights have not been fully implemented and Mi'kmaq' lands rights have been ignored.

However, UNDRIP provides a beacon of hope for the Mi'kmaw Nation. It is hopeful that with Canada's implementation of UNDRIP, Canada's relationship with the Mi'kmaq and other Indigenous nations can truly move toward reconciliation. The work does not need to be difficult if Canada fulfills its legal and ethical obligations to the Mi'kmaq.

I will share examples of the hard work that has been done since Confederation by the Mi'kmaw Nation on rights recognition and UNDRIP implementation. Then I will focus on what two Mi'kmaw communities — Membertou and Elsipogtog — have been doing in the last few years to implement UNDRIP.

It is hoped that UNDRIP will be a catalyst for change in which the Canadian government will act upon, recognize and implement Mi'kmaw Aboriginal and treaty rights. UNDRIP has acted as a catalyst for some Mi'kmaw communities that have advocated for their consent to be sought in megaprojects impacting their lands and in the development of their laws.

3 Minister of Indigenous and Northern Affairs Carolyn Bennett, "Announcement of Canada's Support for the United Nations Declaration on the Rights of Indigenous Peoples" (Statement delivered at the 15th Session of the United Nations Permanent Forum on Indigenous Issues, 10 May 2016).

4 APTN National News, "Justice Minister Jody Wilson-Raybould says adopting UNDRIP into Canadian law 'unworkable'" *APTN National News* (12 July 2016), online: <http://aptnnews.ca/2016/07/12/justice-minister-jody-wilson-raybould-says-adopting-undrip-into-canadian-law-unworkable/>.

5 Pre-Confederation treaties signed between the Mi'kmaq and the British Crown began in 1725.

The Hope: Mi'kmaw Communities

Mi'kma'ki, the traditional territory of the Mi'kmaw Nation, encompasses what is now known as Nova Scotia, Prince Edward Island, Newfoundland, the Gaspé regions of Quebec, the Eastern side of New Brunswick and parts of Maine. The Mi'kmaw title to its traditional territory has never been ceded in any treaty or by any other act or legal instrument.

The treaties that were signed between the Mi'kmaq and the British Crown from 1725 to 1779 were about establishing a relationship based on mutual peace and friendship, not about ceding any Mi'kmaw territory. The Mi'kmaq have never ceded their Aboriginal title nor has Canada ever extinguished Mi'kmaw title over its territory.

For centuries, the Mi'kmaq have been seeking implementation of their treaty rights. Letters were sent to the British Crown reminding it of its treaty promises. In 1841, a letter written by Mi'kmaw Chief Pemmeenauweet to Queen Victoria sadly illustrates the dire circumstances the Mi'kmaq were in during the treaty denial era: "No Hunting Grounds — No Beaver — No Otter — no nothing. Indians poor — poor for ever. No Store — no Chest — no Clothes. All these Woods once ours. Our Fathers possessed them all. Now we cannot cut a Tree to warm our Wigwam in Winter unless the White Man please. The Micmacs now receive no presents, but one small Blanket for a whole family."[6]

Mi'kmaw individuals have been going to the courts to get legal recognition of their Aboriginal and treaty rights with mixed results. Gabriel Sylliboy lost in 1929,[7] as did Martin Francis in 1969.[8] Despite losing in the lower courts, James Matthew Simon in 1985[9] and Donald Marshall Jr. in 1999[10] finally won their treaty right cases at the Supreme Court of Canada (SCC).

In 1926, the Mi'kmaw Grand Chief Gabriel Syliboy[11] was convicted of having pelts (muskrat and fox) in his possession, contrary to the Nova Scotia Lands and Forests Act, 1926. Grand Chief Syliboy's defence was that he had the right to hunt and fish at all times because of his Treaty of 1752 right. The court held that Grand Chief Syliboy was not a beneficiary to the 1752 treaty because he was from Cape Breton. The court then went on to characterize Mi'kmaq as savages: "[T]he Indians were never regarded as an independent power. A civilized nation first discovering a country of uncivilized people or savages held such country as its own until such time as by treaty it was transferred to some other civilized nation. The savages' rights of sovereignty even of ownership were never recognized."[12]

On September 22, 1966, Martin Francis was salmon fishing with a net on the Richibucto River. He was charged with fishing without a licence in violation of the New Brunswick fishery

6 "Letter of Mi'kmaq' Chief Pemmeenauweet to Queen Victoria, 1841", online: *JohnWood1946* <https://johnwood1946.wordpress.com/2011/07/08/letter-of-mi%e2%80%99kmaq%e2%80%99-chief-pemmeenauweet-to-queen-victoria-1841/>.

7 *R v Syliboy*, [1929] 1 DLR 307, 1928 CanLII 352 (NSSC) [*Syliboy* cited to DLR].

8 *R v Francis*, (1969) 10 DLR (3d) 189, 1969 CanLII 848 (NBCA) [*Francis* cited to DLR].

9 *Simon v R*, [1985] 2 SCR 387 [*Simon*].

10 *R v Marshall*, [1999] 3 SCR 456 [*Marshall*].

11 Grand Chief Gabriel Sylliboy's name was spelled Syliboy in this case.

12 *Syliboy*, *supra* note 7 at 313.

regulations. Francis' defence was that he had a treaty right to fish, and he cited three Mi'kmaw treaties, dated December 15, 1725; November 22, 1752; and September 22, 1779.

The court convicted Francis, taking a very restrictive view as to which "bands" of the Mi'kmaw Nation the treaties of 1725 and 1752 applied, and held that Francis had not proven he was a member of those bands.[13] While the court had held that Francis was a member of the Treaty of 1779, it interpreted the Treaty of 1779 as not conferring any hunting and fishing rights.[14]

Regardless of these huge losses and expenses[15] within the Canadian judicial system, the Mi'kmaw Nation never gave up hope that its treaties were valid and that these treaties would be recognized and implemented by Canada. The Mi'kmaw Nation was finally vindicated when, in 1985, for the first time in Canada, the SCC ruled in *Simon*[16] that the Mi'kmaw Treaty of 1752 was valid.

In 1999, the SCC, in the *Marshall*[17] decision, ruled in favour of Mi'kmaw, Maliseet and Passamaquoddy treaty rights. The court recognized those three nations' treaty rights to gain a moderate livelihood from fishing. Sadly, there is not one Mi'kmaw community fishing under a treaty-based commercial fishery. Instead, many are fishing commercially under the interim agreements negotiated by the Department of Fisheries and Oceans soon after the *Marshall* decision was won.[18] Canada has given Indigenous and Northern Affairs the mandate to negotiate a treaty-based fishery with the Mi'kmaq, but there has been no success to date.[19]

Currently, the treaty and Aboriginal rights recognition process, primarily in the courts, is expensive and time consuming.[20] When the Mi'kmaw Nation wins at the SCC level, there are no guarantees there will be implementation, as we learned with the Mi'kmaq in the *Marshall* decision. However, the Mi'kmaq are hopeful that, with Canada's commitment to the implementation of UNDRIP, Canada will spend less time and money litigating with the Mi'kmaw Nation and more time on recognizing and implementing treaty and Aboriginal rights.

In the next few paragraphs, I will share stories from Mi'kmaw communities that are implementing UNDRIP. First, I will share Elsipogtog's struggle to seek free, prior and informed consent. Then, I will share how Membertou made a decision to include UNDRIP within the development of its laws.

13 The term "bands" is a creation of the *Indian Act, 1876*. The Mi'kmaq did not live in *Indian Act*-created "band" entities prior to contact nor during the treaty-making period.

14 *Francis*, *supra* note 8 at 194.

15 Yamri Taddese, "Feds pouring big money into aboriginal litigation", *The Law Times* (11 March 2013), online: <www.lawtimesnews.com/201311113587/headline-news/feds-pouring-big-money-into-aboriginal-litigation>. This article focuses on the expenses of Aboriginal Affairs and Northern Development Canada.

16 *Simon*, *supra* note 9.

17 *Marshall*, *supra* note 10.

18 Parliament of Canada, "The Marshall Decision and the Atlantic Fishery" (20 September 2001), online: <www.lop.parl.gc.ca/content/lop/ResearchPublications/tips/tip63-e.htm>.

19 Atlantic Policy Congress of First Nations Chiefs, "Marshall 10 Years Later: Atlantic and Gaspé First Nations Participation in Fisheries" (September 2009), online: <www.apcfnc.ca/images/uploads/Post_Marshall_report_10_years.pdf>.

20 Kent McNeil, "Stop wasting money fighting aboriginals", *The National Post* (21 October 2015), online: <http://news.nationalpost.com/full-comment/kent-mcneil-stop-wasting-money-fighting-aboriginals>.

Elsipogtog, Fracking and No Free, Prior and Informed Consent

In 2013, the Mi'kmaw community of Elsipogtog challenged the province of New Brunswick on a shale gas exploration project slated to occur within its traditional territory area. The community was concerned about the impacts that project might have on the current and future use of land.

Mi'kmaw groups in Elsipogtog First Nation, New Brunswick,[21] united and stood up against Southwestern Energy (SWN), an oil and natural gas company based in Houston, Texas. The New Brunswick government, under Progressive Conservative Party leadership, had allowed SWN to conduct shale gas exploration within the traditional territory of the Sikniktuk district of the Mi'kmaw Nation. The permission to conduct this exploration was granted by the provincial government without adequate and/or meaningful consultation with the Mi'kmaw groups most impacted by the exploration.

Concerned about the effects of exploration, the Mi'kmaw leaders and members from the community of Elsipogtog First Nation were strongly opposed to fracking and did not want any shale gas exploration to occur within their traditional territory.[22] Many in the community felt their free, prior and informed consent was never sought and, therefore, never given. As stewards of their traditional territory, the Mi'kmaq from the Sikniktuk district stood on their lands and refused access to SWN employees. Chief Aaron Sock of Elsipogtog issued an eviction notice to SWN.[23] As a result, many Mi'kmaw people who joined Elsipogtog in its opposition to SWN's plans launched a protest in an attempt to stop the company.

On October 3, 2013, the Court of Queen's Bench in New Brunswick granted SWN an injunction to end the protests.[24] However, the Mi'kmaw stewards were undeterred, and on October 17, 2013, the RCMP moved in to enforce the injunction.[25] Elders, women and children were pepper-sprayed and more than 40 Mi'kmaw stewards were arrested. The excessive force used against the Mi'kmaq was captured on video and shared internationally through online social media channels.

On December 6, 2013, SWN announced it was halting exploration for a year.[26] On December 18, 2014, newly elected Premier Brian Gallant of New Brunswick announced a moratorium on fracking exploration until numerous conditions were met. The first condition called for a process

21 The First Nation community with the largest population in New Brunswick, located in Kent County.

22 Vidya Kauri, "Elsipogtog man determined to stop fracking", *National Observer* (3 March 2015), online: <www.nationalobserver.com/2015/02/13/news/elsipogtog-man-determined-stop-fracking>.

23 CBC News, "First Nations chief issues eviction notice to SWN Resources", *CBC News* (1 October 2013), online: <www.cbc.ca/news/canada/new-brunswick/first-nations-chief-issues-eviction-notice-to-swn-resources-1.1874870>.

24 CBC News, "Court orders end to shale gas barricades on Route 134", *CBC News* (3 October 2013), online: <www.cbc.ca/news/canada/new-brunswick/court-orders-end-to-shale-gas-barricades-on-route-134-1.1894789>.

25 Melanie Patten, "Elsipogtog First Nation Sees Violence As RCMP Moves To End Protest", *Huff Post Politics Canada* (17 October 2013), online: <www.huffingtonpost.ca/2013/10/17/elsipogtog-photos-rcmp-protest-violence_n_4114506.html>.

26 APTN National News, "SWN ending exploration work in NB, will be back in 2015: Elsipogtog War Chief Levi", *APTN National News* (6 December 2013), online: <http://aptnnews.ca/2013/12/06/swn-ending-exploration-work-nb-back-2015-war-chief-levi/>.

to consult with Indigenous peoples.[27] On May 27, 2016, the province announced it would ban fracking indefinitely.[28]

Despite enormous effort to push them out of the way so that the government could allow companies to develop Mi'kmaw land and resources, the Mi'kmaw people from Elsipogtog never bowed to this pressure. Rather, they stood united with neighbouring communities from Richibucto and Rexton to protect the land for use by current and future generations.

Membertou and Self-determination

Membertou[29] is a Mi'kmaw community that has incorporated UNDRIP provisions in relation to lands, territories and resources into one of its laws. On April 30, 2016, Membertou enacted its Membertou Family Homes Law.[30] The Membertou Governance Committee, which drafted the law, ensured that UNDRIP was referred to and given significance in its law. For instance, in three sections of the preamble, the law states:

> B. Membertou has an unextinguished right to self-determination, as affirmed by the United Nations Declaration on the Rights of Indigenous Peoples, which includes a right to govern itself, its members and its lands;
>
> C. Membertou has an unextinguished and inherent right of self-governance which emanates from its people, culture, language, land and aboriginal and treaty rights, which are recognized by section 35 of the Constitution Act, 1982;
>
> D. Membertou, as an aspect of its unextinguished right to self-determination and its unextinguished and inherent right of self-governance, has jurisdiction to create rules for the resolution of issues regarding family homes and real property located on Membertou lands upon the breakdown of a marriage or common-law relationship.[31]

Membertou is also developing a land code. The land code will recognize Membertou's jurisdiction over its lands, water and resources. The land code will adopt the language of self-determination used in UNDRIP, similar to the language used in the Membertou Family Homes Law. The land code will go to a community ratification vote in the near future. Like Elsipogtog, Membertou is doing the hard work required to implement UNDRIP.

27 CBC News, "Shale gas moratorium details unveiled by Brian Gallant: Five conditions will need to be met before government lifts moratorium on all forms of fracking", *CBC News* (18 December 2014), online: <www.cbc.ca/news/canada/new-brunswick/shale-gas-moratorium-details-unveiled-by-brian-gallant-1.2877440>.

28 Shawn McCarthy, "New Brunswick extends fracking ban indefinitely", *The Globe and Mail* (27 May 2016), online: <www.theglobeandmail.com/report-on-business/industry-news/energy-and-resources/new-brunswick-extends-fracking-ban-indefinitely/article30191515/>.

29 A Mi'kmaw community located on Cape Breton Island in Nova Scotia.

30 *Membertou Family Homes Law 2016*, First Nations Gazette, online: <http://sp.fng.ca/fngweb/26_MPR_law_2016.pdf>.

31 *Ibid*, Preamble B, C, D.

Conclusion

The Mi'kmaw Nation has been advocating for treaty and aboriginal rights recognition for nearly 300 years. The Mi'kmaq are aware of the work required from them to ensure Canada fulfills its legal obligations. UNDRIP would not exist if it were not for the hard work of Indigenous nations from all over the world. UNDRIP is a symbol of what can be accomplished when Indigenous peoples and nation-states work together internationally within the United Nations to ensure our rights are respected and our voices are heard. UNDRIP is another tool that the Mi'kmaq have available to ensure recognition of their constitutional and international Indigenous rights.

The adoption of UNDRIP by Canada is of great importance to the Mi'kmaw Nation. At the heart of UNDRIP is an international recognition of the rights of Indigenous nations to self-determination and all that follows from that.

While the Mi'kmaw Nation has taken important steps, much hard work is required from the government of Canada to implement UNDRIP within Canada. What is needed to implement UNDRIP in Canada is for Canada to stop litigating against Mi'kmaw individuals when they are exercising their aboriginal and treaty rights. Canada needs to recognize and give full meaning to all the existing treaties signed with the Mi'kmaq and other Indigenous nations within Canada. Canada needs to ensure that laws, policies and funding are in place to ensure Indigenous nations are included in discussions of all potential projects that may happen within their traditional territories.

It is hoped that, with implementation, there may be fewer time-consuming, expensive legal battles for Aboriginal and treaty rights recognition. It is hoped that, with the adoption of UNDRIP, Canadian provinces will involve Indigenous nations that are impacted by any potential development within their traditional territory in the entire review and decision-making process. It is hoped that Canada will soon respect Mi'kmaw nationhood, the inherent right of Mi'kmaw self-determination, the right to Aboriginal title and the right to manage land and resources. Ultimately, if these hopes are realized, how can that not lead to reconciliation?

23

The Necessity of Exploring Inherent Dignity in Indigenous Knowledge Systems

James (Sa'ke'j) Youngblood Henderson

The Indigenous concept of inherent dignity is often assumed to be the same as European versions of dignity, yet the many Indigenous concepts of inherent dignity are distinct from the European versions of dignity. Indigenous knowledge systems and languages in Canada are distinct knowledge systems that have in them many diffused and eclectic manifestations of the concept of inherent dignity that have not been systematically explored or unpacked by Indigenous Elders, academics, lawyers or policy analysts. In the collective Indigenous concept, inherent dignity is viewed as inviolable and sacred in all life forms; inherent dignity gives meaning to all of reality and constitutes its supreme value. Grounded holistically in a connected material and spiritual relationship, these Indigenous concepts give meaning and value to all life forms. No clear dividing line exists that separates humans from other life forms. These holistic concepts blend spirituality and consciousness, subjectivity and objectivity, receptivity, relationality, identity and creativity. Inherent dignity generated the Indigenous perspective of ecological, collective, family and individual dignity. It also informs Indigenous law, treaty interpretation and the implementation of the United Nations Declaration on the Rights of Indigenous Peoples (UN Declaration).[1]

1 The UN Declaration was adopted by the United Nations in 2007. *United Nations Declaration on the Rights of Indigenous Peoples*, GA Res 295, UNGAOR, 61st Sess, Supp No 49, UN Doc A/RES/61/295, 46 ILM 1013 (2007).

Human rights are not aspirational or soft law; they are natural rights held by humans, as distinct from artificial governments. They are consensual norms of a non-coercive global legal order that articulate the inherent rights of humans as a remedy to the historical and ongoing racial and cultural superiority of European colonization. Human rights are standards and binding obligations that the consensually ratifying states have promised to respect, protect and fulfill to generate inherent human dignity and protect the self-determination of peoples. Furthermore, the states have no ability to limit these human rights.

Given the diverse views held about and the power relations at play in deciding on the state or the nature of human dignity, an inherent dignity approach to human rights is essential to overcome the past inequalities, discriminatory practices and unjust distributions of power that have impeded developmental progress of peoples. The inherent dignity approach begins with a rejection of violence as a form of social control by the state through its legal system and its administration of justice. An inherent dignity approach to human rights is more than a contextual element that assists in the interpretation of the Constitution, the construction of ambiguous legislation and the filling of gaps in the common or civil law.

The principle of respect for inherent human dignity holds a prominent and canonical position in UN and intergovernmental instruments. It is the starting point, the shaping principle or the overarching principle of the law of human rights. It affirms the centrality of the spirit of the dignity of human beings as persons or of personhood. It emphasizes the significance, uniqueness and inviolability of each human, each person, against the background of their essentially relational dimensions. Inherent dignity is indispensable for living a just life. Yet we are not born knowing how to live or act by this fundamental truth. The spirit and intent of the existing knowledge systems have to teach us how to live and nourish our inherent dignity throughout our lives. The various concepts of inherent dignity of humans need to be boldly, but skilfully, woven and harmonized among distinct knowledge systems to achieve a new national and global order.[2]

Currently, a comprehensive view of the concept of inherent human dignity is explicitly enshrined in international human rights law. The preamble of the Charter of the United Nations states that the peoples of the United Nations are determined "to reaffirm faith in fundamental human rights, in the dignity and worth of the human person."[3] The preamble of the Universal Declaration of Human Rights (Universal Declaration)[4] of 1948 declares that "the inherent dignity" of all members of the human family is "the foundation of freedom, justice and peace in the world." Article 1 of the Universal Declaration declares, "All human beings are born free and equal in dignity and rights." The Universal Declaration established "the idea that human dignity and human rights are core values which should be respected when pursuing any policy."[5] In addition, "it establishes that human dignity and rights are afforded to all human beings" and

2 For sources that examine the concept of dignity in greater depth, see e.g. Patrick Capps, *Human Dignity and the Foundations of International Law* (Oxford, UK: Hart, 2009); Erin Daly, *Dignity Rights: Courts, Constitutions, and the Worth of the Human Person* (Philadelphia: University of Pennsylvania Press, 2012); Michael Rosen, *Dignity: Its History and Meaning* (Cambridge, MA: Harvard University Press, 2012); Oscar Schachter, "Human Dignity as a Normative Concept" (1983) 77 AJIL 848–54.

3 *Charter of the United Nations*, 24 October 1945, 1 UNTS XVI, Can TS 1945 No 7.

4 The Universal Declaration was enacted by the United Nations in 1948. *Universal Declaration*, GA Res 217A(III), UNGAOR, 3d Sess, Supp No 13, UN Doc A/810 (1948) 71 [*Universal Declaration*].

5 Daly, *supra* note 2; Rosen, *supra* note 2.

"that all human action must act in accordance with human dignity."[6] This concept limits the concept of sovereignty and power. The then rapporteur to the Human Rights Commission, Charles Malik from Lebanon, summarized this fundamental issue as whether the state existed for the sake of the human person or the person for the sake of the state: the human rights regime articulates that the state exists for the sake of the human.[7]

The idea of inherent human dignity has been at the heart of the major overarching human rights treaties that grew out of the Universal Declaration, which was initially conceived of as a soft law instrument. Today, the idea of inherent human dignity is widely recognized as the innovative concept of the entire international human rights system.[8] The importance of inherent dignity continued to be foundational in the International Convention on the Elimination of All Forms of Racial Discrimination,[9] the International Covenant on Civil and Political Rights[10] and the International Covenant on Economic, Social and Cultural Rights.[11]

The Universal Declaration paved the way for the adoption of more than 70 UN treaties, which are applied today on a permanent basis at global, regional and national levels. It also served as a model for many constitutions and laws throughout the world and helped to ground countless decisions of national and international courts. The concept of inherent human dignity is prioritized in several subsequent UN laws, thereby helping to expand the intertwining of human dignity with different areas of legal regulation: the rights of children; the prohibition against torture, slavery, inhumane and degrading treatments and discrimination of all sorts; the prohibition against sexual harassment; the regulation of abortion, euthanasia and the handling of mortal remains; the rights of asylum seekers; and so on.[12] The 1993 World Conference on Human Rights in Vienna reaffirmed inherent human dignity as the basis for, and as a fundamental principle of, human rights.[13] References to inherent human dignity in international legal acts spread to the Council of Europe and the European Union and into the constitutions of many European states. Inherent human dignity is the foundation and justification for rights and duties: because of inherent human dignity, human beings have rights and duties.[14]

6 Capps, *supra* note 2 at 107.

7 Charles Malik, "Four Basic Principles" in Habib C Malik, ed, *The Challenge of Human Rights: Charles Malik and the Universal Declaration* (Oxford, UK: Oxford University Press, 2000) at 38.

8 Samuel Moyn, *The Last Utopia: Human Rights in History* (Cambridge, MA; Harvard University Press, 2012).

9 *International Convention on the Elimination of All Forms of Racial Discrimination*, 21 December 1965, 660 UNTS 195 (entered into force 4 January 1969) [*Racial Discrimination Convention*].

10 *International Covenant on Civil and Political Rights*, 19 December 1966, 999 UNTS 171, Can TS 1976 No 47, 6 ILM 368 (entered into force 23 March 1976) [*ICCPR*].

11 *International Covenant on Economic, Social and Cultural Rights*, 16 December 1966, 993 UNTS 3, Can TS 1976 No 46 (entered into force 3 January 1976) [*ICESCR*].

12 See e.g. *Convention Against Torture and Other Cruel, Inhuman or Degrading Treatment or Punishment*, 10 December 1984, GA Res 39/46, UNGAOR, 39th Sess, Supp No 51, UN Doc A139/51 (1985), 1465 UNTS 85 (entered into force 26 June 1987); Council of Europe, *Convention on Human Rights and Biomedicine*, ETS 164 (Oviedo, 1997), online: <http://conventions.coe.int/Treaty/EN/Treaties/html/164.htm>; *Racial Discrimination Convention*, *supra* note 9; *Convention on the Rights of the Child*, 20 November 1989, 1577 UNTS 3, 28 ILM 1456 (entered into force 2 September 1990); *The United Nations and Human Rights 1945–1995* (New York: UN Department of Public Information, 1995); *International Convention on the Protection of the Rights of All Migrant Workers and Members of their Families*, 18 December 1990, UN Doc A/RES/45/158, 30 ILM 1517 (entered into force 1 July 2003).

13 UN, Office of the High Commissioner for Human Rights, *Vienna Declaration and Programme of Action*, 12 July 1993, UN Doc A/CONF.157/23 at para 10.

14 Doron Shultziner, "Human Dignity — Functions and Meanings" (2004) 3:3 Global Jurist Topics at 3.

The UN Declaration[15] implements the customary international law and the existing human rights treaties and covenants that Canada has fully endorsed.[16] Article 1 implements for Indigenous peoples the binding UN treaties on human rights: "Indigenous peoples have the right to the full enjoyment, as a collective or as individuals, of all human rights and fundamental freedoms as recognized in the Charter of the United Nations, the Universal Declaration of Human Rights and international human rights law."[17] In addition, the remaining articles of the UN Declaration clarify and envisage the beginning of a process in the states to actualizing or realizing the interrelated human rights of Indigenous peoples. This flexible process allows countries and their Indigenous peoples to engage in dialogue and gradually become familiar with the global consensus or normative standards to achieve shared consensus on issues that are especially complex or sensitive.

Although the principle of inherent human dignity is at the core of the major international human rights instruments, it is never explicitly defined in the principles or established as a theoretical basis for these instruments. Due to a lack of consensus on the definition of inherent human dignity, the various regional human rights protection systems attribute somewhat similar, but somewhat different, meanings to the idea of inherent human dignity. Consequently, inherent human dignity can be described as a contested concept; this means that it is constantly subject to interpretative analyses from different knowledge systems that need more exploration. A need exists for clearer guidelines from Indigenous knowledge systems and languages in Canada to help clarify the structure and importance of the concept of inherent human dignity in Indigenous human rights. Such clarity could assist in achieving a consistent interpretation of the concept of the inviolability of inherent human dignity.

Instead of providing a definition, the Universal Declaration and other international human rights covenants provide guidance for understanding the principle of inherent dignity as a foundation of justice in the world: first, that dignity is "inherent...to all members of the human family"[18]; second, that all human beings are "free and equal in dignity and rights"[19]; and, third, that human rights "derive from the inherent dignity of the human person."[20] Thus, the meaning of inherent human dignity remains open to all knowledge systems.

The first important consequence of relying on inherent human dignity in international law is that the principle of inherent dignity and its manifestations in the human rights of Indigenous peoples in the UN Declaration has to be carefully understood and unpacked from many Indigenous knowledge systems and languages because it is distinct from Eurocentric concepts of dignity. A careful analysis of human rights law and intergovernmental policy documents, and of the discussion that led to their adoption, provides evidence that the recourse to inherent human dignity reflects a deep concern about the need to ensure respect for the inherent worth of every human being. Eurocentric knowledge systems have a difficult time with accepting or

15 *UNDRIP, supra* note 1.

16 Indigenous and Northern Affairs Canada, "United Nations Declaration on the Rights of Indigenous Peoples", online: <www.aadnc-aandc.gc.ca/eng/1309374407406/1309374458958>.

17 James (Sa'ke'j) Youngblood Henderson, *Indigenous Diplomacy and the Rights of Peoples: Achieving UN Recognition* (Saskatoon: Purich, 2008) at 75.

18 *Universal Declaration, supra* note 4, Preamble.

19 *Ibid*, art 1.

20 *ICCPR, supra* note 10, Preamble; *ICESCR, supra* note 11, Preamble.

defining "inherent," especially the inherent dignity of all members of the human family. Samuel Pufendorf, writing in the natural law tradition in the eighteenth century, claimed that natural rights are derived from human dignity or *dignatio* and not from state authority.[21] However, the contemporary rights systems, in common or civil law, are derived from the sovereign, or state, or are socially constructed as a person's position or status. These legal systems have difficulties in comprehending inherent dignity or rights. European dictionaries usually define inherent as "involved in the constitution or essential character of something,"[22] "intrinsic"[23] or a permanent or characteristic attribute of something.[24] The idea expressed in these shallow definitions, when it is accompanied by the adjective "human," is that dignity is a mysterious endowment inseparable from the diversity of the human condition (but really a gift of likeness to a personal God that intervenes in daily life). These definitions derive from the belief that human nature is exceptional, elevated and distinguishable from other life forms.

The second important consequence of the reliance on inherent human dignity in international law is that basic rights are equal for everyone: if inherent dignity is the same for all and the foundation of all human rights and of freedom, justice and peace in the world, then all human beings possess equal rights. This is the reason why discrimination — the unjust distinction in the treatment of different categories of people — is directly contrary to inherent human dignity. Article 2 of the UN Declaration affirms that Indigenous peoples and individuals are free, are equal to all other peoples and individuals, and have the right to be free from any kind of discrimination in the exercise of their rights, in particular, of their rights based on their Indigenous origin or identity. This is consistent with the Supreme Court of Canada's decision in *R v Oakes*,[25] which declared that the promotion of inherent human dignity is the lodestar for the protection of all the rights guaranteed by the Canadian Charter of Rights and Freedoms.[26] However, subsequently, the court held in *R v Kapp*[27] that the concept of inherent human dignity is too subjective and abstract to be applied as a legal test. Thus, Canadian jurisprudence lacks a principled definition of inherent human dignity. However, the court has continually recognized that the existing Aboriginal and treaty rights of Aboriginal peoples are inherent rights derived from Aboriginal knowledge and laws.[28]

The third important consequence of a reliance on inherent human dignity in international law is the understanding that human rights "derive from the inherent dignity of the human person"[29]; this emphasizes that human rights are not derived from, or given by, state authority, but are distinct and independent from state authority. These human rights are inherent in every human being; thus, they cannot legitimately be taken away by any human, peoples, governments or

21 Eckert Joern, "Legal Roots of Human Dignity in German Law" in David Kretzmer & Eckart Klein, eds, *The Concept of Human Dignity in Human Rights Discourse* (The Hague: Kluwer Law International, 2002) at 44.

22 *Merriam-Webster, sub verbo* "inherent", online: <www.merriam-webster.com/dictionary/inherent>.

23 *Ibid.*

24 See *English Oxford Living Dictionary, sub verbo* "inherent", online: <https://en.oxforddictionaries.com/definition/inherent>.

25 *R v Oakes*, [1986] 1 SCR 103 at para 64.

26 *Canadian Charter of Rights and Freedoms*, Part I of the *Constitution Act, 1982*, being Schedule B to the *Canada Act 1982* (UK), 1982, c 11.

27 *R v* Kapp, [2008] 2 SCR 483 at paras 21–22.

28 James Youngblood Henderson, *First Nations Jurisprudence and Aboriginal Rights: Defining the Just Society* (Saskatoon: Native Law Centre, 2006) at 116–77.

29 Alan Gewirth, "Human Dignity As the Basis of Rights" in Michael J Meyer & WA Parent, eds, *The Constitution of Rights: Human Dignity and American Values* (Ithaca, NY: Cornell University Press, 1992) at 10.

societies.[30] This does not mean that laws are unnecessary to protect initial dignity because it is an integral part of every human being; it means that governments need to respect and protect inherent human dignity to remedy past abuses and wrongs. The UN Declaration is a global remedy to correct past wrongs against the inherent human dignity of Indigenous peoples. The declaration's purposes are, first, to prevent discrimination against Indigenous peoples for being who they are and, second, to advance or realize the full development of the talent, capacities and visions of Indigenous peoples in their chosen paths.

From these three consequences, we can understand that the purposes of relying on the inherent dignity of Indigenous peoples as the source of their human rights is an attempt by Indigenous peoples to generate an Indigenous concept of human rights. It is not an attempt to promote a Eurocentric ideological construct or cognitive imperialism that relies on past philosophies of dignity. The UN Declaration was a hard-won recognition and consensus that inherent dignity is at the heart of every Indigenous person and family.

While the European monologue on dignity and rights is another part of the global dialogue, this monologue cannot or should not be used to construe the inherent dignity or rights of Indigenous peoples. An international discussion began in 2011, during a conference of the Norwegian Academy of Science and Letters in Oslo, Norway. The conference opened a Eurocentric discussion that made reference to "The Concept of Human Dignity in Indigenous Philosophies,"[31] but there has been little follow-up on this concept in Canada or beyond. Similarly, while many Indigenous scholars have begun to address Indigenous understanding in their language and knowledge systems, and in their concepts of well-being and good living, little attention has been focused on their efforts. The conversations and explorations of this concept of the inherent dignity of Indigenous peoples need to be resumed in the implementation of the UN Declaration with the participation of Indigenous leaders, coming from within their diverse and distinctive knowledge systems and languages. Inherent dignity is an integral core of all rights. This concept must be vigorously articulated by Indigenous scholars and peoples.

30 Oscar Schachter, "Human Dignity as a Normative Concept" (1983) 77 AJIL 848–54.

31 See "Conference about the Concept of Human Dignity In Indigenous Philosophies" (2011), international conference organized by the Norwegian Academy of Science and Letters, the Oslo Center for Peace and Human Rights and the University of Oslo, online: <www.norlarnet.uio.no/pdf/events/2011/dignity_background.pdf>.

Contributors

Hannah Askew is an environmental lawyer, and is currently the executive director of Sierra Club British Columbia. For the past 10 years, she has been deeply involved in learning from Indigenous communities about their systems of law and governance. She worked as a researcher on Anishinaabe and Coast Salish legal orders for the Indigenous Law Research Unit at the University of Victoria and also researched Tsilhqot'in and Ktunaxa law as part of the RELAW project (Revitalizing Indigenous Law for Land, Air and Water) at West Coast Environmental Law. The knowledge received from Indigenous colleagues and mentors has been transformative for Hannah and influences every aspect of her work. Hannah holds a master of arts in both history and anthropology, from the University of Toronto and McGill University, respectively, as well as a law degree from Osgoode Hall Law School. She was born on Anishinaabe territory into a family of English and Scottish descent.

Ryan Beaton is a legal scholar whose primary interests include constitutional law, Aboriginal law, Indigenous land rights and legal philosophy. His research focuses on the challenge posed by the evolving conception of Aboriginal title to traditional notions of state sovereignty. Ryan is currently pursuing his Ph.D. in law at the University of Victoria, as a 2017 scholar of the Pierre Elliott Trudeau Foundation. He is also conducting historical and legal research as part of a team preparing an Aboriginal title claim. In 2014-2015, he was a law clerk for Chief Justice Beverley McLachlin at the Supreme Court of Canada. The year prior to that he was a law clerk at the Court of Appeal for Ontario. In 2013, Ryan received his J.D. from Harvard Law School. In 2011, Ryan completed a Ph.D. in philosophy at the University of Toronto. His dissertation examines the secularization of German moral philosophy in the works of Kant, Schopenhauer and Nietzsche. He also holds an M.Sc. in mathematics, having completed a master's thesis on the set-theoretic interpretation of Fregean arithmetic.

John Borrows, B.A., M.A., J.D., LL.M. (Toronto), Ph.D. (Osgoode Hall Law School), LL.D. (Hons., Dalhousie, York and Law Society of Ontario), F.R.S.C., is a senior fellow with CIGI's International Law Research Program. He holds the Canada Research Chair in Indigenous Law at the University of Victoria Law School in British Columbia. His publications include *Recovering Canada: The Resurgence of Indigenous Law* (Donald Smiley Award for the best book in Canadian Political Science, 2002), *Canada's Indigenous Constitution* (Canadian Law and Society Best Book Award 2011), *Drawing Out Law: A Spirit's Guide* (2010), *Freedom and Indigenous Constitutionalism* (Donald Smiley Award for the best book in Canadian Political Science, 2016), *The Right Relationship* (with Michael Coyle, ed.), *Resurgence and Reconciliation* (with Michael Asch and Jim Tully, eds.) and *Law's Indigenous Ethics* (forthcoming), all from the University of Toronto Press. He is the winner of the 2017 Killam Prize in Social Sciences. John is Anishinaabe/Ojibway and a member of the Chippewa of the Nawash First Nation in Ontario.

Larry Chartrand is a professor of law at the Faculty of Law at the University of Ottawa, where he has been a faculty member since 1994, and assumed the role of full professor in 2013. He was born on the western plains and is a proud citizen of the Métis nation. He has previously served as director of the Aboriginal Self-Government Program at the University of Winnipeg, Métis adviser to the Senate Standing Committee on Aboriginal Peoples and director of the Indigenous Law Program at the Faculty of Law, University of Alberta. In 2017, Larry was awarded the distinguished Law Society Medal of Upper Canada in recognition of outstanding service in accordance with the highest ideals of the legal profession.

Gordon Christie has taught in faculties of law and departments of philosophy and Indigenous studies at several universities in Canada and the United States and is currently a professor at the Peter A. Allard School of Law at the University of British Columbia, where he teaches Aboriginal legal issues, legal theory and torts. His research interests lie in Aboriginal legal issues and legal theory. He has published a number of articles on Aboriginal legal issues, including "Who Makes Decisions Over Aboriginal Title Lands?" (2015), "'Obligations,' Decolonization and Indigenous Rights to Governance" (2014) and "A Colonial Reading of Recent Jurisprudence: Sparrow, Delgamuukw and Haida Nation" (2005). He is Inuvialuit/Inupiat.

Aimée Craft is an Indigenous lawyer (Anishinaabe-Métis), an assistant professor at the Faculty of Common Law, University of Ottawa, and an adjunct professor in Native Studies at the University of Manitoba. Her expertise is in Anishinaabe and Canadian Aboriginal law. Aimée is one of the lead researchers on two SSHRC-funded partnership grants: on water sustainability and indigenous laws; and on hydro-impacted communities in Northern Manitoba. Since 2013, Craft has led research on Anishinaabe water law alongside a faculty of Anishinaabe Elders and knowledge holders. Aimée's award-winning 2013 book, *Breathing Life Into the Stone Fort Treaty*, focuses on understanding and interpreting treaties from an Anishinaabe inaakonigewin (legal) perspective. In 2016, she was voted one of the top 25 most influential lawyers in Canada. She is the former director of research at the National Inquiry into Missing and Murdered Indigenous Women and Girls and the founding director of research at the National Centre for Truth and Reconciliation (University of Manitoba).

Oonagh E. Fitzgerald is the director of the International Law Research Program at the Centre for International Governance Innovation (CIGI). She oversees a research agenda that includes international economic law, environmental law, intellectual property law and innovation, and Indigenous law. Oonagh has extensive experience as a senior executive in the federal government, providing legal services and leadership in international law. In her most recent posting before coming to CIGI in 2014, Oonagh served as national security coordinator for the Department of Justice. Oonagh has a B.A. (honours) in fine arts from York University. She obtained her LL.B. from Osgoode Hall Law School, and was called to the Bar of Ontario in 1983. She obtained an LL.M. from the University of Ottawa, an S.J.D. from the University of Toronto and an M.B.A. from Queen's University.

Lorena Sekwan Fontaine is Cree-Anishinabe and a member of the Sagkeeng First Nation in Manitoba. She holds a Ph.D. from the University of Manitoba and an LL.M. from the University of Arizona. She is an associate professor in the Department of Indigenous Studies at the University of Winnipeg. Lorena was a task force member and contributor to the Assembly of First Nations' Report on Canada's dispute resolution plan to compensate for abuses in Indian residential schools. She also acted as a legal consultant to the Toronto law firm Thomson, Rogers for the plaintiffs and as their counsel in the Baxter National Residential School Class Action, as well as to Mother of Red Nations Women's Council in Manitoba on cultural harm issues. She has worked with the Assembly of First Nations as an adviser on Aboriginal languages for a number of years. Lorena was an Equality Rights Panel Member of the Court Challenges Program and has been involved with the Women's Legal Education and Action Fund as a board member and subcommittee member. Currently, Lorena is a National Steering Committee Member for the National Association of Women and the Law.

Brenda L. Gunn is a fellow with CIGI's ILRP. In this role, Brenda explores comparative approaches and best practices for the implementation of the United Nations Declaration on the Rights of Indigenous Peoples (UN Declaration) internationally. Her work at CIGI involves engaging Indigenous peoples on the topic through workshops, conferences and other fora. Brenda is also an associate professor in the Robson Hall Faculty of Law at the University of Manitoba, where she teaches constitutional law, international law and advocacy for the rights of Indigenous peoples in international law. Prior to joining the University of Manitoba, Brenda worked at a community legal clinic in Rabinal, Guatemala, on a case of genocide submitted to the Inter-American Commission on Human Rights. She has worked with First Nations on Aboriginal and treaty rights issues in Manitoba and provided technical assistance to the United Nations Expert Mechanism on the Rights of Indigenous Peoples in the analysis and drafting of the report summarizing the responses to a survey on implementing the UN Declaration. Brenda is co-chair of the Rights of Indigenous Peoples interest group of the American Society of International Law, and a member of the Implementation of the Rights of Indigenous Peoples committee of the International Law Association.

A proud Métis woman, Brenda combines her research with activism. She is recognized for developing a key handbook in Canada on understanding and implementing the UN Declaration. Brenda has a B.A. from the University of Manitoba and a J.D. from the University of Toronto. She completed her LL.M. in Indigenous peoples' law and policy at the University of Arizona and was called to the Bars of Ontario and Manitoba.

Robert Hamilton is a research fellow at CIGI and an assistant professor at the University of Calgary Faculty of Law. He teaches property law, Indigenous peoples and the law, and legal research and writing. His research focuses on Aboriginal rights and title, treaty rights, constitutional history and the history of empire, legal pluralism, and the relationship between the state and Indigenous peoples. Robert is a research fellow at the Canadian Institute for Resources Law. He has worked on research projects with the National Consortium on Indigenous Economic Development, the Centre for Indigenous Conservation and Development Alternatives and the Confederation Debates Project. He has also worked with First Nations on land claims and self-government issues. Robert holds a B.A. in philosophy from St. Thomas University, a J.D. from the University of New Brunswick Law School and an LL.M. from Osgoode Hall Law School. He is a Ph.D. candidate at the University of Victoria Faculty of Law.

James (Sa'ke'j) Youngblood Henderson is a research fellow at the Wiyasiwewin Mikiwahp Native Law Centre of Canada, University of Saskatchewan College of Law. He was born to the Bear Clan of the Chickasaw Nation and Cheyenne Tribe in Oklahoma in 1944 and is married to Marie Battiste, a Mi'kmaw educator. In 1974, he received a juris doctorate in law from Harvard Law School. During the constitutional process in Canada (1978–1993), Sa'ke'j served as a constitutional adviser for the Mi'kmaw Nation and the National Indian Brotherhood, Assembly of First Nations. Sa'ke'j is a noted international human rights lawyer and authority on protecting Indigenous heritage, knowledge and laws and has served as a member of the Advisory Board to the Minister of Foreign Affairs. He was one of the strategists, expert advisers and drafters of the United Nations Principles and Guidelines for the Protection of Indigenous Heritage and the United Nations Declaration on the Rights of Indigenous Peoples. For his achievements, he received the Indigenous Peoples' Counsel award in 2005, the National Aboriginal Achievement Award for Law and Justice in 2006 and an honorary doctorate from Carleton University in 2007. He became a fellow of the Royal Society of Canada in 2013.

Jeffery G. Hewitt (Cree) is an assistant professor at the University of Windsor Faculty of Law. His research interests include Indigenous legal orders and governance, constitutional and administrative law, art and law, human rights and remedies, dispute resolution, and business law, as well as health law and Indigenous peoples. He teaches constitutional law, access to justice and "Indigenous Peoples, art + law." Jeffery holds an LL.B. and LL.M. from Osgoode Hall Law School and was called to the Bar of Ontario in 1998. He has served as a visiting scholar and adjunct faculty at both Osgoode Hall Law School and the University of Toronto Faculty of Law. Jeffery was the recipient of the 2015 Charles D. Gonthier Fellowship from the Canadian Institute for the Administration of Justice and was a 2013/14 McMurtry Fellow at Osgoode Hall Law School, examining the relationship between Indigenous art and law. He is past president of the Indigenous Bar Association of Canada and served as general counsel to Rama First Nation for 14 years, during which time the general counsel's office received a 2011 Canadian General Counsel Award for Social Responsibility for work with First Nation elders and youth.

Cheryl Knockwood is an L'nu and proud citizen of the Mi'kmaw Nation. She grew up within the Sikniktuk District of Mi'kma'ki and currently resides in the Unama'ki District of Mi'kma'ki with her partner Candice and their family. Cheryl received her B.A. (honours) in anthropology from the University of New Brunswick. She later earned an LL.B. from the University of British Columbia and completed her LL.M. in Indigenous peoples' law and policy at the University of Arizona. For 13 years, Cheryl worked as a senior policy analyst with the Atlantic Policy Congress of First Nations Chiefs, where she gave strategic advice in areas such as fisheries, environment, treaty education and economic development to the Mi'kmaw, Maliseet and Passamaquoddy chiefs and communities. Cheryl was called to the Nova Scotia Barristers' Society Bar in 2009, becoming the first Mi'kmaq-speaking female lawyer in Nova Scotia. In 2015, Cheryl was appointed to the Nova Scotia Human Rights Commission and still serves as a commissioner. Since 2010, Cheryl has been the governance coordinator for Membertou, Nova Scotia, where she engages the community in the development of laws in relation to lands and citizenship. She occasionally teaches courses at Cape Breton University on Aboriginal and treaty rights, governance and Indigenous economic development.

Sheryl Lightfoot (Anishinaabe) is Canada Research Chair in Global Indigenous Rights and Politics and associate professor in First Nations and Indigenous Studies and Political Science at the University of British Columbia, where she also serves as senior adviser to the president on Indigenous Affairs.

Sarah Morales is Coast Salish and a member of Cowichan Tribes. She holds a J.D. and a Ph.D. from the University of Victoria and an LL.M. from the University of Arizona and was a post-doctoral fellow at the University of Illinois. Sarah is an associate professor at the University of Victoria Faculty of Law, where her teaching and research focuses on torts, Aboriginal law, Coast Salish legal traditions and international human rights, with a focus on Indigenous peoples.

Joshua Nichols is a fellow with CIGI's International Law Research Program. In this role, Joshua explores the potential implications of UNDRIP's implementation for constitutional law, and consults with Indigenous peoples in workshops and other fora as part of his research. He has researched wise practices in Indigenous community-based economies at the University of Victoria, and is the author of *The End(s) of Community: History, Sovereignty, and the Question of Law* (Wilfrid Laurier University Press, 2013). He is also the author of a forthcoming University of Toronto Press publication investigating the foundations of Aboriginal law. Joshua has a bachelor of political science and an M.A. in sociology from the University of Alberta, a Ph.D. in philosophy from the University of Toronto, a J.D. from the University of British Columbia, and a Ph.D. in law from the University of Victoria. He is a member of the Law Society of British Columbia and the Indigenous Bar Association. He teaches in the Faculty of Law, University of Alberta.

Risa Schwartz is a sole practitioner specializing in international trade and international environmental law and the intersections with the rights of Indigenous peoples. Risa was formerly a senior research fellow in the International Law Research Program at CIGI. She has also held positions as counsel to the Ministry of Aboriginal Affairs and the Ministry of the Environment for the Ontario government, and worked as a legal officer at the World Trade Organization in Geneva, Switzerland. Risa obtained her LL.B. from Osgoode Hall Law School and her LL.M. from the London School of Economics with a specialization in international and environmental law.

Kerry Wilkins, a recovering government lawyer, is adjunct professor at the University of Toronto Faculty of Law. He has edited a collection of essays, and written and published a treatise and several articles, on Canadian law about Indigenous peoples. He accepts speaking engagements and submits written work for publication when he thinks he has something to say. Sometimes he's guessed right.

Artist Credits

Cover

New Beginnings
Christi Belcourt and Isaac Murdoch
2015, 48" x 72", acrylic on canvas
Courtesy of the artists and the Wabano Center for Aboriginal Health

Part I

Piqatiglik BFF
Ningiukulu Teevee
2018, 76 x 58.5 cm, ink on paper
Courtesy of Dorset Fine Arts

Part II

Douglas in Formal Wear (part of the *Romancing Stanley* series)
Kim Hunter
2016, digital vector painting
Courtesy of the artist (www.kimhunter.ca)

Part III

Guud
Ernest Swanson
2015, 14.5" x 22", serigraph edition (110)
Courtesy of the artist

Part IV

Ojiibikaawi (She Has Roots)
Anna Heffernan
2018, 8" x 10", marker and ink drawing
Courtesy of the artist (@miskwaadesigns)

Title Pages

Sweetgrass
Peter Pomart
2017, photograph
Courtesy of the artist

Milton Keynes UK
Ingram Content Group UK Ltd.
UKHW050033011224
451822UK00008B/280

9 781928 096801